The Paul Mellon Centre for Studies in British Art

by

Yale University Press

New Haven & London

Todd Longstaffe-Gowan

The London Town Garden

1740–1840

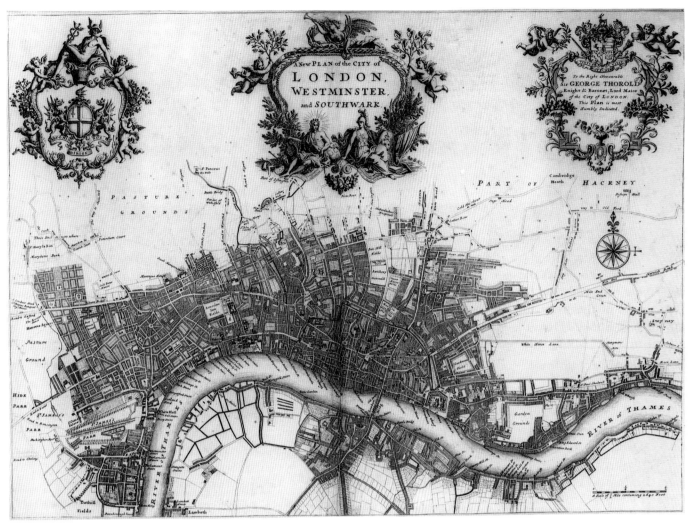

1 John Strype, 'A New Plan of the City of London, Westminster and Southwark', engraving from John Strype, *Survey of the Cities of London and Westminster*, vol. 2 (1720). Paul Mellon Collection, Yale Center for British Art, New Haven.

John Strype credited as being 'no mean cause of preserving Health, and wholesome Air to the City'.[4] Indeed, Hatton recorded that the city had no less than twenty such places – 'mostly very large and pleasant'. They were, moreover, among the city's largest and most conspicuous landmarks, and as such figured, like the City's churches, as primary reference points in the urban geography: Leicester Fields which had an area 'upwards of two Acres' lay 420 yards northwest of Charing Cross; Golden Square – 'a very new and pleasant Square' – lay '240 Yds N. of *Pickadilley*, and 280 near VV. of St. *Anns Church*, in the Liberty of *Westminster*'; and Lincoln's Inn Fields which lay 1,360 yards west of St Pauls, was 'reckon'd one of the finest and largest Squares in the World . . . whose Area is upwards of 10 Acres' (fig. 3).

Each time a square was laid out in the West End the city gained yet another mark of sophistication. While the construction of each of these enclosed spaces was a conspicuous incident in the narrative of urban development, they were created at the expense of open fields, just as the close quarters of the City and the Strand sprang up in the capacious gardens of the city's one-time mansions and palaces. Alongside this impulse towards enclosure was a conflicting desire for open land to insulate domestic and other premises. If we were to sharpen our focus on the cityscape some time in the second half of the eighteenth century we would register that beyond the green shade of the garden squares, bowling greens, small orchards behind taverns, the gardens of the Temple, the Inns of Court, the City livery

2   Unknown artist, *A New and Exact Prospect of the North Side of the City of London taken from the Upper Pond near Islington*, engraving, *c.*1730. Paul Mellon Collection, Yale Center for British Art, New Haven. Daniel Defoe disapproved of London's 'straggling, confus'd' growth, which he remarked in 1726 rendered it 'out of all shape, uncompact, and unequal'.

3   Sutton Nicholls, *Golden Square*, engraving, 1731. British Museum, London.

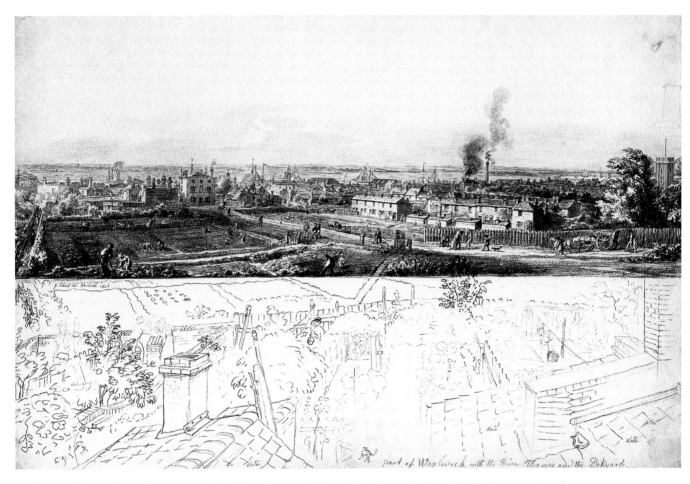

4   George Scharf, *Part of Woolwich with the River Thames and the Dockyard*, pencil, 1825. British Museum, London.

companies, and the royal parks lay areas of green and gravel, summer-houses and statuary, flower-beds and window boxes. Moreover, each one of these thousands of not so anomalous spaces was continuously agitated by the busy-ness of the workaday world – from pruning to sweeping, sawing to skipping. Like the dwellings they surrounded, they were richly animated (figs 4 and 5).

Town gardens were small domestic outdoor spaces which were referred to variously as 'gardens in town', 'little town gardens', 'close Gardens', 'city gardens', 'speck[s] of garden', 'ordinary street gardens', 'little walled gardens in streets', 'Gardens for the Town', 'street-gardens', or 'fourth-rate gardens' (fig. 6).[5] From the early eighteenth century onwards these spaces shared several characteristics: they were small in extent, fragmentary in total expression, regular in layout, flat in situation, considered a miniature 'parade of art', and circumscribed by high, secure and defensive boundaries (fig. 7). The expression was the antithesis of the English landscape garden tradition in which, as the author of an article in

The World (1755) expressed it, 'regularity [is] banished, prospects opened, the country called in, nature rescued and improved, and art decently concealing herself under her own perfections'.[6] The town garden was, above all, a space subject to severe limitations that were not easily surmounted (fig. 8).

The extent of the garden ground was limited by contemporary building practices and patterns of urban estate development. The garden was, in fact, an unforeseen benefit of Nicholas Barbon's 'new method' of town housing. Between 1670 and 1698 Barbon pioneered the technique of casting ground into regular streets in order to 'augment the number of houses' with as little frontage as possible. The formula transformed the structure of old (infill) and new residential quarters of the city and made the terraced house – usually run up in short, discontinuous strings – the dominant housing form for both urban and, in many cases, suburban housing well into the early nineteenth century: earlier patterns of *ad hoc* development gave way to orderly, uniform rows of

5   George Scharf, *View from the back window (1st floor) of No. 1 Torrington Square*, pencil, *c*.1849. British Museum, London.

mass-produced housing as witnessed with the unfolding of the Cavendish-Harley Estate in Marylebone (from 1717) and the Grosvenor Estate in Mayfair (from 1720). This architectural expression was not, however, restricted to the centre of town. London's suburbs in the eighteenth century and early nineteenth century were defined geographically in terms of 'their distance and semi-detachment from the centre', and were 'to a certain extent socially suburban in so far as they were often places of residence divorced from places of work. Physically and architecturally, however, they were extensions of the town, laid out in streets and squares and built in repetitive three- and four-storey terraces whose plain regularity Victorians found monotonous and unimaginative, and whose accommodation was often found too large and expensive for single family occupation'.[7]

The incremental changes to the layout and size of residential premises ultimately resulted in lower building densities, 'airiness', greater spaciousness and 'convenience' – factors which supplied town gardens with attractive amenities, but which did not in themselves promote their creation, or necessarily increase Londoners' desire to garden. Although small gardens were credited by contemporaries as contributing towards the convenience of a townhouse, only rarely were they perceived as surmounting the constraints of poor air circulation and limited direct daylight; and the activity of 'town gardening' was considered throughout the eighteenth century to be a 'diminutive' and 'trifling' pursuit.[8] Such attitudes ensured that the garden remained a secondary planning consideration, and subject to the demands on the ground plot to accommodate the house and its various services.

Thomas Fairchild's *The City Gardener* (1722) marked an important point in the development of the town garden; his little treatise was the first published work by a learned London nurseryman to set down recommendations on 'beautifying the City Gardens', and to chronicle contemporary observations on indoor and outdoor gardening in London (fig. 9).[9] No less significant was

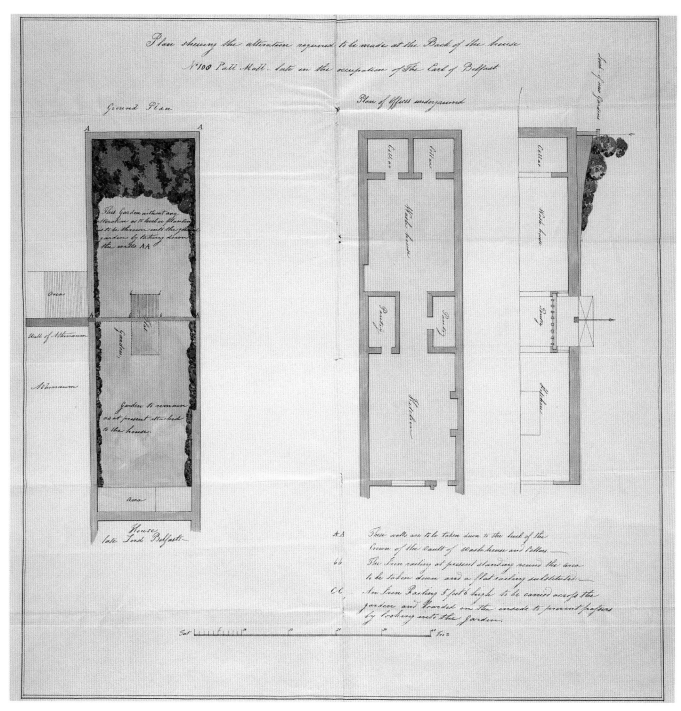

6   *Plan shewing the alterations required to be made to the Back of the house [of] No. 108 Pall Mall, late in the occupation of the Earl of Belfast,* pen and coloured washes, 1828, Public Record Office, Kew.

the book's republication in 1760. *The London Gardener*, as it was then known, was reissued anonymously and with minor amendments: the engraved plates and references in the text to them were omitted, and Fairchild's topographical references were updated to reflect changes in the city's garden geography.[10] The substitution of 'London' for 'City' in the book's title doubtless reflects the prodigious increase in the size of the metropolis, and the fact that the treatise was as relevant for suburban gardeners as it was for their urban counterparts.[11] No revisions, however, were made to the 'method' of cultivating, ordering and 'beautifying' town gardens. This might suggest that little progress had been made in the 'London Practice of Gardening'. By 1760, in fact, the

8 M. Darly, *The Flower Garden*, engraving, 1777. British Museum, London. This *pouffe au sentiment* portrays a flower-garden at its summit. Hannah More recorded in 1777 having seen 'eleven damsels' at dinner, who 'had amongst them, on their heads, an acre and a half of shrubbery besides slopes, grass-plats, tulip-beds, clumps of peonies, kitchen gardens, and green houses'.

7 J. A. Smith, *Plan of a Small Garden*, pen and coloured wash, 1807. British Architectural Library, Royal Institute of British Architects, London.

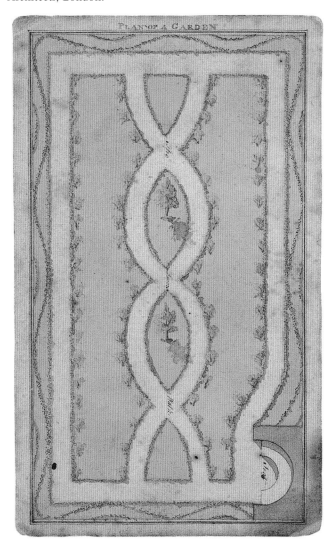

heydey of the London nursery trade had just begun, a number of the central gardens of the city's squares had been recast in the new taste and, most importantly, thousands of new townhouses had been thrown up in Mayfair, Marylebone, Covent Garden and Piccadilly – many of which we shall see possessed 'close Gardens'.[12] By 1760, as a result of these new developments, there were considerably more town gardens and town gardeners in London than there were in the early 1720s. Fairchild's little treatise none the less remained the only *vade-mecum* on the subject of town gardening.

The development of the town garden, like that of the terraced townhouse, required ingenious variation within the inflexible limits of party walls. As the houses were tall and narrow, so the plots were often slender squares or oblongs; and, as the garden was an 'accessory'

9   Frontispiece from Thomas Fairchild's *The City Gardener* (1722). Private collection.

of the house, it could aspire at best to reflect its orderliness and congruity. Isaac Ware commented in 1757, 'a garden enclosed by four high walls is but a great room open at the top',[13] and Lord Kames remarked in 1762, 'perfect regularity and uniformity are required in a house; and this idea is extended to its accessory the garden, especially if it be a small spot incapable of much grandeur or much variety. The house is regular, so must the garden be; the floors of the house are horizontal, and the garden must have the same position.'[14]

The garden, like parterres of city and country houses in earlier centuries, was contrived to be viewed either from the indoors or from a raised vantage point at its end. The summer-house was a favourite and ubiquitous garden feature. Indeed, it prompted Ware – who was sceptical about the benefits of gardening in the city – to declare that 'he who builds high walls about a small garden must climb to his summer-house'.[15] Summer-houses served not only as prospect towers from which to gain views beyond the bounds of one's own diminutive ground, but as places for retirement at a short distance from the house.

The regularity and orderliness of the compartmental style of parterre gardening complemented the layout of the house. This is well illustrated by Joseph Spence's town garden plans conceived between 1743 and 1766, and John Loudon's plans from 1812. Variations of this *regular*, *mathematical*, or *geometric* style – or, as it was then called, *system* of town gardening – remained the mainstay of instances of small urban gardening well into the early nineteenth century, although its simple orderliness was inevitably eroded and enriched through amateur copying, reinterpretation and unlimited personal eclecticism.

Enclosure by high walls was insistently registered as the greatest obstacle to town gardening (fig. 10). It was, of course, impracticable to implement in town what Horace Walpole called the 'capital stroke' of the ha-ha, or for that matter any other 'easy, unaffected manner of Fencing'.[16] A brick garden wall was, as another article in *The Garden* later termed it, a 'necessary horizon'.[17] The garden required defensible boundaries for reasons of protection, privacy and the demarcation and reinforcement of territory; furthermore, in an urban setting there was, in Switzer's opinion, infrequently the opportunity to 'throw' open the garden to view the 'unbounded Felicities of the distant Prospect'.[18] Although town gardeners attempted to conceal the bounds by means of embowered trellises, arbours, displays of foliage, and *trompe-l'oeil* painted walls, they could not dissolve them, so the small plots could not reasonably aspire to the heights of the landscape garden. In fact, most attempts to transgress their prescribed diminutive status and regularity invited more ridicule than praise. As was remarked by an anonymous contributor to *Common Sense* in 1739: 'One can't help laughing at the scanty and abortive Attempts of little Things to equal great Ones.'[19]

The character of town gardens appears to have changed little by the early nineteenth century when Charles Dickens characterised them in his many novels as small, airless, sterile and bleak enclosures – unfashionable and unlovable relics from the 'powdered head and pig-tail period'.[20] When in *Nicholas Nickleby* (1839) Ralph Nickleby gazed 'with an air of abstraction through the dirty window' into the back garden of his 'spacious house' in Golden Square, he contemplated the inhospitable and infertile character of the small enclosure:

Some London houses have a melancholy little plot of ground behind them, usually fenced in by four high whitewashed walls and frowned upon by stacks of

10 John Adey Repton to John Gough Nichols, 7 October 1845, pen sketch of a garden. National Library of Scotland, Edinburgh. Repton satirised Gough's father's new garden at his 'House near *Lunnun* [London] – with a long slip of a garden with two high walls to separate the premises of neighbour A on one side, and neighbour C on the other with a crooked Walk in the middle, which leads to a pea-green gothic Summer House where your father with a white hat, is poring over a gygantic News-paper – having one of the Police to take care of the Geraniums & the tame pheasants'.

chimneys, in which there withers on from year to year a crippled tree, that makes a show of putting forth a few leaves in late autumn, when other trees shed theirs, and drooping in the effort, lingers on all crackled and smoke dried till the following season, when it repeats the same process, and perhaps if the weather be particularly genial, even tempts some rheumatic sparrow to chirrup in its branches. People sometimes call these dark yards 'gardens'.[21]

Dickens registered the garden with a sense of disappointment: every effort to overcome the want of air, light, and 'fresh soil' was vanquished. He saw 'nothing very interesting in the object' which was to him as remote in its origins and layout as it was inconvenient:

It is not supposed that they were ever planted, but rather that they are pieces of unreclaimed land, with the withered vegetation of the original brickfield. No man thinks of walking in this desolate place, or of turning it to any account. A few hampers, half-a-dozen broken bottles, and such-like rubbish, may be thrown there when the first tenant moves in, but nothing more; and there they remain till he goes away again, the damp straw taking just as long to moulder as it thinks proper, and mingling with the scanty box, and stunted ever-browns, and broken flower-pots, that are scattered mournfully about – a prey to 'blacks' and dirt.[22]

So strong was the association of small, airless gardens with the eighteenth-century city that Victorian commentators intermittently mocked Londoners who, in their attempts to garden in the diminutive plots, perpetuated quaint gardening techniques and obsolete 'systems' of planting. As late as 1872 a contributor to *The Garden* remarked that when 'modern citizens of Cockaigne' formed their small gardens they imitated the 'meagre formal prettiness of the old Keepsake, or Souvenir fashion – a prim, pruned, and, as it were, starched and whaleboned beauty'. The essay emphasised the eighteenth-century character of the town garden through a pointedly classicising reference to 'Virgil', 'the irréconciliable uprooter', blaming the Latin poet for the 'many miles of bare brown mould, and rood after rood of naked grey-brick walls, bordering habitations that are assuredly in some need of relief and ornament, in thoroughfares of the city that might have been made gay and gracious'.[23]

'Ignorant amateurs', and women in particular, were, he railed, responsible for the bleak displays which should have been 'oases of beauty and ornament in numberless urban thoroughfares':

Women with a chastened taste for the pastoral have charge of all; and they are swindled and brow-beaten by the professional gardener, and inoculated with the severe notions of the small local Le Nôtres. They hold box sacred as Druid's ivy, a brick wall a necessary horizon, a spic-and-span lawn and weedless beds the highest possible attainment of art, and the brief blaze

of geraniums once a year the very apotheosis of horticultural success. Hideous as such culture makes them, it is no matter for wonder that scarcely any proprietors of urban gardens ever make the slightest use of their domains for the purpose of rest, exercise or recreation.[24]

Such commentary acknowledged that the size of the small garden precluded novel and imaginative designs that surpassed mere 'prettiness'. There was, none the less, a sense of surprise that Londoners did not generally make the most of the potential of their gardens as 'facilities for brightening the aspect and purifying the atmosphere of the legendary *ville vaporeuse*'. The 'great aim of the Cockney gardener' was, the editorial concluded, 'neatness, not health, or beauty *pure et simple*'.

So that his small estate is free from broken bottles and rubbish, he is content that it shall be free from flowers also during the greater part of the year. He enjoys the blank surface of black mould, the trim bare shrubbery, where not one dead leaf remains half a day, the clean gravel walks and the regular box borders, all arranged with the painful nicety of a Flemish kitchen garden. But Flemish kitchen gardens produce very acceptable viands at times, and the city horticulturist's domain contains nothing. It is dingy, dull, and wet and naked in winter, spring and early summer. When the bedding-out period arrives, the professional nurseryman is communicated with, and sends in a cartload of petunias, verbenas, geraniums, and the like to clothe the desert gorgeously for about six weeks or two months in the year.[25]

In early nineteenth-century commentary, one of the most common means by which difference was affirmed between the town garden and the suburban garden was through the construction of symmetrical oppositions. This criticism was no less common a century earlier, when Pope and Switzer invoked it in their repudiation of Dutch gardening techniques on English soil. By the early nineteenth century, however, the emphasis had changed, and commentaries proclaimed the relative merits of suburban gardening over town gardening, establishing powerful contrasts between regeneration and decay, health and morbidity, and freedom and imprisonment.

Although in the eighteenth century city gardens were regularly perceived as trifling, or diminutive, they were assigned a less equivocal – if more mundane – role in everyday urban life, at least from the early eighteenth century onwards. Their proliferation not only celebrated the achievements of horticulture and garden design, and proclaimed improvements in the physical convenience and comfort of city life: gardens were also emblematic of a new spaciousness – the providers of air, sunshine and the goodness and richness of the natural world. Seventeenth-century and early eighteenth-century London had given light and air to the city's wealthiest residents; the growth and success of cities, and the increased affluence of their inhabitants ensured that by the close of the eighteenth century the urban environment would become more spacious and civilised for a greater number of its citizens.

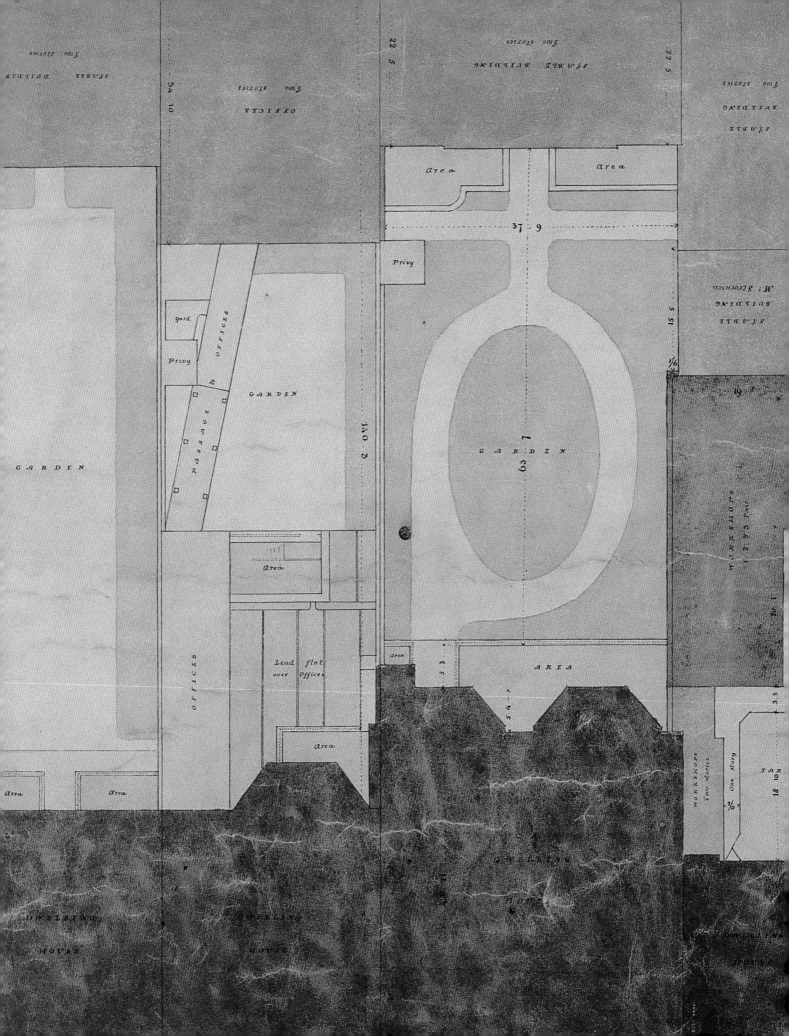

The Garden in the Town Plan

STRYPE'S LONDON

IN this chapter I propose to outline and explore the topographical distribution of town gardens – to examine gardens as spaces, defined by their relationship to other urban spaces, rather than analysing them in terms of their specific aesthetic treatment. Small private gardens are examined as they are represented in three important and influential maps of eighteenth-century and early nineteenth-century London.[1]

Two contemporaries form our first image of the metropolitan fabric: John Strype and Thomas Fairchild. Strype's plan of London, in his *Corrected, Improved and Very Enlarged* edition of Stow's *Survey of London and Westminster* (1720), delineates and describes the morphology of the city subsequent to the beginnings of the spacious planning of London's West End (fig. 11). The plan illustrates the results of the Restoration's building boom, and is among the first surveys to register and distinguish small open garden, yard and court plots behind blocks of building, the existence of which is corroborated by concise descriptive topographical references in the text of his *Survey*. Fairchild, on the other hand, as a practising nurseryman and author of the *City Gardener* (1722), provides specific revelations of the extent of horticultural sophistication and embellishment of particular premises across London, and offers insight into the principal factors which encouraged or dissuaded the practice of town gardening.

The geographical boundaries of our study area in 1720 are established by Strype, who 'set down the distribution of this City in Parts':

The City of *London*, taking that also of *Westminster*, with the adjacent Parts which begirt them, may not improperly be divided into four Parts. The *First* is the City of *London* within the *Walls* and *Freedom*, which is inhabited by wealthy *Merchants* and *Tradesmen*, with

a Mixture of *Artificers*, as depending on *Trade* and *Manufacture*. Secondly, The City or Liberty of *Westminster*, and the adjacent Parts, which are taken up by the *Court* and *Gentry*, yet not without a mixture of eminent *Tradesmen* and *Artificers*. Thirdly, That Part beyond the *Tower*, which compriseth *St Katherines, East Smithfield, Wapping, Shadwell, Ratcliff, Limehouse*, and so Eastward to *Blackwall*. Which are chiefly inhabited by Seafaring Men, and those that by their *Trades*, or otherwise, have their Dependence thereon. And, *Fourthly, Southwark*, which taking in all the *Borough* almost as far as *Newington* Southwards, to *Rotherhith* in the East, and to *Lambeth* in the West, is generally inhabited and fitted with *Tradesmen, Artificers, Mariners, Water-men*, and such as have their Subsistence by and on the Water: Besides abundance of *Porters* and *Labourers*, useful in their kind to do the most servile Work in each of the four Parts.[2]

These four parts cover a vast extent: 'from the farthest End beyond *Petty-France* [fig. 13] Westward, unto *Blackwall* in the East, is reckoned above five Miles; and from the farthest End of *Shoreditch* Northwards, to the End of *Blackmore Street* in *Southwark* Southwards, is about three Miles, making in Circumference above 15 Miles'. The 'great and populous City contains in the whole 6 or 7000 *Streets, Lanes, Alleys, Courts* and *Yards* of Name'; and the total number of houses computed to lie within our study area approximates 78,000 – roughly six times the quantity which stood in the City before the Great Fire. Strype remarks:

In these late Years whole *Fields* have been converted into Builded *Streets, Alleys* and *Courts*; as the great Buildings about the Abby of *Westminster, Tuthill Fields*, and those Parts: Then the greatest Part of St *James's Parish*, as St *James's Fields, Albemarle Buildings*, St. *James's Street, Piccadilly, Golden Square*, all the Streets in the

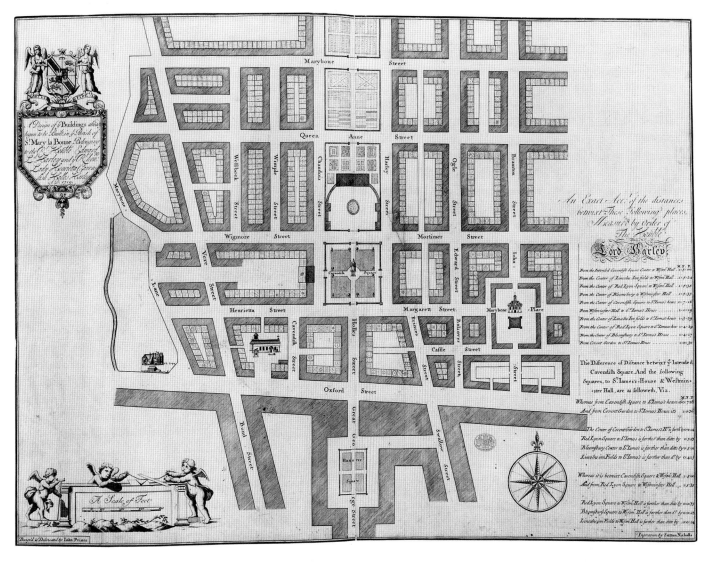

14   John Prince, *A Design of ye Buildings already begun to be Built in ye Parish of St Mary la Bone . . . 1719*, engraving. British Library, London.

north and east of the City walls, towards Hackney, were not redeveloped to the same extent, whilst the area around Charterhouse and the precincts south and west of Drury Lane underwent very little subdivision. Here Strype's map portrays a proliferation of regular rectangular spaces behind thin screens of building which define the city's streets. These spaces are neatly compartmentalised, unlike the built spaces they surround; a symbolic reading suggests that the individuality of premises is read in terms of the open space between and behind buildings and not through the distinction of buildings themselves. Although many of these delineated compartments are undoubtedly conventional cartographic signs, their prominent projection reifies the car-

tographer's view that most settlement beyond the walls was structured in terms of a harmonious consistency of open space and developed land.

Strype perceives gardens in terms of spaces which, like buildings, occupy ground; only as such do they become constituents of the town plan. Gardens are, therefore, valued to the extent that they displace buildings, or spatially insulate domestic premises from one another; they are represented on the plan as white, unelaborated rectangles. Nowhere on the plan is the presence of gardens more evident than in his projection of the yet unfinished estates to the north and south of the Tyburn Road, pivoting on Hanover and Cavendish Squares. The ground plan is transcribed from Sutton

Nicholls's engraving of John Prince's *Design of ye Buildings already begun to be built in ye Parish of St. Mary la Bonne . . . 1719* (fig. 14). It portrays a similar pattern of habitations and gardens rolled out in precise, rational, homogeneous geometry, articulated on the north–south axis connecting the two garden squares, and a broad band of discrete, concatenated walled gardens forged between the garden front of what was intended to be the Duke of Chandos's house and the open fields of St Marylebone.

To our general image of the city may be added the remarks of Fairchild, who has a much wider understanding of the term 'garden'. His claim that 'almost every Body, whose Business requires them to be constantly in Town, will have something of a Garden at any rate' is qualified by his subsequent remarks which make it clear that his garden geography encompasses a great range of gardens that necessarily elude Strype's survey,

such as window boxes, individual plant specimens and fanciful outdoor displays.[6]

Thomas Fairchild, who had 'upwards of thirty Years been placed near *London*, on a Spot of Ground, where I have raised several thousand Plants, both from foreign Countries, and of the *English* Growth', published *The City Gardener* in 1722. His was the first treatise dedicated to the ornamental culture, treatment and improvement of 'little town gardens in London' (fig. 15). The book, which claimed to outline 'the most experienced methods of cultivating and ordering such ever-greens, fruit trees, flowering shrubs, flowers, exotic plants, &c. as will be ornamental, and thrive best in London gardens', was a triumph in gardening circles if only because it persuaded Fairchild (1677–1729) to record his learned observations on growing plants that were suited to the polluted air of the city. His aim was to educate amateur gardeners, 'who do not know how to manage

15 John Kip, *A Prospect of the Cities of London, Westminster and St James's Park*, engraving, 1720 (detail). Private collection. These houses in Pall Mall had their own large gardens with elevated prospect terraces to overlook the expansive gardens of Carlton House. Garden gates gave direct access from the private gardens to those of Carlton House.

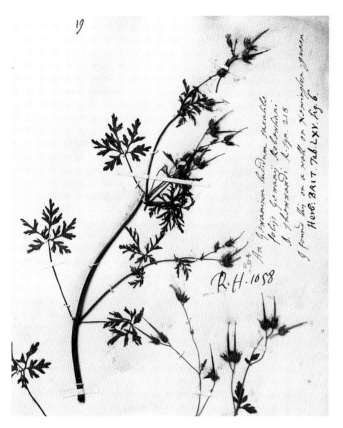

16a Herbarium specimen of a small-flowered form of *Geranium robertianum* collected by Reverend Adam Buddle, labelled 'I found this on a wall on Newington-green' (*c.*1710). Sir Hans Sloane, *Hortus Siccus*, vol. 124, fol. 19. Natural History Museum, London.

16b The leaf of a maple which the Reverend Adam Buddle gathered in 1711, having observed such trees 'in Grays-Inn Garden & severall places about London'. Sir Hans Sloane, *Hortus Siccus*, vol. 126, opposite fol. 35. Natural History Museum, London. Musgrove remarked in 1725 that 'it is very reasonable to suppose that the plants educated in the sulphrous air partaking of London smoke will more readily thrive in or about the town, than those which are bought from distant places where the air is clear and thin'.

their plants when they have got them'. Fairchild, who purported to write his so-called 'Papers' 'purely for the Publick service', remarked that 'I see no Reason why I should not cultivate this innocent Pleasure' among his fellow citizens, 'that from the highest to the lowest, every one may be improving their talent, or even their Mite, in the best Way they can, in order to increase their Quiet of Mind, to be fix'd in a right Notion of County Happiness, when their Affairs will permit them to reach such Pleasures'.[7]

Fairchild's particularised horticultural geography of the City and its suburbs was based on first-hand experience of the city's garden spaces – or what he called 'our close Gardens'.[8] Fairchild, like his contemporaries Sir Hans Sloane, Leonard Plukenet, James Petiver and the Reverends Robert Uvedale and Adam Buddle observed and gathered wild and cultivated plants flourishing in the fields and gardens around London, which were subsequently incorporated into his herbarium.[9] Whilst most of these men cited the occurrence of interesting, rare or outstanding specimens at William Darby

and Fairchild's nurseries at Hoxton, the Bishop of London's garden at Fulham Palace, the Royal Gardens at Hampton Court, the Physick Garden at Chelsea and 'Brompton-park', only Fairchild, Buddle and Petiver documented cultivated plants as they occurred in public places and at modest domestic settings (figs 16a and b); and of these three men, only Fairchild published his observations.

Fairchild divided the metropolis into three distinct areas – each of which was claimed to 'promise' a different 'Success in Gardening'. The areas were distinguished by three factors – proximity to the River Thames, density of development and, most importantly, air quality. The author believed that the most salubrious area of town was 'the Part of London next the River Thames', and in particular the riverside terrain extending westwards from the Temple to the Palace of Westminster, including the Strand. The second zone comprised the 'more Inland Parts of the Town', which constituted most of the City of London; and the third encompassed the spacious residential estates of the West End.[10]

At the eastern and western metropolitan frontiers of the Thames, both margins of the river were lined with clusters of row houses recessed from the banks by long narrow gardens. The greatest concentration of these spacious grounds lay within the stretch of river from the House of Commons to the Temple, which boasted the well-appointed gardens of Whitehall and Somerset House. Fairchild conjectured that gardens immediately adjacent to the river thrived because they lay open to the water, sun and air; he credited 'the constant rising Vapour from the River' as helping plants overcome the effects of 'the poisonous Quality in the City Smoke'. He remarked that at the garden of the Earl of Halifax, near the Houses of Parliament, he saw many plants 'which will not do so well in the Squares, which are situate in the Middle of the Town'. He observed that at Whitehall 'the late Mr Heyman's had several Pots of Flowers, both Auriculas and Carnations, which blossom'd very well', and that at the garden at Somerset House the conditions were so favourable as to 'produce several Varieties of Things, which the more Inland Parts of Town have not generally been garnish'd with'. At the Temple, as in the previous examples, the gardens were alleged to afford a great variety of plants, including a 'good Number of Exotick Plants'.[11]

If gardening on the riverside was apparently easy and delightful, the activity was troublesome and frustrating in 'the Court-Yards, and close Places in the City'. Fairchild asserted that in 'this part of the City Gardening depends upon more Skill than all the rest; for here we have little Liberty of Air'. He remarked that although 'it has been thought difficult to provide such Plants as would barely live in such Places: And also it has been judged impossible, that any Plant should last therein Health for any Time. Now therefore, to remedy this Defect, I shall from Experience give the Names of such Plants as will grow and prosper in the closest Parts of London'. Among the plants were 'The Lime-Tree; The Lylac, with the white Flower; The Lylac, with the blue Flower; The Lylac, with the Purple Flower; the Persian Jessamin; The Bladder Senna; The Figg; The Mulberry; The Virginia Creeper; The Vine; The Common Privet; The Angelica; The Lillies; The Perennial Sunflower; The Martegons; John Tradescant's Starwort; London Pride; Currans; Elder; Gilder-Rose'.[12]

These plants, he claimed 'remain good a long Time, if they are well taken Care of'. To this list he added 'many sorts of Annual Flowers' including 'French Marygold, African Marygolds, and Annual Sunflower, &c'. As further 'Ornament to such Places', he recommended 'such Plants and Flowers as will make a good Summer Show; and these are the French Honeysuckle, Pinks, Daisies of various Kinds, Double-Stocks, Scarlet Lichness, Wall-flowers, Double Rockets, and Pots of breeding Tulips, which will blow much better than the striped Sorts'.[13]

Fairchild wished to inspire in his readers a desire to grow plants in locations in which they were commonly believed to fail. For instance, we are told that lilacs thrived in garden squares as well as in tavern yards, narrow alleys and small courts throughout the City, and Bladder Senna grew well in a court in 'Crutched Fryers'; 'The Scorpion, bladder Senna, and Citissus . . .' could be observed in some little courts and gardens in Lincoln's Inn Fields; and the 'syringe grew very well in *Soho-Square*'. The horticulturist took particular pleasure in relating that figs flourished in some close places about Bridewell 'altho' encompass'd with Houses on every Side, which are so high, that the Sun never reaches them in Winter. These Figg-trees are about fifteen Foot high, and are Green from near the Ground to the Top; for which Reason, I wonder it has not been more generally propagated in the City Gardens; especially since they will not only thrive well in the *London*, but bear good Fruit too, if they are well pruned'. Figs are also reported as having 'ripen'd very well in the *Roll's* Garden in Chancery Lane'.[14]

Other fruit trees also prospered. Pears 'thrive very well in *London*; and besides the fine Show they make when they are in Flower, they will bear very good Fruit, as may be observed in very close Places and confined Allies about *Barbican*, and other Parts about the *Aldersgate-street*, *Bishopsgate street*, &c.' 'Currans' are said to 'conform themselves well to the City Smoak', thriving everywhere – 'even upon Leads on the Tops of Houses amidst the Chimneys'. The mulberry is said to have flourished in the closest courts and alleys: 'There are now two large Mulberry-Trees growing in a little Yard, about sixteen Foot square, at *Sam's* Coffee-house in *Ludgate-street*. There are two likewise, at the Hall belonging to the Worshipful Company of Clothworkers, which have stood there many Years, and bear plentifully, and ripen very well. These may be either planted in Tubs or Cases, and treated as Standards, or nail'd against Walls.'[15]

To these successes we may also add 'the Vine': in

17 A herbarium specimen of 'Virginian Locus[t] Tree' (*Robinia pseudoacacia*), possibly from the celebrated tree in Lady Russell's garden in Southampton (later Bloomsbury) Square, where it was reputed to grow 'over the Wall' (*c.*1700–10). Sir Hans Sloane, *Hortus Siccus*, vol. 180, fol. 3. Natural History Museum, London. Walpole records in his *Essay on Landscape Gardening* that the tree was sold for timber in 1800.

'*Leicester-fields*, there is a Vine that bears good Grapes every Year; and in many close Places, such as Tavern Yards, there are Vines now growing in good Perfection, and even bear good Fruit'. The vine is also credited for fruiting in sunny positions: at 'the *Rose-Tavern* without *Temple bar*, there is a Vine that covers an Arbour . . . [that] has ripe grapes upon it; and at a Coffee-house next to *Grey's-Inn-Gate*, there is now a Vine which grows very well in a small Pot, tho' it is constantly kept in a close Room; this Year it was full of Leaves before *Christmas.*' Hops is also cited as having grown 'very vigorously' and borne fruit in city gardens near Charterhouse.[16]

Fairchild made copious references to trees. The '*Virginia Accacia* makes a good Figure and a large Tree. There was one of them growing in a close Passage between the New and Old Palace-yard *Westminster*, about two or three years ago, and I suppose it may be still growing there; and there is some now growing at *Russel* House in *Bloomsbury* Square'(fig. 17). Fairchild continued, 'we have instances enough of the Elm . . . from the large Trees now growing in the *Temple* and several other Inns of Court'. Among the species of other trees prospering in town we are told that planes were growing at the churchyard of St Dunstan's in the East (above forty feet high), horse-chestnuts make a fine appearance, and give excellent shade at the Temple gardens. Moreover, in a close alley near Whitecross street, toward Bunhill Fields, there is a 'White Thorn . . . [which] I believe is the highest Tree of the Kind in *England* . . . There are good Hedges of this Plant in the *Charter-house* Gardens, altho' surrounded with houses'.[17]

The 'Creeper of *Virginia*' is reported to have been well known throughout the City, 'even where there is no Sun at all': the plant is commended for its rapacious growth, and likewise for its excellent qualities which commend it 'for Ornament of Balconies and Windows, and will grow so well in Pots or Cases, that it will soon cover walls, and shade the Windows, if they lie exposed to the Sun'.[18]

After completing his references to plants growing within the City's close quarters, Fairchild proceeds to expand upon gardening achievements in the spacious streets of the West End. The forms of gardens specific to the West End were, according to the author, balconies, window-boxes and squares.[19] Window-boxes and garden squares are discussed in later chapters, and become central to the tradition of the London town garden; balconies, on the other hand, are more specific to the West End, at least in Fairchild's imaginative topography of the metropolis.

Fairchild recognises a range of diverse elements within London gardens. He distinguishes, first, between what may be termed garden traces, on one hand, and, on the other, gardening achievements wrought through intensive cultivation. Traces – which usually consisted of large, well-known trees – are recognisable as beleaguered relics of the large gardens of the past. Despite the dislocation of these elements, they continue to thrive; they are essentially pastoral images, which produce fruit and flower without apparent cultural work or supervision. Gardening achievements are, on the other hand, georgic, or anti-pastoral, in as much as they require for their existence a high level of horticultural sophistication.[20] Fairchild makes a further distinction in the gardens' codes of signification: City gardens are unexpectedly fruitful, and their plentiful produce is garnered for consumption. Those gardens are therefore part of the mundane and commonplace activities of the domestic round, and contrast sharply with gardens in the less close quarters of town, and especially in the West End. There they are ornamental and showy; their exoticism and innovation suggests that they are symbolic of frivolity and affluence.

The great variety of plants reputed to flourish on the city's balconies includes quantities of spring ephemerals such as tulips, martagons, lilies, iris and crocus, scores of hardy annuals, as well as evergreen displays of bay, box, privet intermixed with flowering shrubs such as lilac, guelder rose and jasmine. Mr Jobber, 'a very curious Gentleman, in *Norfolk-Street*', is credited with having grown an admirable display of aloes, and 'also some of those strange Plants call'd Torch-Thistles, and also some sorts of Fig Marygolds on Ficoides'. In a 'much closer [more confined] Place than this, i.e. *Aldermanbury*, Mr *Smith* an Apothecary has a very good Collection of these succulent or juicy Plants, which he has kept for many Years'.[21]

Fairchild's narrative does not make any mention of the small planted outdoor gardens which are known to have been reasonably common in the more spacious quarters of town, as can be seen in Strype's plan of the parish of St James's (1720; fig. 11) and Zachary Chambers's plan of part of the parish of St James's (1769; fig. 18) which shows gardens depicted in Kip's views of about 1710. This omission is presumably a reflection of several factors. Among them, Fairchild has at heart his self-interests as a nurseryman; he promoted the possibil-

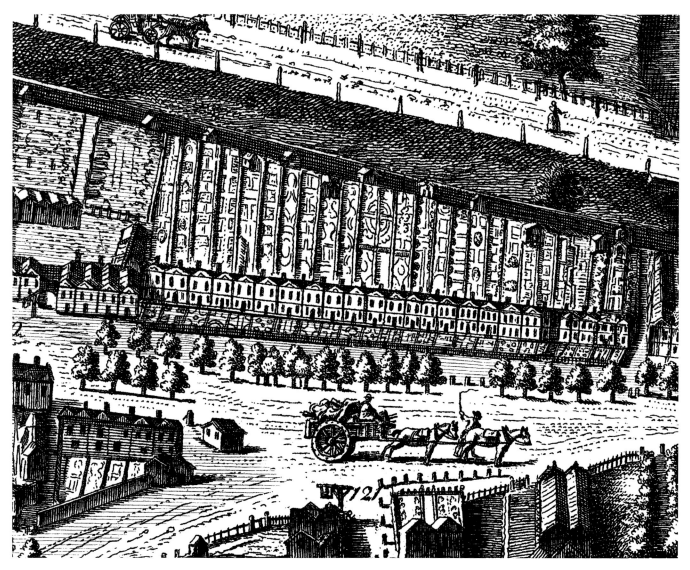

19   Joshua Rhodes, *Topographical Survey of the Parish of Kensington*, engraving, 1766 (detail). Kensington and Chelsea Borough Library. Rhodes's deployment of inventive free-hand geometrical garden plans suggests the infinite array of options possible in the layout of small gardens. See figure 109 for a plan of the forecourts as they appeared in 1811.

At nearly every house in town there was either in front towards the street, or inside the house and building, or also in both places, a little yard. They had commonly planted in these yards and round about them, partly in the earth and ground itself, partly in pots and boxes, several of the trees, plants and flowers which could stand the coal-smoke in London. They thus sought to have some of the pleasant enjoyments of a country life in the midst and hubbub of the town [fig. 19].[27]

Mayfair and Marylebone were laid out and built on a rational, strongly rectilinear geometry which provided for regular and substantial houses, often with equally regular plots behind them (fig. 20). Rocque, however, does not show these spaces. The density of the developed ground in these areas is comparable to the densest quarters of the City. Instead, Rocque's plan suggests that small gardens – as he represents them – are more frequently distributed in the quarters of town where there is the least evidence of rational estate planning. Some explanation of this disparity can be found by reference to Fairchild's definition of the city garden more as a way of handling, developing and elaborating an interstitial space than as a positive spatial entity in its own right. At ground level, gardens of this kind would clearly form

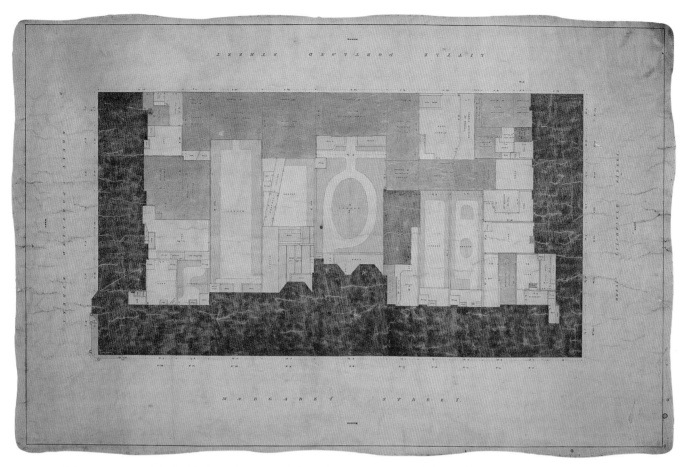

20 Detail from an estate 'Block Plan' on the Cavendish-Harley Estate in Marylebone, showing the gardens of a row of houses in Margaret Street, pen and coloured wash, c.1830. Howard de Walden Estate, London. The 'openings behind' were created when the houses were first erected in the mid-eighteenth century.

a major part of any experience of visiting the city and its houses. To a cartographer, however, such gardens could easily remain invisible – or might actually be viewed as untidy accretions which threatened to disrupt the sense of urban order, and must therefore be excluded from any representation which attempted to range over the city in its totality. In focusing on the civic, public aspects of London rather than on the domestic, individual and private character of the its dwellings, Rocque consigns the small to medium-sized garden to the lowest possible category of domestic mundane-ness, simply by allowing it to be absorbed into the undifferentiated generality that surrounds it.

★   ★   ★

HORWOOD'S LONDON

The elements ignored by Rocque are given ample attention in our next survey. The four editions of Richard Horwood's *Plan of the Cities of London and Westminster, with the Borough of Southwark including adjacent Suburbs*, which appeared in the twenty-seven-year span between 1792 and 1819, make it a unique general guide to a period of rapid growth of the metropolis. Each revised edition depicts immense and scattered tracts of new development and charts successive revisions to the existing fabric (fig. 22).[28] The first survey is reputed to have covered an area containing approximately 110,000 inhabited houses and about 730,000 inhabitants. The first edition of the resulting plan shows that the city has grown only at a modest rate since the time of Rocque; the population has increased more slowly than the country as a whole, and there is restrained expansion on to green-field sites. Most of the new building land

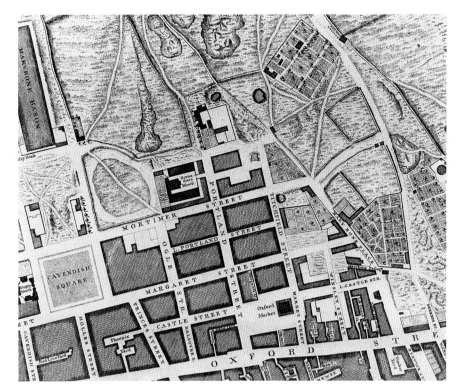

21 John Rocque, *Survey of London and Westminster*, engraving, 1746 (detail). Paul Mellon Collection, Yale Center for British Art, New Haven. In this plan Rocque draws a sharp contrast between the new grid of squares imposed on the landscape, and relict footpaths and fields – traces of a topographical geometry that are about to disappear. Compare with figure 22.

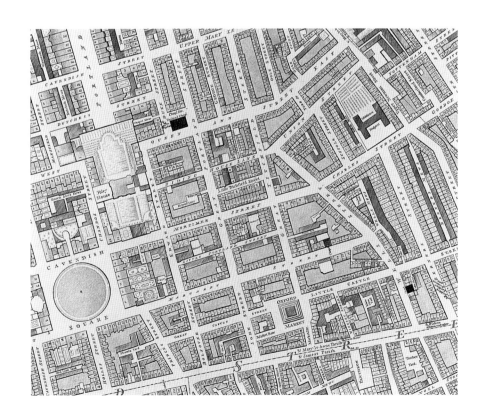

23   Richard Horwood, variant plate from *A Plan of the Cities of London and Westminster* (1799), Peter Jackson. Horwood's panoramic view of 1799 shows newly built strings of terraces at the northern end of Baker Street. The street projected into the open country-side of Marylebone and later joined the perimeter of Regent's Park.

24   View looking south to the newly erected houses at Colebroke Row, Hoxton, mezzotint, *c*.1790. Private collection.

22 (*facing page bottom*)   Richard Horwood, *Plan of the Cities of London and Westminster*, 1792 (detail). Paul Mellon Collection, Yale Center for British Art, New Haven. Compare with figure 21 to see how Marylebone had been transformed by the building of new streets and houses.

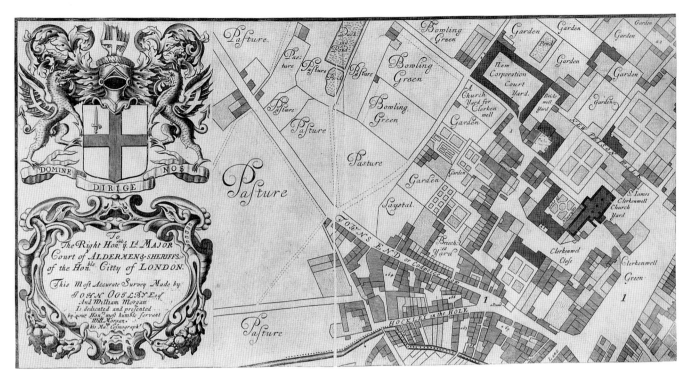

25   John Ogilby and William Morgan, *A Large and Accurate Map of the City of London . . .*, engraving, 1676 (detail). Paul Mellon Collection, Yale Center for British Art, New Haven.

in the second half of the eighteenth century occupied redundant tenter grounds and lightly developed terrain appropriated by the encroachment of metropolitan enterprise.[29] A significant portion of the new building was residential premises (often combined residential and shop premises) created for the middle and lower middle classes – the West End, Knightsbridge, Sloane Square and its environs, and the laying out of Kennington, Walworth and St George's Fields south of the river. Many of these areas were covered by acres of terraced housing, each premises with its own small outdoor ground at the rear. For those dwellings that lined the principal routes from the centre to the suburbs, or streets near the edge of town, shallow front gardens frequently insulated the premises from the noise and dust of the thoroughfare. Areas adorned with gardens contrasted sharply with the smaller, more concentrated developments for artisans, clerks and others of lesser means in the Christchurch district of Southwark, Shoreditch and parts of St Luke's Old Street, and portions of Whitechapel, Bethnal Green and St George's in the East. What is particularly interesting to note is that many of the ribbons of 'suburban' roadside terraces which formerly marched into the open countryside were now the bulwarks of dense backland estate developments – many of which were launched in

the late eighteenth century and conceived of as new 'towns'. Their names, in fact, affirm their status and individuality – such as Hans Town, Camden Town and Somers Town (figs 23 and 24).

The next and subsequent editions of Horwood's map were produced by William Faden (1807, 1813 and 1819) and recorded the city as it experienced rapid expansion and redevelopment: by 1819 the area covered by the original thirty-two sheets contained about 150,000 houses and a population of approximately one million. Of the various editions of the plan, that of 1807 is the most thoroughly revised. First, its content is enhanced to accommodate 9,750 new individual houses, as well as the addition and subtraction of countless other buildings, and second, a number of graphic innovations applied to all the plates increases the level of detail and accuracy of the survey.[30] Such initiatives not only enhance the literal layer of information conveyed on the map, but also lead us to question the processes that galvanised the changes, and to decipher the map's 'iconological' meaning.

To describe the extensive topographical changes to the city is unnecessary. What is more significant is the extensive and systematic application of new techniques to refine successive editions of the map. Among them, vague and fuzzy shadings of premises behind street frontages are given (seemingly accurate) building lines. Architectural details are added to many churches and public buildings, and some private ones are named. Names are added to many fields, gardens, burial grounds and areas of water such as ponds; many more premises are numbered; many unnamed yards and alleys are labelled; and the garden plans of the city's principal squares are revised to reflect their new decorative planting schemes.

Horwood's projection was far more ambitious than any that had preceded it. His was the first map of London since Ogilby and Morgan's of 1676 to claim that 'every Dwelling house is described & numbered' (fig. 25).[31] His urban geography is structured around domestic space, which is meticulously apportioned and numbered (although incompletely) throughout the metropolis. Small individual urban and suburban gardens, or openings, and their plans are represented by conventional signs; signs that bear a visual resemblance

to the features they represent (fig. 26). They are both 'placeless' and universal in as much as their meaning is independent of their positioning on the ground plan. These ubiquitous, carefully delineated and consistent spaces convey a straightforward topographical statement about late eighteenth-century London: small gardens are integral and regular constituent elements of the urban fabric, and, like dwellings, they are representative of homogeneous space. Horwood's map expresses strongly a new assumption that a garden, explicitly defined as such, could be expected to form an integral part of almost every domestic premises.

As a metaphor for the city, Horwood's plan emphasises the role of the mercantile metropolis as a vast multiplicity of individual, semi-autonomous parts, harmoniously integrated into an ordered whole: the overriding and explicit objective of the plan is to attempt to record every dwelling house in the metropolis, and to ascribe to each its number.[32] In supplying a commentary on the task of map-making, the plan defines its own

26   *A View of Lord Bute's Erections at Kew*, engraving, *c.*1780. Private collection. The generalised representation of garden plans in this engraving resembles Richard Horwood's embellishments to his plans of 1792–9: each garden is given an individual and particularised layout. Of particular interest are the amoeba-shaped beds of the garden to the left of 'K'.

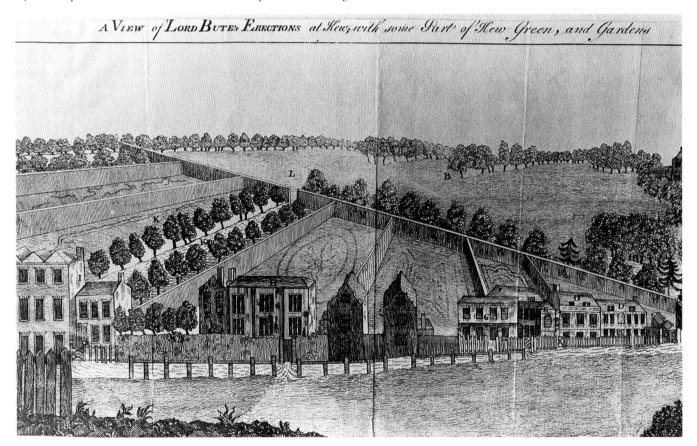

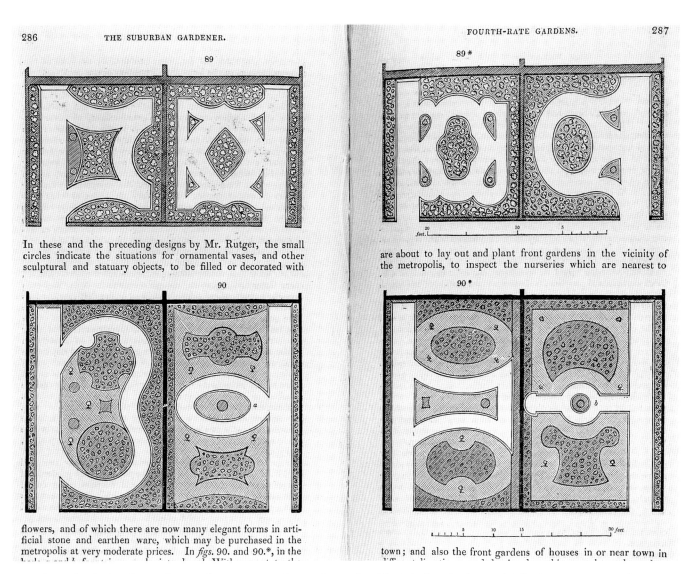

89

In these and the preceding designs by Mr. Rutger, the small circles indicate the situations for ornamental vases, and other sculptural and statuary objects, to be filled or decorated with

90

flowers, and of which there are now many elegant forms in artificial stone and earthen ware, which may be purchased in the metropolis at very moderate prices. In *figs.* 90. and 90.*, in the

89*

are about to lay out and plant front gardens in the vicinity of the metropolis, to inspect the nurseries which are nearest to

90*

town; and also the front gardens of houses in or near town in

28   Plans of eight fourth-rate front gardens, engraving from J. C. Loudon, *The Suburban Gardener and Villa Companion* (1838), figs 89–90.

est must depend on the trees and plants introduced and their culture.[5]

This description suggests that the characteristics of these gardens had changed little from the early eighteenth century when Stephens, Thomas Fairchild and Joseph Spence had addressed the 'trifling' pursuit of town gardening – for then, as now, 'little town gardens' were still generally small in extent, flat in situation, regular in layout and enclosed by brick boundary walls. Loudon, however, took for granted that many of the city's 'fourth-rate' premises – from the artisan's fourth-rate cottage to the aristocrat's first-rate town palace – possessed small front and back gardens – attributes which were not generally common to the average ter-

raced house before the third quarter of the eighteenth century (figs 30 and 31).

The incentive to provide long strips of ground behind houses, and sometimes shallow plots before them, developed during the eighteenth century. Their presence and proliferation reflected a consensus among many architects and commentators on town planning that gardens were capable of improving the character of urban development, and that they were symbolic of a variety of practical and salutary concessions – for example, a recognition of the need for light and ventilation. Private gardens in themselves were not, however, the only purveyors of airiness and spaciousness; for many Londoners, 'from the first persons of quality' downwards, the provision of a garden was less important than a view over a garden square, a park or distant countryside. (This displacement of desire from the private and particular to the public and general is discussed at length in chapter 8.)

Property development practices in Georgian London determined the presence and shape of most of the city's town gardens. Much has been written on the subject of town planning and the development of the 'great estates' during the eighteenth and early nineteenth centuries.[6] The majority of these analyses, however, are concerned with bricks and mortar; few have extended their remit to include the garden. Our interest in the subject is limited to the extent to which these factors explain the existence and nature of these gardens.

Londoners generally rented, leased and/or shared their urban habitations. The most common dwelling type was the terraced house, which, from the early eighteenth century onwards, was constructed in regular and uniform ranges, which gave a dignified unity to what were otherwise rows of small and undistinguished, speculatively built houses (figs 32–5). Within these, many

30 John Swertner, *A View of the Cities of London and Westminster with the Suburbs and Circumjacent County*, engraving, 1789 (detail). Guildhall Library, Corporation of London.

29 Plans of two fourth-rate back gardens, engraving from J. C. Loudon, *The Suburban Gardener and Villa Companion* (1838), figs 70–71.

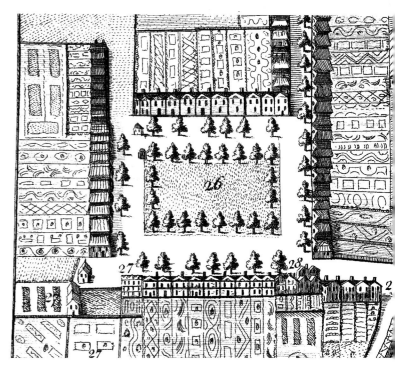

31 J. Rhodes, *Topographical Survey of the Parish of Kensington*, engraving, 1766 (detail). Kensington and Chelsea Borough Library. The small individual garden plans of Kensington Square illustrated are represented by conventional signs that bear a visual resemblance to the features which they represent.

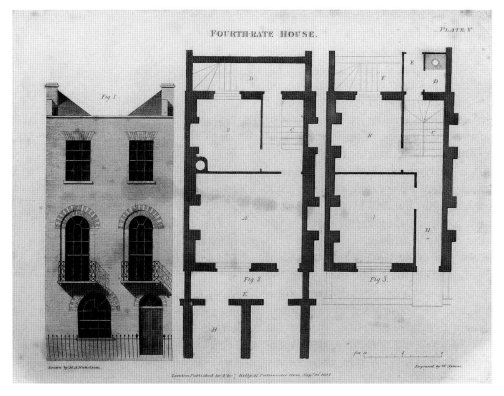

32 'Fourth-rate House', engraving from Peter Nicholson, *The New Practical Builder* (1823), pl. v.
Beinecke Rare Book and Manuscript Library, Yale University, New Haven.

33 'Third-rate House', engraving from Peter Nicholson, *The New Practical Builder* (1823), pl. iv.
Beinecke Rare Book and Manuscript Library, Yale University, New Haven.

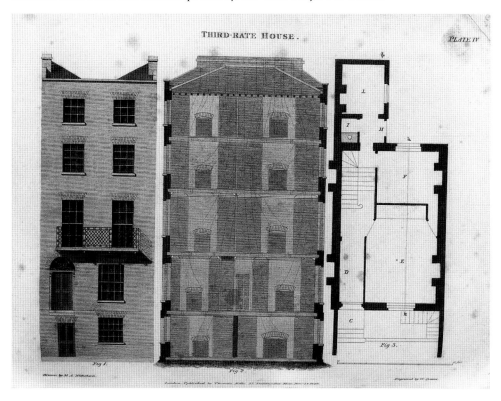

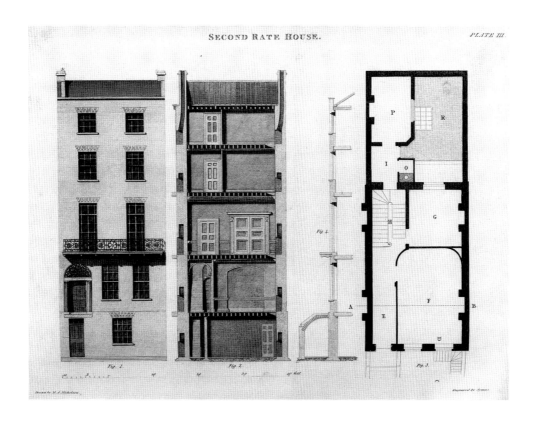

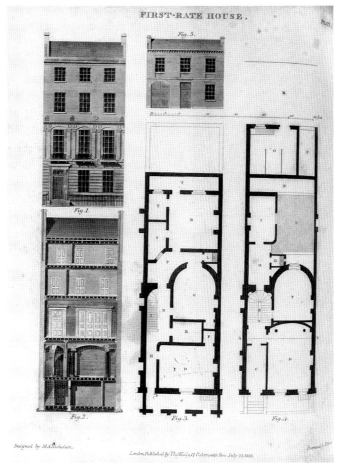

34 (*above*) 'Second-rate House', engraving from Peter Nicholson, *The New Practical Builder* (1823), pl. III. Beinecke Rare Book and Manuscript Library, Yale University, New Haven.

35 'First-rate House', engraving from Peter Nicholson, *The New Practical Builder* (1823), pl. I. Beinecke Rare Book and Manuscript Library, Yale University, New Haven.

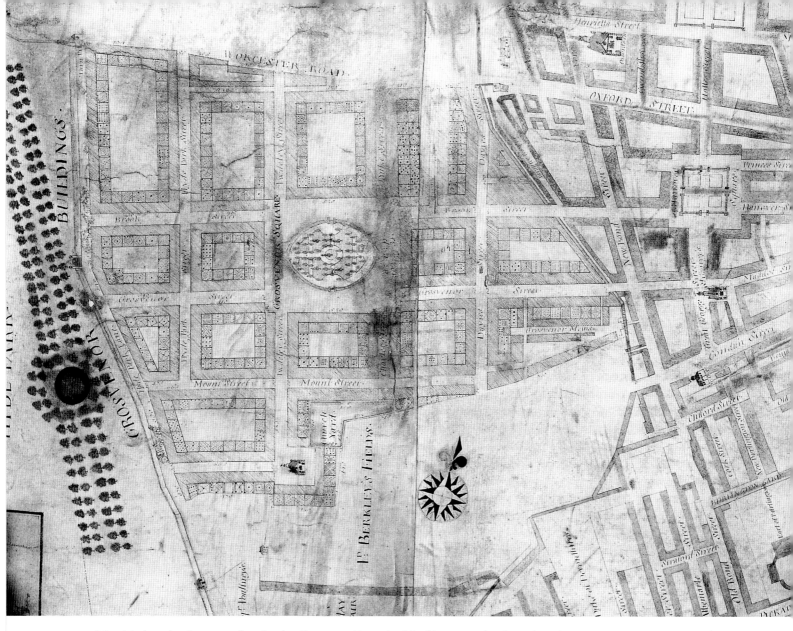

37   John Mackay, development plan for the Grosvenor Estate in Mayfair, pen and coloured wash, 1723. Westminster City Archives, London.

remarked in 1712 'the Extent of Buildings [in town] is more necessary than that of Gardens, on account of being the more usual Place of Dwelling, and of Land bearing a higher Value'.[21] The occupants of modest but spacious houses, however, often required 'openings' behind them for the provision of household offices, stabling and possibly gardens. However, the residents of the grandest houses seldom sought a garden, preferring instead a beautiful view – as John Gwynn remarked in *London and Westminster Improved* (1766), a 'London garden' was 'a thing in itself rather unnecessary' where a house commanded an 'uninterrupted view to agreeable scenery'.[22]

Moreover, Londoners who could afford to maintain large gardens were seldom interested in doing so in the centre of town – especially if they had access to them elsewhere. Defoe commented in 1720 that people who lived in the City were more likely to have second residences in suburbs such as Hackney and as far out as Epsom in Surrey. The gentry and the aristocracy who, on the other hand, resided in the fashionable West End often rented houses in town for 'the season' and, as itinerant visitors, often took little interest in establishing gardens during their tenure.

Nevertheless, a great number of persons did live and garden in the metropolis. The previous examples have shown that by the 1730s a pattern of residential estate development had been established in which garden space in the form of squares and private gardens had been an element. This planning formula, which was aimed at attracting to estates tenants of fashion or at least of respectability, guided 'suburban' estate development in London well throughout the eighteenth century and into the early nineteenth century.

Small gardens were considered sufficiently important for time and energy as well as money to be devoted to them: a number of celebrated architects and intellectuals appear to have been involved in the design of urban garden spaces.

The extent of professional involvement is, however, unknown; while records allude to the consultation of eminent designers there is often insufficient evidence to deduce the extent of their professional involvement. Among those who are documented as having shaped small town gardens are Robert Adam, Richard Bateman, Charles Bridgeman, Lancelot 'Capability' Brown, George Richardson, Henry Holland, Benjamin Hyett, Giacomo Leoni, Sir John Soane (fig. 38), Joseph Spence, James 'Athenian' Stuart, Stephen Switzer and Thomas Wright. For instance in January 1735 Charles Bridgeman received a payment from Lord Glenorchy 'for work done in my town garden' at 46 Grosvenor Square; in 1763 William Chambers advised his client, the 8th Earl of Abercorn, at 25 Grosvenor Square, that his 'Lattice work on the garden' was 'rotten & not worth Painting but I have ordered Your Lordship's Gardener to trim the trees and nail them up where it is wanted to prevent their being blown down and torn to Pieces by the Wind'; Lord Bute employed Capability Brown, in collaboration with Henry Holland, to lay out his garden at 73 South Audley Street (c.1770); Brown also applied himself to the design of the small suburban garden of Frederick Nicolay in Richmond (1770), prompted by the graceful request of the client, who lured Brown by flattery, claiming that he hoped 'it is no offence to wish for a miniature picture from a Raphael'; and Henry Holland probably laid out Spencer House garden in St James's Place in collaboration with Lavinia Countess Spencer in about 1795.[23]

38   Joseph Michael Gandy, detail from a composite view of Sir John Soane's house, Lincoln's Inn Fields. Sir John Soane's Museum, London. The 'Monument Court' created in 1812 by Soane behind his house at 13 Lincoln's Inn Fields contains statues, full-scale models of elements designed for the Bank of England, a Coade stone vase from Carlton House, ammonite fossils and the 'architectural Pasticcio' – a full-scale copy of one of the capitals from the Temple of Vesta at Tivoli.

GARDENS AND THE LAYOUT OF THE HOUSE: THE BACK GARDEN

In his book *A Complete Body of Architecture* of 1756 the practising architect and architectural theorist Isaac Ware condemned town gardening as a pointless and 'very idle' pursuit:

> The common houses in *London* are all built in one way, and that so familiar that it will need little instruction. The general custom is to make two rooms and a light closet on the floor, and if there be any little opening behind, to pave it.
>
> Some attempt to make flower-gardens of these spots, but this is very idle; plants require purer air than animals, and however we breathe in *London*, they cannot live where there is so much smoak and confinement; nor will even gravel continue clean many days from the turning.
>
> In this respect therefore, instead of borders under the walls, the best method is to lay the whole with good sound stone pavement, and at the farther part to build the needful edifice, that cannot in *London* be removed farther off; and something of similar shape and little service opposite to it. An alcove with a seat is a common contrivance in the space between, but it is a strange place to sit for pleasure: all this therefore is better omitted; and the young architect is to have a general caution on this head, that will serve him on many more, which is, that when there cannot be any proper ornament, nothing is so becoming as perfect plainness.[24]

Ware's remarks suggest that by the mid-eighteenth century his readers were sufficiently 'familiar' with the gardens of 'common houses in London' to profit from his pragmatic recommendations. It was, moreover, a measure of the popularity of town gardens, that he addressed the subject of such gardens in his treatise on Georgian architectural theory and practice.[25]

In spite of his censure, and true to his dictum that 'nothing must be esteemed below the consideration of a complete architect', Ware made several constructive remarks on this despised 'room' out of doors when he outlined the layout of the average terraced house; and we should acquaint ourselves with his commentary before embarking on a survey of gardens as it establishes the context for our observations on the planning of the town garden.[26]

Ware considered the 'opening' behind the dwelling one of the principal elements of his vision of the perfect common townhouse of five storeys and about fourteen rooms. When building a house on a London building plot the 'opening, or garden, as it is called, behind' was a significant and necessary concession to achieve the 'greatest conveniency' (fig. 39).[27] The garden – which often occupied as much area of the building plot as the ground-plan of the house – provided air and light, as well as much needed space for external domestic offices including pantries, laundries, larders, privies (and in larger premises, stables and coach houses) which could not be accommodated within the house.

Although the subject of servicing the Georgian house has been explored in great detail elsewhere, it is helpful to recapitulate how the provision of household services, and access to them for regular maintenance, had historically posed constraints on the layout of outdoor domestic space.[28] Until the late eighteenth century most incoming services (water and fuel) and outgoing services (rubbish and sewage) were reasonably independent.

39 English school, *View of a small garden reputed to be near Walthamstow*, watercolour, *c*.1790. Collection of the author.

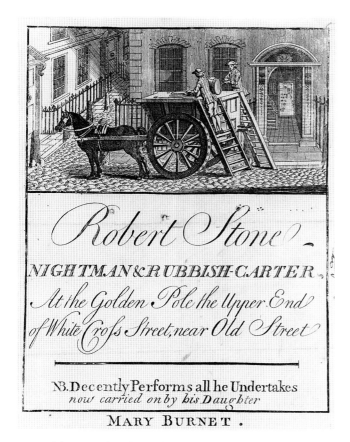

40a and b   A mid-eighteenth-century trade card (and detail) for 'Robert Stone, Nightman & Rubbish-Carter, at the Golden Pole the Upper End of White Cross Street, near Old Street'. The privy, or 'needful edifice', can be seen at the terminus of the back garden. Guildhall Library, Corporation of London.

Many town residences had private wells in their basements or back yards, which supplied them with water. Rainwater was also collected from rooftops and stored in butts or tanks in sunk front areas and courtyards. Although some quarters of London were served by piped water – including most of the West End and parts of the City – the supply of water was 'regular but not constant'.[29] Outgoing services were no less problematic: most townhouses led their drains into a cesspool. The most basic arrangement consisted of an excavation, often located immediately below an outdoor privy, into which liquid waste was discharged in the expectation that it would percolate into the ground. This practice, however, resulted in the contamination of local water supplies. Brick-lined cesspools, which were more common in better quality houses from the late eighteenth century, were only marginally less permeable. Both forms of cesspools required periodic emptying by 'nightmen': 'night soil' was excavated and carried in buckets – often through the house – to tanker carts in the front street (figs 40a and b). This operation took place between mid-

night and five o'clock in the morning, when it caused minimum disruption to the occupants.

The most common location for privies was the back yard or garden. Larger houses often possessed secondary privies for servants in front sunk areas, or occasionally in vaults beneath the street (fig. 41). Water closets, which were popular from the second quarter of the eighteenth century, could be placed inside or outside the house. When they were indoors they were usually accommodated within small projections at the back of the house – sometimes adjacent to reception rooms on the first floor, but more often at parlour floor level (figs 42 and 43).

Ware recommended that the garden should be situated at the lower-storey level ('sunk entirely under ground'), and reached from the rear basement room rather than passing through the ground floor. In so far as the lower storey of the house was conventionally occupied by the kitchen and other domestic offices, and this area was considered damp, 'unwholesome, inelegant, and inconvenient', it was seldom viewed as a desirable point of access to the small garden. Access was more commonly recommended at the 'parlour storey', or ground-floor level: this allowed a more or less imposing connection to be made in the form of a 'flight of easy steps' or a bridge over the back area (fig. 44).[30] Such an entrance was approached by way of a passage, a closet, or – quite often – a small private apartment such as a gentleman's dressing room. In many instances the projecting bays of basement-storey domestic offices provided convenient terraces at raised ground level; these terraces were commonly known as 'leads' on account of the rolled lead employed to waterproof the offices below (fig. 45).

Back gardens were, of course, overlooked by rooms at 'the hinder part of the house'. Where private sleeping apartments and principal reception rooms overlooked the back garden, the area obviously demanded greater attention to its plan. Arrangements were, therefore, recommended with implicit reference to the benefits of the relative tranquillity at the rear of the house – so as to be 'freed from noise and disturbance'. Ware also remarked that where possible the principal apartments should have 'good light' and 'good prospect'. There was, however, in his opinion, little scope to arrange the apartments in 'smaller houses in London' to any great advantage, 'because they are naturally cramped for room, and ty'd down to a particular situation'.[31] (It is worth noting, with reference to this remark, that the distribution of rooms varied immensely, and that views to gardens or distant landscape were taken into consideration when laying out the principal apartments.)

The comprehensive surviving records of one particular early Georgian townhouse – Giacomo Leoni's proposals for Lord Shannon's residence at 21 Arlington Street – demonstrate how the provision of a back garden and forecourt could be significant considerations in planning a town house.[32] The 'Original Draughts, For a new House to be Built in Arlington Street St James' are dated 25 May 1738 and comprise a series of plans, sectional drawings and elevations for a house and garden overlooking Green Park (figs 46–53). Leoni, an accomplished architect, whose authoritative work on Palladio influenced Ware, laid out the forecourt and most of the garden upon a 'Terrass' which was extended over the subterranean domestic offices.[33] In many gardens attached to higher-rated houses, offices were either subterranean, or were located at the end of the garden, and connected to the house by 'arched passage[s] under the garden'.[34] The location of these offices underground provided one way of resolving the difficulties of space

noted by Ware, who remarked that 'conveniencies of all kinds are no where so much wanted as in *London* houses, nor is there any where so little room for them: it is therefore a very proper thing to consider how to add to them'.[35]

Under the forecourt in Arlington Street, and separated from the 'Body of the House' by a ten foot 'Airy', the architect proposed to locate the 'Dorste [dust] Hole', coal vaults, beer cellars, 'a room for powdering ye Wiggs', 'a room for wetting ye Knifes', and a 'House of Offices' (servants' privies).[36] Below the garden were situated the wash-house and laundry, 'a vault for charcoal', the scullery, the kitchen and stoves, a small oven, a water closet, wet and dry larders, and a coal vault. These offices were separated from the house by a small court (21 by 16 feet) flanked by a 'Collonede from ye Offices to ye House, 5 by 21 [feet]', and a small area (7 by 17 feet). A small area, which opened into the 'gravel walck' to the west of the terrace, admitted light to kitchen, wash-house and laundry.

The main section of the garden consisted simply of a terrace, which may have been paved in stone and laid upon lead. Access to the garden was gained from the house at 'Parlour Storey' by a passage off the dressing-room bay window. A level bridge straddled the 'airy' and the water closet (beneath) to join the terrace. The 'airy', and the small court, like that in the forecourt, were probably intended to be enclosed by a balustrade, or a low iron palisade. The terrace – which occupied the entire width of the forty-five-foot garden frontage – extended westwards for thirty feet from the bridge, where it was bounded by another railing, with an opening at the centre which led to a flight of six steps descending to the gravel walk. The walk, a space twenty-two feet long, was flanked on both sides by small, domed pavilions which were linked by a substantial gated palisade overlooking the Green Park. From the wicket, a gravel walk joined the Queen's Walk in the park; such a continuity served to establish an affinity with the rural character of the park itself, and must have made a sharp contrast to the austere and gardenless forecourt in Arlington Street.

Meanwhile, in Mayfair, the bricklayer Thomas Skeat and architect and developer Thomas Shepherd were building a modest house in a range in South Audley Street. The dwelling, completed by 1739, had no attached stables and only a small garden, which was built at parlour storey upon the flat lead roof of the domestic offices. An important feature of the garden was a stuccoed and pedimented architectural façade set against

44   Jean-Claude Nattes, *Mrs Wilson's House, Bayswater*, pen and watercolour wash, *c.*1808. Guild-hall Library, Corporation of London. Stone steps commonly connected the parlour storey to the back garden.

45   Jean-Claude Nattes, *From Admiral Nugent's house, No. 14, Wigmore Street, [Marylebone], July 5th 1810*, pen and watercolour wash. British Museum, London. In order to reach the garden from the house it was necessary to traverse the 'leads'.

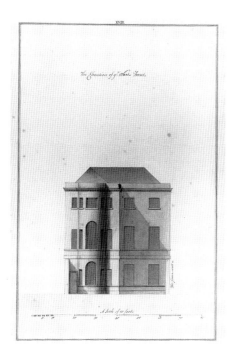

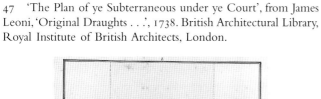

46 'The Elevation of ye Wast Front', Arlington Street, from James Leoni, 'Original Draughts, For a new House to be Built in Arlington Street St James's, for the Rt. Hon:ble The Lord Vis[coun]t Shannon &c', pen and watercolour wash, 25 May 1738. British Architectural Library, Royal Institute of British Architects, London.

48 'The Plan of the [Front] Court', Arlington Street. From James Leoni 'Original Draughts . . .', 1738. British Architectural Library, Royal Institute of British Architects, London.

49 'The Plan of ye Subterraneous under ye Gardin.' from James Leoni, 'Original Draughts . . .', 1738. British Architectural Library, Royal Institute of British Architects, London. This plan clearly illustrates the complex services which were so frequently located beneath small London gardens.

47 'The Plan of ye Subterraneous under ye Court', from James Leoni, 'Original Draughts . . .', 1738. British Architectural Library, Royal Institute of British Architects, London.

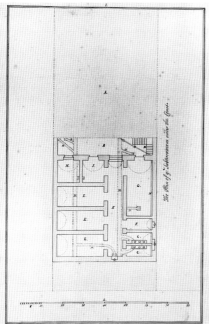

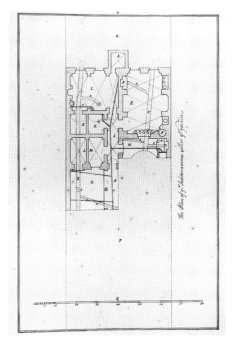

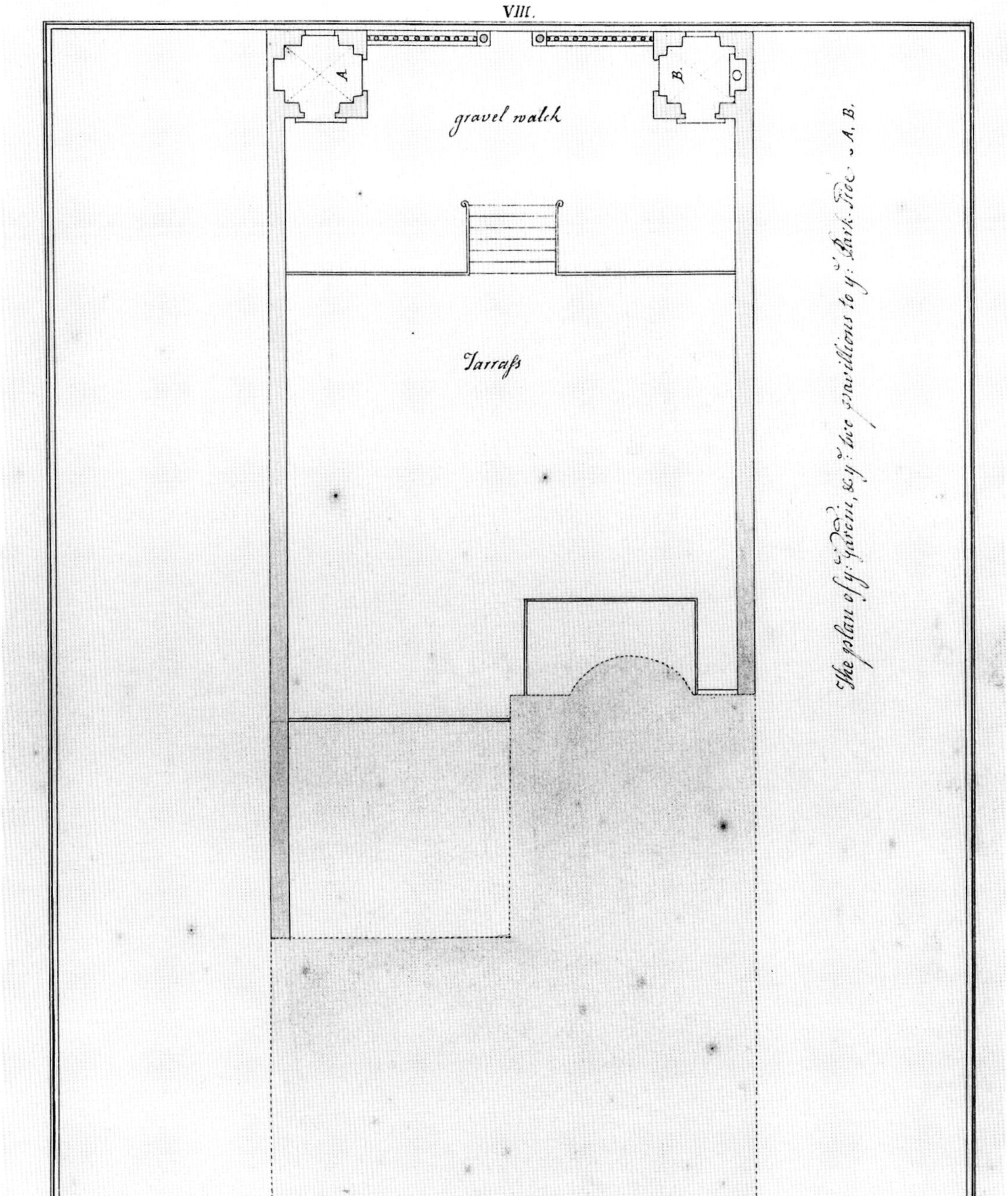

gravel walch

Tarrafs

A.

B.

the plan of yᵉ Gardin, & yᵉ two pavillions to yᵉ Park side. A.B.

5   10   20   30   40   50   60   70   80

A Scale of 80 foot.

50   'The Plan of ye Gardin, & ye two pavillions to ye Park-side', Arlington Street, from James Leoni, 'Original Draughts . . .', 1738. British Architectural Library, Royal Institute of British Architects, London. Arlington
Street was described in 1734 as 'one of the most beautiful situations in *Europe* for health, convenience and beauty;
the front of the street is in the midst of the hurry and splendour of the town, and the back in the quiet simplicity of the country'.

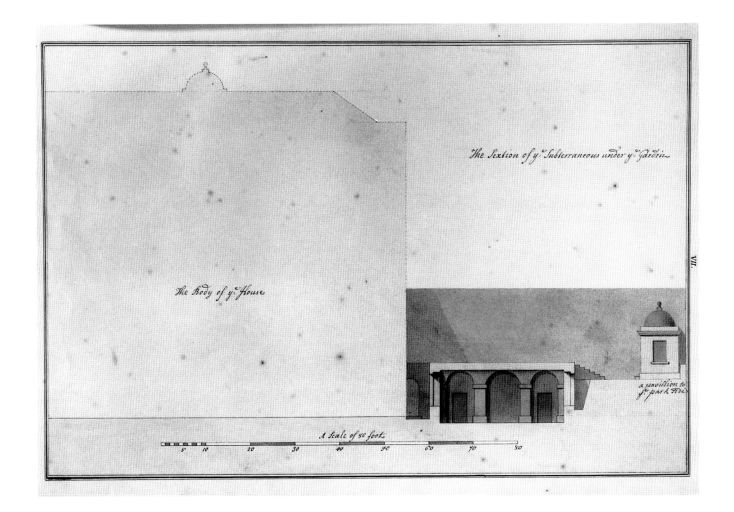

The Sextion of ye Subterraneous under ye Gardin.

The Body of ye House

a pavillion to ye park side.

A Scale of 80 foot.

5   10   20   30   40   50   60   70   80

51 (*above*) 'The Sextion of ye Subterraneous under ye Gardin', from James Leoni, 'Original Draughts . . .', 1738. British Architectural Library, Royal Institute of British Architects, London. The 'pavillion' was one of two small buildings that flanked the iron garden palisade and formed a terminal screen to the garden where it joined Green Park.

52 'The Sextion of the Subterraneous under ye Court', from James Leoni, 'Original Draughts . . .', 1738. British Architectural Library, Royal Institute of British Architects, London.

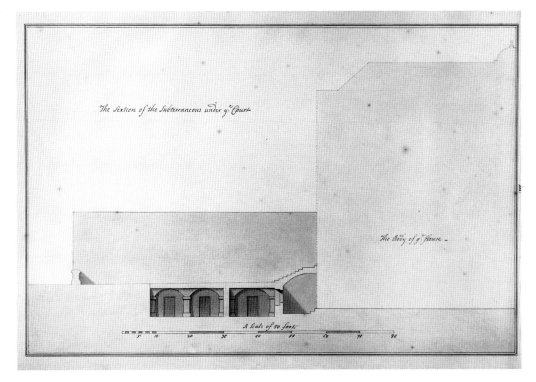

The Sextion of the Subterraneous under ye Court.

The Body of ye House.

A Scale of 80 foot.

5   10   20   30   40   50   60   70   80

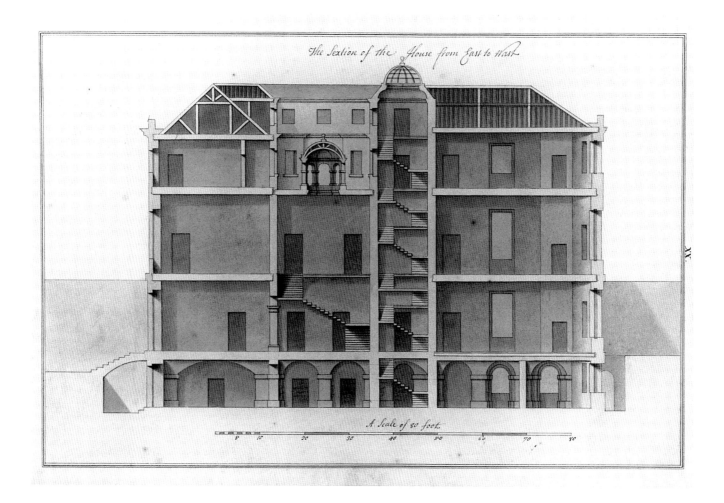

The Sextion of the House from East to West

A Scale of 80 foot.

53 (above) 'The Sextion of the House from the East to Wast', from James Leoni, 'Original Draughts . . .', 1738. British Architectural Library, Royal Institute of British Architects, London.

54 Eyecatcher at 71 South Audley Street, Mayfair, 1990.

the wall of the neighbouring house in South Street. This terminal garden feature, encrusted with three neo-classical reliefs, was designed to carry flues from the basement kitchen.

Although Ware exclaimed that it was 'ridiculous to erect a pompous temple where there was not the extent of a hundred yards from the building', such features occurred with astonishing frequency in London gardens.[37] Not far from South Audley Street, in Hanover Square, the French architect Maurice-Louis Jolivet produced an elegant garden plan for Sir Francis Dashwood's five-bay, four-storey house in Tenterden Street in about 1760 (figs 55–8).[38] The garden was divided in two by a substantial Palladian pavilion surmounted with a balustrade and freestanding classical sculpture. The eye-catcher – possibly a bath house – was erected to embellish the view from the back of the house, blocking views to the stable court and stable block beyond, which communicated directly with Oxford Street. The large garden – framed in the manner of an Italianate courtyard (cortile) – appears to have been laid out at the natural ground level. It possessed a central feature (possibly a basin; over twelve feet in diameter) and a row of trees on its east side. The shallow recesses set at regular intervals in the garden walls were possibly designed to receive decorative panels.

Benjamin West's garden at 14 Newman Street, near Oxford Street, was no less refined. The celebrated painter, and one-time President of the Royal Academy, used his 'Italian garden' as a backdrop for two family portraits.[39] A pencil and wash sketch of the early 1780s shows West, his family and their pets in elegant repose on an elevated terrace beside the artist's studio overlooking the garden (fig. 59). The spatial arrangement of the rectangular plot is, however, more clearly represented in a painted view of about 1808–9 (fig. 60). The garden appears much as it was described by his great-nephew Leigh Hunt, who as a youth spent many a summer in Newman Street in the 1790s. Hunt commented:

Mr West has bought his home, not long . . . after he came to England; he added a gallery at the back of it, terminating in a couple of lofty rooms. The gallery was a continuation of the house-passage, and together with one of those rooms and the parlour, formed three sides of the garden, very small but elegant, with a grass-plot in the middle and busts upon stands under an arcade.[40]

Hunt recollected also that the artist's 'good-sized' parlour with two windows looked out on the 'little garden' which was entered by a 'flight of steps'. 'The garden', he exclaimed, 'with its busts in it, and the pictures which you knew were on the other side of its wall, had an Italian look'.[41] In West's painted view his family – now much expanded – is portrayed in front of the top-lit gallery and surveyed by a pair of heroic busts perched on towering herms. The garden is bathed in the golden light of early evening, and the family's pets – dogs, white pigeons and cat – again feature prominently in the artist's representation of domestic harmony.

At many such houses access to the back garden from the ground floor was formalised as an imposing architectural feature. In Robert Adam's plan for a house (c.1770) on the west side of Portland Place, a centrally placed bridge led up to a portico, which provided the entrance to both coach-houses and stables (figs 61a and b). This approach to the outbuildings was conspicuously more majestic than the back entrance to the house – a simple flight of steps, set to one side. Such an increase in grandeur shows the pre-eminence assigned to views out of the house.

Although the garden plan is not elaborated on the drawing, the layout and choice of plants would have been limited by the depth of soil permitted on the leads over the subterranean office. The garden was ventilated by two narrow sunk areas (approximately six feet wide); this arrangement was used by both Adam and his contemporary James Wyatt at 19 Portman Square, Marylebone.

Adam laid out another town garden between 1771 and 1772 – this time for a fellow Scot, John Grant, Baron of the Scottish Exchequer, who had recently purchased a house at 20 Soho Square (figs 62–4). The architect's scheme formalised the façades of the buildings which overlooked the garden in a manner that evoked the treatment of an Italian cortile. Two sides of the courtyard were formed by the library, which linked the stables to the house and provided the most direct access to the garden. Rows of niches with urns decorated the garden wall, and the façade of the stable-block. As a result, the garden structures, viewed from the house, were once again invested with greater grandeur than the rear façade of the house.[42] Unlike the gardens in Portland Place and South Audley Street, the 'subterraneous' was ventilated by a broad area (over twelve feet wide) and two circular vents set within the garden.[43]

At 29 Old Burlington Street, Piccadilly (c.1770), the conventional arrangement seen in the preceding examples was reversed. Unusually, for a dwelling of such size and status, the garden ended simply in a high wall

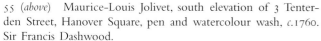

55 (*above*)   Maurice-Louis Jolivet, south elevation of 3 Tenterden Street, Hanover Square, pen and watercolour wash, *c*.1760. Sir Francis Dashwood.

57 (*right*)   Maurice-Louis Jolivet, plan of the garden, bath house and stables at 3 Tenterden Street, Hanover Square, pen and watercolour wash, *c*.1760. Sir Francis Dashwood.

56 and 58 (*below*)   Maurice-Louis Jolivet, elevations of garden screen and stable-block at 3 Tenterden Street, Hanover Square, pen and watercolour wash, *c*.1760. Sir Francis Dashwood.

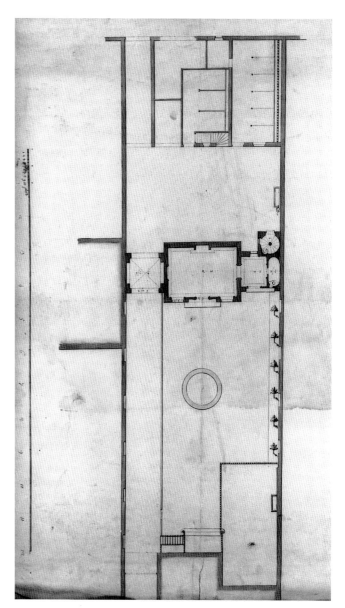

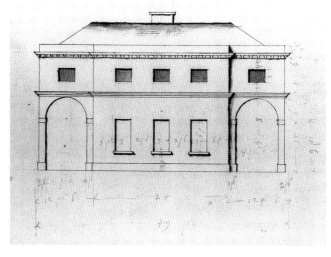

59 Benjamin West, *Mr West's Family in the Garden of their Residence in Newman Street – London*, pen and watercolour wash, early 1780s. Toledo Museum of Art, Ohio.

(fifteen feet), pierced in the centre by a grand gateway opening on to Cork Street, flanked by massive rusticated piers and square pavilions (fig. 65).[44] By contrast, the garden façade of the house itself was highly ornamented: the lower storey being arcaded and the upper one dressed with a Doric order, the whole derived from a design by Palladio for an urban palazzo (fig. 66). The extravagant façade that overlooked such a modest back garden aroused mild amusement from contemporaries who, like Horace Walpole, remarked that the house 'is worse contrived on the inside than is conceivable, all to humour the beauty of the [garden] front'; and reputedly provoked Lord Chesterfield to exclaim 'to be sure he

could not live in it, but intended to take the house over against it [in Cork Street] to look at it'.[45]

Both in this garden and in that at Arlington Street, the pavilions flanking the gateways, which conferred a particular dignity on the garden entrance, were both decorative and utilitarian. While the pair of small garden buildings at Arlington Street served as prospect pavilions, those at Old Burlington Street were described in 1802 as comprising an 'office', a study, a greenhouse and a WC.[46]

The same underlying design principle can be discerned within all the preceding gardens: the most elaborate architectural features were assigned to the

60 Benjamin West, *The Artist's Garden in Newman Street, Marylebone*, oil on canvas, ?1808–9. National Portrait Gallery, Smithsonian Institution, Washington.

garden side of the house, rather than to the public front. In Soho Square, Old Burlington Street, Tenterden Street and Newman Street. in particular, the garden was clearly a domain in which architectural aspiration and invention could be freely indulged in an attempt to evade the usual constraints of the town garden.

The garden of Paul Sandby, the watercolourist, at 4 St George's Row, Tyburn Road, Bayswater, placed the artist's own studio at the end of the garden, in the position of the stable-blocks in more highly rated premises (fig. 67).[47] Sandby's sketch of the two-storey neo-classical studio building – built possibly to the design of his brother, the architect Thomas Sandby – (*c*.1773) is in

sharp contrast to the 'plain built' façade of the house which faced St George's Row, shown in Thomas Girtin's sketch of about 1777 (fig. 68).

Sandby shows his garden as displaying much greater sophistication than his neighbours' to the west at number 5, pointedly emphasising the contrast between the aloof classicism of his own plot and their frenetic horticultural exertions. This superior refinement was established in part through an attempt to create a *cortile* through the introduction of balustrades, statuary and urns. The taste of the neighbours at number 3 would appear from another of Sandby's watercolours to have been more in keeping with his own: the sketch shows

65 Unidentified
draughtsman, garden plan
of General Wade's house
at 29 Old Burlington
Street, pen and
watercolour, c.1770.
Bradford District
Archives.

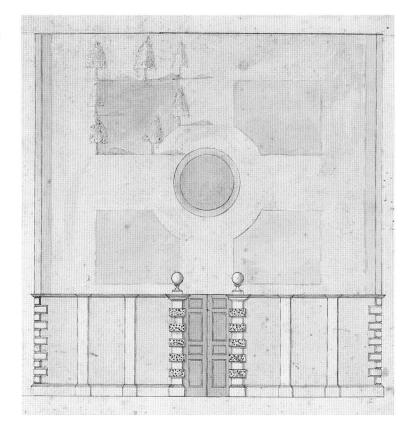

66 Unidentified
draughtsman, design for
alterations and additions
to the garden front of 29
Old Burlington Street,
pen and watercolour
wash, c.1770. Private
collection.

67 Paul Sandby, *Back garden of Mr Paul Sandby's house at 4 St George's Row, Tyburn*, watercolour, *c*.1773. British Museum, London.

68 Thomas Girtin, *View from Hyde Park of Paul Sandby's House St George's Row, Tyburn*, pen and watercolour wash, *c*.1777. British Museum, London.

69 Paul Sandby, *View from the back of 4 St George's Row, Tyburn*, watercolour, *c*.1800–2. British Museum, London.

a timber pavilion with Ionic pilasters at the end of their garden (fig. 69).

Yet another advantage of Sandby's garden layout was that the elevated studio provided a vantage point from which to gaze upon the great view beyond the limits of the garden walls to the open fields of St George's Burial Ground. Ingeniously, Sandby preserved the benefits of prospect from the back of the house by inserting large glazed panels on both sides of the studio.

THE FORECOURT AND THE FRONT GARDEN

The history of the forecourt and the front garden is less straightforward than that of their counterparts at 'the hinder part of the house'.[48] Persons who attempted to garden in these 'close' and 'very close Places' adjoining the open road were subject to what for many years were thought to be insurmountable constraints – most of which were beyond their control. Not only were gardens 'before the house' often subject to severe limitations of space, the want of natural light and the per-nicious effects of dust and the 'poisonous Quality in the City Smoke'; in addition, they were vulnerable to the depredations of the people, pets, vehicles and occasionally livestock that used the rights of way (fig. 70).[49]

A general survey of Strype's edition of *Stowe's Survey* of 1720 suggests that in spite of these limitations, forecourts, or 'pretty handsome open places', were a traditional feature of many town houses.[50] These gardens were, as Kalm reported, 'partly in the earth and ground itself, partly in pots and boxes'[51] and were contrived where space permitted. Fairchild also informs us in 1722 that a wide variety of plants 'make a very good Show in the closest Parts of the Town, as may be observed in Tavern-Yards, and the most narrow Alleys and small Courts in and about the City'. These situations were not, however, considered the best places in which to cultivate a garden, since in 'this part of the City, Gardening depends upon more Skill than all the rest; for here we have little Liberty of Air'. While plants would 'stand in such places', their success depended 'upon the Largeness and Situation of the Places'.[52]

70   James Fredrick King, *Panorama of Kentish Town and Highgate Roads*, pen and watercolour wash, 1848–55 (detail). St Pancras Library, Swiss Cottage, London. These gardens exemplify one of Loudon's most important 'leading rules' on front-garden design: they ascended towards the house, giving an appearance of 'dignity, dryness, and comfort'.

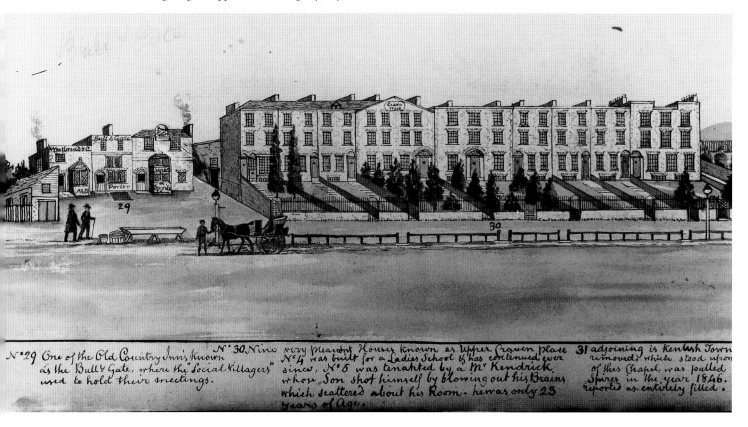

Many of these 'close courts' were relict features of older houses in the City, or former, jumbled street patterns. From the early eighteenth century onward, the depth of the frontage of a 'little common house' was 'limited to a few feet' – most of which was given over to a deep defensive moat – an 'airy', or area, defended at street level by iron railings – over which was thrown a 'flight of steps' which linked the front door to the roadside.[53] Adjoining the area were vaults which extended beneath the pavement, providing space for storage. Although this arrangement served to make the front of the house 'much more secure and ornamental', it did not give much scope for the display of plants.

There were, of course, many exceptions to the rule. From the early seventeenth century spacious courts were frequently found before the city's great aristocratic town houses, such as Leicester House, Lindsay House, Bedford House, Clarendon House, Burlington House, Berkeley House, Monmouth House and Powis House. They were, however, less common before the frontages of 'common houses' prior to the first quarter of the eighteenth century.

We have seen that Leoni provided a deep paved 'court' (46 by 61 feet) enclosed by an iron palisade beyond the front area for Lord Shannon's house in Mayfair. A published account relates that similar features had been introduced to neighbouring houses as early as 1734, which were commended for being 'very convenient . . . the buildings being more retired and quiet'.[54] Isaac Ware, in fact, remarked in 1756 that 'where the proprietor has spirit, and the chosen spot allows of a due extent, the house should have a court before it, and a garden behind.'[55] Large forecourts did not, however, become fashionable in the centre of town on account of the expense of building land; they were almost exclusively confined to Pall Mall, Piccadilly and Lincoln's Inn Fields. The more common method of increasing the distance between the house and the street was to increase the breadth of the area. This practice remained the standard approach throughout the eighteenth century.

The benefits of setting a house back from the road were nowhere more tangible than on the busy roads that linked the city to the suburbs. Many of the ranges of dwellings which lined these highways, turnpikes and 'great thoroughfares' were described as being 'agreeably removed from the noise and hurry of the public street', or 'divided from the road by a forecourt' (fig. 71).[56] These neat, walled front gardens of 'irregular groups of houses at the extremities of the town,' were seldom large, and the houses were not, until the late 1750s, far

71 George Scharf, *William Baker's Gent's Boarding Academy, 1 Frances Place, Holloway*, pen and watercolour wash, 1827. British Museum, London. This sketch shows how building extensions very quickly encroached on the small forecourts of modest terrace houses. Projecting bays were among the most common, but least imposing form of front garden encroachments.

removed from the road.[57] The 'openings', or 'forecourts', as they were commonly known, were found around the periphery of the capital in such thoroughfares as Knightsbridge, Mile End, Ratcliff Highway, Whitechapel, Newington Butts and Lambeth Road, and were valued less for their decorative potential than for their functional use. It should be noted, however, that these premises very often had the added advantage of 'the richness of the prospect backwards'.[58]

These city approach roads were condemned by some critics as 'inelegant' and 'inconvenient', and the narrow passages off them 'disgraced with despicable cottages, embarrassed with obstructions, and clouded with smoke'.[59] Few, however, were so outspoken as John

Gwynn, who 'took a very serious view of the future of London'.[60] In his book *London and Westminster Improved* (1766) – the object of which was to increase the 'Publick Magnificence' of the metropolis – he railed, in particular, against the longstanding habits of covetousness and self-interest which threatened to destroy the benefits of what was intended to be among the greatest public improvements of his time – the New Road from Paddington to Islington.

The New Road (now known as the Marylebone Road), thrown across the open fields in 1756–7, was built to link Islington to the western suburbs and was 'proposed to be the great boundary for restraining the ruinous practice of building, on the north side of the town' (fig. 72).[61] It was unique, and atypical in having legislation that required houses to be set back from the roadway. After the turnpike was completed, however, the Trustees failed to enforce the Act. Gwynn remarked:

> The act of parliament directs, that no building be erected for the future within fifty feet of the New-Road, but some people, in order to evade this judicious clause, have ingeniously contrived to build houses at that distance, but then to make themselves amends they take care to occupy the intermediate space, which was intended to disencumber the road, by a garden, the wall of which comes close upon it, and entirely defeats the original intention. This practice . . . will in time render the approaches to the capital so many scenes of confusion and deformity, extremely unbecoming the character of a great and opulent city.[62]

Clearly the critic himself was forced to reconsider the realities of imposing restrictions which were not easily enforced, nor even generally accepted as reasonable. Front gardens were not in themselves undesirable, but their 'coop'd up brick-walls', which encroached upon the margins of the highway, disfigured the spaciousness of the scheme.

Gwynn proposed an alternative that banished garden walls; his plan acknowledged the need for some kind of

72   Richard Horwood, *Map of London*, engraving, 1799 (detail). Guildhall Library, Corporation of London. The New Road, or 'Islington Turnpike', was planned to provide houses with deep front gardens to diminish the effects of noise and dust on its inhabitants. The *Journal of the House of Commons* (1757) reports that persons living in Great Russell Street and Southampton Row complained that the new road raised considerable dust which obstructed their 'Prospect' and 'spoiled the hay' in the neighbouring fields.

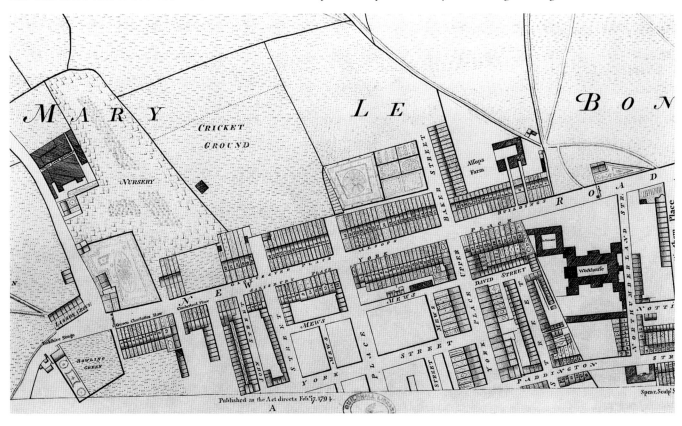

73   George Scharf, *Unity Place, Woolwich*, watercolour, 1825. British Museum, London.

compromise between individual territorial cupidity and the demands of the public good:

> As the New Road is proposed to be the great boundary for restraining the ruinous practice of building, on the north side of the town, so it is to be wished, that no building might be erected nearer than one hundred and twenty feet from the outermost line of it [the New Road] and that this space should be divided by posts and chains, allowing fifty-two feet for the Road, eight feet for a common foot-path, next the fields, and the remaining sixty feet next the houses, to be made equal in heighth to the common path, and laid out with grass-plots, with a convenient space to be gravelled for a foot-path next the front of the houses (This distance from the road would greatly prevent the houses from being annoyed with dust). This method might be observed entirely round the whole city . . .[63]

His solution proposed a function for front gardens: broad green swards, unencumbered by defensive 'dwarf walls', could form spacious buffers between the roadway and the rows of houses. The scheme was, as Gwynn

himself remarked, no less than an elaboration of John Evelyn's proposal of 1666 which envisioned the creation of a broad and scented verdant corridor encircling London, forming a 'most elegant line' round the metropolis, where the adjacent fields composed a beautiful lawn, and made 'an agreeable finish to the extream parts of the town'.[64]

Although Gwynn's retrospective advice was not heeded, the New Road was a success and was extended eastwards to the City in 1761. The front gardens which graced the newly built 'genteel and substantial brick messuages' along the length of the road were described by estate agents at the turn of the nineteenth century as '*cheerful*', 'neat' and 'airy', and averaged eighteen feet in depth.[65] A number of the 'forecourts' were enclosed with 'stong iron railings', had 'Pav'd way[s] to [the] door', and had gardens 'laid out and Planted'. The spaciouness of the road was, by all accounts, remarkable, and persuaded many persons to place their principal apartments on the road-side and to build balconies overlooking their front gardens.[66]

The example of the New Road set a precedent for the planning of new roads and the redevelopment of old

74 George Scharf, *Garden near St James's Park*, watercolour, 1827. British Museum, London. This sketch captures the picturesque character of William Noel Hill's garden at Warwick House, Cleveland Row. The garden was formed in 1770 by taking in land from Green Park; it was enlarged in 1827 when Hill was permitted to enclose a slip of ground ten feet wide between his house and the newly formed public passage into Green Park.

ones. By the late eighteenth century many rows of terraces erected along the major approaches to the capital – Hackney Road, Hampstead Road, Newington Place, Kentish Town Road and the Kensington Turnpike – were being built in a more spacious manner and with the provision of 'street gardens'. Such a phenomenon did not go unnoticed: visitors to London often commented on the 'pretty flower-gardens' that adorned the fronts of houses. In 1814 Hermann von Pückler-Muskau praised the 'rural simplicity' of the 'elegant houses' of South London, which he remarked had 'the neatest gardens in front of them; where round the chequered parterres of flowers, your eye is pleased to behold the laurel, the myrtle, the woodbine, and charming little *thuias* [thujas]' (fig. 73).[67] And in 1829 the French traveller François Philippar noted:

The taste for gardens in England is so pronounced that one finds them before almost every house. In towns and villages, and in London, too, there are gardens in almost all the streets. These small plots are generally the same width as the individual houses, and are as long as they are wide. The garden layouts vary – simple and regular in small spaces, and irregular in larger grounds.

The plants which furnish the gardens are of a variety of species – more so than those which make up our own plantations [in France]; however, one finds many evergreen shrubs, such as laurustinus (Viburnum tinus), Portugal laurel (Prunus lusitanica), cherry laurel (Prunus laurocerasus), yew (Taxus baccata), lots of holly of the Panachures variety, and rhododendron – especially Pontica (Rhododendron pontica). I have also seen lots of very beautiful white broom (Spartium album), and a range of false Scotch ebony (Cytisus scoticus), which makes a very handsome effect with its long clusters of pendant flowers and its elegant outline. One also sees in such gardens new and unusual herbaceous plants.

The gardens are separated from one another by hedges; and when there are walls they are often covered with climbers and sometimes figs or currants . . . They are also elegantly enclosed on the roadside with iron railings of distinctive designs, set on dwarf retaining walls surmounted by convex stone copings to shed rainwater. In several places the paving stones are replaced with cast iron plates. Handsome pillars mark the entrances to these gardens.[68]

In 1828 Loudon remarked that street gardens, or 'common front gardens', were 'a variety so well known as to require no description'.[69] They were, in fact, among the first of the urban garden types that he proposed to reform and modernise when in 1812 he published *Hints*, his first book on the formation of metropolitan gardens and pleasure grounds. For upwards of thirty years Loudon wrote extensively on the subject of street gardens ('these humble scenes'), which he believed could be 'greatly improved in design, and also in cultivation and keeping'.[70]

The front garden was, in Loudon's view, calculated for display – it was 'almost always a garden of pleasure, consisting of a grass plot . . . with a border, or a few patches of flowers in front of the house' (fig. 74). (The plot behind, on the other hand, was suitable for a 'grass-plot', or for 'culinary vegetables and small fruits'.) Maintenance of these small plots was not, however, easy. Loudon suggested to his readers that they employ a jobbing gardener to maintain the handsome permanent displays of 'evergreens and early spring flowers, both of the tree and herbaceous kinds', and 'in summer a display of annuals', as 'plants and turf are soon injured by the smoky and confined atmosphere incident to their situations, the finer plants and trees do not thrive in them, and the sorts which do succeed, and even the turf, require frequent renewal'. The jobber, as shall be discussed in chapter 6, supplied his clients with a succession of flowers over the seasons, kept the grass and gravel in good order, and 'the whole perfectly neat'.[71]

VIEWS, PROSPECTS AND THE GARDEN

Very often the largest London houses, and especially those on the fashionable squares, did not have gardens. Until the late eighteenth century Londoners who lived in these properties were satisfied with prospects, or vistas from their town houses to distant scenery, the city's

parks, squares and even their neighbouring private gardens. A view was an amenity that appealed to all classes of Londoners. While the provision of a view did not preclude the ownership of a garden ground, a private garden was sometimes deemed an unnecessary attribute to the grander houses in town, which overlooked expansive landscapes in town, protected by binding covenants.

Prospects were scenes viewed pictorially, from a position of detachment; whether they were described as beautiful, simple, cheerful or luxuriant, the pleasure derived from them was consistently defined as analogous to that experienced by a spectator in front of a work of art.[72] 'All gardening', remarked Pope in 1734 'is landscape-painting. Just like a landscape hung up.'[73] Virtually everyone had some form of view from his town house. Few, however, possessed the kind of prospects that contemporary auction notices, advertising the sale of town premises, deemed as 'genteel' or 'enchanting'. Views of this superior kind might have incorporated such features as the gardens of the British Museum, Carlton House, Burlington Gardens, Egremont House and the Queen's Gardens, the gardens of the Inner Temple, Drapers' Hall Gardens, private squares or artillery grounds, the royal parks, the Surrey hills, or Highgate and Hampstead.

There was a diversity of prospects available in the city. Those described and praised as the most eligible and fashionable were the expansive views over and into the natural scenery of the great urban parks. These were the uninterrupted vistas over Hyde and Green Park, Kensington and the Queen's Gardens, and the Surrey Hills, which nurtured rustic reflection, and which, Switzer claimed, cleared and relaxed the 'Passages of the Head and Breast'.[74] The next best category of views were those which, in the words of James Christie, combined 'all the chastity of the pastoral serenity, with the variegated busy scene of the capital'. These were the vistas to the varied scenery of built landmarks and monuments of the city intermixed with fragments of extensive landscapes and gardens – the embodiment of *rus in urbe*, which is best characterised by the average London garden square, or the views from the houses in St James's, Mayfair, and those on the edge of town – premises which were praised by Christie as 'agreeable removed from the noise and hurry of the street, catching prospects picturesquely beautiful, forming it into a perfect *Rus in Urbe*'.[75]

There was, likewise, an *urbs in rure* for citizens who lived beyond the 'rich intervening meadows' of the town, and whose suburban properties were praised by

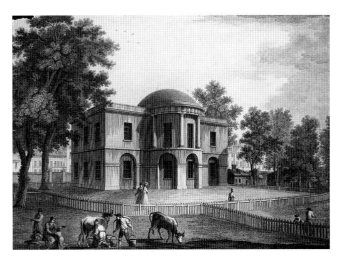

77 Benedetto Pastorini and Giovanni Vitalba after Robert Adam, *The Deputy Ranger's House, Green Park*, engraving, *c.*1778. London Metropolitan Archives.

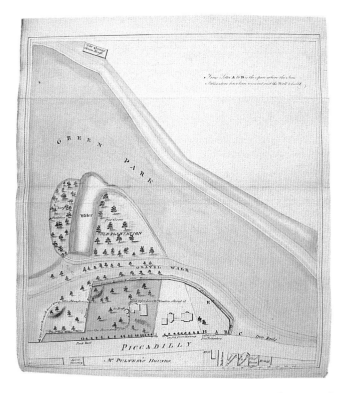

78 Plan of the Deputy Ranger's Lodge, Green Park, pen and watercolour wash, 1785. Public Record Office, Kew.

In June 1785 William Pulteney MP presented a memorial to Augustus Selwyn, Surveyor General of His Majesty's Woods and Crown Lands, endorsed by himself and other 'Proprietors and Tenants of Houses in that part of Piccadilly opposite to the Deputy Rangers Garden and Lodge'. The grievance was submitted on account of

the 'Inconvenience and Injury arising to their Houses from the planting of Trees, and other alterations lately made near the said Lodge'.[84]

The dispute had begun in 1781 when the Deputy Ranger Lord William Gordon[85] bricked up a length of 'Iron Pallisadoes' (a *claire-voyée*) which had been recently 'set up [in the park wall] with his Majesty's permission, and at the expense of the Duke of Queensberry, and other proprietors of Houses near the end of Park Lane, to open a view from their Houses into the Park' (figs 77 and 78). Lord William's misguided improvement was short-lived; 'a few days after the Wall . . . was finished, the Surveyor General of His Majesty's Woods, by his Majesty's Command, caused the same to be taken down, and the Iron Palisade to be restored.' The peer, however, continued to aggravate his neighbours by further alterations to his garden 'Inclosure', compelling them to petition the king again – this time on account of the 'effect of the recent Plantations about the Lodge', which intercepted, and were 'likely in a short time entirely to cut off the prospect of a beautiful part of the Park, from the Houses of the Earl of Cholmondeley, the Duke of Queensberry, and Sir Gerrard Vanneck, and also, in some degree, the Houses at the other Corner of Park Lane'. The aggrieved residents charged that Lord William had 'by obstructing the view greatly lessen[ed] the value of the houses of your Majesty's memorialists which on account of the beautiful prospect of the Park have had large sums of money expended thereon'.[86]

The matter was resolved in 1785 when Selwyn declared that

in order therefore to prevent any real detriment to Lord William Gordon, to the Memorialists, or to the Duke of Queensberry, the Earl of Cholmondeley, or Sir Gerrard Vanneck We humbly recommend that his Majesty be pleased to give directions to the Surveyor General of his Majesty's Woods for the time being not to suffer any tree or trees planted by said Lord William Gordon to remain, or any tree or trees to be hereafter planted, or to remain, within that part of the Inclosure . . . nor to permit or suffer any shrub or shrubs to be grown above the height of six feet from ground, nor to allow any building to be erected within foresaid part of Inclosure, or . . . fence to be allowed or any other thing done that may in any manner obstruct or prejudice the view or prospect from the houses . . .[87]

The right to a view was also enjoyed by tenants of the great estates who were occasionally given the option to purchase restrictive covenants to protect their premises from the depredations of others.[88] Ledgers which record the leasing arrangements of the Grosvenor Estate possess a range of examples. For instance, in August 1806 the Surveyor of the Grosvenor Estate urged the Trustees to honour Mr Boddington's demand that his westward neighbour be prevented from building an extension to the back of his house which would have obstructed the views into Hyde Park of a number of leaseholders. It was argued that permitting such an extension to be built would have set a precedent for uncontrolled expansion by all neighbours who found their views disfigured – all of whom vied for a vista into the park; or, in 1818 one Mr Auriol sought, and was granted, a covenant from the Estate to prevent any development from spoiling his views into Hyde Park from his front garden in Park Street, Mayfair.[89]

The trustees of the city's squares were, perhaps, able to bring about most successful legal enforcement of covenanted, uninterrupted prospects in town. But there were also smaller-scale, or more informal arrangements whereby tenants paid annual subscriptions to keep their views into shared garden grounds temporarily undeveloped. In 1805, for instance, the tenants of numbers 10–40 inclusive in Great Sloane Street paid an annual maintenance fee to the ground landlord 'to prevent any buildings being erected in front of said houses'.[90]

If covenants were, however, assets to those who had options and the money to buy them, they were also discouragements to others who found themselves bound by innumerable restrictions stipulated in 'special penal covenants'. These covenants prohibited alterations to existing houses without permission of the landlord – especially in the opening of new apertures such as window lights and doors, or house extensions and out-buildings.

Some chose to disregard covenants on the grounds that some rights were considered irrevocable – such as views, and access to light and air. These commodities were not, however, guaranteed in the context of a rapidly developing city; such amenities could no longer be taken for granted. These considerations were not new to people who were familiar with the old congested town. Many newly arrived Londoners, however, lacked the fully developed urban consciousness of the likes of the enlightened author John Stewart, who defined the city in opposition the country, and insisted that its metropolitan identity should not be compromised by such ineffectual and anomalous rural reminders as street trees and garden squares. Many bought or leased

properties with the understanding that their environs were not going to be disfigured by development, and were disheartened or distressed by their incapacity to exercise any considerable control over their immediate surroundings.

The difficulties which could arise over tenants' right to a view are characterised by a transaction in the Trustees' Minutes of the Grosvenor Estate in Pimlico. In 1796 the Earl Grosvenor, as freeholder of his estate, decided to exchange a small strip of his property with the Kensington Turnpike Company in order to straighten Upper Belgrave Place. This action caused a furore on the part of his tenants who leased the terraced houses opposite the parcel of land in question. Ten tenants petitioned the Estate trustees, protesting that Lord Grosvenor's actions were injurious to the values of their property; they claimed, furthermore, that his dealings were an infringement of the guaranteed rights of their original leases, which entitled them to a piece of ground planted with trees in the front street, and uninterrupted views to the Surrey Hills.[91]

The dispute was resolved by the Estate lawyer Mr Boodle, who denied that the tenants had been granted any binding covenants in their leases which protected their rural prospects. A few occupants were, however, undaunted by the decision and petitioned repeatedly for compensation. In the end the Estate agreed to compensate the residents by allowing them to extend their back garden grounds – so long as they did not inconvenience their neighbours' access to the mews. Their persistence demonstrates the great importance with which the householders' access to a glimpse of rurality was invested. The compromise suggests an implicit recognition, however, that prospect represented, above all, the privilege of the great landowner: lesser householders were persuaded, with relative ease, to relinquish more grandiose and alluring visions in return for humble but tangible rights of possession.

ASPECT: VIEWS AND THE LAYOUT OF THE HOUSE

Just as there were different varieties of urban prospects, there were divergent expectations of each. The basis for the distinctions was the orientation of the house: the two principal viewpoints to and from the house were from the public street front and the private garden front (or the 'back front'). Views from front windows were typically described as 'animated' or 'enlivened' by the

79 William Hodges and Richard Cosway, *A view from Mr Cosway's Breakfast Room, Pall Mall*, engraving, 1789. London Metropolitan Archives. The prospect enjoyed by Mrs Cosway provides an illusion of pastoral luxuriance and freedom from human intervention which is in sharp contrast to a view of the same terrain from street level.

80 J. T. Smith, *A pictoresque View of St James's Park taken from the Mall in Front of St James's Palace*, engraving, 1807. London Metropolitan Archives. This image, when compared with Mrs Cosway's view (fig. 79), positions the viewer as a humble pedestrian, gazing over the spiked-railings which disrupt any such illusions, and emphasise the intrusive boundaries imposed by urban patterns of property ownership.

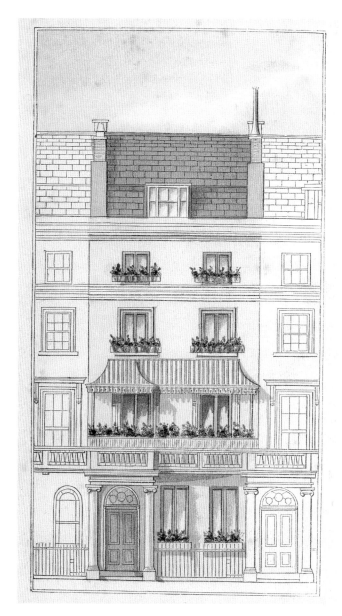

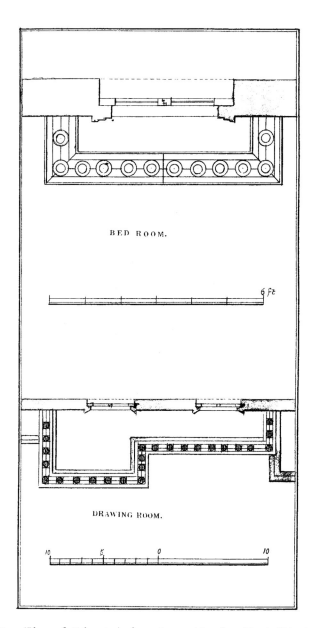

81 'The effect of flowers on the Outside of a House', lithograph frontispiece from James Mangles, *Floral Calendar* (1839). Lindley Library, Royal Horticultural Society, London.

82 'Plan of Balconies', from James Mangles, *Floral Calendar* (1839). Lindley Library, Royal Horticultural Society, London.

'variegated action of the street'; even houses which opened into garden squares experienced a foreground of street activity. The garden front, on the other hand, was often seen as agreeably 'remove[d] from the noise and hurry of the public streets'.[92] Here the views were 'appropriated', and consequently possessed a different quality of animation; they were private and manageable, and were, according to Repton, characterised by the pleasure of seeing life in motion, particularly the wavy motion of trees, or children playing in the garden.[93]

Although the provision and framing of views had long been a concern in the layout of London houses, Humphry Repton was among the first garden writers to address the subject in detail. To calculate views from within the house he placed the viewer in a fixed point in the manner of a landscape painter; for this viewer the prospect was framed and contained. Views from indoors were calculated from the level of the eye of a person seated in the middle of the principal rooms and allowances were made for enhanced cones of vision as the viewer moved toward the window (figs 79–80).

83 George Scharf, *In St Martins Lane*, pencil, 1826. British Museum, London.

Repton's allowance for animation, however, distinguished his prospects from painters' framed views.

In the city it was often desirable to edit out much of the street scene. The urgency to edit the view was greater towards the end of the eighteenth century when window sizes were expanded, sashes lowered, and in some cases picture windows were installed. The most common means of ensuring adequate privacy was to embower the foregrounds of these enlarged apertures. Prospects were framed by living plant displays staged on lead flats, prospect-balconies and verandahs, which buffered the inside apartments from the street (figs 81–2). The new improvements not only brought greenery closer to the indoors but also helped 'beautify the frontispiece of the house'; and the whole combined with 'an uniform ornamental exterior a most pleasing and attractive object from within'.[94]

The aspect, or 'situation', of the house determined its comfort and convenience, and the options for developing the garden.[95] Aspect was the most important consideration when dealing with terraced houses, as it prescribed the views and defined the house and garden's exposure to the rays of the sun. In town many houses were built with little consideration given to aspect. Repton gave precedence to aspect over prospect, advising his readers to manipulate whatever light they did get in town to their advantage. He also claimed that the difficulty of obtaining comfort and cheerfulness in a town-

house arose from the pursuit of two incompatible aims: seeking to increase lighting and attempting to reduce noise and visibility from the street.[96]

The principal rooms, at the front of the house, were said to deserve most particular consideration to aspect. Repton and Loudon agreed that a south-east aspect was best, followed by south, and then due east. The worst was south-west, as the rainy weather came from this direction; north was too gloomy for want of sunshine, and due west was annoying as the occupants' eyes were dazzled by the glare of the setting sun. When there was no alternative to a western aspect the sunlight could be filtered through Venetian blinds, coloured glass screens or the natural foliage of trees. Nevertheless, there were redeeming features of some unpopular aspects when prospect was taken in account: a view to the north overlooking trees and gardens was agreeable as 'verdant objects look best when viewed from rooms so placed, because all plants are most luxuriant on the side of the sun'.[97]

The prospects from the front offered gratification of curiosity, rather than pleasures of a primarily aesthetic character. They also raised a problem: at the same time as the householder gazed out upon the passers-by, those outside the house, including neighbours, were similarly prompted to gaze in upon the householder. A drawing by George Scharf (1826) offers a detailed, intimate view of the activities of a family in a house across the street in St Martin's Lane, as viewed by the artist from his own front window (fig. 83).

Robert Noyes, when writing in the *Gentleman's Magazine* (1753) on the management of a fine and genteel London house, advised the young proprietress (to whom the essay was addressed), that the respectability of a house was projected through its windows and doors which opened on to the public street. He remarked that although her windows – if always kept clean and bright – would prove a great ornament to her house by commanding extensive prospects, she should be cautious not to look through them at everything that passed by, lest by some misfortune it should lead to an indelicate exchange with someone on the street, which might in turn draw scandal upon the house.[98] Scharf's 'Memorandums of windows early and during day' (*c*.1820) depicts a timetable of blind-drawing, shutter-closing and window-opening which attempts to ensure privacy, security and protection from sunlight over the course of various days' observations (fig. 84).

A way of mitigating this problem was to add balconies and verandahs; even in Scharf's view of the family

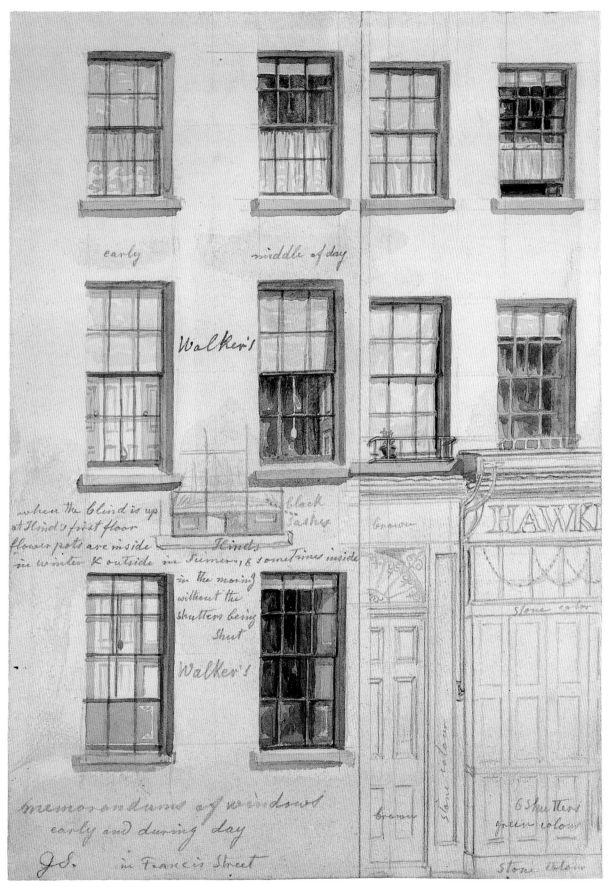

The following text appears within the drawing:

early   middle of day

Walker's

when the blind is up
at Hind's first floor
flower pots are inside
in winter & outside in summer, & sometimes inside
in the moring
without the
shutters being
shut

black
sashes

brown

Walker's

Hinds

HAWK

stone colour

stone colour

brown   stone colour   6 shutters
green colour

memorandums of windows
early and during day

J.S.   in Francis Street

stone colour

84   George Scharf, *Memorandums of windows early and during day in Francis Street*, pencil, *c*.1820. British Museum, London. Scharf depicts a timetable of blind-drawing, shutter-closing and window-opening which attempts to ensure privacy, security and protection from sunlight over the course of various days' observations.

85   William Henry Hunt, *A distant view of St Martin-in-the-Fields from Pall Mall*, pen and watercolour wash, 1826. Private collection.

opposite him, the balcony and the plants placed upon it provide a symbolic barrier behind which the occupants of the house can enjoy a sense of privacy, however illusory. Balconies and verandahs screened the front windows and at the same time increased the breadth of views up and down the street (fig. 85).[99] They were often, in fact, elaborated into open air conservatories, and at times aviaries, which were more part of the indoors than the outdoors. The treatment of both was the same: French, or low sashed windows opened into balconies and verandahs that contained a small garden on a lead flat planted with shrubs and enclosed with railings.

Christie's declared in 1802 that people were fortunate to have 'the peculiar advantage of the windows opening into a virandah [sic], which happily blends all the picturesque and enchanting beauties of the Park, with the interior splendour of the apartments'.[100] Planting up a balcony or a verandah was a means by which 'the desponding amateur might enjoy a spice of "*Rus in*

Urbe;" and if it is accompanied by classical associations "*Recubans sub tegmine fugi*," still he may create in front of his windows a florid and glowing scene – a tessellated surface of enamelled hues, whose dazzling splendour, while refreshing his sight and cheering his senses, may assist to reconcile him to his doom of being an urban, and not a sub-urban resident'.[101] (Robert Southey, writing as Don Manuel, condemned the London 'fashion' for verandahs, 'lately introduced from better climates'; writing in 1807 he remarked that it was a foolish conceit, especially in 'a country where physicians recommend double doors and double windows as precautions against the intolerable cold!!')[102]

Views were often categorised in terms of propriety. The Grosvenor Estate received complaints from residents in Chester and Chapel Streets, Grosvenor Square, who objected to dust and ash heaps behind their gardens. The Surveyor agreed that these inconveniences must also be a 'very great nuisance to the houses ... especially in the summer & at all times a very unpleasant & improper object to be seen from such houses'.[103]

Eighteenth-century architects commenting on the design of London townhouses recommended that the layout of fashionable apartments should be based on the provision of views. Isaac Ware remarked in *The Complete Body of Architecture* (1756):

> Where there is a garden of tolerable extent, some of the principal apartments, supposing the situation proper, may be very conveniently placed in the hinder part of the house. They will by these means be freed from noise and disturbance, and will have a good light; the garden will also be a good prospect.[104]

He also claimed that in laying out a townhouse with a garden behind, 'the best disposition possible is to throw the whole first floor of back rooms into a string, or suit[e]; these should consist of a saloon, an antichamber, a drawing room, a bed-chamber, and a dressing room; the windows of all these being to the garden will be very pleasant; and the looking through the whole range at once has an air of magnificence and elegance'.[105] Some years later, in the 1790s, Repton recommended very much the same enfilade of rooms terminating in a conservatory or a small conservatory. He, however, placed greater emphasis than Ware on bringing the garden indoors by carefully positioning mirrors which made the indoors more cheerful and expansive by brightening it with reflected daylight. The mirrors were also an excellent means by which 'to introduce views of

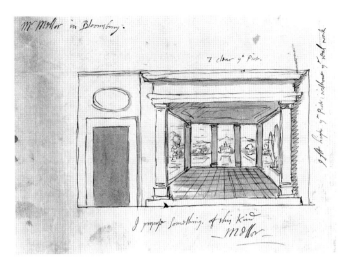

86 John Mellar, *trompe-l'oeil* painting proposed for his garden in Bloomsbury Square, pen and watercolour wash, *c.*1712. Yorke Collection, Erddig, Clwyd.

88 James Thornhill, design for a *trompe-l'oeil* backdrop for a garden wall, pen and watercolour wash, *c.*1712–15. Private collection.

87 James Thornhill, *Sketches for ye Garden in Bloomsbury Square*, for John Mellar, pen and watercolour wash, *c.*1712. Yorke Collection, Erddig, Clwyd.

89 James Thornhill, *Sketches for ye Garden in Bloomsbury Square*, for John Mellar, pen and watercolour wash, *c.*1712. Yorke Collection, Erddig, Clwyd.

scenery which could not otherwise be visible from a particular point of view'.[106]

Another popular means of combining the indoors and the outdoors, or extending the garden both spatially and associationally, was through the introduction of landscape murals on garden walls, on drawing-room and rustic tea-room walls which opened into balconies, verandahs or private gardens. These prospects combined illusionistic (painted) with actual (real) scenery. An early occurrence of such an effect is recorded by John Evelyn at Mr Porcy's house in Lincoln's Inn Fields, where the garden courtyard was 'extended' by a 'Perspective . . . painted by Streeter . . . indeed excellent, with *Vasas* in Imitation of *Porphyrie*; & fountaine . . .'[107]

In 1712 Sir James Thornhill proposed an equally remarkable series of sketch designs for *trompe-l'oeil* paintings for the garden wall at John Mellar's house on the east side of Bloomsbury Square (figs 86–7 and 89). The first design may represent a working up of an initial pencil sketch by Mellar himself, the other more fully developed proposals are very French in charcter; the one with the fountain resembling Jacques Rousseau's Saint-Cloud vignettes, while that with the balustrade and loggia recalls the contemporary work of Isaac de Moucheron.[108] Another unidentified scheme of roughly the same date depicts a more architectural Roman scheme (fig. 88).

Among the most impressive surviving examples of

92   Thomas Rowlandson, *Road Building*, pen and watercolour wash, *c.*1790. Private collection.

93   Frederick Birnie after Robert Barker, *Blackfriar's Bridge from Albion Mills*, hand-coloured aquatint, 1792. Paul Mellon Collection, Yale Center for British Art, New Haven. Birnie's view shows the prim surroundings of Albion Place, Southwark, built shortly after the completion of the neighbouring Blackfriars Bridge in 1769. Albion Street was the gateway from Fleet Street in the City to the densely populated southern suburbs of Lambeth, Newington and Walworth.

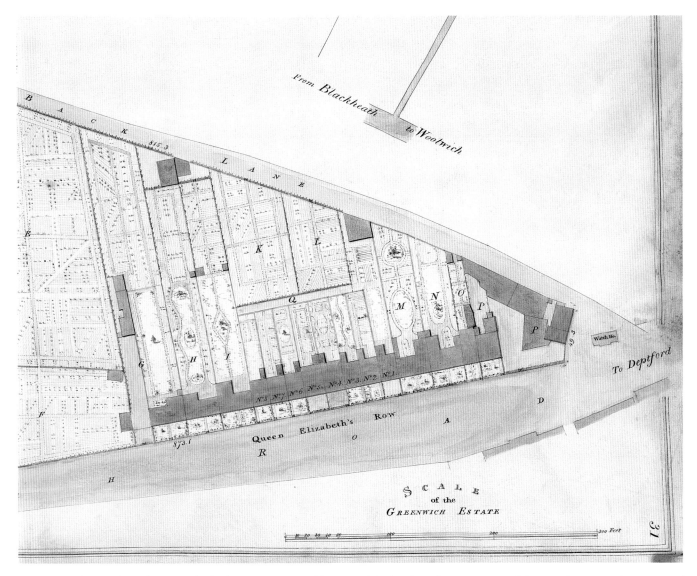

94 Jesse Gibson, 'Plan of Queen Elizabeth Row, Greenwich', pen and bodycolour, from *A Survey of the Several Estates Belonging to and under the Trust of the Worshipful Co. of Drapers'* (1819). Company of Drapers, London.

to maintaining the respectability and prosperity of their estates in order to sustain building activity, stimulate healthy development and subsequently to see rising returns on their investment.

The Company of Drapers invoked the authority of St George's Parochial Paving and Communications Act of 1777 to bring about improvements to Betts Street, Ratcliff Highway (fig. 95).[120] As the short-term leases fell in, the 'old, decayed and inconvenient tenements' were demolished and the street was rebuilt over a thirty-year period with uniform third-rate houses and a public house.[121] Twenty small houses were erected, each with a deep back garden containing a privy (fig. 96). The new building lines were recessed five feet from the edge of

the public highway to provide for raised stone footpaths, and the street was paved by 1792.[122] The houses were not given sunken areas or forecourts.

The building of the Lambeth Road over the Archbishop of Canterbury's estate in south London brought about the development of what was known as the 'Twenty-one Acres'. The ground was leased in 1805 to Sir William East who, with the approval of estate surveyor, Samuel Pepys Cockerell, pulled down 'old houses, poor cottages, sheds and buildings of a very inferior Quality' to build regimented rows of second-rate and third-rate houses laid out on spacious streets (figs 97 and 98). Cockerell's 'general improvement' entailed providing new houses with back gardens ('ground behind'),

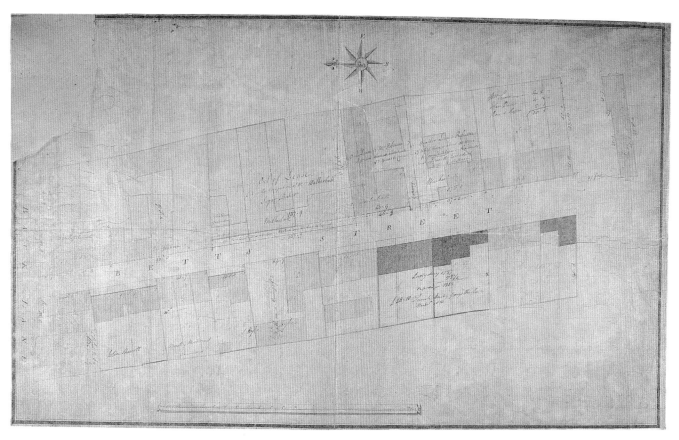

95   Survey of Betts Street, pencil and watercolour, ?1780. Company of Drapers, London.

96   Jesse Gibson, 'Plan of Betts Street', pencil and bodycolour, from *A Survey of the Several Estates Belonging to and under the Trust of the Worshipful Co. of Drapers'* (1819). Company of Drapers, London. Betts Street after it was 'improved' in the early 1790s.

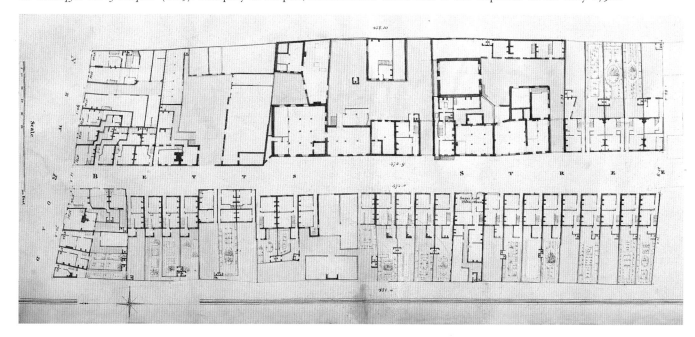

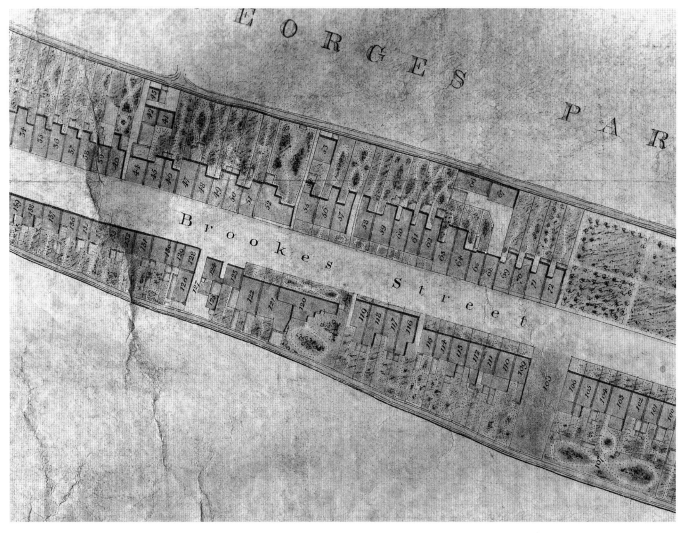

97   Plan of Brookes Street, Lambeth, pen and watercolour, *c.*1812 (detail). Lambeth Palace, London. Survey drawing of houses and gardens on the Archbishop of Canterbury's estate, in Lambeth.

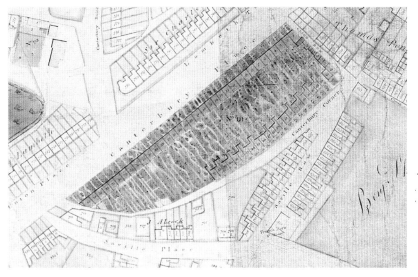

98   Plan of Canterbury Place, Lambeth, pen and watercolour, *c.*1812 (detail). Lambeth Palace, London. The serpentinised layouts of the gardens before and behind the houses of Canterbury Place, Lambeth, are reminiscent of Loudon's 'layouts for Small Plots' published about the same time (figs 106 and 107).

and where possible the dwellings were 'situated . . . in the *Centre* of the Premises'.[123] At Union Street, Canterbury Street, Brookes Street and Lambeth Terrace the houses were given small planted forecourts and back gardens, while the remainder of the rows of terraces were given only long narrow openings behind.

There were, of course, just as many instances where gardens were reduced in size for the sake of 'public convenience'. William Porden, surveyor of the Grosvenor Estate, had recommended such measures at Millbank in Pimlico. In 1793 he suggested 'that in all future or reviewed leases of houses facing the Thames the Gardens or Court yards in front of these houses should be resumed and the leases confined to an area of not more than 5 or 6 feet at most to be inclosed with an iron rail and the remainder of the Court Yards of Gardens to be thrown into the Street in order to render the Terrace more spacious and uniform'.[124]

This pattern of orderly garden development was in sharp contrast to the equally ubiquitous practice of encroachment. Encroachment was practised by all classes of Londoners and was characterised by the invasion, use and enclosure of vacant land or disused ground for the purpose of commerce, agriculture or recreation. The temporary enclosure and management of land for ornamental or productive gardening, when carried out with the consent of the landowner, was a common means of

99 'View from the gallery of the Steeple of St Mary, Islington', engraving from John Swertner, *A View of the Cities of London and Westminster with the Suburbs and Circumjacent County* (1789). Guildhall Library, Corporation of London. This detail depicts what appears to be a garden encroachment.

protecting ground from potential nuisances. This practice, often referred to as 'inclosure' or 'enlargement' on the payment of a 'grass rent' was a popular means of acquiring a garden or extending the townhouse garden, and records of it abound in estate papers (fig. 99).[125] Some estates were disposed to letting small parcels of ground on short leases for garden building or for the purpose of 'preventing Nuisances' contingent on a range of conditions: among them, that the land was surrendered for building when required; that the lease did not interfere with the estate's plan for building; and that the tenants bore the expense of removing fencing and other garden structures erected during their tenure.[126]

In 1796, on Lord Grosvenor's estate in Pimlico, one Mr Perks applied for leave to enclose the 'piece of ground behind his building ground in Ebury Street' and the vacant ground 'adjoining westwards to his house and garden' for the purpose of extending his garden and 'preventing nuisances'. The estate agreed to his proposal in so far as 'the enclosure [was] not to be considered as occupation of the Ground by Mr Perks as tenant to Lord Grosvenor' and that he is to 'give it up without notice whenever it is wanted'.[127] Perks raised potatoes in his new garden.

Although tenants were obliged by guarantee to surrender their encroachments without compensation, some refused steadfastly to honour their agreements. Among the more protracted and well-documented examples of the potential problems which could arise from such arrangments was the seventeen-year conflict between the Grosvenor Estate and one Henry Hamblett. In 1795 Hamblett had leased a small piece of vacant ground adjacent to his terraced house in Ebury Street, Pimlico, with an undertaking to build three 'full third-rate houses, each at 18 feet wide'. Immediately upon engrossing the 'peppercorn' lease, and with the agreement of the Estate, he enclosed his ground with a pale and planted a garden. When, by late October 1807, Hamblett had failed to throw up a single building the estate accused him of deliberately causing 'considerable inconvenience', and frustrating their efforts to develop the building line in Ebury Street. They alleged that 'he evidently wished not to cover it but enjoy it as a garden'.[128] The dispute was terminated by the timely death of the tenant in October 1812 – days before his scheduled eviction. Hamblett died without having built a single house or paid a guinea's ground rent.

Another option open to landowners faced with such disputes was to cede permanently the enclosure under new terms (fig. 100). For example, the decision by the

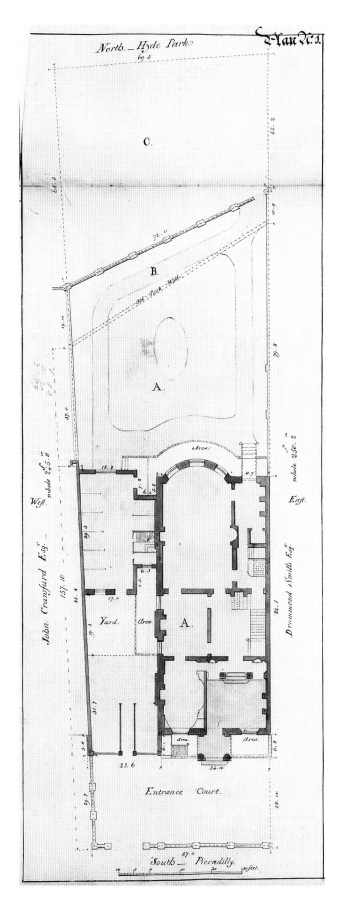

Commissioners of Wood and Forests in 1795 to give leave to the aristocratic residents of St James's Place and Arlington Street to extend their small gardens behind their houses into Green Park was a reconciliation of a century of piecemeal encroachments; the same was true for the noble lords at the west end of Piccadilly who in 1797 were granted permission to 'enlarge' their already capacious back gardens by taking in the 'freeboard' of Hyde Park (fig. 101).[129]

Where the landlord considered proposed encroachments to be beneficial to his estate they were legitimised through changes to title deeds. In March 1789 Sir John Stanley appealed to Lord Grosvenor on behalf of himself and the rest of the tenants in Grosvenor Place 'for a slip of Ground behind their Houses for the purpose of making Gardens or outlets to their Houses and to keep off the Cattle belonging to the Tenants of the Fields who make Laystalls close up to the Stables'. Their wish was granted as the estate surveyor remarked that their proposal was 'not inconsistent with Lord Grosvenor's Plan for the improvement of that part of his Estate'.[130]

More frequent, and most difficult to prevent were unauthorised encroachments. For instance, the building speculator Mr Willis was advised by the Grosvenor Estate in February 1794 that he had 'exceeded the bounds of what was granted to him [in Ebury Street] by enclosing as court yards the ground that was intended to be thrown into the street which will now defeat the object of what is now called 5 Field Row a handsome Street'.[131] Further encroachments were reported eight years later in the same street, and nearby Eccleston Street when a group of residents 'encroached on the width' of the highways by planting poplars and 'extended their footway beyond the proper and convenient width'. They also 'encumbered the streets with timber, have kept cows and have occasioned considerable nuisances to the neighbourhood'. The encroachments were attributed to the fact that the streets were 'not properly formed and paved'.[132] The 'Twenty-one Acres' estate in Lambeth, like so many other estates, experienced similar difficulties: it was reported in 1804 that William Dymock 'enclosed a piece of waste – [and that] said encroachment was converted into a garden'. There were also various records

100 *Survey of a House in Piccadilly*, pen and watercolour wash, 1797. Public Record Office, Kew. This survey shows the 'Plot of Ground in the [Hyde] Park marked C, designed to be enclosed for the enlargement of said Garden'. The area marked 'B' on the plan had been 'enclosed from the Park with Iron Rails, and used as part of the Garden' some years earlier.

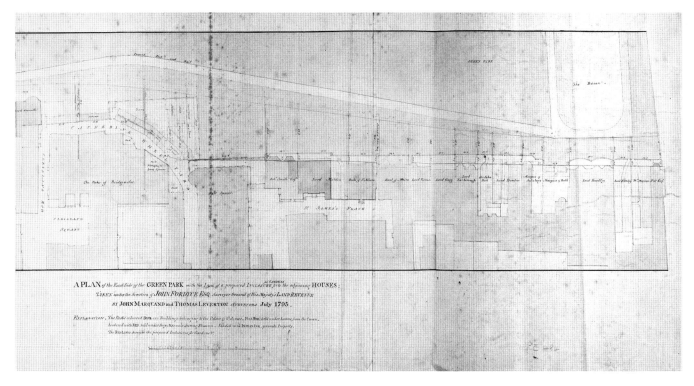

A PLAN of the East Side of the GREEN PARK with the Line of a proposed INCLOSURE &c to the adjoining HOUSES; TAKEN under the direction of JOHN FORDYCE ESQ. Surveyor General of His Majestys LAND REVENUE BY JOHN MARQUAND and THOMAS LEVERTON Surveyors July 1795.

101 John Marquand and Thomas Leverton, *Plan of the East Side of the Green Park with the Line of Proposed Inclosures for Gardens &c. to the Adjoining Houses,* pen and watercolour wash, 1795. Public Record Office, Kew. The plan formalised what had been a series of gradual encroachments in the royal park.

of land having been enclosed 'by post & chains' for plantations, gardens and pleasure grounds.[133]

While encroachment was one way of acquiring or forming a garden, the more conventional means was to lease or purchase a designated garden opening. Auction notices and sale particulars published in London newspapers suggest that from the early eighteenth century 'very neat small garden[s], in good order' were available throughout London, and that 'the Conveniency of a Garden' added distinction, and value to a town premises (fig. 102).[134]

Most notices describe gardens in Belgravia, Bloomsbury, Covent Garden, the City, Marylebone, Mayfair, Piccadilly, Westminster and the suburbs and occasionally corroborate the delineation of small gardens on contemporary maps and plans – Horwood's *Plan* (1799) in particular. Where the notices prove most informative is, however, where topographical or cartographic evidence is wanting. Roque's *Plan* (1746), for instance, is at once animated when we discover that in April 1739 'A Good and Convenient House, in extraordinary good Repair . . . situate in the Passage leading out of Bartlet's Buildings into Fetter Lane' had a 'pretty garden before it'; that in January 1745 a 'ready furnish'd . . . Very good House,

completely fitted-up, fit for a large Family, in the broad Part of St James's Place, in St James's Street' boasted a 'Garden before the Parlour Window' and a 'Door in[to] the [Green] Park at the End of the Garden'; or that in 1752 the surgeon Mr Bogue's 'Genteel and Commodious House, fit for any Gentleman's Family' at the 'upper End of New Bond-street' possessed a 'spacious Yard . . . decorated with Trees and Borders for Flowers'.[135]

Although the rhetoric of contemporary advertisements is often hyperbolic, the fact that gardens featured prominently in descriptions of some town premises suggests that they were noteworthy attributes of certain classes of premises. 'Genteel' and 'commodious' houses 'fit for a small Family' were, for example, often described as possessing 'a pretty little Garden', or with 'Gardens behind'. Gardens in these advertisements were accorded equal stature with their premises' geographical location and their buildings' rating.

Less common, until the late eighteenth century, were notices which went beyond mere generalised descriptions, to elaborate upon the layout of the openings. Where these descriptions survive they paint a more vivid picture of a premises as they enumerate a garden's most distinctive attributes. For example, a 'large garden'

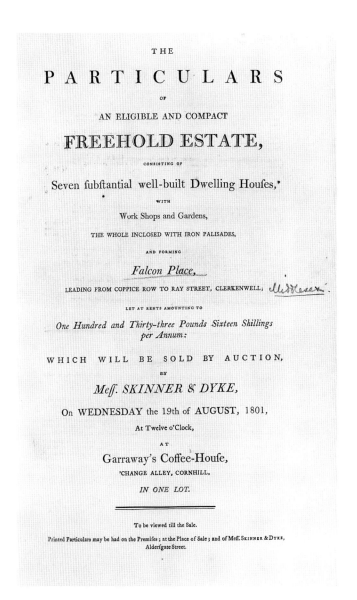

THE

PARTICULARS

OF

AN ELIGIBLE AND COMPACT

FREEHOLD ESTATE,

CONSISTING OF

Seven fubftantial well-built Dwelling Houfes,

WITH

Work Shops and Gardens,

THE WHOLE INCLOSED WITH IRON PALISADES,

AND FORMING

Falcon Place,

LEADING FROM COPPICE ROW TO RAY STREET, CLERKENWELL; *Middlesex.*

LET AT RENTS AMOUNTING TO

One Hundred and Thirty-three Pounds Sixteen Shillings
per Annum:

WHICH WILL BE SOLD BY AUCTION,

BY

Meff. SKINNER & DYKE,

On WEDNESDAY the 19th of AUGUST, 1801,

At Twelve o'Clock,

AT

Garraway's Coffee-Houfe,

'CHANGE ALLEY, CORNHILL,

IN ONE LOT.

To be viewed till the Sale.

Printed Particulars may be had on the Premifes ; at the Place of Sale ; and of Meff. SKINNER & DYKE,
Alderfgate Street.

102 Sale particulars advertising seven houses in Clerkenwell with enclosed gardens. Gough Collection, Bodleian Library, Oxford.

which lay behind the house of the late Princess Amelia in Harley Street, Cavendish Square, was described in 1797 as being 'agreeably laid out with shrubs, trees and gravel walks, at the extremity of which is a uniform building'; the garden and 'inner courts' were reported to 'give scope to the premises' (fig. 103). 'Immediately opposite the Queen's Gardens [Buckingham Palace Gardens]', the garden of a house in 'Stafford Row' was described in 1801 as 'extensive', and its 'two walls planted with fruit trees; and two alcoves'. Half a mile away in Mayfair, a 'capital leasehold MANSION' at the junction of Grosvenor Square and North Audley Street

was described in 1802 as having a 'spacious garden neatly laid out and planted with lofty trees and shrubs; in the garden is a capital strong-room or study'. In 1803 a house in York Street, St James's, had a 'extensive garden, walled and cloathed with fruit trees'; and in 1806 a premises at the north end of Manchester Street overlooking the square had a 'capacious garden tastefully laid out' containing a 'small fish pond'.[136]

The advertisements suggest gardens occurred less frequently, and were often smaller in the City. Dwellings in the City generally had yards, or paved courts, although exceptions abound.[137] In January 1745 a 'Large Convenient House [in Aldersgate], four rooms on a Floor, sash'd, wainscotted, and in good Repair, with good Warehouse-Room and large Wine Vaults' is reported to have had 'a small Garden behind, and an airy Court-Yard before the House'.[138] Not far away, at 1 Broad Street Place, or 'Old-Bethlem', 'nr. Royal Exchange', the garden was described some fifty-six years later as possessing a first-floor 'balcony in front', a terrace, 'ornamental garden space and railing[s] in front'; and in 1802 the forecourt of a 'Genteel and substantial brick messuage' on the 'East side of the City Road, [a] 10 minute walk from the Royal Exchange', was 'inclosed with strong iron railing, and Pav'd way to door, and garden laid out and Planted'.[139]

From the late eighteenth century a number of sale particulars included the garden's dimensions where the gardens were considered unusually large, or where they occurred in places in which they were unexpected. In 1797 the 'carcases', or 'those capital and truly desirable houses', at 5 and 7 Southampton Terrace, St Pancras, were advertised as possessing 'extensive gardens behind, about 84ft in depth'.[140] In August 1800 the 'roomy gardens backwards' of six 'compact and substantial well built' houses in Stafford Place, Buckingham Gate, were described as being 'sixty feet deep'. The 'EXCELLENT GARDEN' at 45 Great Ormond Street, Bloomsbury, was described in 1801 as '34 [ft] in breadth and extensive depth' (fig. 104);[141] and the 'back garden' of the residence of the late Sir Henry Grey Cooper at 7 Cavendish Square was described in 1802 as 'spacious' at '53 ft by 33 ft'.[142]

Some notices went so far as to assert that a garden was, in fact, a 'requisite' for a genteel or substantial town house.[143] This was particularly true if the house, or row of houses, was newly built. In these advertisements the 'neat walled garden' featured prominently among the 'advantages' of a premises. The garden was, moreover, mentioned repeatedly in the advertisements – some

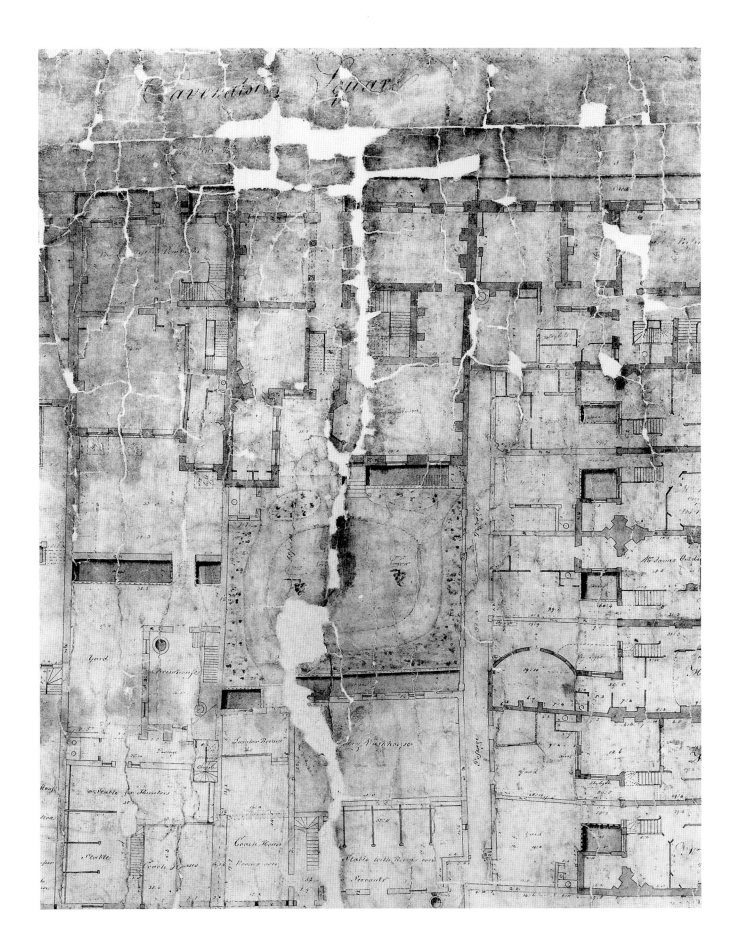

times as many as five times – each time emphasising the 'convenience', gentility and dignity that the garden ostensibly conferred upon the property. In 1801 John Vyse advertised the lease of three newly completed 'genteel brick dwelling houses' in Upper Belgrave Place – each premises was possessed of a forecourt and a 'garden neatly laid out'. In October of the same year Messrs Skinner, Dyke & Co. offered four newly erected houses for sale in the same street – each premises containing a 'spacious forecourt enclosed with railings and a garden'. In both instances the gardens were presented in the particulars as giving a finished look to the new properties. There are, in fact, a number of sale particulars which advertise the lease and sale of whole ranges of terraced houses where the garden featured among the conspicuous benefits of the new premises. For instance, in July 1805 Mr Smith advertised the sale of twenty 'substantial houses . . . nr. the Turnpike at Holloway', and five premises in Cornwall Place, Marylebone, all of which had front and back gardens and cellaring.

A handful of sale particulars also promoted the potential of a garden to be improved, and in some instances went so far as to make recommendations. In January 1752 the owners of a house on the 'South Side of Bloomsbury-Square, newly put in good Repair' had a 'Garden behind, [which] can make ten or more Beds, if requir'd'.[144] In June 1801 the roof terrace of General Poyntz's house at 12 Hinde Street, Manchester Square – from which one gained an 'uninterrupted view of the villages of Highgate and Hampstead, and the rich intermediate Valley' – was advertised as a place which could benefit from the addition of 'an observatory or tea room' which 'could be added at a trifling expense'. At a 'newly built' dwelling in neighbouring Manchester Street (1806) a 'large capacious garden, tastefully laid out', was claimed 'from its extent capable of very great improvement'. Lord Cawdor's paved courtyard at his house near Hyde Park, which was in 1799 'now occupied as a museum . . . might be converted into a Green House'; and at the bottom of the garden at the 'singularly neat and eligible residence for a small genteel

104   John Roque, *Plan of the Cities of London & Westminster*, engraving, 1746 (detail). Private collection. The houses on the north side of Great Ormond Street were described in 1780 as possessing 'extensive walled-in gardens'.

family' at 7 James Street Terrace, near St James's Palace, there was in 1805 a 'piece of vacant ground that might be applied to various convenient purposes (dust and ash are conveyed out this way without soiling the house)'.[145]

In the outer suburbs such as Islington, St Pancras, Chelsea, Newington or Stepney, we are perhaps less surprised to discover that many rows of houses had small gardens. In 1796 a dwelling 'facing Colebrook Row, on the banks of the New River Islington, nr. the bottom of Camden Street' possessed an 'excellent garden well planted and a genteel forecourt next to the River'; at Owen's Place, Goswell Street Road, near Sadlers Wells, 'a VERY NEAT GARDEN' was described in 1804 as being 'walled all round and planted with several choice fruit trees, the south wall is upwards of nine feet high, and an excellent wall for early fruit'. The forecourt and the garden of 19 Cheyne Walk, in Chelsea, were in 1794 'planted with fruit trees'; and at a modest house in Lower Clapton, near Hackney, the 'extensive walled garden [was] 140ft. deep more or less, [and was]

103   Plan of the Earl of Macclesfield's garden at 19 Cavendish Square, pen and watercolour wash, c.1795. Howard de Walden Estate, London. Described in June 1795 by a Christie's sale notice as 'LARGE', this contemporary plan shows that it was formed at parlour floor level, was accessed by a pair of bridges thrust across the 'airys' and possessed a pair of mulberry trees. The trees may have been planted by Lady Mary Wortley Montagu when she was resident in the 1770s.

110 'Rustic Rockwork and Fountain at Peckham', engraving from *The Gardener's Magazine* (1838), p. 463. 'This rockwork . . . and the jets of water which are intended to add to its interest, are on a small scale, and have no pretensions to rank high as works of art.'

introduced into 'masses of rockwork' (fig. 110). The writer explained 'what may be done by very common materials, put together with little or no other artistical knowledge, than that of what constitutes the difference between grouping objects, and indiscriminantly scattering them about'. The irregularly shaped basin 'composed of vitrified brick, flints, spars, &c.' had a jet of water 'rising in its centre by means of a leaden pipe, carried up through a convolvulus-shaped figure', as well as 'various 'adjutages in brass, forming different devices for throwing out of water'. 'Creeping plants' were introduced in the interstices, and a 'large *Yucca* gloriòsa' occupied the space between the two principal masses of rockwork.[172]

Few small gardens were as impressively eccentric as that of the anatomist Joshua Brookes in Blenheim Street,

111   C. Hullmandel after George Scharf, *A view of the Vivarium in the garden of Joshua Brookes in Blenheim Street, near Oxford Street*, engraving with watercolour, 1830. London Metropolitan Archives.

A VIEW OF THE VIVARIUM,
Constructed principally with large Masses of the ROCK of GIBRALTAR, in the Garden of Joshua Brookes Esq.
Blenheim Street Great Marlborough Street

off Great Marlborough Street (fig. 111). Brookes's Vivarium, which 'was constructed principally with large masses of the Rock of Gibralter', was home to a variety of exotic birds and beasts including a pair of egrets, an ibis, a raccoon, an eagle, a large owl, pheasants and a fox.[173] The rockwork menagerie and its pendant gothic hermitage lay in the small walled garden between Brookes's house (and 'Anatomical and Zootomical Museum') and his stable block in Blenheim Mews. An iron grille gave into the garden, allowing passers-by to gaze in. This public-spirited gesture, however, had its drawbacks: when the Pantheon in Oxford Street was consumed by fire on 16 January 1792 'the heat was so violent that his doors and sash frames were blistered, and the eagle, hawks, raccoons, foxes, and other animals, terrified by the scene, and incommoded by the heat, were panting and endeavouring to break their chains. The mob assembled and, fancying that the poor animals were roasting alive, kept up an alarming yell, and threatened to pull the house about his ears'.

Among the most memorable accounts of a small roof-top garden was recorded by Henry Phillips in *Sylva Florifera* (1823). The author could not forebear relating the singular devastation that was committed 'on some rural scenery, on a street, leading out of the Strand':

where the wife of a respectable tradesman, who never passed her – 'Brick-wall bounds / to range the fields and treat her lungs with air, / Yet felt the burning instinct-over head,' on the leads of her house contrived to form a grove of myrtles, geraniums, and other such plants as Covent Garden affords. Thus she managed a peep at nature, without the fear of fences being broken by neighbouring cattle, or trampling sportsmen treading down her fairest hopes, which, however, were soon spoiled by a host of enemies as ravenous as unexpected. The adjoining house was occupied by a furrier, who finding his muffs and tippets required air, placed them on his leads also, where the heat of the sun soon gave birth to numerous insects, which escaping from their eggs concealed in the hairs of the fur, flew to the newly created Babylonian garden, and there fixed themselves until every leaf was destroyed; and it was only by the interference of mutual friends and neighbours that damages were not sought in the Court of the King's Bench.[174]

3

Garden Theory

THEORIES AND ASSUMPTIONS

SMALL GARDENS were clearly regarded as an amenity of both symbolic and practical importance, and great attention was paid to their appearance. Although there was little explicit discussion of the aesthetic principles which might have governed their design, they were not entirely ignored by theorists, who frequently referred to such gardens in aesthetic treatises in the course of their discussion of landscape.

Throughout the period, theorists such as Francis Hutcheson, Henry Home (Lord Kames), Thomas Whately, Edmund Burke and Archibald Alison examined gardens as spaces which presented the gardener with the task of exciting a sense of beauty, surprise, curiosity, sweetness, gaiety, melancholy or wonder through the manipulation of proportion, order, colour, harmony, variety and utility.[1] Similarly, garden writers such as John James (translating the work of Antoine-Joseph Dézallier d'Argenville), Joseph Spence and Sir John Dalrymple devised rules for the perfection of garden planning. However, the small garden became the object of popular, informed discussion not for its aesthetics but, rather, as an instrument which contributed to the enjoyment of city living (as it did in the writings of John Trusler, William Cowper and later Leigh Hunt). Others made it the object of discourses which sought to reconcile aesthetic satisfaction with the needs of health, outdoor recreation and utility.

The small garden is what might be called a 'floating concept' – meaning that there was neither a theoretical basis, nor a single source which offered an area of consensus in defining the principles which governed practical town gardening. Therefore, although small gardens were subject to actual or presumed tenets of taste, they were much more powerfully determined by the private aims and desires of their owners. This independence of small garden design from the trends which governed the layout of rural parks and gardens might seem surprising to anyone familiar with contemporary treatises on landscape gardening, which draw confidently upon a well-established body of aesthetic theory. However, throughout the eighteenth century the design of small gardens was only intermittently governed by principles derived from this larger discourse. It was not until the nineteenth century that the explicit theorising about such gardens became widespread; the writings of John Dalrymple and John Loudon, for example, draw on aesthetic theory with a confidence and sense of relevance that are entirely lacking from earlier works on small gardens.

Small garden design was not transmitted through pattern books and other publications which so noticeably enriched and popularised the neo-Palladian idiom in domestic building. Town gardens were invariably the product of their owners' particularised notions of appropriate character and use of their premises; as such, they were, above all, advertisements of the power of technique, and not the art of composition. Virtually all eighteenth-century and early nineteenth-century English gardening and horticultural literature was dominated by practical knowledge disseminated through manuals, dictionaries, 'daily assistants', remembrancers, journals, handbooks, pamphlets, pocket-books, and above all 'kalendars', which were calculated 'not so much to make, as manage a garden'.[2] The objective of each work was the transmission of horticultural instruction, compiled and presented to provide easy directions for the proper management of all forms of gardens.

Stephen Switzer was among the earliest commentators to view the town garden as a distinct horticultural category, when he remarked in 1715 that it was 'compos'd of Flowers, Greens, and choice Exoticks'. He believed that town gardening was no more than a decorative and inconsequential domestic art, which he denounced as 'flower gardening'. He considered flowers trifling and fading beauties that corrupted nature's *simplex munditiis*: spoiling unaffected simplicity, elegance and decency by introducing costly artifice.[3]

Switzer's condemnation did not, however, diminish the art as an essential urban pastime for both men and women. He remarked that 'all Enclosed and Flower-Gardens . . . are absolutely necessary in Cities, [and] Towns . . . he could not possibly employ himself in the narrow Limits of a City-Garden, without such little busy Employs'. Town gardening was, he reflected, an imperfect solution, which he 'hop'd [at] some future Time will give an Opportunity of humbly publishing more Thoughts to the World on that Subject, and reducing that into a correcter Method than has yet appear'd.'[4] Sadly, despite his intentions, Switzer never did so. He failed also to reform what he labelled as the 'Diminutive and wretched Performances we every where meet with, so bad and withal so expensive, that other parts of a Gentleman's Care is often by unavoidable Necessity left undone; the Top of these Designs being in Clipt plants, Flowers, amid other Trifling decorations . . . fit only for little Town-Gardens.'[5]

If Switzer perceived small gardens as problems it is largely because they did not coincide with his greatest interest, which he called 'Rural and Extensive Gardening' – which allowed the 'Beauties of Nature' to remain 'uncorrupted by Art', and where 'all the adjacent Country be laid open to View, and that the Eye should not be bounded with High Walls . . . and several Obstructions, that one sees in too many places, by which the eye is as it were imprisoned'. Switzer believed it was difficult, if not ridiculous, to invoke the aesthetic theory of 'Extensive Gardening' when discussing and designing small gardens. Thus, where landscape gardening provided models, and rules as to adaptation of these models, small garden design had few.

Dalrymple, in his *Essay on the Different Natural Situations of Gardens*, composed in the 1750s, did not refer directly to town gardens, but to 'small gardens' in 'dead flat' situations.[6] This category, however, included the town garden, as this, above all others, was the place where 'affectation [was] to be exposed'; in other words, where artifice was laid bare. As such situations raised 'little or no sentiment, so the whole fancy of the gardener should be employed in carrying the thought, by a parade of art, from attending to this defect of nature.' The 'flat' garden was 'more proper when in the neighbourhood of a great city, and thrown open to all the

world, than when in a remote province . . . [as] a garden, like this, is a kind of fairy land'.

The contrivances of artifice which were invoked to supply the defects of natural topography and natural prospect were 'pardonable here'.

> As there is but little pleasure to the imagination, arising from this situation itself, so it should be contrived to give as much pleasure to the senses as possible: for this reason, the flowers should be sown in beds and parterres, to be more obviously seen, and to throw out their sweets more strongly into the air: fruits of the finest kinds should be spread throughout the compartments: the flowering shrubs should be planted in clumps, and assorted in their colours and flowers with all the nicety of a well made up flower-pot; to strike with the stronger surprize; the trees should all be exotics, and of the rarest kinds: and to create greater variety, through the Chinese form from its fantastical appearance, and the CORINTHIAN order from its magnificence, be, in general the properest for such an adorned garden; yet buildings of all species under the sun, that have dignity in them, should here find place.

Dalrymple concluded that 'in short, every agreeable object, that creates surprize, and that exhibits a view of magnificent art, should enter into the composition of such a garden'. As a site of unbridled whimsicality, the flat garden 'should not be judged of by the ordinary rules of experience, or taste; but by the capricious ones of variety and fancy'.[7]

Loudon doubtless drew upon Dalrymple's *Essay* when in 1812 he produced *Hints on the Formation of Gardens and Pleasure Grounds*. Loudon was as obsessed with the true expression of 'progress' and modern garden design as he was with the rational ordering of knowledge. He remarked in *Hints* that

> It follows, that small spots, from being less adapted to this system of improvement [i.e., the Picturesque], and the detail of country seats in general, from being less the subject of the artist's studies, have been completely neglected. Thus, while the quartos and folios have been sent forth on landscape gardening, picturesque improvements, or country residences, we have been upwards of a century without seeing any work to supersede the ancient plans and treatises on parterres and kitchen gardens, by Switzer and Le B[l]ond: or the 'Gardens for the Town,' by Batty Langley, Le[onard] Meagre, and others [fig. 112].[8]

112 Leonard Meager, design for a small garden, engraving from *The English Gardener* (first published London, 1670; London 1688), pl. 6. Lindley Library, Royal Horticultural Society, London.

Loudon offered the following account of his predecessors' efforts:

The designs in those works being wholly adapted for clipt trees, shorn hedges, and groves, are too obsolete, as well as too expensive in execution, for the present day. The prevailing taste, however, must be imitated; the modern style, therefore has been applied in town villas without science, and the grounds of the retiring citizen filled up with clumps and strips of trees, after the undigested ideas of his builder or upholsterer; or planted out with borders of rare shrubbery, by his nurseryman. Such is the general taste in the vicinity of the metropolis.[9]

The object of *Hints* was to 'prove that taste may display itself to advantage, where there is neither great extent to work on, nor an immense sum to be expended'; and to show 'a display of a superior taste in the small places and garden scenes' about town, to reflect the general progress of the age.

Loudon reflected that it was 'natural for a mind unacquainted with the powers of art, to suppose that professional assistance can effect little in laying out small gardens . . . but this is to infer, that nothing can be beautiful that is not also extensive. Beauty or expression depend no more on dimension than on expence, but

are the result of a combination of parts forming a whole, calculated by its fitness and utility to gratify the mind, and by its effect to charm the eye.' The 'small spot', he remarked, 'is a blank, depending for its effect wholly on the skill and ingenuity of him who undertakes to fill it'.[10]

Among the plans he published 'for small places, gardens and parterres' Loudon introduced 'some in the ancient geometrical style of rural improvement.' He felt that to commend designs in a style which 'has been a century laid aside', required an apology. This was, however, unnecessary, as he was not, as he was probably aware, attempting to 'revive' so much as perpetuate a system of gardening. In the spirit of Dalrymple's 'fairy lands' he recommended grotesque and fantastical miniature gardens, scenes of 'heath, furze, brambles, hollies, thorns, briars, fens, thistles, with rocky pits or dingles, and in a place of covered seats, mud huts, or turf hovels'.[11]

These recommendations serve to show how little town gardening had, in fact, changed since the early eighteenth century, and how the so-called 'system' of town gardening was, in fact, and had historically been, exempt from the strictures of taste: every contrivance, every affectation was, as Dalrymple reminds us, 'proper' and 'pardonable' in a small garden.[12] As Loudon remarked in 1812, gardens, parterres and 'such small subjects' seen at one view were incapable of surpassing the 'ancient mode' in so far as 'they must always be, characterised by avowed art of some description'. In such a 'flat situation', where there was little or no distant prospect, the 'modern style' could 'effect nothing, but simple variety'.[13]

TOWN GARDEN MODELS

There were two main models of garden design that provided points of reference for the London town garden: the Dutch and the French. Emphasising one at the expense of the other denies that both tastes were, on the scale of small gardening, relatively interchangeable.[14] It is, none the less, possible to distinguish a variety of differences between the opposing models from The Netherlands and France.

Seventeenth-century and eighteenth-century Dutch gardens have recently been the subject of protracted investigations, which have yielded a great many insights into what was previously a much misunderstood and maligned taste.[15] Some of the new findings have stressed

113 Cornelis Troost, *An Amsterdam Town Garden*, oil on canvas, *c*.1743. Rijksmuseum-Stichting, Amsterdam.

the spatial ordering and garden vocabulary as they were perceived by contemporary observers as being 'ontologically Dutch'.[16] Among the Dutch characteristics which appear to have been adopted within early eighteenth-century town gardens in Britain, as well as in larger gardens, was the enclosure of the garden by high walls, and a fastidiousness and ingenuity in the arrangement of garden artefacts and natural elements. Above all, the gardens were perceived as diminutive decorative spaces, which often had a remote relationship to the house, and were furnished with an *ad hoc* assortment of garden imagery – such as trellis, statuary, potted plants, topiary, pavilions and furnishings.

French formalism was, on the other hand, based on the repudiation of the disjointed clutter which characterised the Dutch taste: it promoted the integration of house and garden, and commended simplicity of overall design. It also encouraged restraint in the appointment of garden elements and the modelling of natural materials, which had the general effect of surpressing sumptuous excesses and fussiness.

The Dutch garden was suited for bourgeois life, being perfectly adapted to the modest city premises. Switzer

remarked in 1741 that it was 'the People of the common level of Understanding [who] grew so fond' of the '*Dutch* Taste . . . being delighted with the little Niceties and fantastical Operations of Art, always thinking that the finest, which was least natural'.[17] The Dutch expression was, at its simplest, a basic rectilinear configuration of beds and gravel walks in an enclosed ground adjacent to the house. At its most exuberant, it was characterised by geometrical scrolls or straight-sided quarters of box-edged flower-beds, 'grass-platts', broad rolled gravel and shell walks, and displays of 'cliped [sic] Evergreens,. and such low expensive things', all laid out on a ground which was 'reduced to exact Levels.'[18] Cornelis Troost's painting of an Amsterdam garden of about 1743 shows a scene of domestic harmony enacted within a lavishly appointed flower-garden (fig. 113). This little theatrical setting, complete with covered seat, statuary, fruiting trees and shrubs, small pool and luxuriant backdrop of foliage, shows that the garden could be, perhaps more than any other part of the domestic topography, the locus of affluence. It was the showcase of abundance, and the object of a high level of horticultural and decorative sophistication.

Troost's painting and an earlier evocation of Gerard van Rijp's town garden (*c*.1700) in Noord Holland, provide very detailed painted views of small premises, which were seldom depicted in contemporary English paintings (fig. 114). They are among the best views of gardens, which in a number of ways provided a model for small well-appointed London gardens at the time of Thomas Fairchild. The layout of the flower-beds and the smaller decorative baubles are features which are known to have occurred within planted town gardens in the eighteenth-century London town garden.[19] Plants and garden artefacts are typically laid out on a simple plan, as if to portray a truthful picture of the Georgic reality of the scene: if the gardens are scenes of abundance, then every ingredient is commodified, as each one requires for its existence intensive cultivation and management. Likewise, the simple, commodified scene is one of ingenuity, neatness and frugality, which reflects that a well-ordered garden is a product and symbol of a well managed soul. The garden was not, in fact, necessarily a display of extravagance, but one of an artfully contrived assemblage of commodities which were perceived by the owners as an outward display of their spiritual and material comfort.

The English equivalents to the garden plans portrayed by Dutch artists were published by Leonard Meager in *The English gardener; or a Sure Guide to young Planters and*

114 Unknown artist, scene with Gerard van Rijp standing in his modest town garden in Noord Holland, c.1700. Kerkeraad van de Verenigde Doopsgezinde Gemeente, Amsterdam. Although many London gardens of the same period may have resembled this small plot, such intimate topographical views are now rare.

Gardeners (1670; figs 112 and 115).[20] Meager's plans of 'Knots' depict the comparative pragmatism, plainness and lack of sophistication of English small garden design: an expression which had not substantially changed since the time of Robert Smythson (1534–1614) and William Talman (1650–1719), when the models were derived from the compartmental parterres of Renaissance Italy and France.[21] Worlidge remarked in *Systema-Horti-Culturae: or the art of gardening* (1677) that this 'new mode of Gravel Walks and Grass-plots' was 'fit only for such Houses, or Palaces, that are scituated in Cities and great Towns, although they are now become presidents for many stately Country Residencies'.[22] Until the end of the first decade of the eighteenth century, English gardenists had only the work of Meager to draw upon for published sources to guide the layout of their city gardens, while in The Netherlands there were several informative publications, including Jan van der Groen's *Den Nederlandtsen Hovenier* (1669).[23]

Examples of what Switzer termed '*decent*' and '*plain*' Dutch-inspired gardens abound in early eighteenth-century topographical views. Kip's bird's-eye views of

115 Leonard Meager, design for a small garden, engraving from *The English Gardener* (first published London, 1670; London 1688), pl. 7. Lindley Library, Royal Horticultural Society, London.

116 John Kip, *Aerial View of the Cities of London and Westminster and St James's Rark*, engraving, 1720 (detail). Private collection.

117 Unknown artist, *Pierrepont House, Nottinghamshire*, oil on canvas *c.*1708–13. Paul Mellon Collection, Yale Center for British Art, New Haven.

118   Leonard Knyff, *Old Palace Yard, Westminster*, pen and watercolour wash, after 1718. British Museum, London.

London (*c.*1710–20) show dozens of gardens in the West End, and particularly in the vicinity of St James's Park – most of which are enclosed by walls (sometimes covered with vines or espaliered fruit trees), and the ground cast into simple geometric quarters studded with shaped shrubs and encompassed and dissected by gravel paths (fig. 116). Likewise, many of the houses, and especially those in Petty France and Pall Mall, had summerhouses perched atop raised mounts or terrace walks; the latter 'being necessary for the proper Elevation of any Person that walks round his Garden, to view all that lyes round him'.[24]

In Leonard Knyff's more detailed topographical view of about 1718–19 the viewer looks north into Old Palace Yard, Westminster (fig. 118). The artist portrayed a small walled enclosure, decorated by a flower-garden composed of small retangular beds, dotted with clipped shrubs, and what appears to be an urn in the centre; the walls are lined with fan-trained fruit trees. This garden has been described as a representation of the perfection of the Dutch tendency 'to be local, parochial, traditional and customary'.[25] John Dixon Hunt compares the garden to the 'extravagant' Dutch garden at Pierrepont House, Nottingham (fig. 117); 'both', he remarks, 'are examples of how the Dutch style provided ideal town gardens'.[26]

The Pierrepont garden is a sunken garden linked to a perimeter terrace walk by four flights of steps. The walk is framed on the inside by a raised parapet wall, which is surmounted with a profusion of part-glazed terracotta vases filled with colourful blossoms. The sunk 'level' garden is cast into symmetrical beds edged with either stone or deal, which contain uncluttered displays of low flowering plants (some of which were undoubtedly exotics) interspersed with regular, but less frequently occurring, corresponding rows of obelisk shaped evergreens. The garden is divided by one main and one transverse axis, at the junction of which is a statue of Flora. Flanking the circumference of the perimeter walk of the sunken garden are lines of regimented square flower beds etched in a gently sloping bank, or glacis. The top of the glacis forms the edge of a border of variably shaped evergreens which hug the garden walls. While the garden is that of a large provincial town house it contains all the elements of a London garden. The 'extravagance' of the garden lies in its scale and the proliferation of costly decorative features; the plan of the flower-beds, if viewed in isolation from the raised *terras*, is characteristic of that of many smaller London town gardens.

A London garden executed in the Dutch style, which

119 Unknown artist, *The Gardens and Yards of the Officers' Terrace at Chatham Dockyards*, pen and watercolour wash, 1774. British Library, London.

might have approached the layout of a modest quarter of the Pierrepont sunk garden was that of Mrs Delany at 48 Upper Brook Street, Mayfair. Mrs Delany wrote in 1734, when keeping her provincial sister abreast of the activities at her own garden:

> You think, madam, I have no garden, perhaps? but that's a mistake.; I *have one* as big as your parlour at Gloucester, and in it groweth *damask-roses, stocks* variegated and plain, some purple, some red, *pinks, Philaria*, some dead some alive; and *honeysuckles* that never blow. But when you come to town to weed and water it, it shall be improved after the new taste, but till then it shall remain dishevelled and undrest.

Whether she went ahead with her proposed improvements is unknown, although we are informed by a subsequent missive that equipped with her 'little bird' and Mrs Pott, Mrs Delany journeyed to Upton in Essex to pay a visit to the celebrated horticulturist Dr

Fothergill, where she alleged that '[I] crammed my tin box with exoticks, over-powered with such variety I knew not what to chuse!'[27]

The Officers' Terrace at Chatham Dockyards, Kent, exemplifies the manner in which Dutch spatial planning promoted a relative lack of relation of parts to the whole – contrasting sharply with the French advocacy of their dynamic integration. A variety of topographical images, plans and an outstanding model of 1774 portray how the row of twelve early eighteenth-century houses and their back courtyards were separated from the their individual rear gardens by a single-lane carriage-way (figs 119 and 120). The compartmentalised orchestration of the domestic topography was derived from a Dutch country house – that is, from a method of garden planning which had been fostered by the need to establish pleasure grounds beyond the necessary obstacles of fortifications, and canals.[28] However, the plan of the houses and gardens at Chatham was not directly derived from

120   Model of the Officers' Terrace, Chatham Dockyard, Chatham, Kent, painted wood, 1774 (detail). National Maritime Museum, Greenwich.

The Netherlands, but from the Officers' Terrace at Portsmouth (designed 1692); nor was it the last to be built on such a plan, as the Officer's Terraces at Woolwich and Devonport soon followed suit.

The Chatham Officers' Terrace and its gardens remain relatively unaltered to this day. The gardens lie on a gently sloping hillside east of the range of terraces, raised an average of nine feet above the level of the road, and supported by a long high retaining wall. The row of 'depending' terrace walk gardens were conceived about 1715 and built as a grand gesture by the Navy Office, beginning in 1722. Despite the uniformity and congruity of the houses, each garden was conceived on a slightly different plan, and was modified by successive householders. Like so many contemporary examples, the simple geometrical patterns of the flower-beds are derived from Meager.[29]

If we return to Mrs Delany's letter, in which she stated that her intention was to create a garden in the 'new taste', we may take it that she referred to the French taste – and particularly from John James's translation of Dézallier d'Argenville's *La Théorie et la practique du jardinage* (1709).[30] The book had a profound influence upon English gardens, especially on the design and layout of small gardens. The extent of its influence is discussed in the following section.

It is sufficient to say here that the proponents of the French taste did not, of course, dwell solely upon the design of flowerbeds, but commended simplicity and unity of composition. It was remarked that 'a garden . . . if not of great extent, will not admit dissimilar emotions. And in ornamenting a small garden, the fastest course is to confine it to a single expression'. Thus if 'the whole be very small, so as scarce to fill the eye at one look, its division into parts will . . . make it appear still less. The minuteness of the parts is, by an easy transition of ideas, transferred to the whole. Each part hath a diminutive appearance, and by the intimate connection of these parts with the whole, we pass the same judgement upon all.'[31]

The new tenets neither simplified garden design, nor made the tasteful design of a small plots appreciably easier – for as Switzer remarked in 1715: 'if the [garden] Room be but small, there requires the more Judgment in laying it out well', and he continued to remark that 'even in the least and meanest Design there is some Judgment, Thought, Frugality, and Contrivance'.[32] As grounds were often taken in at a single glance, every embellishment was integral to the composition of the whole: 'the whole Art of Designing consists in a just Agreement of the several Parts one with another; and the adapting the whole to the Nature and Uses of the Place, for which your Design is formed.'[33]

JOSEPH SPENCE'S PLANS: 'VERY PROPER FOR A TOWN GARDEN'

Having examined the generalities of garden theory, we can now turn our attention to a range of plans contrived for small London gardens and the very specific models, concepts and influences which determined the way in they were to be laid out on the ground. Our central point of reference is the corpus of garden plans produced between 1743 and 1766 by the Reverend Joseph Spence (fig. 121).[34] In so far as Spence was both a practical gardener and a garden theorist, his work offers an unusually wide range of material for analysis: his garden proposals can, therefore, be examined in relation to his own well-formulated design principles, as well as in the context of contemporary writings and topographical material.

Spence (1699–1768) was Professor of Poetry and, later, of Modern History at Oxford, and dedicated much of his early life to the study of garden design theory. He is remembered for his record of the conversations and ideas of his many friends and acquaintances, which were collected in *Observations, Anecdotes, and Characters of Books and Men*; which, although not published until 1820, was widely circulated and acclaimed and quoted in the eighteenth century. Among the most interesting aspects of the book is the record of Alexander Pope's remarks on the English landscape garden, which influenced Spence's own garden precepts, or 'materials' for garden design.

Though distinguished in many spheres, it was Spence's gardening accomplishments at Byfleet, Surrey,

121 George Vertue after Isaac Whood, *Joseph Spence*, engraving, 1746. National Portrait Gallery, London. Spence (1699–1768) was both a practical gardener and a garden theorist. He formed a range of small garden layouts for his friends' London houses during the period 1743–66.

that gained him considerable reputation and earned him numerous landscape commissions across the country.[35] Horace Walpole 'esteemed him a man of taste and judgement in Gardening';[36] and Edward Rolle claimed that Spence became 'so celebrated, & his character herein so well settled & established, that his Decisions upon any controverted point of this Sort, were generally implicitly Submitted to & acquiesced in; as carrying a kind of stamp of Conviction with them: who indeed has Hardiness enough, to doubt of the Propriety of any little intended alteration, after it was know to have been Suggested by Mr Spence!' A young lady who visited Spence at Byfleet wrote enthusiastically to her fiancé that her host was 'well known in the literary world as an author, a perfect critic in poetry, painting and gardening; I mean the *Landskip garden*, which is a kind of painting. It was he and Mr Pope, and another or two of his friends, who introduced the present taste in gardening, and rescued them from the imprisonment of high walls and clipt hedges.'[37]

In his writings Spence was concerned with formulating 'general rules' in order to banish what he described as 'all confined, gloomy, regular and flat' forms of gardens. However, in his designs for town gardens he devised garden plans which often perpetuated concepts and models directly at odds with this explicit aim.[38]

He was familiar with, and indebted to, a variety of contemporary or earlier garden writers; among them Leonard Meager, John Worlidge, Stephen Switzer, George London, Henry Wise, Thomas Fairchild, Richard Bradley, Batty Langley and Philip Miller. His approach to composition was also, although less obviously, influenced by his familiarity with the letters of the Jesuit missionary Jean-Denis Attiret published as *Lettres édifiantes des missions* (1749) and illustrated with thirty-six engraved plates.[39]

Spence's general rules, like those of his contemporaries, were theoretical guidelines only. He often broke them to comply with the demands of comfort and convenience, and to accommodate his patrons' taste.[40] He also remarked that people 'don't mind what is right, but what is the fashion, so to please in laying out a friend's grounds one must not mind what the place requires so much as how to adapt the parts as well as one can to what he wants'.[41] For instance, Spence invariably attempted to increase his clients' enjoyment by carefully considering their various views, their places of rest and contemplation within their grounds, and the means by which they might be exposed to the maximum effect of combining and changing colour, scent, topography and ornament. The outcome of one such consideration led Spence to perpetuate the use of lattice-work in contravention of prescribed taste, as it was agreed that in gardens, one was often 'so much exposed to heat, that ladies who are careful of their complection, dare not walk in them till after sun-set'.[42]

Spence designed a total of seven London gardens between 1743 and 1766, one of which was for his own house in Piccadilly.[43] A series of plans, each with fragmentary scribbled notes, gives us an unusually rich source of information on his small garden work. The garden plans were not commissioned designs, but favours for friends; this was characteristic of Spence's affection, benevolence and unremitting liberality, which he lavished on both close acquaintances and needy strangers.[44] Recipients of his plans included: Lady Falmouth, Alexander Pope's friend Dr Noel Broxholme,

and two personal friends of Spence, Robert Dodsley and Baron Atkyns. The following gardens are discussed in our analysis of Spence's work: Dr Noel Broxholme, Bond Street, Mayfair (1743); Lady Falmouth's 'London-Garden' in Albemarle Street, Piccadilly (1744); Spence's own garden in Stratton Street, Piccadilly (1744); Buckingham Gate, near St James's Park (1747); 'Exchequer-garden' in Parliament Street, Whitehall (1751); Robert Dodsley, Richmond (1753); Baron Atkyns's garden modelled on Le Sage's garden in Paris (1763); and 'John's Plan for Baron Atkyns, Fulham' (1763).[45] Gardens that lie beyond the metropolis, but that are discussed in terms of their influence on Spence's town garden designs, include Mrs Bart[hol]emew's, in Shalford (1751), and Mr Boleby's, at Ferryhill (1766).

Before beginning this analysis of Spence's work it is worth taking particular note of what is possibly his last small garden plan, which in many ways summed up his approach to their design. Spence described the suburban Parisian garden of the novelist Alain-René Le Sage in 1763 – twenty-two years after having seen it. He entitled the vignette 'The Manner of Laying out a Garden; like old Mons. Le Sage's in the Rue de S: Ja[c]ques; at Paris'; a note on the reverse reads 'very proper for a Town Garden: Albemarle Street' (fig. 122).[46] When Spence was in Paris in 1741 with Lord Lincoln, the former 'ever alert to an opportunity to converse with a literary celebrity, sought out the aged Le Sage, living in retirement and in comparative poverty in the Faubourg St Jacques. He was charmed with the old romancer's pretty little garden, and looked with reverence at the room in which most of *Gil Blas* had been written.'[47]

And an extreme pretty place to write in it was. His House is at Paris in the suburbs of St Ja[c]ques, and so, open to the country air, and the garden laid out in the prettiest manner that ever I saw for a town garden. It was as pretty as it was small, and when he was in the study part of it he was quite retired from the noise of the street or any interruptions from his own family. The garden was only of the breadth of the house, from which you stepped out into a raised square parterre, planted with a variety of the prettiest flowers. From which you went down a flight of steps, on each side, into a berceau which led to two rooms, or summerhouses, quite at the end of the garden. These were joined by an open portico, the roof of which was supported with columns so that

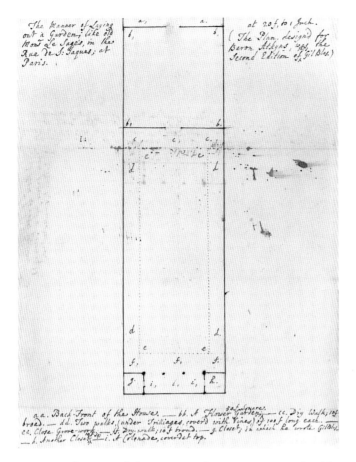

122 Joseph Spence, 'The Manner of Laying out a Garden like old Monsr. Le Sage's, in the Rue de S: Ja[c]ques; at Paris. (The Plan design'd for Baron Atkyns . . . Very proper for a Town garden: Albemarle Street)', pen, 1763. Beinecke Rare Book and Manuscript Library, Yale University, New Haven.

he could walk from the one to the other, all under cover, in the intervals of writing. The berceaux were covered with vines and honeysuckles, and the space between them was grove-work. It was in the right-hand room as you go down that he wrote *Gil Blas*.[48]

In another, shorter description, he referred to 'His pretty little Garden: rais'd ground at first; then a Green Cage Walk, on each side; & a Logietta (with Portico in the midst . . .)'.[49]

Le Sage's garden served as a model for Spence's town gardens proposals. There were, of course, some stylistic modifications to his approach – *berceaux*, or arbours, were rejected in favour of more fashionable alcoves and garden seats, the plantings became more natural and assorted, and the topography became more varied. However, the conventional propriety of ordering of house and garden remained fairly consistent, and responded to contemporary theories and assumptions on the relationships which were held possible between art and nature in the garden.

What applied to the extensive garden also applied to the small plot: Shaftesbury posited that gardens required a graduated sequence of design whereby regulated nature near the house gradually gave way to the untouched forms of nature on the horizon.[50] Spence generally endorsed what has been called in our own time, this 'scale of diminishing artifice', which he may have acquired from Dalrymple. It was Dalrymple's belief, like Shaftesbury's, in the need for a 'transitional' effect from the regularity of the house to the wilderness in the distance, which formed a bridge between the ideas of Switzer earlier in the century and those of Repton towards its close.[51]

Although, in the case of the small garden, it was difficult to achieve a fluid graduation of designed spaces, some designers of small gardens – and Spence, in particular – often invoked this 'transitional' effect in their attempts to systematise the art of town gardening. A system of some sort, it seems, was regarded as useful, if not essential for the development of rational principles to bring about further improvement of the art of town gardening.

facing page Detail from fig. 137.

4

Garden Elements

'THE DISPOSITION AND GENERAL DISTRIBUTION
OF GARDENS'[1]

SPENCE, WHEN DISCUSSING 'Materials for Designing a
Garden', set out twelve 'articles that he sees as central
to the theory and practice of garden design'. Spence's
categories provide useful starting points for a more
general discussion of eighteenth-century assumptions
about the design of small gardens, and for an analysis of
the ways in which various aspects of the London garden
were handled in practice. He lists them as follows: 'What
a ground wants –; What it demands –; What to take away
– Boundaries, y^t seen to imprison you; What to take in
– views, sun & good air; what to shut out – Disagreeable objects, Sun & bad air'; and 'What to provide for
– alternative openings, & solids, lights & shades, p[leasing
objects (for the different seasons) in [a] word, variety &
use intermixt.'[2]

The 'articles' are discussed by Spence under twelve
headings, which refer to the principal considerations of
laying out and building a garden, and the features which
were incorporated within them.

GENIUS LOCI

To consult the *genius loci* was to identify the character,
spirit or meaningfulness of the place. D'Argenville
observed that 'To make a complete Disposition and
Distribution of a general Plan, Respect must be had to
the Situation of the Ground: For the greatest Skill in
the right ordering of a Garden is, thoroughly to understand, and consider the natural Advantages and Defects
of the Place; to make use of one, and to redress the
other: Situations differing in every Garden.'[3]

The small town garden did not, strictly speaking,
possess a *genius loci*: the ground was invariably artificial,

the natural ground level and profile being disfigured
with heaps of building rubble, and raised or altered with
excavated fill. Furthermore, the average enclosed plot
was often too small to contain, within its bounds, a
'disposition and distribution' which commanded the
designers' 'Respect'. Nevertheless, this general rule was
invoked, and did not contravene another concomitant
premise: that it is

> the great Business of an Architect, or Designer of
> Gardens, when he contrives a handsome Plan, with
> his utmost Art and good Œconomy to improve the
> natural Advantages, and to redress the Imperfections,
> Shelvings, and Inequalities of the Ground. With these
> Precautions he should guide and restrain the Impetu-
> osity of his Genius, never swerving from Reason, but
> constantly submitting, and comforming himself to
> that which suits best with the natural Situation of the
> Place.[4]

Spence advised persons wishing to lay out a garden
'to study the ground & things and views round it, many,
many times, before you begin (a month is scarce enough
to do this as thoroughly as it should be.)'[5] His methodi-
cal and thorough approach applied to gardens of all
scales, and is corroborated by the fact that he produced
a number of preliminary and alternative designs for
many of his small gardens (figs 123, 131–5).

Spence had a pragmatic definition of the *genius loci*
which was readily applicable to the small garden:

> The first and most material is to consult the Genius
> of the place. What is the great guide as what ought
> to be. The making of a fine plan for any place
> unknown is like Bay's saying 'that he had made an
> excellent simile, if he did but know how to apply it'.
> To study the ground thoroughly, one should not only
> take a view of the whole and all its parts, and con-

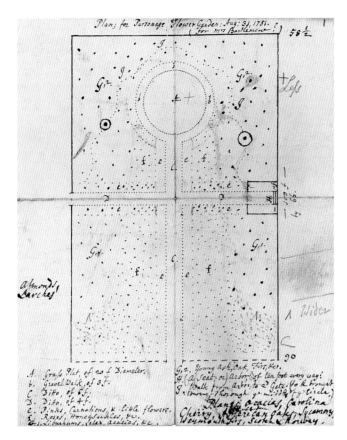

123 Joseph Spence, *Plan: for Parsonage Flower Garden: August 31, 1751 (for Mrs Bartlemew?)*, pen. Beinecke Rare Book and Manuscript Library, Yale University, New Haven.

sider the laying of it in general, and all its beauties and advantages or inconveniences and impediments, in particular, but also walk around it in the line without your own bounds; to see what beauties may be added by breaking through your outline.[6]

To conceal the bounds, or at least to render them less conspicuous, was the overriding, if implicit, determinant of every general rule. While it might have been difficult to delude the viewer as to the frontiers of a small plot, it was perceived as possible and essential to invoke illusionistic effects which diminished or dematerialised the intrusiveness and imprisonment of hard boundaries. The emphasis put on the *genius loci* suggests that small gardens were not just inward-looking – their character was often perceived as being influenced or determined by the character of terrain beyond one's own boundaries.

★   ★   ★

The 'easie and plain Directions, very useful for a Learner [and professional], how to level and bring a Garden into some Order and Form' had not substantially changed since the mid-seventeenth century.[7] Leonard Meager (1670) briefly outlined the steps as follows: first, 'put your Garden into Form' – planning it on paper, or working directly on the site, after having levelled the ground; secondly, set out the pattern of the ground with 'a quantity of handsome straight stakes' (four to five feet long, being sharpened at one end); thirdly, form the border edges for a peripheral walk, setting the outer edge of the path at a minimum of two and a half feet from the garden wall; fourthly, 'cast out your Walk'; fifthly, level the ground (again); sixthly, dig over the ground (breaking clods and weeding, digging and raking); and lastly, set the edges and proceed to plant (fig. 124).[8]

John James remarked in 1712 that 'a fine Garden' is 'no less difficult to contrive and order well, than a good Building'.[9] Spence's small gardens were carefully surveyed and plotted, substantiating Switzer's claim (1718) that 'if the [garden] Room be but small, there requires more Judgment in laying it out well'.[10] Every reputable

124 Leonard Meager, 'Geometry of laying out beds', engraving from *The English Gardener* (London, 1688), pl. 2. Lindley Library, Royal Horticultural Society, London. 'Nets of squares' were used to lay out small gardens.

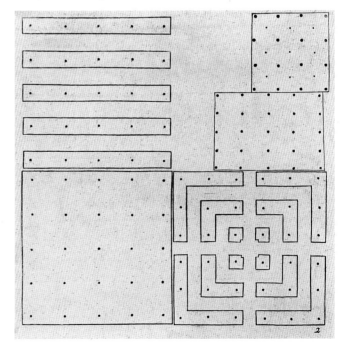

garden designer was expected to perform the same preparatory surveying and planning exercises regardless of the size of his project. Spence completed all his commissions in the professional manner defined by the various treatises on geometry and planning.[11] James describes the credentials of professionalism:

A Man should know something of Geometry and Architecture, and be able to draw well; he should understand Ornament, and be acquainted with the Properties and Effects of all the Plants made use of in fine Gardens; should design readily; and, with all this, have a right Judgment, and natural good Taste, form'd upon the Contemplation of Things that are excellent, the Censuring of those that are ill, and a consumate Experience in the Art of Gardening.[12]

Spence employed a grid-based template for all of his small town gardens designs: each ground was neatly plotted on a 'net of squares'. Thomas Breaks, commenting on the well-established tradition of dividing the ground into a series of 'squares', remarked in *A Complete System of Land Surveying* (1778) that 'Division of ground is a very useful and necessary branch of practical Surveying, teaching us to divide any Plot or Draught into any number of Parts, equal or unequal, according to Quantity and Quality of the Ground about to be divided'.[13]

The size of the grid squares was determined by the dimensions and proportions of the garden-front and its apertures (doors and windows), which in turn proportioned the extent of the several elements of the garden, such as walks, loggiettas, hedging, fish ponds, flower-beds and porticos. John Rutter and Daniel Carter recommended in *Modern Eden* (1767) that where the 'ground is smaller, the parts must be fewer in number, that there may be got so much extent for each, as will keep it from being ridiculous'.[14] Spence based the scale of his grid units on the breadth of his garden walks; therefore even his smallest garden which measured only eighteen by forty feet (his own ground in Stratton Street) was laid out upon five-foot square modules, whilst his largest town garden at two hundred by four hundred feet (Buckingham Gate) was formulated on a twenty-five-foot square grid (figs 125, 126a and b).

★   ★   ★

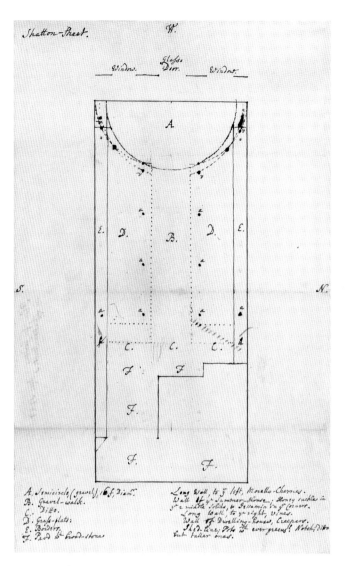

125 Joseph Spence, *Stratton Street*, pen, 1744. Beinecke Rare Book and Manuscript Library, Yale University, New Haven. Spence's plan of his own town garden in Piccadilly.

REGULARITY

Switzer remarked in his 'explanatory notes upon the general Disposition of the [building and garden] Plan', that 'Little Gardens that lye contiguous thereto [next to private apartments and offices], may be easily observed to answer to their Designs and Use, which is Decency and Plainess'.[15] The garden was an 'appendage' or 'accessory' of the house, and as such could aspire merely to succeed in reflecting its orderliness and congruity. Lord Kames explained the rationale: 'nothing happens without cause. Perfect regularity and uniformity are required in a house; and this idea is extended to its accessory the garden, especially if it be a small spot inca-

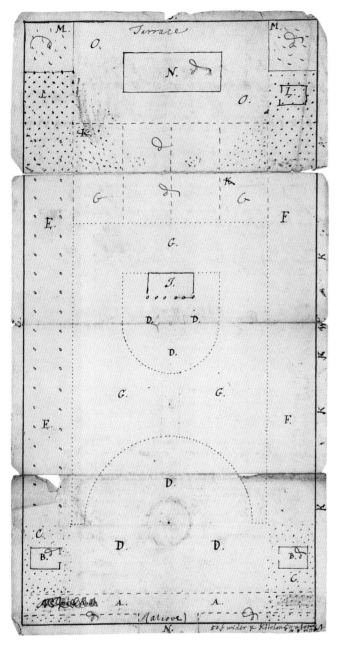

126a Joseph Spence, *Plan of a Garden for a house in Buckingham Gate, London*, pen, 1747. Beinecke Rare Book and Manuscript Library, Yale University, New Haven.

A. Gravel-Walk. 150 f, by 12.
B. Two Arbours; to dine in, &c. 15 f, by 12.
C. Lime-Trees; w Woodbine, or Jessamin, up each trunk.
D. Lawne, or Plaine.
E. Chesnut-Walk; 200 f, by 25.
F. Open-Walk; Ditto.
G. Grove-work, with Serpentine Walks; seats; &c.
H. A Fountaine: 25 f Diameter.
I. A Loggietta, or Summer-House: 20 f, by 10.
K. Kitchen Garden; with Espaliers. 100 f, by 50.
L. Two Quincunx's, of Cypress & Ever-greens.
M. Two little Mounts; with large Hedges
N. Fish-pond: 50 f, by 20.
O. Low withys; & low flowering Shrubs: If the latter, Violets & Primroses, about the Mounts.

126b Joseph Spence, *Plan for a Garden for a house in Buckingham Gate, London*, pen, 1747 (verso of fig. 126a). Beinecke Rare Book and Manuscript Library, Yale University, New Haven. Spence's specifications for his garden design at Buckingham Gate.

pable of much grandeur or much variety. The house is regular, so must the garden be; the floors of the house are horizontal, and the garden must have the same position; in the house we are protected from every intruding eye, so we must be in the garden.'[16]

In *Observations on Modern Gardening* (1770), Thomas Whately alleged that it 'has always been supported that *art* must interfere [with nature]; but art was carried to excess when from accessory it became principal . . . when ground, wood and water were reduced to mathematical figures; and similarity and order were preferred to freedom and variety'.[17] He continued:

So strange an abuse probably arose from an idea of some necessary correspondence between the mansion, and the scene it immediately commanded; the forms therefore of both were determined by the same rules; and terraces, canals and avenues, were but so many variations on the plan of the building. The regularity thus established spread afterwards to more distant quarters: there, indeed, the absurdity was acknowledged as soon as a move towards natural disposition appeared: but a prejudice in favour of art, as it is called, *just about the house*, still remains. If by the term *regularity* is intended, the principle is equally applicable to the vicinity of any other building; and every temple in the garden ought to have its concomitant formal slopes and plantations; or the conformity may be reversed, and we may as reasonably contend that the building ought to be irregular, in order to be consistent with the scene it belongs to. The truth is that both propositions are erroneous; architecture requires symmetry; the objects of nature freedom; and the properties of the one, cannot with justice be transferred to the other. But if by the term, no more is meant than merely *design*, the dispute is at an end; choice, arrangement, composition, improvement, and preservation, are so many symptoms of art, which may occasionally appear in several parts of a garden, but ought to be displayed without reserve near the house; there nothing should seem neglected; it is a scene of the most cultivated nature; it ought to be enriched; it ought to be adorned; and design may be avowed in the plan, and expense in the execution'.[18]

Regularity of design, meaning geometric or rectilinear patterns, was the recurrent characteristic of most small gardens; regularity, however, consistently introduced conflicting arguments about the propriety of ordering nature in the 'Mathematical Style', or nature 'Laid out by the Rule and Line'.[19] Regularity denoted mensuration, uniformity, harmony, proportion and other geometrical properties. In the strictest sense it invoked precision, congruity and orderliness, and was the recommended character for scenes or objects created from topography or materials which did not immediately commend themselves to the imagination and the senses.

Regularity was also equated with uniformity, although the terms were not entirely interchangeable. Uniformity expressed the similarity of parts considered separately, and regularity the similarity of parts as constituting the whole. There might, however, be uniformity without regularity, because there might be similarity between any two or more parts of a form,

without a general similarity among the whole. But there could not be regularity without uniformity, or without this general resemblance of the parts to each other.[20]

Regularity was ultimately contingent upon the magnitude of the object perceived, the distance at which the object was perceived, and the vantage point of the viewer. For instance, a series of three small rectangular beds seen from the drawing-room window at parlour storey might appear regular in outline and homogeneous, but from a different vantage point the compartments might be perceived to be variably planted with contrasting textures, hues and forms.

Spence's small garden compositions were generally 'regular' and geometrical.[21] In the ordering of larger spaces he perpetuated, as we have discussed, the conventional 'transitional' effect from the regularity of the house to the natural landscape in the distance – only rarely allowing aspects of the natural landscape to approach the house without a prefatory regular, ornamental buffer. In proceeding from the house to the garden the general formula dictated that 'there should always be a Descent from the Building to the Garden, of three Steps at least; this renders the Fabrick more dry and wholesome . . .'[22] Rutter and Carter commented that 'there is something poor in the method of walking strait out of a parlour into the level of a garden walk . . . [as with a] little ascent we see the garden agreeably from the house, even when we are not walking in it'.[23]

The designs for the gardens of Robert Dodsley and Baron Atkyns suggest great subtlety of ordering, and design complexity (figs 127 and 128). Spence maintained that all scenes of nature possessed uniformity and regularity amidst variety: in composing imitations of nature, it was therefore quite acceptable to introduce contrasting elements of regularity and irregularity, and similarity and dissimilarity of parts. Under the guise of regularity, combinations of conflicting qualities were successfully interplayed to create an appearance of coherence and unity; as a buffer between the uniformity of the building and the naturalness of the scene beyond, the garden was seen as a space that might be legitimately composed of variable gradations of regularity.

VARIETY

The small garden required variety to enliven it; it needed to be 'highly and variously ornamented, in order to occupy the mind, and to prevent its regretting the insipidity of an uniform plain'.[24] Variety was one of the

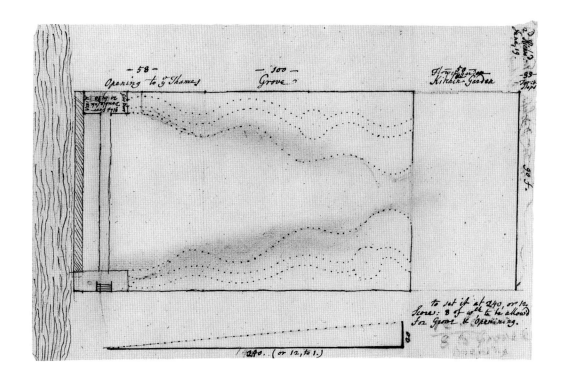

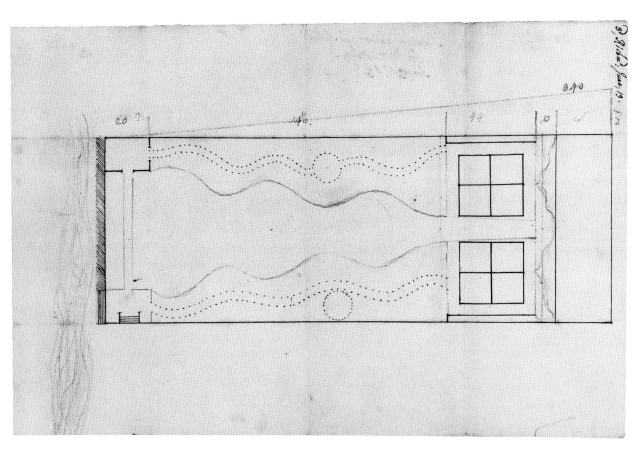

127 Joseph Spence, two plans of Robert Dodsley's garden in Richmond, pen and pencil, 1753. Beinecke Rare Book and Manuscript Library, Yale University, New Haven. Spence introduced contrasting elements of regularity and irregularity, and similarity and dissimilarity of parts into the plan in order to inject the layout with dynamism.

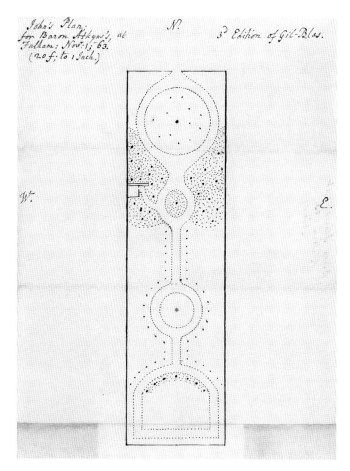

128 Joseph Spence, *John's Plan: for Baron Atkyns's, at Fulham*, pen, 1763. Beinecke Rare Book and Manuscript Library, Yale University, New Haven.

most important concepts in eighteenth-century aesthetic theory, and was recommended in all scenes to alleviate the displeasure of boredom or indifference incurred by suffering the mind 'to dwell too long, and waste itself on any particular Object'.[25] Lord Kames remarked that 'In every beautiful work of Art, something more than mere Design is demanded, *viz.* Elegance of embellished Design. The only material sign of this is Variety. It is this which distinguishes, in general, beautiful from plain Forms; and without this, in some degree, Uniformity is only dullness and insipidity.'[26] Addison remarked:

Every thing that is *new* or *uncommon* raises a Pleasure in the Imagination, because it fills the Soul with an agreeable Surprise, gratifies its Curiosity, and gives it an Idea of which it was not before possest. We are indeed so often conversant with one Sett of Objects, and tired out with so many repeated Shows of the same Things, that whatever is *new* or *uncommon* con-

tributes a little to vary human Life, and to divert our Minds, for a while, with the Strangeness of its Appearance: It serves us for a Kind of Refreshment, and takes off from the Satiety we are apt to complain of in our usual and ordinary Entertainments. It is this that bestows Charms on a Monster, and makes even the Imperfections of Nature please us. It is this that recommends Variety.[27]

Variety was not, however, just the result of spatial invention and manipulation inside the garden: it was also a question of what could be seen outside its boundaries: the prospect. This point is discussed in 'Boundaries', and elaborated to a greater extent in subsequent chapters.

The enormous enthusiasm with which variety was pursued in garden design is emphasised in Whately's warning that his readers should exercise restraint in their use of variety, lest it degenerate into inconsistency; furthermore he cautioned his readers to be subtle in their use of contrast – which he paired with variety – as resulting in contradiction.[28]

Closely related to variety, surprise and novelty were two secondary concerns, which were viewed as qualities to be applied sparingly in the small garden. Although both offered an immediate gratification, familiarity, it was assumed, soon dulled this initial pleasure.[29] Variety and contrast ensured that although the viewer might have been familiar with each particular feature of a scene, each experience was sufficiently diversified through seasonal, temporal, physiological and sensuous changes to create a sustained emotional interest.

For writers attempting to rationalise garden design in theoretical terms, the smallness of extent of town gardens was defined principally as a constraint, and not as an opportunity. When laying out a small premises, persons opted either for rectilinear configurations, or fragmentary and whimsical decorative compositions. Among the most common garden configurations was a degenerated or eccentric geometrical solution; a garden in which fancy subverted reason, or ingenuity conspired with inventiveness to disfigure tidy solutions. In order for observers to deal with the variable and inconsistent designs of small gardens, Sir John Dalrymple suggested that these compositions were to be judged not by reference to the ordinary rules of experience or taste, but by capriciousness of variety and fancy.[30]

What is evident in the gardens of Aaron Hill and William Stukeley is that it was possible, within the scope of conventional propriety, to form gardens which invoked numerous discordant concepts at the same time.

Hill's garden in Petty France, Westminster, was conceived by Hill himself as a testimony to Addison's disquisitions on taste. When the poet described the success of his own efforts to Lady Walpole in a letter dated 30 May 1734, he alleged: 'it is the imagination that does all, in this amusement.' He then proceeded to describe 'the shadowy beginnings of a rock-work, in my speck of garden'.[31] We are told that his servants informed him that her Ladyship was desirous of knowing what *compositions* he used in 'cementing the *pebbles*, and shell-work, and where and at what rates, the *blue-stones* are to be procured'. Hill replied that his embellishments required – besides an imagination – a trifling and inconsiderable expence, and 'not so much as *Terras* is necessary, except on the *roofs* or *copings* of places.' As for the materials: the cement was a mixture of sand, lime and a moderate proportion of hair; the blue-stones were 'chosen *clinkers*, from the *glass-house . . .* produced from the breaking of melted pots, filled with metal, for the finest sorts of glass'; and the shells were obtained, 'at very chargeable rates, from the *toy-shops*, here in town.'

Hill continued:

My intent was, to cover a little town garden, by way of a model for a design, which I have some thoughts of executing, at large, where I have more room in the country. But I find myself so crowded, as to want space, even for a model.

In the mean time, I ought to have, in my eye, the example of a *coquette haymaker*, who would not allow herself to be called *pretty*, at present; but confessed she should be worth *looking at*, when she came to church next *Sunday*. I will, therefore, sketch out for your Ladyship, a little idea of the *Temple of Happiness*, as I proposed it, from that rude foundation, with four entrances, in the middle of the garden; but your Ladyship saw it undressed, and as void of ornaments as the *haymaker*.[32]

He indicated that 'the whole space was intended to be a square of 300 feet, in which was inscribed a circle 100 feet in diameter. The *inner division* of the circle was *quite private*, being separated from the rest by a wall round the circular cloister, whose piazzas in front, open, on all sides into the garden.' In the centre of the circle was a mount topped by a Temple of Happiness, from which point views were gained of the whole garden. At the foot of the mount there was a 'ring of corn fields, and meadows, round a thatched country cottage. This prospect is extended, by rural paintings *in fresco* upon the inner cloister wall.' Four great passages, in the guise of

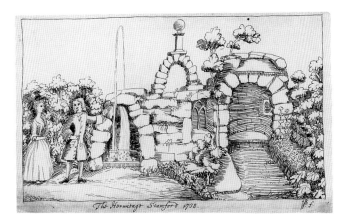

129 William Stukeley, hermitage in his town garden at Stamford, pen, 1738. Bodleian Library, Oxford. Stukeley's hermitage incorporated architectural fragments gleaned from demolished churches.

130 William Stukeley, rockwork in his garden at Barnhill, Lincolnshire, pen and watercolour wash, *c.*1747. Bodleian Library, Oxford. This feature recalls the character of Aaron Hill's 'rockwork' at his garden in Petty France, near St James's Park.

irregular rockwork grottos, led into the cloister – of which only one eventually snaked its way to the Temple of Happiness.[33]

Only a fragment of Hill's laboured allegorical project was completed before he abandoned London for the attractions of the suburbs in 1738. In the absence of a view which illustrates Hill's curious London rockwork, we may look to William Stukeley's depiction of his own similar construction, forming a hermitage in his town garden at Stamford (1738), and his design for a rockwork at Barnhill (c.1747) (figs 129 and 130). Stukeley was a prolific and imaginative designer of gardens, especially his own at his various town residences in Stamford, Grantham and Kentish Town in North London – all of which convey strong literal and symbolic meanings.[34] Besides the design of geometrical compositions of box-edged intersecting auricule *plates-bandes* dotted with flowers and shapley shrubs, set in capacious green swards amidst broad gravel paths, Stukeley's greatest preoccupation was the projection and building of rockworks and hermitages.

VISTAS

Spence paid the utmost attention to providing good vistas from the house into the garden, and from one part of the garden to another.[35] The 'principal point of view' in a small property was invariably established from the rooms which faced the garden. Spence's gardens invited the viewer to enter and participate in the garden; intricate ground patterns of low-growing plants and gravel were rejected in favour of bolder three-dimensional projections which obscured the clarity of the geometrically laid out ground plan. The secondary point of view was determined either indoors looking into the garden, or outdoors looking into the garden, or, in the event of a good prospect beyond the bounds of the property, looking without.

Spence's plans for the 'Exchequer-House' prepared for John Tracy Atkyns, Baron Atkyns, show the extent to which vistas determined the garden composition.[36] His final plan for this small garden in Whitehall was the result of numerous consultations and subsequent revisions: in all there are five plans for 'the Ground between The Exchequer-House, & the Thames'.[37] The first two plans of 10 April 1753 established the ground and the boundaries, annotating and positioning the windows on the outline of the house (172 feet long) so as to identify the prospects from the house into the property (figs 131 and 133). The preliminary plan was straightforward and rectilinear incorporating gravel walks, a 'Square of Grass' (140 by 70 feet), and flower-beds (optionally paved) immediately beside the house.

Revised drafts dated 11 April show how the plan was elaborated, and how it was developed into an annotated

working drawing and planting plan (figs 132 and 134). Spence recast the garden plan, rotating the axis and the 'Square of Grass, to point N[orth] & S[outh], instead of E[ast] & W[est]', and realigning the paths. The new broad gravel walks were cast perpendicular to the river, and 'answered' to the Venetian window and to the 'middle parlour-window'. The widths of the paths corresponded to the width of the windows. It was also proposed that the watergate should be shifted towards the centre of the river's embankment; the short ends of grass plot (now 98 by 58 feet) were to be flanked by 'Two Rows; of Almond, & Double Blossom[e]d Cherries; alternatively' to link the riverside to the building. The 'Gravel-Walk by the Thames; 168f[t] by 20.' was shaded by an 'old Row of Trees', and seats were placed at either end of the walk.[38]

The final plan, produced on 16 April, was a refined and formalised solution (fig. 135). A large square lawn sat centred on the levelled ground between the north and south garden walls, on each side of which long 'studs' (island flower beds) of mixed evergreens and flowering tree and shrub grove-work bordered on long gravel paths answering to the parlour and Venetian windows.[39] Two new seats, or 'Shells, or Grots?' (based on 'Mr Walpole's, by Robinson, little summer houses, &c.') were proposed for the waterside walk, to be sheltered by a mixture of weeping willows, planes, acacias and other 'Aquatics'.[40] 'Windsor-Chairs' were set at the east and west ends of the paved and gravelled terrace, and were to be 'sheltered, as much as can be afforded, by the Evergreens in the Urns; that are to be scatter'd, about this Opening.' The final choice of some of the planting, as indicated on the reverse of the third plan, included '8 Almonds, and 6 Early blossom'd Cherry trees alternatively; for the 2 Quarters of Flowering-shrubs'. Notes in the plan margin suggest that the studs were to be planted alternately with scattered flowers, and the narrow grove-work verges of the studs were to be turfed.

Spence took similar care in planning the vistas in his own east-facing, kerchief-sized garden in Stratton Street (1744). His plan was plain and functional, and proposed throwing a five foot central gravel walk across the length of the garden from the back of the house to the summer-house at the east end. Where the walk joined the house it was terminated in a 'Semicircle' gravel apron sixteen feet in diameter, while the far end was laid to an irregularly shaped terrace 'Pav'd wth broadstones' which gave on to a garden shed and the summerhouse.

141 A decorative basin of *c*.1774 found by archaeologists in the garden of 12 the Officers' Terrace, Chatham Dockyard, in June 1990. Private collection.

142 Model of the gardens of the Officers' Terrace, Chatham Dockyards, painted wood, 1773 (detail). National Maritime Museum, Greenwich. The gardens were supplied with water by a central pumping station, which encroached on the back lane.

number 12 at the Officers' Terrace, Chatham Dockyard, archaeologists discovered a small oval basin surrounded by a larger rectangular pool. The structure is built of brick, and finished with a waterproof render of *terraz* or *pozzolana* (figs 141 and 142).[70] Although a lead conduit led into the basin, it is not known whether it circulated water – like a small 'Jett' – in the basin, or transported water into it. In any event, the basin was probably filled with water up to the bottom of the coping of the rectan-

gular brim, and its perimeter may well have been decorated, like similar contemporary features at Dr Grevile's town garden in Gloucester, with potted plants (fig. 143).

Although Spence disparaged the fashion for creating artificial water features, he used the view to naturally occurring water to great advantage. At Baron Atkyns's gardens at Whitehall and Richmond, and those of Mr Dodsley at Richmond, the orientation of paths, borders and tree planting, and the positioning of seats, 'shells' and 'Grots' took account of the view to the river. While Spence appears to have favoured leaving the view to the river open, or framed by planting, many others sought to enclose their waterside garden boundaries with brick walls, which they pierced with water-gates and sometimes surmounted with summer-houses. Such overhanging pavilions can be seen in George Lambert's view of the Thames at Old Montagu House (*c*.1746); Jacob Knyff's view (*c*.1675–80) of the garden of Old Corney House, Chiswick (fig. 144); or Pieter Andreas Rysbrack the Younger's view (*c*.1740) of the gardens of Herring House and its neighbours.[71] In either case, the view of the water was defined as a major pleasure.

At Dodsley's garden, not far from Herring House, in Richmond, Spence projected a pair of summer-houses at the water's edge. In contrast to his treatment of the gardens just cited, however, he proposed a sinuous and concealed approach from the house to the Thames. The spectator was guided through the formal gardens which

143 C. Lewis, *Dr Grevile's Garden, 2 Barton Street, Gloucester*, pen and watercolour wash, *c*.1763. Private collection.

144 Jacob Knyff, *Garden of Old Corney House, Chiswick, seen from the River Thames*, oil on canvas, *c.*1675–80. Museum of London. Summer-houses were common features of many riverside premises, where they were set into the embankments, or hung over the river at the ends of small gardens.

adjoined the house, and descended from either the right or left hand side of the bottom of the parterres, by a small verdant portico into a grove (replicated on either side of the garden, and symmetrical on the central axis). From there it meandered down the slope until it opened in one of the two the summer-houses overlooking the Thames.

GARDEN STATUARY

Although Spence had a sophisticated sense of the correct ordering of garden statuary, he seldom recommended its inclusion in any of his small garden schemes.[72] Statuary and other forms of decorative ornament were commonly placed in gardens with the intention of elevating or distinguishing a premises. Many contemporaries, such as William Chambers and James 'Athenian' Stuart, invoked similar principles (fig. 148). Statuary was placed 'to compleat an area, end a vista, adorn a fountain, or decorate a banquetting-house or alcove'.[73] Much of the stock of the city's garden ornament was procured from the shops and yards of John Cheere, William Collins and the Thomas Carters. Their establishments were known collectively as the

Statuaries, and stood in Park Lane between Devonshire House and Hyde Park Corner (fig. 145).[74]

The quality of the works produced was variable; at their worst it was alleged that they 'afford a judicious foreigner such flagrant opportunities to arraign and condemn our taste'. 'Among a hundred statues', wrote James Ralph in 1734, describing London gardens, 'you shall not see one even tolerable, either in design or execution; nay even the copies of the antique are so monstrously wretched, that one can hardly guess at their originals' (fig. 146).[75] At their best they were the competent if clumsy works of John Cheere or John Nost. Regardless of the workshop, the supply of copies was indisputably affordable, hastily mass-produced and coarsely finished.

The popularity of ornament was the subject of dozens of spirited accounts – few of which were favourable (fig. 147).[76] Critics like Stephen Switzer did not wish so much to discourage the use of garden ornament as to rectify 'some Mistakes in their Local Distribution, Magnitude, and general Proportion'; they hoped, instead, that enthusiasts would curb their vulgar caprice of appropriating the 'Leaden lame Copies' of the antique without the least understanding of their significance, and the propriety of their placement.[77]

145 William Hogarth, 'The Statuaries, Hyde Park Corner', engraving from *The Analysis of Beauty* (1753), pl. 1. British Museum, London.

146 (*below left*) C. Lewis, *The Venus de Medici at Dr Grevile's garden, 2 Barton Street, Gloucester*, pen and watercolour wash, *c*.1763. Private collection.

147 (*right*) 'Stone Tables for Gardens &c', engraving from Batty Langley, *The City and Country Builder's and Workman's Treasury of Designs* (1740). Paul Mellon Collection, Yale Center for British Art, New Haven.

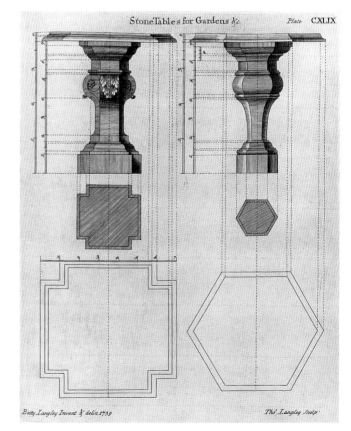

148 James 'Athenian' Stuart, plan and elevation of garden eyecatcher for a London house, pen and watercolour wash, *c.*1764. British Architectural Library, Royal Institute of British Architects, London.

149   Robert Adam, *A Second Design of an ornamental Screen on the back Wall of the Yard between the House and Offices of Sir Watkins Williams Wynne[']s House, St James's Square*, pen and watercolour wash, c.1770. Sir John Soane's Museum, London.

Their injunctions were, however, futile. As citizens acquainted themselves on their excursions with the lapidary deities of the landed classes, and were exposed to the statues and monuments which populated the city's squares and courtyards, the urge to embellish their own premises with copies became insatiable. Such demand was met by the Statuaries. Indeed, so great was the proliferation of gods of Athens and Rome from Hyde Park Corner that one author, meditating upon the decline of the established state religion, feared that 'the poor and the vulgar, when they find all other worship ridiculed and laid aside, may foolishly take to these molten images, and adore every leaden godhead they can find'. To staunch the swell he proposed invoking a poll tax, which 'be their representation what it will, suns, dogs,

moons, or monkies, is absolutely necessary, and would infallibly bring in a large revenue to the state' (fig. 149).[78]

The demand for statuary never ebbed. By the 1790s Mrs Eleanor Coade's campaign, which vaunted the virtues of her artificial stone, had begun to pay off, with the effect that consumers interested in garden ornament were replacing their 'dull Apollo, limping Diana . . . knock-kneed Hercules or . . . impotent Mars' with more durable and expertly formed Coade stone reproductions.[79]

Statuary, and ornament in general, played a powerful role in the ordering and the associational meaning of the garden. The successive town gardens of William Stukeley exemplify the paradoxical nature of artefact:

although he believed that everything in the cultural landscape had its place, he treated the sense of place as something which in the context of gardening could be regarded as transferable. His gardens at Grantham (1726–9), Stamford (1729–37), Barn Hill (1737–47) and Kentish Town, London (1747–65), were full of diverse objects – curious plants, 'mechanical artificialls', 'old reliques', antiquities and utensils plundered from the landscape – which, although invested with precise associations by their original siting, were none the less unhesitatingly transplanted from one garden to the next. His desire to take these objects with him when he moved about the country was, in fact, strongly endorsed by contemporary assumptions about the symbolic ordering of the garden: a space which permitted specifically personal forms of display, bearing the imprint of the owner's personality. The 'curiosities' which Stukeley collected not only preserved their original associations, but acquired new highly particularised meanings as a result of their place in his life.[80]

PLANTS AND PLANTING DESIGN

To Spence, like others, the design of the smallest flower-garden called for the painterly techniques of attracting, distancing and mixing lights and colours, and the application of such techniques with a knowledge of perspective to create contrasts and harmonies between texture and colouration of vegetation and architecture.[81] He formulated numerous injuctions which dealt with the range of options available to the gardener: for instance, to comprehend the compatibility of plants, one had 'to observe the different friendships and enmities of different colours, and to place the most friendly ones next to each other'. 'In the mixing of lights and shades [he wrote] . . . let the former have the prevalence or, in other words . . . give the whole a joyous air rather than a melancholy one.' He also had strong views on a garden's setting: 'Buildings' should be 'white and accompanied with trees' to provide a strong contrast between green and white (the trees should be 'lively evergreens – not to look townish, or house-like').[82]

These general 'materials' were supported by specific prescriptions for achieving the desired effect. Among his most common planting techniques was the combination of woodbine or jasmine, entwined and trained up the trunks of the trees in 'grovettes'. This procedure would, he claimed, enhance the natural character of a planta-

tion. As Langley remarks, 'where standard-trees are planted in Hedge-lines of Walks, and Hedges also, . . . [they] should never be suffer'd to grow very high . . . [and should be] filled with the several Kinds of Jessamines and Honey-suckles to run up and down in a wild and rural Manner'.[83]

Spence's planting designs for small town gardens were conventional and undistinguished; they have been analysed in some depth by the garden historian Mark Laird.[84] The usual pattern and treatment was similar to that outlined in the *Dictionarium Rusticum* (1717): 'agreeably disposed of and filled up with Borders of Flowers, Dwarf-trees, flowering Shrubs, or Ever-greens; or . . . with little Wildernesses of Trees rising one above the other . . .'[85] Among Spence's innovations in flower gardening was his use and promotion of island bedding.[86]

Spence imposed geometry and symmetry on his town garden plans, and perpetuated traditional, and in some instances old-fashioned, planting patterns, such as hierarchical 'staging' (graduated arrangement) of plants, which owed much to the classical French structure of planting. Typical ordering began with the lawn, or from the margins of a garden walk, graduating to low shrubs, to small trees and subsequently to forest trees, moving away from the house.[87] He proposed to implement this convention at Mrs Bartholemew's garden (1751): at the path's edge there was an enamel of pinks, carnations and 'little flowers', which faded into studs of roses and honeysuckles, succeeded by laburnums, cherries, lilacs, acacias, canopied by a backdrop of clumps of ash, oak, planes, Scotch and Weymouth pines, and Norway spruce.[88]

One of Spence's earliest town flower-gardens was executed for Lady Falmouth, widow of Hugh Boscawen 1st Viscount Falmouth (fig. 150): the plan 'for a London-Garden' was prepared for Lady Falmouth's house in Albemarle Street, which she leased for the year in 1744.[89] The layout was attuned to the demands of the gregarious and social-climbing peeress, who desired a showy, colourful and theatrical outside drawing-room for entertaining during the London Season. The garden-front of the house opened into a gravel terrace which split into two six-foot walks circumscribing a twenty-four by twenty-eight foot double quincunx 'Grovette' of almond trees, carnation cherries and green-painted Windsor chairs – arranged around a stone table (4 feet in diameter).[90] The north and south sides of the gravel paths were flanked by shallow (2 feet deep) 'Beds, for Flowers' where 'there might be Six fruit-trees, on each side wall, at 8[f[t]] dist: from one another: & two trees with

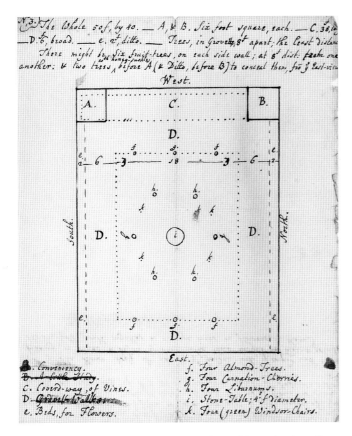

150 Joseph Spence, plan for Lady Falmouth's garden 'in Albemarle Street', Piccadilly, pen, 1744. Beinecke Rare Book and Manuscript Library, Yale University, London.

honey-suckles' before the 'Conveniency' and the 'Little Study' (A and B on the plan) 'to conceal them, fro[m] yᵉ East View.' The end of the garden was screened by a 6 foot deep by 38 foot 'Covered-way, of Vines' bridging the two small square outbuildings. Spence recommended that of the trees marked F and G at the far end of the garden could be placed to form 'a couple of Arches, wᶜʰ will look as if there was more ground on; especially if A & B were coverᵈ in front, with Jessamin & Honey-suckles.' He also remarked that 'the House itself wᵈ add to yᵉ Garden-look if coverᵈ with creepers, filleray, or vines: & before yᵉ Iron-rales [to the area] there might be (blew & gold) flower-pots; (with myrtles & orange trees, or flowers in them).'[91]

Like Langley, Spence employed plants and other ornaments to create illusionistic effects aimed at making the small garden appear larger than it actually was.[92] At Lady Falmouth's he proposed a screen of floral embroidered treillage at the end of the garden in order partially to conceal the view from the house by a middle distance of a staggered arcade of alternating trees and Windsor chairs, against a background of jasmine and honeysuckle.

The range of plants which Spence proposed was generally endorsed by Fairchild and Miller as being able to prosper in town. He also formed his own lists, or consulted other sources such as 'Mr Chip's list of flowering shrubs and Evergreens that will stand the London Air' (undated), which contained a larger selection of hardy plants than is recommended by the Society of Gardener's *Catalogus Plantarum: A Catalogue of Trees, Shrubs, Plants, and Flowers both Exotic and Domestic, Which are propogated for Sale, In the Gardens near London* (1730).[93] One cannot over-emphasise the importance attached to recommending plants which were proven to 'thrive in the smoke of London'. Indeed, inventories of plants, and factors which affected their health, were among the very few subjects which prompted explicit discussions on town gardening.[94]

William Curtis commented in *Flora Londinensis* (1777) that the city gardener was beset by problems. He remarked that although 'even professional writers upon gardening have contributed to keep up the prejudice against its practice in the cities . . . complaints of consumptive geraniums, languishing through the summer, to die in October, and show the desolating view of rows of pots, containing blackened and dusty stems'.[95] He recommended prescriptions to combat the foremost problems of gardening: blackened foliage could be kept free of soot by frequent syringing; the injuries of wind could be attenuated by erecting 'close pale fencing' (painted green), or privet hedges; and netting would discourage the 'serious annoyance' caused by cats.

It is particularly important to acknowledge Philip Southcote's influence on Spence's later planting design. Southcote, who was Spence's neighbour at Byfleet, is credited as the 'founder' (Walpole's word) of the *ferme ornée*, and was celebrated for his discriminating, innovative and informed amateur horticultural expertise. His emphasis on flowers and colour in natural gardening may be attributed to his knowledge of English landscape painting, and played a significant role in Spence's theoretical and practical work.[96]

★　　★　　★

Attitudes towards enclosure were, unsurprisingly, of immense importance in determining the form and function of the town garden.[97] Spence thought nothing so oppressive and imprisoning as brick walls or wooden pale boundaries.[98] The raw and unornamented brickwork of back façades and garden walls was known as 'dead walls'.[99] Switzer remarked that 'the First Thing Gentlemen commonly do after their Houses are built, is to set out their Garden Walls: In this there is some Surveyor or Bricklayer that is very ready, it being some of the best pickings they can have; and the Gardener himself is doubtless as fond of them as any thing, and thinks his Garden can't be fine, except it has a Brick Wall round it.'[100]

Rutter and Carter remarked in 1767: 'In general nothing is so sad a sight in a garden as a brick-wall. Nothing else shews the absolute termination of the ground; and of all the things we should conceal the boundaries of a garden' (figs 151 and 152).[101] John Gwynn opined in 1766 that such structures were both melancholy and dangerous, and he could see no other remedy than that of 'making dwarf walls with iron rails . . . which occasions an unnecessary expence, and when done becomes inconvenient and ungraceful'.[102]

Secure and opaque enclosure restricted opportunities for physical and aesthetic expression. Barriers were criticised for precluding passive sociability – meaning, as one mid-eighteenth century ironist put it, that the citizen was denied 'an opportunity of displaying his best wig to every one that passes by'. Lloyd's 'cits',[103] who inherit a 'town garden' when they buy their new suburban box, repudiate the townishness of the layout:

> I cannot bear those nasty rails,
> Those ugly, broken, mouldy pales;
> Suppose, my dear, instead of these,
> We build a railing all Chinese.
> Although one hates to be exposed
> 'Tis dismal thus to be enclosed,
> I wish you'd fell those odious trees.
> Objects continual passing by
> Were something to amuse the eye,
> But to be pent within the walls –
> One might as well be at St Pauls.[104]

Horace Walpole also claimed a 'partiality . . . for moving objects', remarking that 'A park-wall with ivy on it and a fern near it, and a back parlour in London in summer, with a dead creeper and a couple of sooty sparrows, are my strongest ideas of melancholy solitude.'[105]

Walls and pales, however maligned, were regarded by all critics as necessary for the protection of the premises, especially at the rear of the townhouse. On the other hand, a contributor to the *Connoisseur* reported in 1754 that the planting of the front garden (when there was one) was 'levelled' so 'Nothing its view to incommode, / But quite laid open to the road; / While every traveller in amaze, / Should on the little mansion gaze.'; and so sparsely planted that it was 'So desart, it would breed a famine'.[106]

Fencing, like other garden attributes, was susceptible to the vagaries of fashion. When in 1756 the 'cit' proposed to replace his 'ugly, broken, mouldy pales' with a 'railing all Chinese', he was invoking the mid-eighteenth-century rage for a style of fencing purported to be 'most common in the Emperor of China's garden'. Spence, however, informs us in 1751 that the English imitations which were 'so much in fashion in town as well as country' were insipid and 'ridiculous things', and not at all like their oriental prototypes.[107]

Privet hedging was, throughout the eighteenth and early nineteenth centuries, among the more common means of 'dividing up [small] gardens for shelter or ornament'; either acting as a substitute for a wall, or used in conjunction with timber palisading. William Curtis, in *Flora Londinensis*, commented on this shrub: 'It is found to thrive better in the smoke of great cities than most others; so that whoever has a little garden in such places, and is desirous of having a few plants that look green and healthy, may be gratified with the Privet, because it will flourish and look well there'.[108] Spence's preferred solution was equally simple and inexpensive: he advised his clients to mask their garden walls with vines and rows of dwarf, and espaliered trees, as we have seen at Lady Falmouth's and his own garden in Stratton Street. At Boleby's garden, he proposed 'Espaglia's for fruit-trees made of 'smooth ash –, painted lead colour; 6 feet high; the posts, 6 Inches square & cross pieces 2'.[109]

Other contemporaries, such as James and Langley, recommended that walls and other disagreeable objects might also hidden by garden architecture and built and embowered ornament. James remarked in 1712:

> Arbors, Cabinets, and Porticos of Lattice-work, are commonly made use of to terminate a Garden in the City, and shut out the Sight of Walls, and other disagreeable Objects; this Kind of Decoration making a handsome Sight, and serving well to conclude the

151 Unknown artist, *View of the back garden of 14 St James's Square, Bristol*, watercolour, *c.*1805. Bristol Museum and Art Gallery.

152 Unknown artist, *Back elevation of the Pole house and garden at 14 St James's Square, Bristol, from York Street entrance*, watercolour, *c.*1805. Bristol Museum and Art Gallery. Shallow borders filled with displays of flowering herbaceous plants and mature vines flank both sides of the gravel walk. Many late eighteenth-century London gardens were laid out in a similar manner.

153 (*left*) Detail of a treillage/garden cabin at the Officers' Terrace, Chatham Dockyards, 1990.

154 (*below*) C. Lewis, *A garden 'shell' in Dr Grevile's Garden, 2 Barton Street, Gloucester*, pen and watercolour wash, *c.*1763. Private collection.

155 Stephen Duck, details of treillage for Spence's house in Byfleet, Surrey, pen and pencil, 1750. Beinecke Rare Book and Manuscript Library, Yale University, New Haven.

Prospect of a principal Walk. They are likewise used in Groves, Sinkings, and Niches, where Seats and Figures are proper to be set, and are often cover'd with Rose-Trees, Jasmin[e]s, Honey-suckles, and wild Vines for the Conveniency of Shade [figs 153 and 154].[110]

Spence recommended lattices, *berceaux* and arbours until the late 1740s (figs 125, 126a, 150, 155 and 156). These features were, however, perceived as unfashionable from the late 1720s onwards.[111] Miller commented in his *Dictionary* (1737 ed.) that the arbour is 'formerly in greater esteem with us than at present; few Gardens were without cover'd Arbours and shady Seats; but of late they have been much rejected . . .'[112] Their decline may be attributed to the fact that these 'artificial arbours' were regarded as unhealthy, on the grounds that they

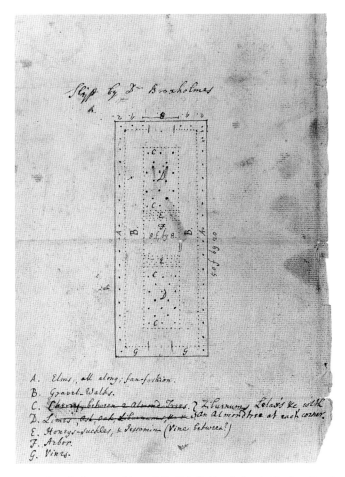

156 Joseph Spence, *Plan of Dr [Noel] Broxholmes's Garden, Bond Street, London*, pen, 1743. Beinecke Rare Book and Manuscript Library, Yale University, New Haven. This was among Spence's first and smallest garden designs.

harboured damp air, and, being built out of wood, they very quickly decayed. Ephraim Chambers remarked in 1728 that they have 'now gone much into disuse as their seats, apt to be moist, are unwholesome'.[113] In their wake appeared the 'healthier' and more practical alcoves and garden seats, embowered by naturally formed grove-work edges and small clumps of specimen plantings.

Lattices and screens did not, however, entirely disappear from the vocabulary of garden ornament. They experienced a revival in the early nineteenth century, with the popularity of aviaries, and decorative flower-garden screens characterised by the designs of Loudon and Papworth. Lattices also, were, still sufficiently common in the late 1760s to prompt a contributor to the *Gentleman's Magazine* (1769) to remark that although 'our moden lattices are approved of, because it is pretended that they give to places chearfulness, light, air, and views abroad. All this may be had in an open field,

if we would chuse to dwell there under a tent. If lattices give you the pleasure of seeing what passes abroad, they also give the uneasiness of being seen, however you may happen to be employed, by all who pass by.' They were similarly judged as promoting a false sense of protection from the dangers of the street: 'You think yourselves very retired at home, and in perfect security by a barrier of iron rails, not considering that the hundred openings of this inclosure deprive you of that security, and that you have a hundred gates displayed, which leave a free communication from without, and expose you to plunder.'[114]

Garden walls close to the house were frequently painted white, or white-washed.[115] Given the enduring, vehement and critical attacks on conspicuous garden boundaries, it is remarkable that white-washing appealed to town gardeners. Spence, for instance, suggested that white was a 'Townish' and 'Houselike' colour. It is possible that painting walls white was, as Spence recommended, to 'give the whole [garden] a joyous air rather than a melancholy one'. White was described from the early eighteenth century onwards as producing a strong and desirable contrast between garden buildings and evergreen plants; it was, likewise, believed that whiteness gave the impression of neatness. White paint also reflected daylight, brightening small gardens and yards.

Other ways of managing the boundaries were to occlude the views without, and to keep the visitor's gaze fixed on what lay contained within the garden, or to exaggerate the sense of enclosure by erecting eye-catching pavilions, banqueting houses, summer-houses or arcades. Architectural conceits were the most potent and lasting contribution to the imposition of order in the court, garden or yard. Screens and arcades were commonly built to link the house with external offices, disguise, embellish or surmount outbuildings and diminish the monotony of brick garden walls or high wooden *palisados* (fig. 149).

There are plentiful examples of such exercises: the builder John Gorham produced a design for a domed pavilion with triple-arched openings and a broken pediment on four sides for 34 Old Burlington Street at the junction of Burlington Gardens (1730; fig. 157); and a house in Grosvenor Square was described in 1742 as possessing 'an Alcove at the end of Garden after the dorick order covered with lead, the alcove back and sides wainscotted quarter round and raised pannells with a seat, Portland pavement before ditto'.[116] James 'Athenian' Stuart formulated a three-bay Ionic garden loggia for Thomas Anson at Litchfield House, 15 St

157 John Gorham, *Eyecatcher for a London garden*, pen and watercolour wash, 1730. British Architectural Library, Royal Institute of British Architects, London.

158 Garden screen of 20 St James's Square, London, *c*.1920. The screen was designed by Robert Adam in 1772 for Sir Watkins Williams Wynn.

159 Robert Adam, ornamental screens decorating the offices at the back of houses on the west side of Mansfield Street, Marylebone, *c*.1950.

160 Joseph Michael Gandy, composite view of Sir John Soane's house, watercolour, 1822. Sir John Soane's Museum, London. The two central views show how the garden courtyards were contrived as extensions of the interiors.

James's Square (c.1764); Robert Adam erected a decorative screen in the back garden of 20 St James's Square for Sir Watkins William Wynn (begun 1772; fig. 158), as well as forming a number of similar illusionistic screens for houses in Mansfield Street, Marylebone (from 1770; fig. 159); Benjamin West had erected a 'house-passage' along the long side of his back garden wall at 14 Newman Street (built c.1780); and Sir John Soane formed his own elaborate courtyard gardens for his residence in Lincoln's Inn Fields (fig. 160) – and his office produced a number of decorative wash-house and courtyard screens for a variety of London houses (from c.1808).[117]

5

The Francis Douce Garden:
A Model Town Garden of the Late Eighteenth Century

ONE ORDINARY London town garden occupies an important place in this study on account of the extensive surviving documentation which animates the plan, its recipient and the garden designer: Richard Twiss's proposal of 1791 for Francis Douce's garden at 13 Upper Gower Street in Bloomsbury.[1]

Francis Douce (1757–1834) was one of the most eminent antiquaries and bibliophiles of his age, whose amateur pursuits included entomology, angling and botany. Apprenticed as an attorney at the King's Bench, he decided in 1791 to devote himself entirely to research and collecting manuscripts. Between 1799 and 1812 he was Keeper of Manuscripts at the British Museum, but 'his independent spirit could not brook the pragmatical interference of one of the Trustees . . . and he resigned his situation'.[2] His means were for many years modest, his appearance was 'singular and strange', and his manner vaguely eccentric yet gentlemanly.[3] He disdained travel, preferring the surroundings of his own home in Upper Gower Street; and his attachment to these premises – and particularly his library – was such that when circumstances obliged him to dispose of his property in 1806 he found it difficult to find a suitable house in a comparable location.[4]

Douce's interest in gardening was possibly first aroused by his friend, the essayist and travel writer Richard Twiss (1747–1821). Having inherited an ample fortune as a young man, Twiss devoted himself to travelling abroad and publishing accounts of his cultural and botanical observations. His works achieved reputable acclaim. Twiss and Douce shared a variety of interests, among them natural philosophy, topographical writing and the classics; indeed, they operated a book and periodical exchange, loaning each other works on a range of subjects, including botany and gardening.[5]

Twiss had for some time been urging Douce 'to cultivate his garden'. He wrote in December 1790: 'je vous conseille . . . de vous marrier auplutôt, et ensuite de *cultiver votre femme et votre jardin*', to which Douce replied that he flattered himself that although he might consider cultivating a wife, he did not possess the wherewithal to cultivate a garden. Twiss's injunction was not, however, merely a reference to gardening; he invoked the moral of Voltaire's *Candide* (1759): practical action must replace idle speculation – 'il faut cultiver notre jardin': 'We must cultivate our garden'.[6] Twiss took his own advice very literally and in 1789 abandoned his premises in London to rusticate in suburban Bush Hill, Edmonton; and, like Voltaire at Les Délices, he immediately began to remodel his estate on a grand scale.

Douce was not in a position to cultivate a garden until late 1791 when he leased a large house at 13 Upper Gower Street, north of Bedford Square – a street that was, in his own words, 'well known' for having some of the 'most eligible' houses in the metropolis (fig. 161).[7]

He moved into his newly completed terraced house on 2 November 1791, after having quit his rooms at Gray's Inn on the eve of his marriage to Isabella Price.[8] As soon as Douce moved into his premises Twiss hastily supplied him with a garden plan, copious explanatory notes and a friendly assurance that 'Should you wish to do anything about your garden you may at all times command me, & I shall wait on you whenever you please' (fig. 162). He also pronounced: 'You will take as much delight in your garden, as I do in mine, & you will amuse yourself with a rake & a hoe, and I hope never suffer a weed as big as a pin's head to appear with impunity, but destroy *him* directly.'[9]

Twiss regretted that in forming his design he was obliged to conjecture the dimensions of Douce's ground

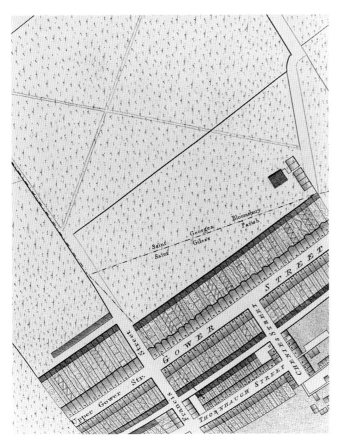

161 R. Horwood, *Plan of the cities of London and Westminster* engraving, 1794–9 (detail). Paul Mellon Collection, Yale Center for British Art, New Haven. Douce's east-facing garden opened on to the fields of the parishes of St George Bloomsbury and St Giles, which provided clear prospects as far as Highgate, Hampstead and Islington.

and its aspect: 'if I had the exact dimensions of the ground, I would make an accurate plan of it which might be *wholly*, *partly* or *not at all* used.' Notwithstanding this uncertainty, he conceived a plan for an east-facing garden plot twenty-five feet wide by fifty feet long. He implied that the garden could be formed through a bricolage of elements included on the plan, so long as the ultimate design was simple and neat: 'the more such a small spot is simplified, the more beautiful it will be.'[10] He outlined the steps by which Douce was to build the garden in detail:

> The soil ought to laid along the wall & for the great Bed, (but not under the Gravel) 3 feet deep, of manure, or a compost of Dung & Loam & rotten mould, sifted from bricks, stones & other rubbish. the beds along the wall should gently decline from it thus ⌐, & the great bed should be 8 or 10 inches higher

in the middle than on the sides ⌒. when these beds are made the trees should be planted; & the box too, for edging, & lastly the Gravel laid which will then be clean, (no flagstones in the garden). gravel is sold at 7/6 p. Load, deliv'd. home, and I suppose 4 Loads will do. A London garden must be made to please the Eye only, fruit is out of the question, as it will not ripen well, & if it did, the whole produce would not be worth half a crown, whereas by planting it with ornamental trees, the eye is gratified, and after the first Expence no other is incurred nor any other trouble than keeping it free from weeds, & watering it in dry weather, a man to work it once a month will suffice.[11]

He submitted a schedule of plants which could be bought at 'Mess.rs.Gordon, Dermer & Thomson of Mile-end [who] are the very first Class of Nursery men & the most reasonable in their charges', as well as a list of basic garden tools to maintain the garden (fig. 163).[12] The cost of the garden was estimated at 'about £20.-.', of which 'labour & other small charges' was £4 8s. 6d. The expense was, Twiss remarked, trivial for the gratification that it was certain to give.

> If all this [his recommendations] should be completed, your little slip of ground will be *un lieu à voir*, which will super-eminently and super-abundantly eclipse all your neighbours in Gower Street, even unto Sommers' town, nay perhaps as far as Pancras, may be Kentish Town! The garden will continually be growing more beautiful, & will not cost above 30 shill.s. p. ann[um]. to keep it.[13]

The whole scheme was, of course, contingent on the garden's orientation. Twiss proposed that in the event that the garden lay on the 'West side [of the street], you can have nothing but the Poplars and a grass plat, or a Skittle-ground if you prefer it'.[14]

Twiss had great enthusiasm for botany from at least the mid-1770s. He did not, however, indulge in garden building until 1789. This first-hand experience, which was encouraged through his acquaintance with James Lee ('*the most intelligent nurseryman in the Kingdom*'), Conrad Loddiges and Philip Miller, appears to have transformed his considerable interest into an obsession, as in June 1791 he equated his enthusiasm for the 'science' of gardening to a 'deep contemplation', remarking that persons were apt to look upon such 'men of deep speculation with some sort of pity, judging them to be a little touched in their brain, and under a degree of madness'.[15]

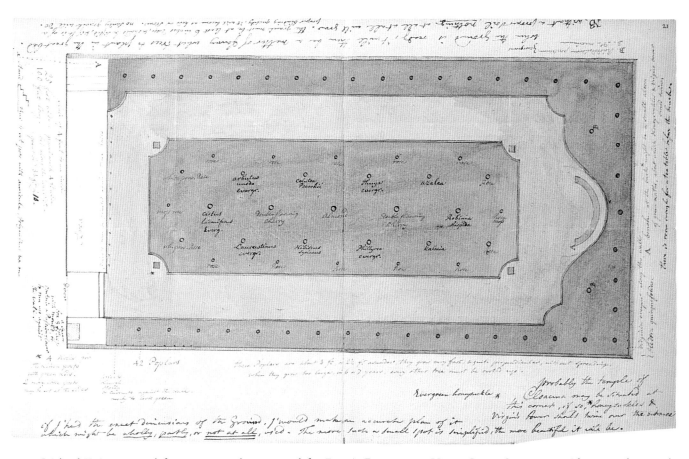

162 Richard Twiss, proposal for a town garden prepared for Francis Douce at 13 Upper Gower Street, pen with watercolour wash. MS Douce, c.11, fol.18, Bodleian Library, Oxford.

In the same letter he implored Douce to plant a garden, as it was an economical and rewarding activity which would provide them with a subject of mutual interest.

I believe I shall hardly trouble you any more ab[ou]t Botany; but what I have hitherto told you, is what every person that delights in the science ought to know. In May or June you shall have a practical Lecture, and we shall (tho' you never said you should like it) perhaps visit Chelsea [Physic] garden together, & Kew, too, if you please. I have specimens of all the 24 Classes, & of most of the Orders, in the Garden.

I have *all* the *Necessary* books. They cost me ab[ou]ᵗ £15.- & my plants ab[ou]ᵗ £25.- more so that I learn this science cheap enough, & at the same time have my money's worth . . . the plants (unless they die) will never grow worse, but always better, & as for seeds I have enough of them for my own plants, all I have to do is to keep the soil properly manured, watered and weeded. I wish you had a garden with some

plants within 10 Miles of this, [Bush Hill] there would then be some competition. Whereas here I stand alone, no censure, no praise, except the Ladies say 'this flower is vastly pretty, what nasty pricks this plant has!' & then they laugh at Pappy Lion Acy us (papiliona-ceous) & at the Dracunculus and Quamoclit.[16]

It is a curious coincidence that when Twiss was entreating his friend to cultivate a garden, the *Gentle-man's Magazine* was publishing a series of short articles on town gardening – a subject so rarely addressed in the press that it deserves to be quoted at length.

The first correspondent commented on Miller's *Gar-dener's Dictionary* (1768 ed.), which he regarded as the 'catalogue [which] comes nearest to one which I wish to see, and which is probably a general *desideratum*; that is, a list of such plants, &c. as will grow in the *confined air of a* TOWN-GARDEN'.[17]

In this great city there are many patches of garden-ground in which their opulent owners would wish to

was encompassed by four-foot-wide gravel paths, the easternmost of which opened into an semicircular area for a bench or a 'small alcove of green Laths, about which Honeysuckles & virgins bower should twine'. Twiss remarked that here there was 'room enough for a tea table before the bench'.

Three sides of the garden were enclosed by a peristyle of forty-two Lombardy poplars, to be planted about '3 ft., or $2\frac{1}{2}$ ft. asunder, they grow very fast, & quite perpendicular, without spreading. when they grow too large, in 6 or 7 years, every other tree must be rooted up'. A variety of herbaceous plants was to be planted in the borders: 'suppose 36. perennials, the most curious sorts all different & one with another . . . & likewise *all* the annuals in England, 192 sorts. Of these you shall seeds of the best.' As for 'kitchen herbs', he recommended 'Thyme, Mint, Lavender, Southernwood, Sage & Rosemary. these are enough, they are all odoriferous, & I can supply you with them all'. He also added: 'I had almost forgotten that 2 or 3 guineas should be spent on Bulbs, such as Hyacinths, Tulips, Iris, Ranunculus, Anemone, Lily, Peony, Ornithogalum, Crocus, Snowdrop, Martagon, &c &c.'

The fourth side of the garden, beside the house, was to be planted with a line of privets to screen the rails that contained the sunk area. Along a short section of the garden wall, east of the bridge over the area, Twiss recommended placing 'privets Laurel Holly or currants' at regular intervals 'merely to look green'. To the right of the door, at the bottom of the area (probably over six feet deep) was placed a 'Square box 3 ft deep with mould, to contain a Passion flower to run up against the wall', and at the far end of the garden Virginia creeper was placed along the west-facing wall. Quite curiously, he proposed to erect a staged auricula and polyanthus stand in the depths of the sunk area.

Twiss's planting design was less inspired, adhering to the conventions of 'hierarchy, symmetry and regularity' outlined in Mawe and Abercrombie's book *Every Man his own Gardener* (10th ed., 1784) – a treatise which appears to have had a considerable influence upon the designer.

The planting design was both anachronistic and modern. There was a 'residual sense of geometric order', and a 'desire to satisfy picturesque principles'. In his enthusiasm to create a small garden which would rival his own, Twiss disregarded his own formal injunctions – particularly that which asserted that the garden 'must not be crammed, but every plant must stand insulated & have room to grow'. The plan is annotated with a flurry of spontaneous scribblings – each one recording an afterthought that imposed a new level of horticultural complexity to the plan, and threatened to disrupt the clarity of the original design. Had the plan been planted as it is shown, with its various amendments, the 'formal and distinct' manner of planting would have given way to a careless, natural and unkempt appearance. An early nineteenth-century view of the garden of the antiquary William Upcott in Islington shows how informal mixed planting within a uniform framework could give the impression of natural disorder. Although Upcott's west-facing garden at 102 Upper Street – or 'Autograph Cottage' as it was known in his own time – was similar in layout to Douce's plot in Upper Gower Street, it contrasted sharply in character on account of its irregular, if somewhat serendipitous arrangement of shrubs and herbaceous plants (fig. 164).

As Laird and Harvey point out, although the palette of plants used in Douce's garden was unexceptional – most having been available in the seventeenth century – Twiss applied the idea of a shrubbery to the central bed. The shrubbery was a traditional attribute of the landscape garden; from 'around 1750 [it] had become appealing for the urban as well as the rural gardener'. He attempted to 'accommodate this new "theatrical" form within a framework traditionally allocated to the formal *plate-bande* or flower garden. His curious arrangement of shrubs came naturally from a desire to emulate the variety and horticultural diversity of the picturesque plantation.'[26]

It is tempting, given the wealth of information available on Twiss and Douce, to speculate on possible sources for the design. Given their mutual and enduring interest in Pliny the Elder's *Natural History* (and the Antique in general), it is possible that Twiss may have invoked the author's injunction to produce *in opere urbanissimo subita velut illati ruris imitatio* – which Horace Walpole translated as 'Something like a rural view . . . contrived amidst so much polished composition [the city]'. He may also have borrowed elements from the 'narrow and enclosed' gardens of the Antique to form the basis for the antiquary's town garden plan – where the garden was 'enclosed with walls . . . to the exclusion of nature and prospect' – a characteristic which Walpole considered to be a great shortcoming of the gardens of Rome and Herculaneum. Only six years before Twiss devised his plan, Walpole had published his *Essay on Modern Gardening* (1785) in which he esteemed the 'small square enclosures [of Herculaneum], formed by trellis-work, and espaliers, and regularly ornamented

164   T. H. Shepherd, William Upcott's back garden at 102 Upper Street in *c.*1835, with the spire of St Mary, Islington, in the distance, watercolour. Guildhall Library, Corporation of London.

with vases, fountains and careatides, elegantly symmetrical, and proper for the narrow spaces allotted to the garden of a house in a capital city'.[27] Although Twiss's plan lacks the decorative sculpture and structures which appeared in small walled gardens of the Antique, Douce appears to have modified the garden plan to include treillage, and possibly some sculpture.[28]

Douce and Twiss frequently exchanged anecdotes and queries regarding plants' scientific and symbolic properties: Twiss, it would seem, took great pains to interest the antiquary in his scheme by reinforcing the associational value of some of the planting. *Rhamnus paliurus* recalled Christ's thorns and reminded the beholder that 'our blessed Lord & Saviour was crowned withal: this classical and religious plant will cost 2/6.-';[29] Alexandrian Laurel was 'said to be the plant which the wreathes were made to crown Poets & Orators, among the Romans'; and the yew was described as the tree from which 'long bowes were wont to be made, which were of great account, as well with us, as with other nations, long agoe for Virgil georg[ic] 2 saith *Ityreos Taxi torquentur in arcus*'.[30] The taste for the Antique also extended to the features of everyday living: Twiss's annotations register a strong impulse towards a classicising, allegorising, ironic elevation of the 'low' and the mundane. Most notably the privy, at the far end of the garden, was christened the 'temple of Cloacina', with 'Virgin's bower' and 'Evergreen honeysuckle' twined over its entrance.[31]

Despite these inducements, Douce probably contrived his garden to meet his own high standards of comfort and convenience rather than Twiss's ambitious scheme – especially as he was uncommonly particular in all matters which threatened the dignity, comfort and peaceful retirement of his domestic establishment.[32]

Few 'inconveniences' caused him greater irritation than noise, which disturbed him to an abnormal degree, and especially so in his old age: street cries, ringing bells, screaming parrots, yelling children and, above all, barking dogs, 'caused him to remove his ever increasing possessions four times between 1812–25'.[33] It was, in fact, the nuisance of dog fights held in the waste fields behind his garden which compelled him in 1806 to abandon his house in Gower Street and retreat to what he believed was a more retired situation in Charlotte Street, Portland Place. However, at his new premises he was just as much aggravated by the insistent noise generated by his neighbours, whose garden was the playground of '6 or 8 children always out & screaming', 'gates always shutting violently', the 'house door banging', and the 'perpetual noises of horses, dogs barking and children screaming'; even within the house he was disturbed by the 'children's wails' which were 'plainly heard' through the walls of his stairs and study (fig. 165).

Douce remarked in his 'Miscellanies II' that 'it is to be presumed that another century or two will improve the condition of mankind and do away entirely [with] some of the following nuisances & absurdities of modern times which are a disgrace to a civilized society'.[34] He listed nine 'inconveniences', most of which appeared repeatedly in different forms in his 'maxims' and memoranda, and pertained to the poor layout, orientation, aspect and construction of London townhouses, and their relationship to neighbouring houses and gardens.[35]

His foremost maxim was: 'before you buy or lease a house examine its situation as to the adjoining houses and endeavour to discover what possible means your neighbours may have of annoying you, whether by accident or design. Never take a good house with one next to it that is considerably inferior in like or value.' Finding a 'good house' was in itself a difficult objective, as 'most of the houses in London that have been built in the present day are erected in clusters on one inconvenient & formal plan & by common carpenters without the least attention to the real comforts of life'. He remarked on the subject of aspect: 'Never take a house whose back part faces the North. It will be damp, cold, & uncomfortable in winter time. a house standing N[orth] & S[outh] is not half as valuable as one E[ast] and West.'[36]

He was, however, particularly obsessed with privacy, and was hostile towards 'the abominable fashion of formally pulling the windows down to the ground':

It is a very common thing to hear people, & especially women, complaining of being overlooked by their neighbours, they themselves seldom reflecting that they are generally at the same time doing the same thing. The new & monstrously absurd fashion of cutting windows down to the floor that originated in the vanity of shewing the person tricked out in useless finery, or of standing in a balcony in the summer months to look at every carriage that passes is an excessive nuisance altogether, & in our cold-catching climate often fatal to the fools who delight in the above practices. In winter a great deal more cold air is let into the room that is either provident or necessary.

London terrace houses, he believed, were contrived

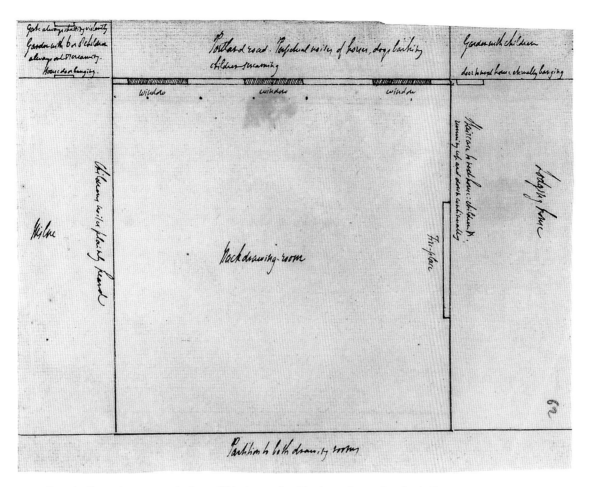

165 Francis Douce's annotated plan of his house in Charlotte Street, Portland Place, pen, 1791, MS Douce, d.87, fol.62, Bodleian Library, Oxford.

to frustrate their occupants, who wished to live in quiet and secure premises.

> The Old Dutch & German houses were admirably constructed in this aspect for health, privacy & comfort. You could hardly see the street without mounting a chair. The light was softer & much pleasanter, much internal advantage was gained & more place for furniture.
>
> I would like a house without any opening to the street as in the Eastern cities, but looking only towards a garden or back open place. When people are indoors they should literally be at home & abstracted from the streets altogether. This is in the opinion at back [?] of those who love peace & tranquillity. There is time & opportunity enough of feeling the world outdoors.[37]

Douce invoked his maxims as best he could at Upper Gower Street. We know from an auction notice adver-

tising the sale of his house in March 1806 that the antiquary made various refinements to his premises.[38] The house was described as being 'most Substantially Built, abound[ing] with Convenience, and . . . remarkably Airy'. Douce's greatest improvements appear to have been made to the apartments on the garden front: on the ground floor, the 'Morning Parlour of Octagon Shape 14 Feet 6 Inches × 14 Feet 6 Inches' had a 'Venetian Window'; and on the first floor the 'Back Drawing Room [the bibliophile's library] 20 Feet 6 Inches by 14 Feet 8 Inches' had a 'Venetian Window to the Floor and Balcony.' From the ground floor there was 'a Lead Flat with Descent by a Flight of Stone Steps to a Spacious Garden, at the bottom of which is a Substantial Detached Building, comprising a Coach House and Stabling for Four Horses, opening into a Mews behind'. It is interesting to note that Twiss's 'temple of Cloacina' had been superseded by a water closet off the 'Morning Parlour', built atop the 'small Wash-house' which con-

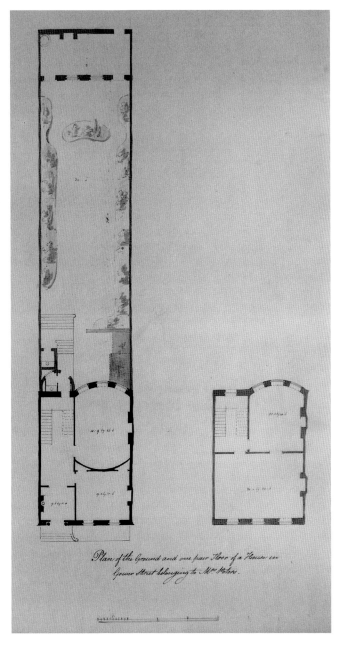

This arrangement might be compared with a survey made in about 1808 of Mrs Peters's garden up the road at 34 Gower Street (fig. 166). Here the garden measured approximately 30 feet by 110 feet and was terminated at the east end by a small symmetrical building (possibly a summer-house?) with a door to the fields behind. Access to the garden was gained by a broad set of steps that projected twenty feet behind the house. To the right of the steps was a service court, hidden from the garden by a wall. The garden was laid out with two long beds along the walls and a single kidney-shaped bed at the far end.

The 1806 prospectus is the last description of Douce's Gower Street premises. It does not, unfortunately, provide a detailed account of the garden. We know, however, that Douce did cultivate a garden; which one hopes he did with greater success than his marriage, which was 'not productive of happiness'.[40] Twiss indicated in 1792 that he intended to visit the antiquary's garden, and that he 'shall be glad to know what plants you have got'. In 1793 he hoped that his friend was watering heavily during the drought; and in 1794 he expressed surprise that Douce should wish to have 'two trees of a sort in your small garden'.[41] There is no further discussion of gardening in their surviving correspondence: both men appear to have lost all interest in the subject, preferring to discuss entomology.[42] We are left to conjecture how far Douce carried out his friend Twiss's proposals, what his garden actually looked like and the significance he attached to the activity of gardening.

Some of the reasons that commended gardening to Voltaire might also have convinced Twiss and Douce to cultivate the latter's garden. Gardening was, in the French philosopher's own words, 'an occupation which destroys boredom', but a more obvious and literal interpretation of *Candide* might in fact suggest another way of endorsing this activity: to cultivate a garden was to cultivate one's own character. When he counselled his friend to 'cultiver votre femme et votre jardin', Twiss was doubtless reflecting upon his own experience and contentment at Bush Hill, as Voltaire was doing at his Epicurean garden at Les Délices. Perhaps he thought that Douce – the irritable bookworm – could be persuaded to take up gardening as a serious and all-consuming pursuit. Voltaire had, after all, confided to Madame du Deffand in April 1760 that there was only one pleasure to be preferred to literary ones, and that was 'seeing vast prairies turn green and beautiful crops grow'.[43]

166 Office of Sir John Soane, 'Plan of the Ground and one pair Floor of a House in Gower Street [No. 34] belonging to Mrs Peters', pen with watercolour wash, from *Drawings of Plans for Town Houses* (c.1808). Sir John Soane's Museum, London.

tained a 'force Pump' that supplied water to the water-closet.[39] Douce had evidently at some point extended his domestic offices eastwards into the garden to accommodate 'a small Servant's Hall' and the wash-house which were 'detached' from the house by an area and covered by a 'lead flat'.

6

Gardeners

TOWN GARDENERS

EIGHTEENTH-CENTURY and early nineteenth-century gardening and horticultural literature was dominated by practical knowledge disseminated through manuals, dictionaries, 'daily assistants', remembrancers, journals, handbooks, pamphlets, pocket books and above all 'kalendars', all of which were calculated, 'not so much to *make*, as *manage* a garden'.[1] Many people formed their gardens without the necessity of external advice. They presumably had their own particular notions of the appropriate character and use of their premises, and were confident in their abilities to create order and manipulate their own gardens without fear of critical censure. Technical aspects of gardening, however, were considered more complex than the art of composition, as was the ability to cope with the cultural prescriptions for the ever-expanding range of plants available and with improving garden technology.

The subject of maintenance is among the most interesting aspects of urban gardening, as it has the potential to reveal the scope and variation of domestic social practices. Domestic order broke down in the garden: every player was to some extent able to intervene in the range of gardening activities. This makes the hierarchy of garden management unclear. What is clear is that from the early eighteenth century onwards many Londoners engaged 'jobbing gardeners' to perform the formal and mechanical aspects of gardening.

Jobbers were typically itinerant and self-employed 'garden operatives' or 'tradesmen gardeners', who solicited their own custom, used their own tools and supplied their own plants or seeds (frequently from their own gardens) to make, mend and manage small to medium-sized town gardens, and garden squares (figs 167 and 168). They worked on a casual contractual basis, catering to building contractors, nurserymen and private householders by providing cheap, practical and quick gardening services.

Middle-class Londoners did not often engage full-time serving gardeners to maintain their small city premises: the grounds were too small to require daily attention. Both male and female household servants were capable of carrying out small garden chores such as sweeping, refreshing potted displays, jardinières and scouring garden furnishings. It was, however, expedient to contract jobbers to carry out the arduous task of setting out gardens, or to perform perfunctory maintenance chores such as raking and rolling gravel walks, and tending flowerbeds, pots and boxes.

Wealthy citizens with larger premises, on the other hand, often kept a full-time gardener: a qualified journeyman, who usually lived off the premises. He was responsible for hiring jobbers to assist with seasonal or difficult tasks including hedge clipping, gravel turning or planting (fig. 169). Only very rarely were gardeners brought up from people's country houses to cultivate their town garden. The London gardener provided an important liaison between city seed and plant suppliers and the family's head gardener in the country: he ascertained and checked the prices of goods, ensured the quality of available plant stock, arranged and supervised the safe and prompt delivery of orders and advised his rural counterpart about the most up-to-date gardening technology, plant culture, production techniques and plant introductions available in the capital.

The prospect of freelance contracting induced many serving gardeners to quit their professional indentures to attempt jobbing in the metropolis. By opting out of the traditional apprenticeship they became free agents, and were immediately self-propelled from labourer to 'nurserymen without having the means'.[2] Because jobbing required little investment and nominal practical training, the trade attracted both accomplished journeymen

167 Paul Sandby, 'The Gardener', crayon and watercolour, from *Cries of London* (*c*.1770). Cecil Higgins Art Gallery, Bedford. Loudon remarked in 1822 that the city's smaller gardens were 'managed by jobbing-gardeners by the day or year'. The jobber's 'great object' was 'to keep up a succession of flowers, and to keep the grass and gravel in order, and the whole perfectly neat'.

169 (*facing page*) George Scharf, *Back of Houses in Sloane Street*, pencil, July 1827. British Museum, London. This gardener at work at a garden in Sloane Street in 1827 is shown dressed in a short tailcoat and a top hat. Note the verandahs at the backs of the houses.

168 (*below*) Thomas Rowlandson, *The Jobbing Gardener*, pencil and watercolour, *c*.1805. Private collection. Contract gardening entailed weekly, monthly, quarterly or annual inspection by professional and jobbing gardeners who pruned, syringed and replaced wilted specimens, bringing renewed freshness to clients' plant displays.

Backs of houses   in Sloane Street July 1827 g.S.

wishing to abandon their servitude and a larger proportion of unskilled opportunists who hoped to reap a fast profit. This practice had long disgruntled London's garden professionals, who from the thirteenth century onwards had attempted to regulate and to render exclusive the trade of gardening in the City of London.[3] In 1605 the Worshipful Company of Gardeners was established by Royal Charter for 'the Publick Good'. It granted that 'Gardeners, then inhabiting in *London*, and within six Miles of said City . . . should be one Body Corporate, by the Name of Master, Wardens, Assistants, and Commonalty of the Company of Gardeners of *London*'.[4] The Charter empowered the master and wardens of the City livery company to destroy and confiscate goods that were grown in violation of the Company ordinances, and to regulate gardening services by inspecting the worth of people who practised without the prescribed training, experience and knowledge.[5]

In 1701 the 'mystery of gardening' included the trades of 'potegery' ('kitchen herbs and salads'), 'florilege' ('flowers and evergreens'), orangery ('foreign plants grown in stoves or hot-houses'), 'sylvia' ('the planting of lawns, avenues, &c'), 'Nursery-work' ('the propagation & raising of all greens, fruit trees, and trees for avenues, fit for planting out'), botany and designing ('or the making of grounds, parterres, &c.').[6] The seven categories reflected a streamlining of the trade, which as it was described in the 1605 charter encompassed the following tradesmen: botanists, florists, foresters, fruiters, fruit-growers, garden implement dealers, greengrocers, herbalists, horticulturists, horticultural sundries-men, nurserymen, market gardeners, plant merchants, seedsmen and sowers.

The reduction of the trades from sixteen to seven categories was intended to consolidate and standardise the profession; to redefine the degrees of specialisation without major overlaps of professional skills. Shortly after the reorganisation of the trade, a proposal was made to extend the influence of the Gardeners' Company over the whole of England and Wales by forming a national network of gardeners. The executive recommended incorporating 10 garden designers, 150 noblemen's gardeners, 400 gentlemen's gardeners, 100 nurserymen, 150 florists, 20 botanists and 200 market gardeners to establish a national system of technical correspondence, employment agencies and supervision of all gardeners and apprentices. The scheme was never implemented.[7] The London Company had enough problems keeping

its own house in order, without the additional difficulties of expansion. It was, for instance, remiss in enforcing its own protective ordinances – especially in keeping stragglers and 'foreigners' (predominantly '*Northern* Lads') from saturating the London market.[8] It appears that as far as the Company was concerned, it was impracticable for the Court of Assistants to prosecute the great numbers of higglers, costermongers, forestallers and other 'rude persons', who effectively violated the Company's monopoly.[9]

London's skilled master gardeners and journeymen first began to feel the squeeze in the 1660s, when hundreds of unskilled labourers were recruited by the designers of large gardens and plantations to work in and about the city. The untrained men, on completion of their contracts, would, according to Switzer, 'immediately put on an Apron, get a Rule and pair of Compasses, with other things belonging to this Work; thus equipt, what Wonders are we not to expect from so profound a Sett of *Mathematicians* and *Designers*?'[10] Again, in the 1690s, the city found itself awash with the immigration of hundreds of common garden labourers who were recruited to build the gardens of Hampton Court, Kensington Palace and the pleasure grounds of the Duke of Beaufort and the Earls of Chesterfield, Sunderland, Rutland, Bedford, Devonshire and Craven.[11] It is estimated that out of five hundred gardeners employed to carry out these works, ten were 'able masters', forty were professed gardeners and the remainder were common labourers.[12] Many of these men remained in London after their contracts were terminated and turned to jobbing.

Much to the annoyance of professionals-gone-jobber, many Londoners were unable to distinguish between qualified journeymen gardeners, common garden labourers and thinly disguised sharpers.[13] Switzer noted in 1715: 'several Artizans or Mechanicks that elope their own Province, and by pretending to give *Designs* in Gardening, are guilty of a great Crime.'[14] It would appear that when a jobber presented himself at the door of a potential customer he was seldom required to produce professional credentials or personal recommendations to seek casual labour.

Switzer identified the 'several misfortunes that tire some in Performance, and deter others from ever meddling' with gardening, and proposed to trace 'these Mishaps . . . from their Original Source, and endeavour to give such general Advice as will help to reform them'.

170a   Detail of the frontispiece engraving to Thomas Fairchild, *The City Gardener* (1722). Here a gardener is portrayed working in a decorative parterre at Fairchild's nursery at Hoxton.

170b   Detail of the frontispiece engraving to Thomas Fairchild, *The City Gardener* (1722). Another of the gardeners at work in Fairchild's nursery in Hoxton.

The first is, the too great Haste I have often observ'd Gentlemen to be in; and sometimes, on a mistaken Notion of their own Judgment, lay hold on the first Opportunity that offers in making their Gardens, without consulting some experienc'd Workman, whose Judgment may be depended on; and to make the Matter yet worse, there is too often some awk[w]ard, ignorant, I might add dishonest Person and Pretender to a great deal of Knowledge in this matter at hand, and ready to offer their Advice, tho' never so weak or false.[15]

This deficiency compelled some professional gardeners to attempt to educate their customers as to how to distinguish a tradesman of quality. They did this through advertising the dignity of the mystery, and the morality,

integrity and learning of its *bona fide* practitioners. In 1722 Thomas Fairchild advised his readers that they should contract 'a Gardener of Judgement to manage a City Garden' (figs 170a and b).[16] The nurseryman, who declared that his advice was 'purely for the publick Service', defended men of the trade who were fair dealers: 'Bred Gardeners, who have study'd the Art . . . rather than trust to those who have never had the Opportunity of improving or knowing what a garden is . . .'[17] He stressed that 'a Gardener that had been bred in the Country, and has not had Practice about the Town, knows little more of managing a Garden in *London* than one that is bred to Plow and Cart'.[18] Like George London, Henry Wise and Stephen Switzer, he denounced the 'many ignorant Pretenders, who call at Houses where they know there is any Ground, let it be in Season or out of Season, and tell the Owners it is a good Time to dress and make up their Gardens; and often impose on them that employ them, by telling them every Thing will do when perhaps it is a wrong Season; for most sorts of Things they plant, and even more sorts of those Plants they recommend, will grow, tho' they were to be planted in a right season. This is a great Discouragement, which makes those Persons, who delight a little in a Garden, neglect doing any Thing at all, thinking all their Labour and Cost thrown away.'[19]

Switzer commented in 1715 that the city gardener was particularly susceptible to the abuses of dishonest and unqualified tradesmen.

> If the Gardens are to make, the first thing they fall on is probably some little Court-yard, or other small Division of the Garden; for by the Largeness of their Scale, and the Narrowness of their *Genius*, their Sheet of Demy and Heads are both so wonderfully fill'd with the Contrivance of those minute Parts, that 'tis impossible they should lay such a general Scheme, as that the Part now making, may any way correspond or agree with what may follow after: In short, when their Designs come to their intended Perfection, they are often full of an indigested heap of Absurdities, scarce ever reducible (without a total Revolution) into any tolerable Figure, tho' they happen afterwards to fall under the Direction of the most skilful in this Way.[20]

Despite these cynical appraisals of the character and abilities of ordinary jobbers, there were many genial and lasting collaborations between this form of gardener and his employers. These often arose from personal recommendations, occasionally through casual encounters over the threshold of the front door, and perhaps even less frequently through advertisements placed in local newspapers (fig. 171). London newspapers carried notices of openings for jobbers or places for persons with gardening skills who sought employment as household servants.[21] These advertisements, which appeared infrequently until the third quarter of the eighteenth century, do not, however, appear to have supplanted the more conventional informal means of seeking employment.

The most common form of notice was placed by gentlemen seeking to hire young and versatile males who had an interest in gardening. Not surprisingly many Londoners who wished to employ a gardener, but whose diminutive grounds or limited income precluded the engagement of a full time operative, sought the assis-

171 Tradecard of William North, nurseryman and seedsman, *c.*1810. Sloane/Heal Collection, British Museum, London.

tance of a sober, reliable and literate servant who was capable of undertaking a range of tasks. The role he was expected to fulfil was that of a steward or bailiff – both of which positions were commonly filled by gardeners in larger, modest country gardens. In 1743 Mrs Norton, of Colchester Street, Goodman's Fields, placed a notice in the *Daily Advertiser* seeking 'A single Man, not above Thirty-five Years of Age, that can drive a Coach, and work in a Garden, or can do any other sort of Business upon Occasion'. A similar notice of April 1745 advertised the wish to engage 'a Gardener that is a single sober man, and whose knowledge in the Management of Flowers, to have Care of a little Garden, a Horse, and do the necessary Business of a small family'.[22] The practical skills expected of a town gardener do not appear to have changed considerably by the later part of the century, as a notice in the *Morning Chronicle* of February 1789 confirms: a gentleman advertised a place for 'a steady young man, 24 years of age, of light weight, as Coachman; understands the management of horses, and knows something of town; would have no objection to look after a small garden; knows how to behave, can write a plain hand, and can have a good character from his last place'.[23]

Married men were occasionally employed as full-time town gardeners, but only when their wives were prepared to work at the same premises as indoor servants. This form of indenture, sometimes known as 'Places together', usually entailed 'a Gardener and his Wife; the Man to look after the Gardens, and the Woman to dress Victuals, or get up Linnen, &c.'[24] Although this practice was known in town, it was more common in the outer suburbs and the country.

172 Thomas Rowlandson, *The Hedger and Ditcher*, pencil and watercolour, *c.*1800. Paul Mellon Collection, Yale Center for British Art, London. Hedgers and ditchers were among the lowest ranks of garden labourers who served in town and country.

Persons seeking gardeners or garden labourers for part-time employment also advertised in the local press. This type of engagement appealed principally to gardeners who either by circumstance or design found themselves jobbing. Dr Hill of St James's Street placed a notice in the *Daily Advertiser* in May 1760 requesting the services of 'a Number of Labourers for a Garden; they must be able Hands; there is immediate Work for them; and the Pay is Ten Shillings a Week' (fig. 172). The local press also provided an outlet for jobbers or garden tradesmen to promote their own services. For instance in October 1747 a notice in the *London Evening Post* announced 'Gardens made and Handsomely kept by the year by Edward Cooper at the corner house leading to the square in Kensington near London'.[25]

Country house muniment rooms are a rich source of London garden history; their records occasionally provide us with elaborate records of garden activities at London premises. We know, for instance, from Sir Thomas Hanmer's private accounts that between 1726 and 1727 he was paying one Mr Bunning £5 14s. 6d. for 'flowers put into my garden [at 12 Old Burlington Street] and keeping it', and 'to Louis Dutoi the french Gardener half a year's wages for looking after my Garden'. Some of these men were evidently jobbers, as Hanmer was also paying his full-time gardener Mr Symonds £8 per annum, or 'Gardeners full serv'ts wages'.[26] Similarly, Lord Glenorchy's family muniments record that between 1733 and 1738 gardeners performed a number of chores in his small garden at 46 Grosvenor Square. In 1733 he paid £3 5s. for the material and labour for gravelling his garden, and he disbursed another fifteen shillings in January 1735 'to [Charles] Bridgeman a Gardener for work in my Garden in town'.[27]

Records of the maintenance of less august town premises, on the other hand, are less abundant. Although the practice must have been relatively common, we know far too little about the role of jobbers in the making and keeping of small gardens. What we do know dates primarily from the early nineteenth century, and suggests that they made regular visits to their places of employment and performed a prescribed range of duties. For instance, from 1798 to 1806 George Hopkins tended the 'Squar[e] Beds ye Terrass . . . Grass-Platt and Fruit-trees' of a gentleman's 'walled garden' at 6 Bedford Street, 'within 1 door of Bedford-Square'; and between 1807 and 1813, the 'jobbing gardiner' Mr Thomas Phillips was regularly tending the 'large walled garden, planted with several fruit trees' at 8 Russell Square for Mr Denton.[28]

According to John Loudon, who in 1822 was among the earliest popular garden authors to publish a simplified and refined categorical hierarchy of professional gardeners, jobbing gardeners occupied the lowest grade of professional tradesmen gardeners.[29] They were succeeded in ascending rank first by contracting gardeners – 'jobbers on a large scale' who undertook extensive landscape and gardening work: forming plantations, pieces of water, roads and even hot houses – and, secondly, by nurserymen. Throughout the eighteenth century the professional training of a jobber was claimed to be remarkably lacking in rigour in comparison to that required of a comparable rank of serving gardener.

Serving gardeners in the eighteenth century were men who had undergone strict and protracted indentures under master gardeners. Labourers occupied the lowest end of the scale of serving gardeners. They performed the common drudgery of gardening – trenching, digging, hoeing and weeding. These labourers – both men and women – gained all their experience from casual observation, and not through instruction. Their lack of education meant that they seldom graduated to a more elevated status. The next step up in the hierarchy was occupied by the apprentices: youths who served under tradesmen or serving gardeners for a prescribed period under terms of mutual benefit. The master contracted with the apprentice's guardians to provide instruction, food and lodging, or a weekly sum as an equivalent, in exchange for the service of their son. The average contract was three years, being of longer duration if the apprentice was under sixteen years of age when the agreement was entered. In any event, a youth's apprenticeship never extended beyond the attainment of his majority. Subsequent to this stage, the apprentice was admitted as a journeyman, at which time he was required to intern for at least one year in three distinct situations: a public botanical garden, a public nursery and a private garden. On completing this stage he would, at the age of twenty-five, be promoted to the professional status of master gardener, and was free to pursue the senior offices of head gardener, nursery foreman, botanical curator and, ultimately, royal gardener. Few gardeners achieved such an exalted station; the great majority remained in the middling ranks.

Many gardeners had humble origins. In London a small number of operatives were trained through charitable foundations such as the Foundling Hospital and Bridewell. From the early eighteenth century Bridewell administered its own school for the trades, where 'ordinary officers' called 'Task-masters', 'Task-mistresses' and 'Arts-masters' – 'such honest persons as are expert in such sciences and occupations as shall there be exercised' – instructed poor boys, 'masterless men', vagrants and disorderly persons in the trades.[30] The governors of the Foundling Hospital, on the other hand, had from 1758 arranged for their friends to take on young men as apprentices in 'Household Service and Gardening'.[31]

Regardless of the background of the gardener, there was an apparent consensus from the eighteenth century onwards that there was no class of rural or urban tradesmen, or masters, possessed of such exemplary moral character, integrity and intellect, who went so unrewarded and unappreciated.[32] This assumption was justifiable: apprentice and journeymen gardeners could read and write (they sometimes had some knowledge of the rudiments of Greek and Latin), and were proficient in the practical arts of geometry, land surveying and botany – a breadth of knowledge that was not expected of comparable tradesmen, such as, journeymen bricklayers, carpenters, masons or smiths.[33]

For all their training, journeymen gardeners scarcely earned half as much as other tradesmen. In the mid-eighteenth century, apprentices were given the sum of £5 to £10 per annum – comparable to the wages of an apprentice embroiderer, horner or fish-hook maker. Unlike many tradesmen who worked six to eight-hour days, gardeners' working hours were determined by daylight – summer days being long and arduous stretches of twelve to fourteen hours.[34] Moreover, it was relatively expensive to set up as a master – costing between £100 and £500 (comparable to similar costs incurred by glaziers, or joiners). Nor did the remuneration of gardeners improve by the first quarter of the nineteenth century; independent tradesmen often earned less than their serving brethren, and journeymen gardeners earned between two shillings to two shillings and sixpence a day (in 1825) – compared to a carpenter's daily wage of five shillings and sixpence to six shillings. Even a successful jobber's wages are reputed never to have exceeded three shillings a day.[35]

By the late eighteenth century the defence of the dignity of professional gardening was not simply a matter of deterring unscrupulous pretenders, but of protecting the rights of the lower ranks of tradesmen from the abuses of commercial nurserymen: gardeners accused commercial nurserymen, among others, of perpetuating the poor treatment and remuneration of fellow gardeners by endorsing a policy of discrimination. Tradesmen argued that nurserymen falsely claimed that the profession was oversubscribed, and that there were few or no openings for skilled workers – only to do an about face and offer them work on the condition that they accepted labourers' wages, remarking that they were fortunate to secure any work at all.[36]

There were, of course, advantages to the friendly collaboration of nurserymen and jobbers. The benefits for the nurserymen were the percentages they recovered from their subcontractees' wages and the promotion of their goods and services. To the gardener there were the bonuses of regular employment and income and the credibility of professionalism. Professionalism, above all, was from the early nineteenth century onwards believed in the trade to encourage regular patronage.

Regular income was the jobber's greatest and most persistent concern. Finding work was not generally as difficult as collecting payment from private customers –

173　J. Hill after Henry William Pyne, 'Gardiners', aquatint from *Microcosm: or, a Picturesque Delineation . . .* (1808), vol. 2, pl. 97. Paul Mellon Collection, Yale Center for British Art, New Haven. Their attire and the scope of their activities had changed little since the early eighteenth century.

many of whom employed tradesmen on credit. The obstacles gardeners had to surmount to collect their payments were common to most independent tradesmen.[37] It was easy for unscrupulous clients to default since they reckoned that small itinerant tradesmen often found it impracticable to litigate. Gardeners occasionally in despair or in anger were tempted to undo their work by reclaiming costly specimens and displays, but under the law this constituted the punishable offence of larceny.[38] Switzer had advised as early as 1718 that clients should 'set apart such a portion of the Revenue as can be conveniently spar'd' to be regularly applied 'to the Discharge of the Expence; for that Labourers Unpaid, are of course the most Impertinent, Troublesome Persons that may be'.[39]

The precarious career of anonymous jobbers who built and tended town gardens seldom received the attention of garden writers until Loudon began in 1826 to publish their grievances. In the *Gardener's Magazine* he expressed his belief that progress in gardening depended on the liberal and professional education of gardeners; accordingly the *Magazine* addressed technical, aesthetic and economic aspects of the gardening trade, and published notes on contemporary wages, hours and living conditions. Many of Loudon's sympathies were directed particularly towards the plight of unfortunate journeymen jobbers. In September 1826 he published 'On the Life of a Jobbing Gardener – By Mr Archibald M'Naughton, of Hackney' as a leading article in the first issue of the *Magazine*. We are informed that the contributor, having occupied a number of respectable gardening posts from Edinburgh to Epsom, quit the comfortable security of servitude for the freedom of jobbing. The result was disastrous; the wages were poor and the work was unsteady. After several years of jobbing at Paddington he moved to Hackney 'on account of the air, where I have been ever since, being just able to gain a livelihood, by laying out the gardens for new buildings going on in the neighbourhood'.[40]

In the early nineteenth century there were in London only limited opportunities for self-employed jobbers to collaborate with builders in the laying out of simple gardens for house carcasses, or working with private clients in planting, reordering or maintaining small gardens (fig. 173). The jobbers' traditional door-to-door business was being superseded by large, organised garden contracting businesses. The scope of services provided by the jobbers of the kind described by Hammer and Glenorchy was being carried out much more efficiently and often more reliably by garden operatives deployed by professional London nurserymen's retinues of gardeners. Opportunities still abounded for full-time gardeners in extensive gardens, but small-time jobbers found themselves increasingly beleaguered. The method of conducting business had changed: town gardening was now a powerful and polished service industry dominated by nurserymen who operated wholesale and retail goods and service monopolies. Moreover, from the early nineteenth century readers of the popular garden press were encouraged by the likes of John Claudius Loudon to develop a greater interest in the laying out and management of their own premises, without the assistance of a gardener.[41] This subject is examined in greater detail in chapter 9.

PLANT AND GARDEN CONTRACTING

Contract gardening was a desirable alternative for many classes of persons who had a town garden but had little or no time to garden, or spent most of the year in the country but kept up a townhouse. These people, who required seasonal help, or were frustrated by harmful effects of the city air, had plant displays which were regularly supplied and managed by contracting with London nurserymen.[42]

Among the entrepreneurs who profited from professional contract gardening was James Cochran (1763–?1825), of whom we know a great deal through the survival of his accounts, which document the business of a successful florist and plant contractor operating in early nineteenth-century London.

Although Cochran's records cover the years 1811 to 1822, the firm's accounts can be taken as representative of earlier plant contracting businesses which had been operating in London since at least the mid-eighteenth century.[43] The Cochran manuscripts comprise six day-books, two receiving books and one ledger, all of which comprehensively record eleven years of his business transactions in Duke Street, near Grosvenor Square.[44] The documents are remarkable for their thorough and descriptive inventories of the leasing of plant and garden accessories, which give us insights into the creation – costs, constituents and display – of imaginative temporary indoor and outdoor townhouse gardens.

James Cochran went into business in 1800 as a nurseryman, seedsman and land-surveyor operating from the New Road, Marylebone.[45] His business might have been undistinguished, although successful, had he not bought out a flourishing plant contracting partnership around 1815; at the same time he set up a retail shop at the hub of fashionable London. The result of his enterprise was that in the space of four years (from 1816) Cochran saw the profits of his florist business increase seventeen-fold. His astonishing success was due to a combination of his location and his practice of supplying flowers and shrubs for hire to the fashionable world.[46]

Cochran's large clientele comprised aristocrats, successful merchants and tradesmen resident within a one-mile radius of his shop. The largest subscribers of leased plants were members of the *beau monde*, which I. M. Cruikshank, in his 'Corinthian Order of stratified society', described as the 'Flowers of Society' – roses, pinks and tulips – the Prince Regent being at the top of the tree (fig. 174). Their patronage was regular and sustained.[47]

Contract gardening was recommended by practising gardeners and garden writers from the early nineteenth century onwards as the only assured procedure to sustain vigorous and robust flowering in the town garden and greenhouse. Contracts entailed regular visits by professional and jobbing gardeners who pruned, 'syringed' (washed) and replaced wilted specimens, bringing renewed freshness to clients' plant displays.[48] James Mangles, who, like many London gardeners, supported contract gardening, remarked in 1839 in *The Floral Calendar Monthly and Daily*: 'all plants after flowering in London, will inevitably die, unless taken the very care of by a practised gardener; they therefore, if purchased, become very expensive . . .'[49]

174 I. M. Cruikshank, 'The Corinthian Capital', aquatint from Pierce Egan, *Life in London* (1821). British Museum, London. The 'Corinthian Order of stratified society' satirised the *Flowers of Society* – roses, pinks and tulips – the Prince Regent being at the top of the tree.

Cochran specialised both in extended contract hire and in leasing 'for the night'. In order to realise every possible advantage from the location of his shop in Mayfair, his services included the provision of land surveying, garden construction and maintenance, and the supply of sundries ranging from Wedgwood flower baskets to copies of William Aiton's *Hortus Kewensis*.[50]

To meet his customers' demands Cochran owned a small nursery in Paddington, and supplemented his own stock with that of neighbouring nurserymen and

farmers. He acted as middleman to many nurserymen in the vicinity of his own grounds, buying and selling the flowering plants of those who did not have the wherewithal to retail in the West End. He bought hard-to-sell plants from nurserymen at discounted prices and subsequently leased them to his clients, with the salvageable plants returned to his greenhouses to be reused in contracting.[51]

This practice was common among many of his contemporaries, who raised flowers to augment their income. Most growers cultivating great quantities of plants could not rely on chance buyers and private custom to dispose of all of their nursery stock. According to Loudon they would first attempt to sell to London markets – such as Covent Garden – distributing their plants a fortnight before they blossomed (fig. 175).

> If he fails there, the hawkers come to him every morning and see what he has got a bargain and his next resource is the green-houses, cabinets, or chamber-stages, which he supplies by contract; and when he removes them from thence in their last stages of beauty, he sends them to a rout [party], where one night in general kills or half kills alike the best and worst of plants; and for which he gets the plant returned and half its price.[52]

Cochran employed a variable number of gardeners, whom he in turn subcontracted for the building of new gardens, garden refurbishment, or maintenance services at his clients' premises. He had a minimum of seven regularly employed gardeners – Messrs Hodgkins, Howard, Ryan, Edwards, Thursby, Carter and Holding – each of whom served a roster of private customers. For instance between 1818 and 1820 Mr Thursby regularly spread mould, planted 'roots', potted plants, 'propped up trees' and 'cleaned the grass' at Mr Davis Davenport's garden 28 Lower Brook Street, while Messrs Ryan and Howard together laid out, planted and maintained Mr Champeny's garden in Maida Hill, Paddington.[53]

If people had the means, and commensurate enthusiasm, they gained the greatest benefit from contract gardening. They had large seasonal contingents of flowers and shrubs which were plunged into their gardens, balconies, greenhouses, conservatories and the window sills of their libraries, drawing-rooms and parlours, in order to heighten and 'exaggerate' the experience of the current season (figs 176a and b). Spring was, above all, the most celebrated and popular garden season. Lawns were grubbed up and re-turfed, gravel paths were turned

175 Thomas Rowlandson, *Covent Garden Market*, watercolour, c.1800. Paul Mellon Collection, Yale Center for British Art, New Haven. Covent Garden market was London's principal fruit and flower market. It was established in the central open space of the piazza in the early seventeenth century.

or replaced, and hundreds of spring-blossoming shrubs and flowers were planted out for instant effect.[54] Almost every flowering plant was forced; and since spring was celebrated as 'perpetual', nothing was displayed to portend the ensuing seasons. A small variety of favourites was displayed and sustained through constant replenishment and plant replacement, to keep the garden in a state of suspended climax (and this was kept up for weeks, if not months). If customers wanted perpetual spring, then nurserymen and florists were eager to oblige. Nothing was easier and cheaper for commercial gardeners than growing enormous quantities of a limited assortment of plants.

While Cochran would create plant displays to any specification, his customers were compelled either by convenience or cost to choose from a range of standard plants and arrangements which may have been on show in Duke Street, or illustrated in a customised 'pattern book'. The most popular plants ordered for May were heaths, rhododendrons, azaleas, heartsease, mignonette, rose-trees, Persian lilacs and ranunculus. In June the choice altered only slightly, with the addition of pinks, stocks, hydrangeas, heliotropes and sweet briars. As the season progressed the choice narrowed substantially – most displays were planted in combinations of stocks, heartsease and mignonette with sprinklings of evergreen foliage (ivy or myrtle). During the winter months Cochran primarily provided displays of bulbs, the most popular of which was hyacinth.

A popular leasing arrangement was the short-term maintenance contract: customers hired portable plant displays by the week for the duration of the summer or the London Season. The displays were transported by waggon to the client's townhouse, where they would remain for five to ten weeks. The cost of such a service was assessed either by reference to the quantity and variety of the specimens and their containers or, in the case of simpler arrangements (such as boxes of mixed

A MINIATURE FLOWER GARDEN,
18 feet by 12 feet, on the sloping bank of the Grand Junction
Reservoir'—as seen from the back Dining-room Window.

(vide page 28.)

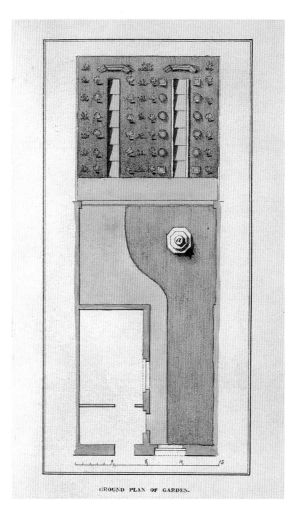

GROUND PLAN OF GARDEN.

176a 'A miniature flower garden', lithograph from James Mangles, *Floral Calendar* (1839), verso p. 28. Lindley Library, Royal Horticultural Society, London. This corresponds with the 'Ground plan of a flower garden' (fig. 176b).

176b 'Ground plan of a flower garden', lithograph from James Mangles, *Floral Calendar* (1839), vide p. 60. Lindley Library, Royal Horticultural Society, London. Mangles's ground plan characterises the composition of many of the small 'temporary' gardens which James Cochran was creating for his London clients from the early nineteenth century.

mignonette and stocks), by reference to the running foot.

The expense of hiring a few window boxes ranged from ten to fifteen shillings a week. Every second week in May from 1816 to 1821, for instance, a gardener and a painter (and occasionally a carpenter) arrived at Owen Williams's house at 41 Berkeley Square to install twenty-one leased plant boxes which were painted and planted *in situ*. The planters were stationed on window sills, balconies and leads. The order for planting the boxes remained constant from year to year: two-thirds mignonette and one-third stocks. The cost was roughly five pounds. This form of contract was inclusive of all maintenance, and included the care of the displays, as well as the replacement of blown, wilted or dead specimens. Williams, like dozens of other customers, hired his displays for the Season, after which time the boxes were collected and carted back to Cochran's for replanting and re-hire.

Cochran often encouraged his customers to extend the lease of their temporary displays once they were in place by offering substantial savings in contract costs. For instance, when the Duke of Grafton leased 104 plants for the night in June 1816 he was persuaded to keep them a week, at a cost of £7 16s.[55] The expense of leasing twenty-one plants for the night in 1816 was twenty-two shillings, and the lease could be extended for another week for an eleven shilling supplement. It

177 Thomas Rowlandson, 'All a-growing, a-growing, here's flowers for your gardens', pen and pencil with watercolour wash, 1799, from *Cries of London* series. Henry E. Huntington Library and Art Gallery, San Marino, California.

was cheaper still to lease by the month at a three pounds, as did Sir John and Lady Beresford at 48 Harley Street during the Season of 1817.[56] Larger plants were, on the other hand, usually more costly to hire, and customers could expect to pay a few guineas a week for a small garden full of flowering plants, or leads dotted with a dozen elegantly potted lilacs, rhododendrons, azaleas and laurels.[57]

Cochran's nursery carried out only limited new garden construction. The records of their contracts do, none the less, provide detailed insights into the cost of creating small gardens, and the plants which were supplied for them. In September 1818 two men spent two days 'taking up privets' and carting them away from Mr Fielden's garden at 20 Charlotte Street, Portland Place. They subsequently planted '2 vines in pots, 18 Irish iveys, [and] 16 white jessamines', and on 2 October laid '70 turfs'. Four days later '200 crocus, 50 double daf-fodils, 50 tulips, 12 pinks, 12 wall flowers, 6 heartsease, [and] 6 sweet williams' were planted. The garden cost, inclusive of labour, £7 2s. 6d. In September 1818 one of Cochran's men planted '4 rhododendrons, 2 laurel stineys, 2 red cedars, 2 aucubas, 4 vines in pots for [the] wall, 4 irish iveys . . . 10 china asters, 4 Indian pinks, [and] 4 globes' at Mr Sidney at 58 Newman Street, near Oxford Street, at a cost of £3 1s. 6d (fig. 177).[58]

For those perons who required only regular garden management there was a range of standard contracts. Mr Merrick engaged the nurseryman to 'look after' his garden at 43 Lower Grosvenor Street at a cost of four guineas per year; 'all plants, gravel, roots, mould, et. & extra labour extra to be paid for separate'. There were also arrangements for the over-wintering of plants: in spring 1821 Mrs Phillips of 45 Montague Square paid Cochran £2 19s. for keeping fifty-nine plants over the previous winter.[59]

178   W. Butler, 'Section of a conservatory', from James Mangles, *Floral Calendar* (1839), verso
p. 38. Lindley Library, Royal Horticultural Society, London.

7

Artificial Gardening

THE 'TOWN GREEN-HOUSE', THE CONSERVATORY AND THE MANAGEMENT OF PLANTS IN 'ARTIFICIAL SITUATIONS'

A FLOWER IN THE open parterre, though beautiful and gay, has yet something less endearing, and is less capable of receiving especial regard, than a plant in a pot, which thus acquires a sort of locomotion; and becomes, as it were, thoroughly domesticated. After choice things were planted in pots, things rare would be planted in them; and from things rare to things rare, foreign and tender, the transition would be natural and easy. Tender plants would be taken into the house for shelter, and set near the window for light, and hence the origins of the Green-house.[1]

Loudon remarked in 1824 that 'a Green-house, which fifty years ago was a luxury not often met with, is now become an appendage to every villa, and to many town residences; – not indeed one of the first necessity, but one which is felt to be appropriate and highly desirable, and which mankind recognise as a mark of elegant and refined enjoyment'.[2] If Loudon compared the greenhouse of his own time to 'a work of Art', the eighteenth-century 'town green-house' was, by comparison, little more than a poorly heated and poorly ventilated cabinet formed to 'preserve choice Plants . . . against the Extremity of the Season'.[3] These modest brick, timber and glass structures were often appended haphazardly to walls, buildings or parapets – regardless of aspect, light or ventilation. Raising plants in such constricted 'artificial situations' was expensive and difficult; as one author remarked in 1764, 'plants inclosed are in the most artificial situation in which they can be placed, and require constant and unremitting attention to counteract the tendency of that artificial state to destroy them'.[4] Although a range of garden writers of the period compiled treatises to the subject of how to

'nourish and succour your Plants in their Confinement', none, until the early nineteenth century, addressed the subject of the 'town green-house, or conservatory'.[5] Instead, writers discussed tender plants and their display in terms of their role as expendable 'Ornament'.[6]

George Tod's handsomely illustrated *Plans, Elevations and Sections of Hot-Houses, Green-Houses, an Aquarium, Conservatories, &c.* (1807) is among the few surviving publications to have described and illustrated what appears to have been a modest town greenhouse before such little 'Horticultural Buildings' were transformed by the advent of cheaper glass and wrought-iron glazing bars. The town greenhouse erected for Sir George Farrant (fig. 179) 'adjoining to the drawing-room of his house at no. 52 Upper Brook-street' was described as follows:

> constructed eleven feet above the surface of the yard behind the dwelling, that the floor may be on a level with that of the drawing-room, with which it communicates. The floor is framed with strong timbers, on which are laid rough boarding, and on the boarding are laid foot tile paving, bedded in Roman cement, to prevent the water, when watering the plants, from filtering through. It has a span roof of glass; one side is formed with sashes hung with weights, to slide down; and the other side is brickwork, which terminates the adjoining premises. The furnace is placed underneath, and the flue ascends perpendicularly till it reaches the Green-house, when it continues round above the floor, and returns upon itself on that side which is brickwork to a chimney placed at the north-east corner to discharge the smoke. There are fancy stages placed within; and the whole has a novel and pleasant appearance from the drawing-room, particularly in the evening when lighted with lamps.[7]

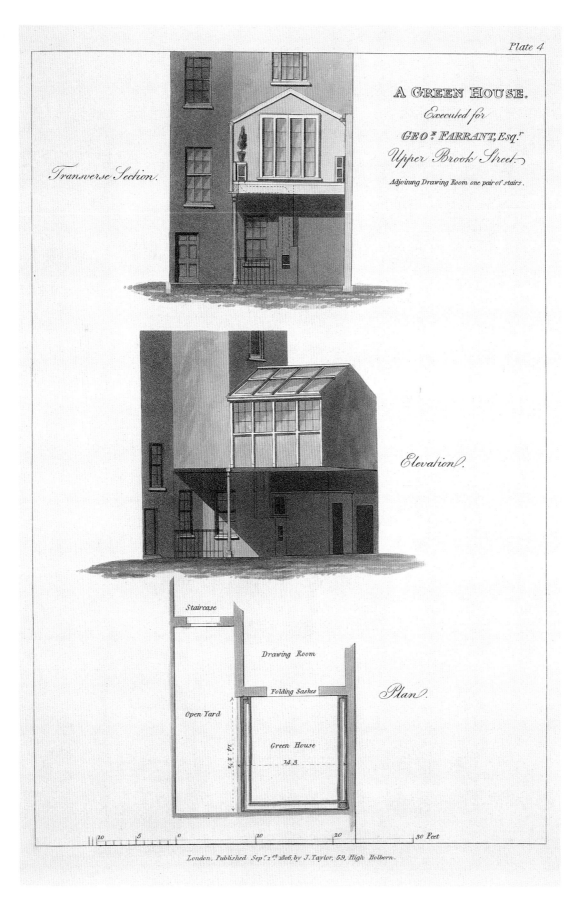

Plate 4

A GREEN HOUSE.

Executed for

GEO. *FARRANT, Esq.*

Upper Brook Street.

Adjoining Drawing Room one pair of stairs.

Transverse Section.

Elevation.

Staircase

Drawing Room

Folding Sashes

Plan.

Open Yard

Green House

14.3

10   5   0   10   20   30 Feet

London, Published Sep.* 1* 1806, by J. Taylor, 59, High Holborn.

179 'A Green House Executed for George Farrant, Esq.', adjoining the drawing room of his house in Upper Brook Street, London, aquatint from George Tod, *Plans, Elevations and Sections of Hot-Houses, Green-Houses, an Aquarium, Conservatories, &c.*(1807), pl. IV.

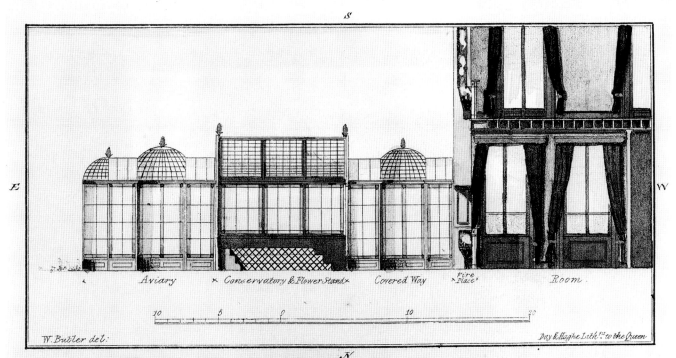

SUGGESTION FOR A MORNING OR BREAKFAST ROOM, WITH AN ATTACHED CONSERVATORY AND AVIARY,
visible through an upsliding window of plate-glass over the mantel-piece (which must be very low), with an Arnott's stove covered
with porcelain, and the flue leading up on one side.

180 W. Butler, 'Suggestion for a Morning or Breakfast Room, with an attached Conservatory and Aviary', lithograph from James Mangles, *Floral Calendar* (1839), vide p. 126. Lindley Library, Royal Horticultural Society, London.

This humble closet appears to be contrived less for the cultivation of plants than the extension of the inside apartments. Indeed, it may, in fact, have been put up for the same reason as Mr John Elliot's greenhouse at Pimlico, which Tod 'constructed for the purpose of preventing the prospect of some offices from the dwelling house'.[8]

George Tod was one of a number of 'surveyors and hot-house builders' who emerged at the turn of the nineteenth century, and whose business spanned an important period in the improvement of the glasshouse. He, like William and Daniel Bailey of High Holborn, Messrs Loddiges of Sion Lodge and John Cushing of Hammersmith, were specialist tradesmen who, in Loudon's estimation, were 'accustomed to build greenhouses, to regulate their flues, paths, drainage, chimneys and ventilation, &c. and who be responsible for its answering the purposed ends'.[9] Improvements in building technology, and in particular heating, ventilation and the development of the wrought iron glazing bar (1816), made possible the creation of modest and inexpensive glazed garden rooms which communicated directly with the house.[10]

Repton was among the earliest garden writers to recommend that the greenhouse should be treated as an elegant reception room dedicated to the assembly of large parties. Writing in 1816, he suggested that the greenhouse could be a vibrant terminus or 'visto' to an enfilade of modern apartments.[11] This concept was subsequently adopted and refined by Loudon, who in 1824 charted a more elaborate, hierarchical set of rules which determined the relationship of the room with other interior apartments. He recommended that the greenhouse – which might take the form of a corridor, or an apartment – should communicate directly with – in order of precedence – the library, breakfast parlour or the drawing-room; or the porch, entrance hall, saloon, or billiard room (fig. 180). From the outside the glasshouse had a curiously detached, or independent expression from that of the dwelling, and yet when viewed from the indoors it was able to blend seamlessly with the interior. This was especially true where the greenhouse was linked by 'spacious glass doors' to the parlour or library – here the indoor garden achieved its full splendour: the complement of neighbouring apartments, when 'judiciously furnished with mirrors,

Section of Conservatory, shewing Flower Stand &c

W. Butler del.   Day & Haghe Lith.rs

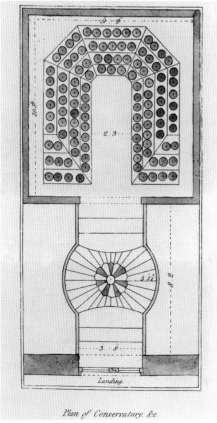

Plan of Conservatory &c

and bulbous flower in water glasses', greatly enhanced the effect of the 'growth, verdure, gay colours, and fragrance'; vegetation was felicitously 'blended with the books, sofas, and all the accompaniments of social and polished life' (figs 181 and 182).[12]

Town greenhouses were, from Loudon's point of view, 'adjuncts' to the house – glazed internal apartments for the display of flowering plants, which were 'generally on a small scale, and seldom accompanied by sheds for potting and shifting, stock and mould, and a platform for setting out the plants in summer'.[13] Their direct and intimate communication with the house, in fact, compelled the author to suggest that persons who intended to erect these 'artificial environments' should give the matter as much serious consideration as the rest of the layout of the house lest they receive 'what tradesmen call a bungling job', and 'if not approved of by the gardener, form a sort of scape-goat for his errors or neglect'.[14]

It should be noted that from the early eighteenth century onwards, the terms 'town greenhouse' and 'conservatory' were often used together or interchangeably. The building types were not, however, the same, when used in a specialised, technical context, and later came to be seen as distinct in everyday parlance as well: glasshouses contained potted plants which were displayed on 'stages', whilst conservatories, on the other hand, had plants bedded directly into the earth in borders. There was, moreover, a range of smaller decorative devices which could be fitted in the townhouse – plants could also be grown and displayed in cases, cabinets or on chamber-stages (figs 183a and b).[15] Loudon remarked in 1838 that many ardent urban botanists had amassed astonishing collections of exotic plants which they arranged with particular ingenuity 'under glass' at their small premises: 'Mr [Nathaniel] Ward of Wellclose Square, a distinguished botanist, grows a considerable hardy flora, in troughs, or boxes, on the tops of the walls which enclose his back yard, on the roof of the outbuildings in it; and in the different rooms in his house, he grows upwards of a hundred specimens of ferns, indigenous and exotic'.[16] He asserted, with some amazement: 'we know a gentleman whose back garden is hardly 30 feet square; nevertheless he has a dry stove in it, in which he cultivates a collection of succulent plants, one of the richest in species of any neighbourhood of London'.[17]

Loudon's interest lay not in curious displays, but in the greenhouse, and as such he made specific recommendations on the building, purchasing and mainte-

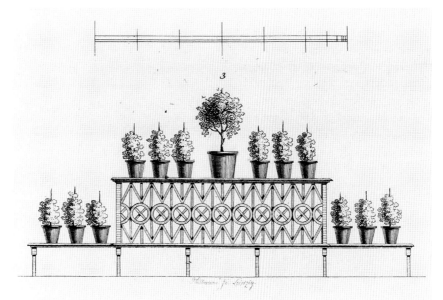

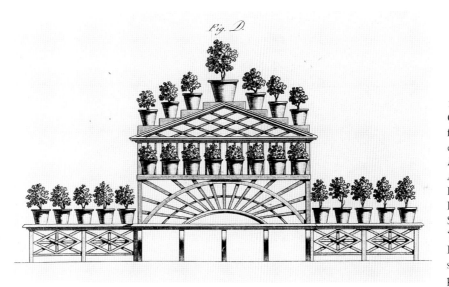

181 (*facing page top*) W. Butler, 'Section of a conservatory', from James Mangles, *Floral Calendar* (1839), verso p. 38. Lindley Library, Royal Horticultural Society, London.

182 (*facing page bottom*) 'Plan of a Conservatory, &c.', lithograph from James Mangles, *Floral Calendar* (1839), p. 39. Lindley Library, Royal Horticultural Society, London.

183a J. G. Grohmann, 'Gradin chinois – sopha de Jardin', engraving from *Recueil d'Idées* (1802), 41, pl. 4, no. 3. Lindley Library, Royal Horticultural Society, London. Grohmann's magazine published a variety of designs for garden buildings and flower stands which were copied in England from the early nineteenth century.

183b J. G. Grohmann, 'gradin de fleurs formant sofa', engraving from *Recueil d'Idées* (1802), 44, no. 3, fig. d. Lindley Library, Royal Horticultural Society, London. This 'gradin' was similar to English 'chamber stages' of the same period.

nance of buildings for 'plant habitation' in town. 'Malleable iron' was, he believed, the 'cheapest and strongest' material available for the purpose: 'for a green-house or conservatory we have no hesitation in giving the preference to metal over wood, as producing more light, elegant and durable fabric, and admitting of greater latitude of form and dimension than timber.' Building a greenhouse with iron components also meant that they could be 'more easily taken to pieces and replaced in the case of a change of plan, or residence'.[18]

The 'cheapest and best method' of erecting a glasshouse was first to consult an architect 'as to the sort of form which will best accord' with the house; 'next,

a good gardener or nurseryman as to the situation and position; and thirdly, having fixed on these, let him call in a manufacturer of green-houses, and, stating the date given by the architect and gardener, require of him a plan and estimate of expense'.[19]

Although the 'cultivation of Exotic plants' was considered to 'hold the highest rank in horticultural science', the activity of greenhouse gardening was not restricted to the rich, or to botanists, but extended to middle-classes amateurs.[20] By the early nineteenth century indoor gardening had evolved as a fashionable pursuit, invested with the attractions of gentility. Loudon in 1824 warned would-be greenhouse gardeners in *The*

Greenhouse Companion that they should temper their enthusiasm and extravagance, and restrict the range of plants which they grew: 'we wish we could impress sufficiently upon our readers the importance of selecting a few choice sorts [of plants], rather than aiming at a great number of species, or what gardeners call a greater variety. The truth is, that within the last fifty years the accession to our stock of exotics has been so great, that gardeners are quite bewildered among them, and the nurserymen at present, in their recommendation of plants, act as if every purchaser were a botanist.'[21]

The 'general culture of green-house plants, and the management of the green-house' was a serious consideration; Loudon remarked in his practical manual of 1824 that it 'required a higher degree of knowledge, than is called for in the management of the open garden'.[22]

184 John Raphael Smith, *Lady on a Terrace tending a Carnation Plant*, chalk, *c*.1790. Paul Mellon Collection, Yale Center for British Art, New Haven. The cultivation of flowers was defined as a proper exercise of the female virtue of modesty and the female inclination for leisurely reflection on nature.

All that can be said with advantage on town greenhouses might be comprised in very few words: viz. that the only way to have them look well is to agree with a nurseryman to keep up a supply of verdant flowering plants for such a part of the year as the family is in town. We are confident that there is no other mode that will be attended with success, till the nature of plants or the nature of a coal fire is considerably altered.

A number of London green-houses placed behind the house on the tops of kitchens and other offices, and of plant cabinets communicating with living-rooms, are maintained in order by nurserymen in this way; and a number also are kept in order, as it is called, by jobbing gardeners, who call occasionally to see that the plants are properly watered, who supply pots of mignonette, and who shift plants in spring, and prune them in the autumn . . . The green-houses managed in the latter mode are wretched vegetable abodes, – hospitals, or pest-houses of plants; and to any person who knows what a green healthy plant is, they are deformities rather than ornaments.[23]

James Mangles reiterated Loudon's injunction in 1839, remarking that 'the difficulties which beset the amateur florist in London are great and almost irremediable; day and night he has to contend incessantly [both outdoors and indoors] with a poisonous atmosphere – no skill or art – no assiduity or care – will protect his plants from the destructive infection of the pernicious *blacks*; their withering influence will baffle all his precautions . . .'[24]

It was not, however, the wish of either author to alarm London's 'amateur florists', but to educate them in the 'general management' of the town greenhouse. In his introduction to *The Greenhouse Companion* Loudon reassured his readers that it was 'the object of this little work to enter into the details of the subject in such a way, as may enable any lady or gentleman, with the assistance of a footman or common labourer, to manage their own green-house as completely as if they employed a regularly bred and skilful gardener.' The directions he prescribed, and the reasons for them, were 'so ample, and so plain, that no lady or gentleman can be at a loss fully to comprehend them, or discern when they are properly acted on'.[25]

As the greenhouse became linked to the house, so too did its management, like that of the open parterre, become 'pre-eminently a woman's department' (fig. 184).[26] Loudon remarked: 'A green-house is in a peculiar degree in the care of the female part of the family, and forms an interesting scene of care and recreation to the mother and her daughters, at a season of the year when there is but little inducement to walk in the kitchen-garden, and nothing to do in the parterre or the shrubbery.'[27] This demarcation of the pursuit as feminine was reinforced by the proclaimed fragility of the potted displays, and their weak dependency upon regular heat, shelter and nutrition. The potted plant was a symbol and institution of women's containment: 'it was marriage which would safely domesticate the burgeoning flower-garden into an indoor pot plant; the beautiful object potentially open to all men's gaze became the possession of one man when kept within the house like a picture fixed to the wall.'[28]

It should also be remembered that according to Loudon the potted plant had also acquired 'a sort of locomotion'. A plant in a pot may not have been in a 'safer state than a plant in the open ground'; it was, however, 'often more convenient for the cultivator', certainly more convenient for people who expressed little interest in keeping or cultivating plants, and extremely convenient for those persons who had an ardent interest in using potted flowering plants for instant and temporary decorative effect at *routs*, or parties. Loudon opined that 'the only true way to have a fine display on the chamber-stage is, never to bring the plants there till they are just coming into flower, and to remove them when the flowers show the first indications of decay'.[29]

TEMPORARY INDOOR GARDENS: THE INDOOR STAGE

Private indoor temporary gardening reached its heady climax with Londoners' fanciful interpretations of the French *fête-champêtre*. The novelty of the *fêtes* lay in the symbolic blurring of boundaries between the indoors and the outdoors: drawing-rooms were traversed by gravel paths, interior walls were embowered in laurel, and aviaries, pavilions and herbaceous floral borders littered the indoors, displacing regular room furnishings, which were placed in the garden.

The rule of thumb was that when nature was staged it was improved; when manipulated it was subordinated to effect; and as foil it dutifully enhanced the status of the performers and the audience. 'Nature' was the malleable accessory of the accomplished flower designer, or *festarolo* (who might have been either the florist, the hostess or even a gardener) and was the ephemeral complement to radiant and vital beauty.[30]

It is not known at what point in history Londoners began devising large and costly planted-up stages in their townhouses for masquerades and routs. Certainly the practice was flourishing by the mid-eighteenth century, perhaps reaching its acme in the early nineteenth century. Whilst there are records of the Duchess of Norfolk's metropolitan masquerades in the late 1740s, and reports in the correspondence of Mrs Delany in the 1750s, the first well-documented examples of exotic private entertainments in the manner of the indoor *fête-champêtre* are those of the adventuress Mrs Theresa Cornelys in the 1760s and 1770s.

Mrs Cornelys's masquerades at Carlisle House, Soho Square, were advertised amusements that attracted hundreds of select subscribers at two guineas a head. The dazzling parties were invariably staged in fanciful temporary indoor gardens. Newspaper accounts described the interior decoration of her apartments for the *fêtes* as exceptional. On one occasion in 1765 'the Bridge-Room was converted into an elegant garden, the sides were full of shrubs and odoriferous flowers, at the extremity was a kind of Arbour filled with green-house plants and pots of flowers, and in the center was an elegant pavilion hung with festoons of silk . . .'[31] Other accounts of her entertainments chronicle elaborate indoor scenes formed of *allées*, green regular hedges, fish ponds, large potted trees and grottoes and springs which were contrived to make subscribers believe they were frolicking *en plein campagne*.

Mrs Cornelys, like the many private socialites who attempted to stage similar festivities, was declared bankrupt in 1772. Between the demise of her sumptuous parties and the private revels of her successors in the early nineteenth century, there intervened a period of popularity of public centres of amusement such as Ranelagh and Vauxhall Gardens, The Pantheon, Sadler's Wells, Marylebone Gardens and Finch's Grotto – resorts which boasted the attractions of fireworks, 'new and elegant transparencies' and the latest mechanised stage scenery and effects executed by the 'first artificers of the kingdom'. The success of these centres for public amusements also coincided with the assimilation of thousands of Londoners into the swollen ranks of the gentry, but by the early nineteenth century the *ton* had tired of the indiscriminate mingling of the classes at the public meetings, and had withdrawn to the comfort of their townhouse drawing-rooms, where they could privately entertain a select company of guests.

London's greatest entertainments invariably took place during the period from late April to late June known as the Season.[32] Although many of the city's residents divided their time between town and country, fashionable London was never dead; celebrated visitors came and went throughout the year. Movement to and from the country transcended class and income; a large number of gentry, and many hangers-on participated in the seasonal migrations. The *beau monde* alone punctiliously observed the inflexible Court calendar. The Season entailed a complicated and ceaseless series of social events which kept the *ton* in a tail-spin. The days were long and filled with elaborate daily rounds of amusements, and the evenings were often longer, as *divertimenti* began at sunset and ceased at daybreak.

As in Mrs Cornelys's day, during the Regency private entertainments like theatrical spectacles, were seldom staged without the setting of a contrived landscape, usually drawing on one or the other conventional types: the pastoral landscape and the wilderness. Such settings were based on the model of the court masque, both in their dramatic effect of lighting and in their use of a standard range of features: the triumphal arch, the portico, the decked table and the fountain.[33] As in the seventeenth-century court masque, the landscape mapped out a space of removal and of allegorical intensification and elevation: within the drama enacted, Olympian gods and goddesses were usually among the main protagonists, while the simplest and least ceremonious activities of the daily round were portrayed as heroic feats.[34]

The success of a landscape setting was determined by the technical virtuosity with which it was devised, and by the skill deployed in producing illusionistic effects which reinforced the impression of a domain of heightened reality. The gardens invariably incorporated ingenious perspective distortions. Enormous displays of living plants were also employed as instruments of intensification and illusion. These plants served to intensify the theatrical space not by virtue of any inherent exoticism but, rather, through the scale on which they were employed, and through their appeal to at least two of the senses at once – those of sight and smell.

Cochran raised large quantities of a limited variety of flowering and fragrant plants consisting mainly of familiar garden species such as mignonette, stocks, pinks, violets, roses and geraniums. The range was largely determined by the need to create displays in which all of the constituents were in a state of simultaneous perfection, and could be sustained as such for a prolonged period. Although some blossoms – particularly pelargoniums ('Barryingtonia', 'Prince Regent' and 'Waterloo')

– evoked strong associations, and some foliage plants such as myrtle and laurel were possessed of emblematic qualities – the specific identity of individual plants was much less important than the general effect of overwhelming abundance and luxury which they served to create.

The luxuriousness of such displays was further emphasised by the fact that one night of festivity usually rendered the plants useless, either for planting out or for further ornamental purposes within the domestic interior. Walter Nicol in 1809 characterised the plants used as 'starved . . . dumb innocents [which] should not be returned to the gardener, or the florist, after two or three days privation, perhaps, in a state more fit for the hospital than the green-house'.[35] His assessment was echoed by Loudon, who in 1818 also appropriated the metaphor of the 'plant-hospital' when he contemplated the fate of hired plants after being crushed, bruised and ill-fed at townhouse routs. Nevertheless, the florist was more a set-designer than a plantsman when it came to creating an instant garden: plants were his stage props, and he strove only for effect.

The artisans were among the greatest beneficiaries of the new house parties, and the florist played a major part in setting the scene, second in importance only to the suppliers of furnishings and lighting. We have only to examine the thousands of entries in the working papers of Cochran to attest that his role was seminal in the interior decoration of the London townhouse.

Cochran's day-books and the 'Fashionable World' column of the *Morning Post* confirm that it was very often the woman of the household who hosted and organised parties in the London Season.[36] As the manager of domestic duties, she was also charged with the responsibility of hospitality at home. Women often supervised the decoration of the house, appointing a florist among other specialists, to design and build spectacular settings subject to her recommendations which 'displayed all the luxuriance of the present season's prolific growth'.[37]

Clients lavished great sums of money on Cochran's ephemeral floral displays. In 1819, for instance, out of a total of fifty-eight orders for 'plants for the night', seven were over ten pounds, five over twenty pounds and four over forty pounds. The leasing scheme was immensely lucrative, as his account books indicate. His contracting, beginning in 1816, totalled 555 plants for the night and peaked at 9,429 plants for the night in 1819. The orders varied from the lease of a single yellow azalea to Davis Davenport Esq. of Lower Brook Street, to the creation

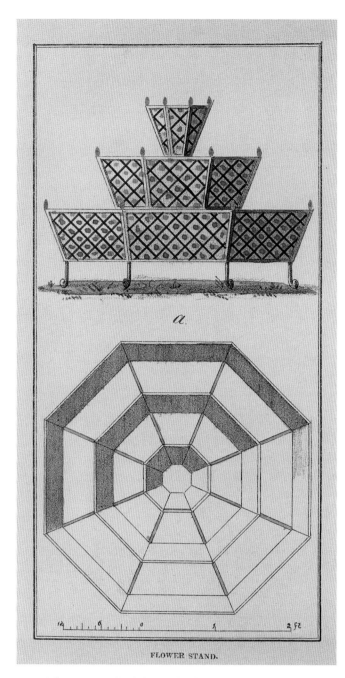

185 'Flower Stand', lithograph from James Mangles, *Floral Calendar* (1839), verso p. 43. Lindley Library, Royal Horticultural Society, London. This stand decorated with a 'running pattern' of Copeland porcelain tiles set in a wrought-iron framework, was made by Mr Butler of Edgware Road.

convenient location of his retail establishment in Mayfair.[38] While the floral effects of his contemporaries were seldom discussed, Cochran's accomplishments were praised extensively: he was frequently cited in the 'Fashionable World' column of the *Morning Post* for his 'ingenious' disposition of plants at routs and *fêtes*, or his superintendent duties as florist, nurseryman and 'botanist'.

Cochran employed a variety of props to create his instant gardens, including boxes, stands, baskets, Wedgwood garden pots, pillars, red and black basketwork, as well as tin-lined oval, double oval and semicircular decorative boxes (fig. 185). The displays – usually fitted with castors – were hired on a nightly basis or on long-term contracts. Clients were charged for the use of plants and stands separately. Customers selected their floral compositions by paying a visit to the nurseryman at his premises in Duke Street, where they would examine ready-made displays, or peruse a manuscript pattern book. While Cochran seems to have exercised complete control in the supply, delivery, display and collection of his plants, the extent to which he collaborated with other tradesmen and professionals was variable, and subject to the arrangements with the client.

Short-term plant leasing flourished from May to July and occasionally in April and August, the busiest times corresponding with the Season. Dozens of balls and routs were held at which the host or hostess would throw open his or her house for the evening. Typically the doors would open at 10 p.m., amusements and quadrilles would follow at midnight, the repast would begin at 2.30 a.m. and *divertimenti* and dancing would carry on until dawn. For such *fêtes* it was the fashion to furnish one's residence as sumptuously as possible, and Cochran's clients vied for conspicuous and grandiloquent settings. Doors and windows were removed, layouts of interior apartments were altered through construction works, and furnishings and lighting were hired for the events – including items as large as chandeliers, sideboards, consoles, sofas and tables. Everywhere living wildernesses were created indoors: passages became alcoves embowered with evergreen and laurel, appointed with mirrors, lanterns and fragrant flowering shrubs. The settings resembled the backdrop scenery of popular contemporary stages, and particularly the designs for the Toy Theatre (figs 186 and 187).

When a house was decorated for a *fête* the interior's splendour spilled into the courts and gardens through lavish balcony displays of flowering shrubs and trees which framed prospects into illuminated town gardens.

of a scene of Heliogabalean splendour at Sir Charles Cockerell's house in Hyde Park Terrace on 10 June 1818 through the arrangement of 1,240 plants and cut flowers at a cost of £63 15s.

Cochran's success was a result of his business acumen, imaginative flair and, perhaps most importantly, the

186 Backdrop from *The Harlequin Brilliant*, from West's Theatre, Strand, aquatint, 1815. British Museum, London. Theatrical settings, the 'living wildernesses' which were created in London drawing rooms of the Regency, were not the subject of surviving topographical views. The household settings were, however, similar to those which were appearing on the popular stage.

187 Backdrop from the fifth scene of *Bluebeard*, from West's Theatre, Strand, aquatint, 1825. British Museum, London. This luxuriant vegetative display evokes the character of the green theatres in miniature which were thrown up in London drawing rooms and were the subject of ecstatic descriptions in the *Morning Post*.

In July 1821 an article in the *Morning Post* praised the genius of the duc de Gramont, the French Ambassador, for his party held in honour of the coronation of King George IV.

> The Promenade Saloon . . . represented an enchanted grove. Pomona and Vertumnus themselves might have been proud to acknowledge it for their favourite garden. The finest flowers in every species bloomed in beds of a semi-circular form along the sides; and behind them arose, in great abundance, the most beautiful shrubs and orange trees, growing in a state of nature – there were forty waggon-loads!! All above were enlivened by festoons of artificial flowers, inter-mixed with 670 wax-lights, placed in fanciful giran-doles . . . In this enchanted garden, apparently on fairy ground, the visitants took their station at half-past ten o'clock.[39]

Plants leased for the night were, where possible, intended to supplement the pickings from the hosts' own gardens. Garden pavilions and conservatories were assembled for the night to enclose tender, or exotic plants, and existing conservatories' glazing was partially replaced by stained glass (fig. 188).[40] Variegated lamps and Chinese lanterns illuminated terraces and gardens, drawing people from the heat of the rooms to the fragrant air outside.

For grander events, floral displays enhanced real and *trompe l'oeil* (or illusionistic) follies. Roman ruins were etched on transparencies, floors were painted in water-colour to illustrate mythological scenes, mock-up gothic conceits and pagan temples were assembled and decked in festoons and wreathes of jasmine and evergreen. At Mrs West's ball of 13 June 1818 the boudoir was 'fancifully decorated with shells and flowers; [and] a transparency in the background resembling the ruins of a Roman temple . . . The garden was lighted up by variegated lamps, with trellis work, and a full length figure of Wellington mounted on his charger. The *tout ensemble* was perfectly novel, and much admired'.[41]

Mrs Henry Baring was one of the foremost enter-tainers of Regency London. Her many *divertimenti* were lauded in 'The Fashionable World' with generous dis-tinctions and praise. Perhaps one of her most remark-able festivities was held in June 1818, when six spacious apartments in her newly constructed house at 48 Berke-ley Square were thrown together to form the 'drawing-room *suite*'. The domestic interior was described as being 'at once *nouvelle* and beautiful':

> Draperies of white muslin, relieved by pink rosettes, festoons of artificial flowers, rare exotics, blooming in beds of moss around, the latter extending to the extremities of the balconies, and filling the chimneys

facing page Detail of fig. 231.

and other interstices. The three finest apartments were illuminated by the finest specimens of cut glass in Europe, consisting of Grecian chandeliers, lustres, and girandoles (such as have never before been seen) . . . Mirrors of vast dimensions, viz. 150 inches by 96, reflected every object *ad infinitum*. The end of a vast perspective was terminated by a saloon, or, more properly speaking, the *Temple of the Sun*.

Two of the principal rooms were appropriated for the ball: the floors being chalked for quadrilles . . . all the windows were removed; and to prevent too great a current of air, a temporary awning was erected in front of the house . . . The grand staircase was decorated with wreaths of laurel entwined around the balustrades. The hall was enlivened by all kinds of flowering shrubs. The passages communicating with several temporary rooms, represented an alcove, being entirely filled with branches of the laurel. The two great rooms on the ground floor, namely the parlour and the library, had the addition of a temporary room for the Princes of the Blood Royal . . . The supper tables [laid for six hundred guests] were superbly decorated with *or-molu*; the most striking were flower-baskets, supported by female *caryatides*.

We have witnessed nothing so splendid and beautiful since the days of Mrs Walker – the same liberality in the expenditure, and the same taste. Never was anything so effective as the disposition of the plants.[42]

Mrs Baring's Arcadian evocation, at which the 'visitants extolled the chandeliers and lustres, the plants and the disposition of them', was constructed in part by 1,004 plants leased from Mr Cochran (fig. 189).[43] It took five men two days to transport and assemble, with moss, wire, twine, nails and sticks, the large quantities of cut laurel and evergreen, dozens of green baskets, stands and china cut-flower jars used to furnish the house for the party; it took one day to take it all down. The *Morning Post* credited Cochran's achievement as 'evidently the work of a superior artist'.[44]

Frances Trollope gave a full account of an early nineteenth-century party in *The Days of the Regency* (1848). The novelist described the redecoration of the fictional Mr and Mrs Cuthbert's townhouse in Cavendish Square – from the silken drapery hung to disguise the antiquarian books, to the architect's interventions, which

188   The Chinese Pavilion at Montagu House, Whitehall. The Duke of Buccleuch and Queensberry, K.T. This timber-framed structure with its decorated oilcloth skin was erected each spring in the garden from the 1740s to the late nineteenth century.

189 (*right*)   Account from the ledger of James Cochran, pen, 5 June 1818 (detail). Public Record Office, Kew.

involved removing a wall between the dining-room and the library for the creation of a grand banquet hall.

> The scene that greeted her seemed, to her [Mrs Harriet Cuthbert's] fancy, to be much more like one of magical delusion than sober reality ... When Harriet walked into the beautifully decorated rooms, which were, now in many respects, much more richly furnished than she had ever see them before, she felt as if the whole show was perfectly new to her. The brilliancy of the lighting; the graceful arrangement and lavish profusion of the flowers; the soft shade and the delicate twilight of the beautiful conservatory; together with the elegant and fanciful decorations bestowed on the canopied elevation prepared, very nearly in the form of a throne, for the Regent, produced as effect that was altogether dazzling ... .[45]

The expenditure for such a party, inclusive of all the costs was £2,400, of which the cost of the floral decorations constituted roughly five to ten per cent. The total bill, in this instance, was apparently disproportionate to Mr Cuthbert's annual income, and proved to be an extravagance from which his estate never recovered.

There were, of course, economical prescriptions for achieving comparable effects. Capricious and exuberant plant displays may have begun as an aristocratic conceit, but the fashion was quickly taken up by the middle classes. In 1818 Loudon published *The Greenhouse Companion*, which included a chapter on the 'Management of ... Plants in Chambers at Routs', in which he described how 'much romantic splendour may be produced ... with little expense of green-house plants'.[46]

> Plants at routs require little management while there, but must be tastefully arranged individually by rods and threads, and well syringed, and also watered at the root. The soil should be covered with moss, and the pot either cleaned and painted, in any appropriate body colour, or chalked, or covered with coloured paper. An earthen brown with black and gray lines is among the most suitable colours, whether for the temporary painting, chalking or papering. Where the plants are only to remain one night, they need not be set in saucers, but only on paper or small carpets of the size of the bottom of the pot; but where they are to decorate the apartments for two or three days in succession, they should be set on a little gravel, and over the gravel the saucer filled brimful with moss or fine green turf. This looks well, and the space occupied by the gravel admits of giving the plants daily a

little water, which greatly refreshes them in this state of trial.[47]

In 'common cases', Loudon recommended that plants should be stationed in recesses and on side tables, and near 'glasses which may reflect them; he proposed, too, that a few choice specimens should be scattered over the floor as single objects' (figs 190 and 191).[48]

Loudon projected grander prescriptions for more select entertainments: 'During dinner pots of fruit-bearing shrubs, or trees with their fruit ripe, are ranged along the centre of the table [presumably on a *surtout-de-table*], from which, during the dessert, the fruit is gathered by the company.' Likewise, he recommended that 'sometimes a row of oranges, or standard peach trees, or cherries, or all of them, in fruit, surround the table of guests; one plant being placed exactly behind each chair, leaving room for the servants to approach between. Sometimes only one tall handsome tree is placed behind the mistress; and sometimes only a few pots of lesser articles are placed on the side-board, or here and there round the room.'[49]

Loudon's subsequent recommendations were increasingly dramatic and extravagant:

> The drawing room is sometimes laid out like an orange-grove by distributing tall orange trees all over it in a regular quincunx, so that the heads of the trees might be higher than those of the company: seats are also neatly made over the pots and boxes to conceal them, and to serve the purpose of chairs. One or two cages with nightingales and canary-birds are distributed among the branches, and where there is a want of real fruit, that is supplied by art. Sometimes also art supplies the entire tree, which during artificial illumination is hardly recognised as a work of art, and very few real trees and flowers interspersed with these made ones, will keep up the odour and the illusion of nature.
>
> Sometimes large picture galleries are laid out in imitation parks in the ancient or modern style, with avenues or with groups and scattered trees. At masqued routs, caves and grottos are formed under conical stages, and covered with moss and pots of trees, in imitation of wooded hills. In short, there is no end to the arrangement of plants at routs: and the reader is not to suppose that only real plants with roots are necessary for this purpose; for, provided a few of these be judiciously introduced, the rest can be effected by branches of box, laurustinus, laurel, juniper, holly, &c., decorated with artificial flowers

8

Garden Squares

EARLY GARDEN SQUARES

Tʜᴇ ɢᴀʀᴅᴇɴ sqᴜᴀʀᴇ evolved between about 1630 and 1680, and coincided with the conversion of dozens of acres of agricultural land into planned residential estates which had as their focus 'handsome open Places, with very good Buildings well inhabited'.[1] Open spaces abounded in seventeenth- and eighteenth-century London, and took the form of cloister gardens, college quadrangles, closes, sheep-walks, paddocks, kitchen gardens and waste common fields. Few of these, however, had great bearing on what became known as garden squares. It should be noted that throughout the period 1700–1840 garden squares were defined as more visible than the city's private gardens, and that eighteenth-century writings and topographical accounts register them as such: not only were they the subject of countless descriptions by Londoners and English visitors, but also by foreign travellers, who found them a point of comparison with the public open spaces of their own countries of origin.

There were two significant precedents to the development of the square. The first was the integration of a large rectangular open space within an axially related plan of uniformly fronted terraced houses. This established important aesthetic and practical lessons for future builders in the metropolis, who either chose to work within these constraints or were forced to observe them. The second precedent – which was to a great extent contingent upon the first – was the regular enclosure of open waste fields, where the new formal enclosures preserved or modestly enhanced the rural character of the former landscape. This often meant little more than keeping the fields in turf, but inscribing them with gravelled paths and enclosing the resultant 'Grass Platts' with post and rail fences. These two precedents were established by the late 1650s. It was not, however, until the

early 1680s that the first square garden was formed – where the residents of the square created and maintained the enclosed area 'in the Midst', which was laid out as a pleasure ground planted with ornamental flowers, shrubs and trees.

Covent Garden was London's first residential square and formal open space. The area in which Covent Garden now stands – circumscribed by Long Acre, St Martin's Lane, Drury Lane and an irregular parallel line with the Strand – was once enclosed pastureland belonging to the Abbey (or 'Convent') of St Peter at Westminster. This seven-acre field had been confiscated by the Crown during the Dissolution of the Monasteries and was granted to John Russell, 1st Earl of Bedford, in 1552. Upon the south side of the site the 3rd Earl built Bedford House in 1586, where it faced the urban palaces and gardens of the noblemen and courtiers in the Strand. Four decades later Francis Russell, 4th Earl, encouraged by the extensive development of the surrounding quarters, embarked upon an ambitious speculative building venture. In 1627 he secured for two thousand pounds a licence to erect to the north of his garden wall a number of dwellings 'fitt for habitacions of *Gentlemen* and men of ability'.

According to a contemporary account, 'many ancient buildings were demolished, and other new buildings were erected by special direction of the then King and his Council with much ornament and beauty and to a vast charge'.[2] The resultant square, or piazza as it was then known, conceived by Inigo Jones, was an astonishing application of Italian urbanism in late seventeenth-century London (fig. 192). The square area was defined on the north and east sides with buildings of strictly uniform and classical character. On the west side a church linked to two separate houses, and to the south the piazza backed on to the earl's own private garden. The houses, which were completed in 1639, had

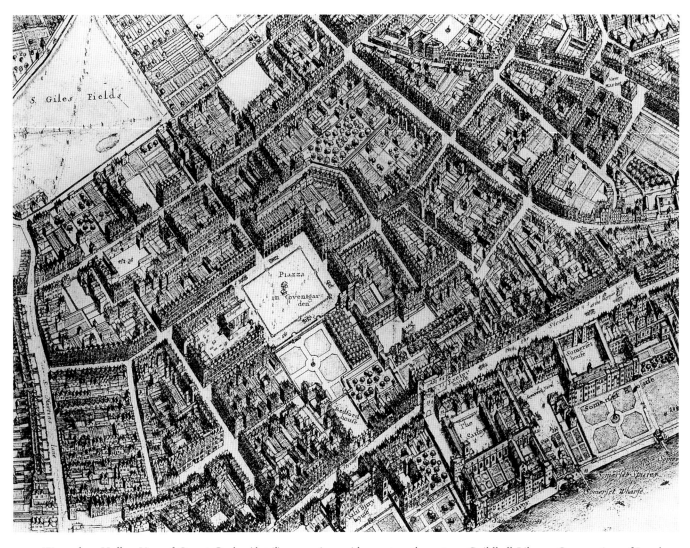

192 Wenceslaus Hollar, *View of Covent Garden* (detail), engraving, mid-seventeenth century. Guildhall Library, Corporation of London.

front doors opening into a vaulted arcade, and gardens with coach houses and stabling at the back. The composition was derived from the Place Royale in Paris (begun in 1605, and now known as the Places des Vosges).[3] Covent Garden's central area and its context square were, however, distinctive. Whilst at the Place Royale the whole of the square was encompassed by buildings, at Covent Garden there were houses on three sides; the southern side remained open. This arrangement undoubtedly satisfied Lord Bedford, who would otherwise have been deprived of his garden and his privacy, and must also have pleased the residents of the square, who gained a prospect into the earl's extensive pleasure ground.[4] Moreover, while the centre of the open square at Place Royale was adorned with an heroic equestrian statue of Louis XIII,[5] there stood at the hub of Covent Garden piazza a 'Mount': a small tree perched upon a square elevated pedestal, fitted round with modest wooden benches (fig. 193).[6]

The second precedent for the garden square was established with the regular enclosure of waste common fields, and in particular Leicester Fields and Lincoln's Inn Fields. These were enclosed common fields within or adjacent to the city, where parishioners enjoyed rights-of-way and the use of the open space for drying clothes or pasturing cattle. From the beginning of the seventeenth century onwards, both Lincoln's Inn and Leicester Fields were threatened by speculative builders and their proposed encroachments. Most attempts at expropriating common fields met strong organised community opposition: the middle classes objected to such encroachments because the amenity provided by open

193   Jan Siberechts, *Covent Garden* (detail), oil on canvas, c.1650. The Earl of Pembroke.

fields was often their only recourse for active recreation; and the upper middle classes, on the other hand, contended that development threatened to destroy their views out to the distant countryside. Until the mid-seventeenth century, the Crown and commoners resisted approaches by some landowners – notably Lords Bedford, Southampton and Leicester, and the Inns of Court – to build over open fields; some of the fields in question enjoyed common rights, and were lands over which the Crown exercised eminent domain and/or freehold possession. The Crown did, however, eventually agree to sell building licences to large estate developers who promised to provide open space for recreation and grazing to commoners and wayfarers.

An early precedent for the preservation of common fields was set in 1607 by the improvement of Moor Fields (land to the north of the city outside Moorgate). Much to the contentment of the inhabitants of Moorgate and the adjoining parishes, the fields were drained and laid out in walks, with the result that the once marshy and insalubrious area was transformed into an agreeable place for public recreation.[7] This example was not lost on those who were opposed to the development of the open land at the centre of the fields.

In the wake of Charles Corwallis's unsuccessful application of 1613 for a licence to build in Lincoln's Inn Fields (comprised of Purse-field, Cupp-field and Fickett's-field) a second petition was presented to James I in 1617 from the gentlemen of the Inns of Court and Chancery and the four parishes adjoining the Fields. The petitioners requested 'that the feildes commonly called Lincolnes Inn Feildes, being parcell of His Ma[ties] inheritance, might for their generall Commoditie and health be converted into walkes after the same manner as Morefeildes are now made to the greate pleasure and benefite of that Citty'.[8]

The king, who endorsed the 'special benefits and ornamental value' of Moorgate Fields, was eager to encourage a similar initiative at Lincoln's Inn Fields. Accordingly, the Privy Council circulated a letter to the Lord Mayor, the city aldermen, the Justices of the Peace for Middlesex and the members of Gray's Inn, Lincoln's Inn, Middle Temple and Inner Temple, urging them to solicit subscriptions to meet the cost of 'so worthie and commendable a work'. In 1618 a Commission on Buildings was established (and reformed and enlarged in 1620), which included the names of the Earl of Pembroke, the Earl of Arundel and, among numerous others, that of the Surveyor, who was the Commission's executive officer.

The purpose of the Commission was to ensure that the fields were set out into 'faire and goodlye walkes, would be a matter of greate ornament to the Citie, pleasure and freshnes[s] for the health and recreation of the Inhabitantes thereabout, and for the sight and delight of Embassadors and Strangers coming to our Court and Cittie, and a memorable worke of our tyme to all posteritie'.[9] The Patent Roll specified that this entailed clearing the fields of encroachments and rubbish so that they could be 'framed and reduced both for sweetnes, uniformitie and comlines into such walkes, partitions or other plottes and in such sorte, manner and forme both for publique health and pleasure'.[10] The design for the planting was undoubtedly in part derived from the fashionable lower walks of Gray's Inn, which in 1621 were embowered by long shady avenues of elm, and were alleged to be 'the pleasantest place about London'.[11]

The Commission was empowered to lay out only the grounds that now constitute the open space of Lincoln's Inn Fields. They could not exercise any authority or influence over development around the periphery of the enclosure. Consequently the inner area of the fields was protected but the environs were not. William Newton of Bedfordshire was therefore able to petition Charles I in 1636 for a licence to build fourteen large houses (each with a forty-foot frontage) in Purse-field – which he was immediately granted. In 1638 he obtained yet another licence, to build thirty-two houses on the west side of the Fields – most of which were complete by 1641. Newton envisaged a bold, symmetrical, classical composition for his scheme, based on the plan of Covent Garden.

194   G. Bower, design for a silver medallion, showing west side of Lincoln's Inn Fields, pen and watercolour wash. Pepsyan Library, Magdalene College, Cambridge.

By 1659 the Fields were enclosed on three sides by buildings – most of which had been built illegally during the turmoil of the Civil War. The fourth side (east) was bounded by the garden wall of Lincoln's Inn and the palisade of Lesser Lincoln's Inn Field (Fickett's-field). The central area was 'levelled plained and cast into grass plots and gravell walks of convenient breadth, railed all along on each side, and set with rows of trees'.[12] A painted view of about 1683 shows the enclosed field set to turf and dissected by transverse and diagonal paths, and Bower's design for a medallion of 1688 depicts the contents of the Portuguese ambassador's chapel being burnt in the centre of the square (fig. 194).

In the neighbouring parish of St Martin-in-the-Fields, Leicester Fields experienced similar improvements. Formerly the common fields of St Martin, Leicester Fields were first partially enclosed in 1616 by the Military Company for an exercise yard. In 1630 Lord Leicester negotiated the lease of the Fields, where he planned to build his own private house. He pledged at the same time to improve the remainder of his leasehold 'into Walkes and planted with trees along the walkes, and fitt spaces left for the Inhabitantes to drye their Clothes there as they were wont, and to have free use of the place, but not to despasture it, and all the

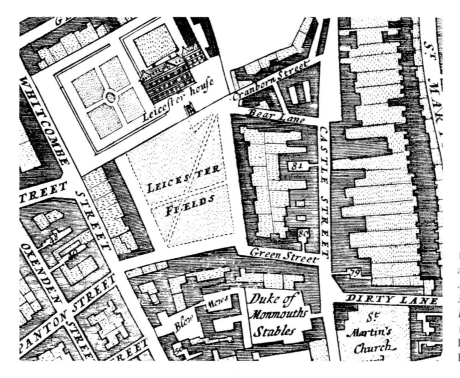

foote wayes through that Close to bee used as now they are'.[13] By 1670 the earl had begun to develop houses around the periphery of the fields, and through an agreement entered with ten speculators he contracted to have the centre portion of the fields enclosed and planted with 'younge trees of Elm'.[14]

The central areas of Leicester Fields and Lincoln's Inn Fields were not converted from turf to gardens until the early eighteenth century: Lincoln's Inn Fields was enclosed and planted by 1700, and Leicester Fields remained unfinished and unplanted – with the exception of its several trees – until it was enclosed with 'pallisadoes and fence', and planted in about 1720–25 (fig. 195).[15] Covent Garden, however, remained obdurately paved. The central area of Covent Garden had by 1654 suffered the first incursions of mercantile premises in the 'portico walks'. The square rapidly became a resort of popular concourse, and was by 1667 afflicted with 'great ffylth' caused by the volume of business transacted on the south side of the piazza. The 'roote of the old tree in the broad place' was dug up in 1666/7 and was replaced in 1668/9 by a stone sundial column; in 1670 the market was legally established by the authority on the royal prerogative.[16]

Soho Square – also known from the early eighteenth century as King Square, was possibly the earliest London square to be built around a purposely laid out and enclosed garden (fig. 196).[17] The site of the square

formed part of Kemp's Field, or Soho Fields, which were leased in April 1677 by Joseph Girle of St Marylebone to Richard Frith, citizen and bricklayer. The plan of the square and the surrounding streets in Soho Fields was probably contrived by Frith, who with his asso-

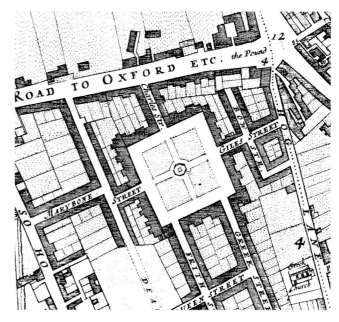

197   Sutton Nicholls, *Sohoe or Kings Square*, engraving, *c.*1750. British Museum, London.

ciate William Pym had engrossed their first lease in 1679/80.[18] In any event, Frith and Pym were granting house leases in 1680/81 which contained clauses charging lessees garden rents of ten shillings per annum 'towards the makeing and keeping in repaire the Rayles, Payles, Fountaine and Garden in the middle of the said Square'.[19] We can presume with certainty that lime trees were planted in the garden, since Fairchild reported in 1722 that 'all the Squares in London which are already made, are proof that the Lime-Tree will bear the *London Smoke*'; he also added that 'Syringe [*Philadelphus*] grew very well in *Soho-Square*'.[20] The statue at the centre of the square was carved by Caius Gabriel Cibber in 1681, and placed there soon afterwards. According to Strype the garden was in 1720 'a very large and open Place, enclosed with a high Pallisado Pale, the Square within being neatly kept, with Walks and Grass-plots, and in the

Midst is the Effigies of King Charles the Second, neatly cut in Stone, to the Life, standing on a Pedestal' (fig. 197).[21]

'THE ADORNING OF SQUARES IN THE RURAL MANNER'

Shortly after the pleasure ground was laid out in Soho Square in 1680/81, the developers of Golden Square proceeded to establish their own garden. Sir Christopher Wren's 'modell' or plan of 1673, which formed part of the royal licence to build Gelding Close (later Golden Square) did not provide for a central garden enclosure. A lease assignment of 1684 indicates that a householder was obliged 'to pay his share towards railing in the said Quadrangle . . . when thereunto requested'.[22] The rails

GOLDEN SQUARE

Published according to Act of Parliament 1754, for Stowe's Survey.

Sutton Nicholls delin: et sculp:

25

198   Sutton Nicholls, *Golden Square*, engraving, 1754. British Museum, London.

and posts were specified to be made of good oak 'as large as the rail of the Quadrangle in Leicester feilds'. A similar covenant was engrossed the following year, where a lessee bound himself 'to pay the rates and proportions with others interested in any other building fronting the place, for all charges in posts, rayls and other ornaments or materials fixed, or employed . . . for dividing, distinguishing and adorning the same'.[23] The garden may have been completed by 1688, when one Mathew Capell in number 25 paid one pound 'towards Gravelling the Square'.[24] The original layout of the square is reproduced in an engraved view of about 1727 and shows the middle area dissected by gravel paths and cast into five grass plots. Four large rectangular plots, bounded by hedges and interspersed with small trees, encompassed a small turfed area at the centre of the square. The layout and planting of the garden and its

perimeter wooden palisade were identical to Leicester Fields (fig. 198).

This 'plain way of laying out Squares in Grass Platts and Gravel Walks', remarked Fairchild in 1722, did not 'sufficiently give our Thoughts an Opportunity of Country Amusements'. He continued: 'I think some sort of Wilderness-Work will do much better, and divert the Gentry better than looking out of their Windows upon an open Figure'.[25] St James's Park was 'as much oppres'd with the *London* Smoke, as almost any of our great Squares; yet the wild Fowl, such as Ducks and Geese, are conformable to it, and breed there; and there is an agreeable Beauty in the Whole, which is wanting in many Country Places'. Citing the example of St James's Park, and the various royal and private gardens near the park, Fairchild asked 'why may we not in many Places, that are airy in the Body of *London*, make such Gardens

SOUTHAMPTON OR BLOOMSBURY SQUARE

Great Russell Street

Published according to Act of Parliament 1754 for Stowes Survey

18

200   Detail from fig. 199a.

as may be dress'd in a Country manner? There is St *James's* Square, *Lincoln's Inn* Fields, and *Bloomsbury* Square, besides others which might be brought into delightful Gardens' (figs 199a and b).[26]

In order to redress this deficiency, Fairchild dedicated a substantial section of *The City Gardener* to the layout of the centres of London squares in 'the Rural Manner'. His first chapter was entitled 'Of Squares, and large open Places in London and Westminster: The Plants Proper to adorn them', and charted a course for the improvement

of the city's squares. He outlined in five steps how to improve the quality of the areas by listing the useful functions that they might fulfil:

> In the *first* place; If a Square was planted in the Manner of a Wilderness, it would be a Harbour for Birds. *2dly*, The Variety of Trees would be delightful to the Eye. *3dly*, Groves and Wildernesses would be new and pleasant in a *London* Prospect. *4thly*, The Walks, tho' regular as the Walks in the common Squares, would be more shady and more private, and the Hedges and the Groves of Trees in every Quarter would hide the Prospect of the Houses from us; every House would command a Prospect of the Whole, as well as it was lay'd out in plain Grass Platts and Walks. And *5thly* Every Fountain made in such Places, would have double the Beauty it would have in plain Squares, as is now the Fashion; and notwithstanding what may be objected to Fountains in this Wilderness-Work, that a Fountain cannot be discover'd in the Prospect of every House ; I say, that it may be done with Ease, to make it appear or shew it self as well to one House as another, as my Draught will show.[27]

As a 'small Example of what may be done', Fairchild supplied a 'Draught' plan which 'may be varied by those who make or fit up such Squares', and proceeded to list plants which he professed would make the garden 'look well in the Winter, and that Part of the Spring, when Persons of Distinction are in Town' (fig. 201).[28]

201   Plan of a garden square, engraving from Thomas Fairchild, *The City Gardener* (1722). The London Library.

199a (*facing page top*)   Sutton Nicholls, *Southampton or Bloomsbury Square*, engraving with watercolour, 1754. Paul Mellon Collection, Yale Center for British Art, New Haven. The garden square was planned as the centre of what John Evelyn described as 'a Little Towne'.

199b (*facing page bottom*)   British School, *Bloomsbury Square*, oil on canvas, eighteenth century. The National Trust, London, This view of Bloomsbury Square *c.*1787 shows the bleak garden of the central enclosure before it was recast by the 6th Duke of Bedford in *c.*1807. James Ralph remarked in 1734 that the square was 'remarkable for nothing but its being a place capable of great improvements: there is not a tolerable house in it, and the area in the middle is almost as much neglected as the buildings'.

202   John Alston, 'The Garden Ovall [plan of Grosvenor Square]', pen and watercolour wash, 1725/6. Grosvenor Estate, London.

203 Thomas Bowles, *A View of Grosvenor Square, London*, engraving, 1751. British Museum, London.

the Equestrian statue of King George I, finely gilt; which together with the noble Houses that are building, and those already finished, makes this the most magnificent Square in the whole Town' (fig. 203).[46]

Other commentators were less enthusiastic. James Ralph remarked in 1734 that 'as to the area in the midst; tis certainly laid out in a very expensive taste, and hitherto kept with great decency and neatness: the making it circular is new in design, and happy in effect: the statue in the centre makes a very good appearance in prospect, and is a fine decoration: but, in itself, is no way admirable, or deserving applause.[47]

Contemporary critics do not report that the 'Wilderness worke' was perhaps a greater achievement than the surrounding houses: while attempts to give the square architectural uniformity had been ineffectual, the proposed formality and regularity prevailed in the central garden.[48] Doubtless the total effect of the area was pleasing in its moderate architectural variety, but the chief impression of the square must have been its spaciousness, which derived from the lowness of the buildings in relation to the expansive formal garden they surrounded.

ST JAMES'S SQUARE: A MODEL IMPROVEMENT ACT

The 'plain way of laying out Squares in Grass Platts and Gravel Walks' prevailed for practical reasons: an 'open Figure' contained within a securely enclosed and defensible enclosure was easy to guard and inexpensive to maintain. London's squares depended upon exclusion of undesirables for their sustained respectability.

In March 1661 Henry Jermyn, 1st Earl of St Albans, obtained half of the freehold of forty-five acres of pasture known as St James's Fields in the Bailiwick of St James's.[49] By November 1662 the area, which since the early seventeenth century had been used for grazing and recreation, was being cast into streets and building plots to create a fashionable Court suburb centred upon a great residential square. Although St Albans intended the square – known at the time as Place Royale – to contain not more than twelve or thirteen 'great and good houses, fitt for ye dwellings of Noble men and other Persons of Quality', by 1680 twenty-three 'stately uniform Piles' had been erected on the east, north and west sides of the square.[50] The south side, backing on Pall Mall, was less uniformly developed and presented an irregular building line to the square.

The somewhat inward-looking plan on which the area was laid gave an orderly, dignified and convenient pattern for a fashionable but not wholly exclusive residential neighbourhood. Three centrally entrant streets converged on the square; the Church of St James's (completed c.1680) lay to the north in Piccadilly, and the market to the east. The 'Great Square Place' (what is now the garden) was, however, until 1727 a large featureless expanse possessing a single carriage-builder's shed, and a few 'trees', probably planted by individual residents before their houses (fig. 204a).[51] The simplicity of the area was doubtless at first effective, and did much to contribute to the regularity and the surrounding buildings, but by 1726 it was observed that it 'hath lain, and does lie, in a filthy condition and as a common Dung hill', littered with ashes, rubbish, offal and the occasional dead cat and dog.[52]

Dissatisfaction with the condition of the square led residents to petition Parliament in 1725/6 for leave to present a bill for better maintenance of the square. The Act received royal assent on 26 April, making it the first legislation of its kind for the maintenance of a London Square.[53] The Act empowered the residents, who were said to be 'desirous to clean repair adorn and beautify the same, in a becoming and graceful Manner', and who were observed to be in general both occupiers and owners of their houses, to levy a rate on themselves (at ten shillings per foot frontage) for this purpose. The Act neither vested them in the soil of the square, nor did it sanction the exclusion of all non-residents from the central area.

As residents of the square were entitled to exercise control over the use, function and design of their square, they developed a loyal desire to maintain and enhance their private and shared amenities. In the summer of 1726 the Trustees, who had been considering 'the best method of beautifying the Square', engaged one Thomas Ackres to make a general survey in order to determine whether 'the sd Square shall be inclosed, or open by levelling or paving'.[54] The following July the Trustees agreed to create a 'bason' in the centre of the square – to be 'sunk to the level of ye Pavement', 150 feet in

diameter and four feet deep – and to be enclosed by a five-foot-high iron railing 'to be joyned to 8 stone Obelisks to carry lamps'.[55] The reservoir was ornamental and functional (for fire-fighting).[56]

The layout and construction of the square was entrusted to the 'landskip gardener' Charles Bridgeman, who was paid £5,630 for the work.[57] The refurbishment was completed in 1728, and the area was subsequently described as 'finely paved all over with Heading Stone, and has a large, beautiful oval [round] basin of water, surrounded with a broad Gravel Walk, and Iron Rails, on a Dwarf-wall, forming an Octagon, and at each Angle are Stone Pillars, decorated with Lamps'.[58] Outside the railings the square was paved in Purbeck stone – 'Square Cubick Stones, commonly called French Paving' (fig. 204b).[59] In the centre of the basin a fountain played daily.[60] Two night and two day watchmen, or constables, were appointed by the Trustees and provided with two moveable watchhouses. The constables were charged with policing the square and enforcing the statutes, which entailed preventing encroachments and the dumping of rubbish, and keeping disorderly people out of the square.[61]

The new square layout won instant and universal approbation, and was celebrated in panegyrics which exalted the grandeur of the area, which was to a large measure due to 'the neatness of the pavement and the beauty of the bason'.[62] The plaudits also precipitated a spate of square improvements, as one by one resident groups of city squares petitioned for, and were granted their own Acts: Lincoln's Inn Fields (1734), Red Lion Square (1736), Charterhouse Square (1742), Golden Square (1750), Berkeley Square (1766) and Grosvenor Square (1774). The St James's Act also created the city's first square to be planned from the outset, and to have at its centre an exclusive private garden.[63]

Although the nature and extent of the city's dozens of squares varied as much as the layout of their respective central areas, it was generally agreed from the second quarter of the eighteenth century onwards that they were all distinct from apparently similar public resorts where citizens took delight in 'the Walking Exercise'. The principal difference was that whilst the large and pleasant walks in the gardens of the Charterhouse, Drapers' Hall, Moorfields, the several Inns of Court, Somerset House, St James's Park and the Temple were generally open 'to every person above inferior rank', and the fine walks and shady groves of the Royal Gardens of Kensington open 'only for persons of Distinction', the gardens of the city's best squares were almost all

204a   Sutton Nicholls, *St James's Square*, engraving, *c*.1750. British Museum, London.

204b   Sutton Nicholls, *St James's Square*, engraving, n.d. British Museum, London.

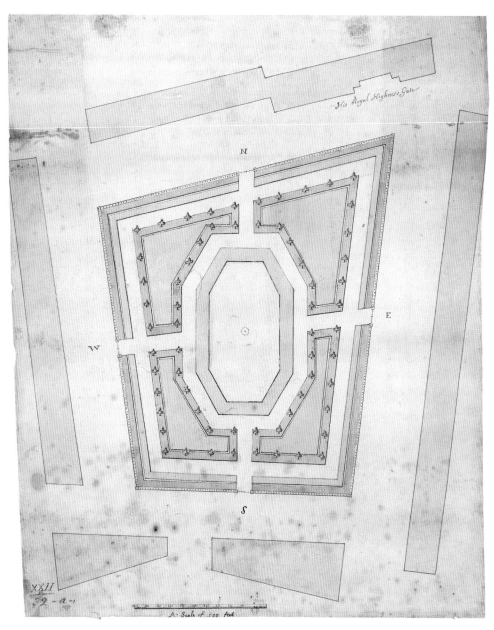

His Royal Highness Gate

N

W

E

S

XXII

A Scale of 500 feet

205   Sutton Nicholls, plan of Leicester Fields, pen and pencil with watercolour wash, 1737.
British Library, London.

private. They had controlled access and were open to key-holding residents of the respective squares.[64]

From around 1725 onwards, squares were consistently registered as the most fashionable urban precincts, their residences and inhabitants distinguished by a social pre-eminence. These people profited from the obvious exclusivity of their garden sanctuary, and also often benefited from the privacy of their own back gardens. Only marginally less fashionable were streets, rows and places which adjoined the large 'garden enclosures'.

IMPROVED GARDEN LAYOUTS

The force of the various Acts to 'inclose, pave, repair, enlighten, adorn and beautify' squares was often sufficient to effect momentous changes to their physical layout and appearance. Central areas which were enclosed were in almost every instance levelled and zealously overhauled, in order to reaffirm the respectability and exclusivity which were implicit in post-Act square improvements.

206   Sutton Nicholls, *Leicester Square*, engraving, *c*.1748. British Museum, London.

207   Thomas Bowles, *A View of Leicester Square, London*, engraving, 1753. British Museum, London.

When the inhabitants and proprietors of the houses in Lincoln's Inn Fields were in receipt of their Act of 1734, which enabled them to 'make a Rate on themselves for raising money sufficient to inclose, clean and adorn the said Fields', they resolved to advertise for tenders to carry out their redesign. The central area, which had been described in 1710 by Zacharias Conrad von Uffenbach as boasting 'handsome, tree-bordered walks and a fountain', was in 1734 believed to be 'capable of the highest improvement . . . no place could be more contemptible or forbidding; in short, it serves only as a nursery for beggars and thieves, and is a daily reflection on those who suffer it to lie in its abandon'd condition'.[65] In the same year it was reported that

> great mischiefs have happened to many of his Majesty's subjects going about their lawful occasions, several of whom have been killed, and others maimed and hurt by horses, which have been from time to time aired in the said fields; and by reason of the said fields being kept open, and many wicked and disorderly persons have frequented and met together therein; using unlawful sports and games, and drawing in and enticing young persons into gaming, idleness, and other vicious courses; and vagabonds, common beggars, and other disorderly persons resort therein, where many robberies, assaults, outrages and enormities have been, and continually are committed, notwithstanding the watch or guard allowed by the several parishes . . . for preventing the same.[66]

Sometime shortly after June 1735 the fields were laid out with grass and gravel walks, enclosed with an iron palisade upon a stone plinth and 'ornamented in the Middle with a fine Bason of Water'.[67]

On 16 April 1737 it was announced in *The Country Journal: or The Craftsman* that Leicester Fields – and 'the inclosure in the middle, which alone affords the inhabitants round about it, something like the prospect of a garden' – was going to be 'fitted up in a very elegant Manner . . . after the Manner of Lincoln's Inn Fields' (fig. 206).[68] The improvements were to be paid for by voluntary subscriptions from the inhabitants. According to the plan drawn up for the residents a new parapet and railing were to be erected, and the ground was to be cast into regular grass plots around an octagonal basin (to 'contain 700 Tons of Water'); and 'in the middle of the bason there will be a pillar with a shell or bowl to bring the water into the Reservoir and contrived in that manner that whenever it is required it may throw up a jet d'eau 4–5 ft. above the bason, the jet to rise 20 foot

or more' (fig. 205).[69] A view by John Bowles shows that while most of the garden proposal was executed, the basin and the fountain were not. A statue of George I 'on horseback in Armour', with 'Trophies of Warr' on the panels of the pedestal was erected at the centre of the garden in 1748 (fig. 207).[70]

When Golden Square received its private square Act in 1750, its formal garden layout, created in the late seventeenth century and incorporating a leafy grove of semi-mature trees, was swept away in favour of a new design. An engraved view of 1754 portrayed the 'inside' of the 'small but neat' octagonal square. The garden was described in 1768 as 'adorned with Grass Plots and Gravel Walks', surrounded by a 'handsome Iron' railing (which replaced the former 'wooden Rails') and possessing a statue of King James at its centre.[71]

Soho Square experienced a similar cleansing in 1748/9. Ralph commented in 1734 that the square possessed a 'little, contemptible garden in the middle of the area, and worse still a statue, if it be possible, in the middle of that. The place . . . indeed, is not so intirely neglected, as many others of the same sort about Town . . .' (fig. 208).[72] After a meeting in May 1748 of the inhabitants and the landlord, the 2nd Duke of Portland, Robert Hardcastle, mason, submitted a plan of proposed improvements and alterations. This involved reconfiguring the shape of the garden enclosure to an octagon, the erection of an iron railing and gates in place of the old wooden palisade, and the fixture of lamp-irons at the corner angles. In the following months the plan was revised by Benjamin Wood, carpenter. The new design retained the existing shape of the enclosure and provided for new railings and gates with eight lamp-posts, one at each of the four corners, and one to be supported by 'a strong handsome and convenient Scroll of Iron Work', over each of the gates.[73] The erection of the new wall and railings was complete by January 1748/9, and in February a contract was entered with Humphrey Terry for the improvement of the garden at a cost of £52 10s. By August 1749 the existing beds of flowers and dwarf trees were uprooted (except for the limes, which were allowed to survive), and the paths were levelled and gravelled. The grass plots were re-sown with Dutch clover and grass seed in the following season. The stone statue of King Charles II, the fountain and the four stone pedestals remained unmoved and unchanged.[74] Two nearly contemporary views show distinct phases of the garden refurbishment: Thomas Robins's aerial view of about 1750 gained from a vantage point in Monmouth House on the south side

208 Sutton Nicholls, *Kings Square in Soho*, engraving, 1754. British Museum, London.

210 Sutton Nicholls, *Kings Square in Soho*, c.1760. British Museum, London.

209 Thomas Robins, *View of Soho Square from the South*, pen and pencil c.1750. British Architectural Library, Royal Institute of British Architects, London.

of the square, portrays the old fencing, and the new simplified circular basin (fig. 209), and Sutton Nicholls's bird's-eye view of about 1760 shows the scheme as it was completed. The redesign did not appear to have elicited much favourable criticism. It was reported that the 'area in the centre' was 'too small, and the avenues to the east and west . . . [were] . . . very indifferent' (fig. 210).[75]

'COOP'D-UP BRICK-WALLS' AND SECURE ENCLOSURE[76]

The unmistakable urban quality of the garden of the mid-eighteenth century London square is affirmed in a novel of the period: Samuel Richardson's *Sir Charles*

Grandison (1754). Reeves's account of Grosvenor Square assumes that reader must be aware of the discrepancies between the garden of the square itself, as an evocation of *rus in urbe*, and the authentic rurality of the countryside outside town. This assumption is endorsed, moreover, by a more general sense of the impossibility of the dream of the urban pastoral; the knowledge that the cosy orderliness of a London square could never be mistaken for the rural or semi-rural terrain which lay dangerously beyond the boundaries of the city imprints itself on the dialogue between the heroine and her abductor in a grimly ironic manner.

Miss Harriet Byron is intercepted by the agents of her villanous ravisher Sir Charles Pollexfen as she attempts to make her way to Grosvenor Street after a masquerade in town. She soon finds herself captive in a sedan chair, and is spirited off to the countryside. The young lady only realises her plight after some time, when she draws aside the side curtain of her carriage, and sees that she is 'in the midst of fields'. She is, in fact, in Lisson Green. After screaming for succour, she composed herself sufficiently to beg to be carried home:

> She asked for Grosvenor Street. She was to be carried, she said to Grosvenor Street.
>
> She was just there, that fellow [the chairman] said. – it can't be, sir! It can't be! – Don't I see fields all about me? – I am in the midst of fields, sir.
>
> Grosvenor-square, madam, replied the villain; the trees and garden of Grosvenor-square.[77]

As the reader is all too poignantly aware, poor Harriet could hardly have been deceived. There could clearly have been no mistaking the open and bucolic surroundings of suburban Lisson Green for the formal garden of Grosvenor Square.

Far from being open and spacious, Grosvenor Square was in fact densely planted and enclosed by garden walls. Contemporary writers were critical of the garden's high 'fence-wall', which prevented the residents from having a view into it, thereby substantially impeding the full enjoyment of the pleasure ground. Ralph remarked in 1734 that 'the inclosure round the area is clumsey, the brick-work not only superfluous, but a blemish to the view it was intended to preserve and adorn'.[78] John Stewart registered similar grievances in 1771:

Grosvenor square, which is generally held out as a pattern of perfection in its kind ... is doubtless spacious, regular and well-built; but how is the spaciousness occupied? A clumsy rail, with lumps of bricks for piers, to support it, at the distance of every two or three yards, incloses nearly the whole area, intercepting almost entirely the view of the sides, and leaving the passage round it as narrow as most streets with the additional disadvantage at night of being totally dark on one hand. The middle is filled up with bushes and dwarf trees, through which a statue peeps, like a piece of gilt gingerbread in a green-grocer's stall.[79]

Only from the 1780s onwards, when more invisible forms of fencing were in place around the city's squares, were views into the gardens no longer encumbered by inelegant, solid and ineffectual barriers.[80] The replacement of 'wooden palisadoes' by metal railings in many instances brought about further rounds of improvements to the gardens which reflected the residents' confidence in their ability to protect their gardens from 'loose or disorderly' characters. The new form of fencing also did much to open the scenery of 'shrubbery-walks and grass-plats', which 'afforded very seasonable relief, the eye being wearied of the sameness of colossal piles of bricks and mortar'.[81] We have already seen that the gardens of Soho and Golden Square were reformed when their iron railings were erected in 1748 and 1768 respectively.

The residents of Grosvenor Square procured a private Act in 1774, which authorised them to 'inclose the said Garden in a more substantial Manner, and to alter and embellish the same'.[82] Changes to the garden were made contemporaneously to renovations of the houses in the square.

The plan for the garden refurbishment is attributed to the architect George Richardson (fig. 211).[83]

211 George Richardson, design drawing for the garden of Grosvenor Square, pencil and watercolour wash, 1774. Kedleston Archives.

Richardson reduced Alston's wilderness work to four quarterings arranged around a central raised grass platform crowned with a statue. Each quartering was appointed with eight oval shrub clumps of variable size arranged symmetrically on the longitudinal axis of the garden square.[84] The layout was evidently striking: it prompted the German clergyman Carl Philip Moritz to remark in 1782 that 'in Grosvenor square, instead of the green plot, or area, there is a little circular wood, intended, no doubt, to give one the idea of *rus in urbe*'.[85]

In the summer of 1785 Abigail Adams, wife of the American ambassador, described the garden in two accounts: the first was written soon after she took up residence in the square, and conveys a sense of the wonder typical of the response of newcomers to the metropolis:

My Habitation here is in one of the pleasentest squares of London. We are in the same Row if not in the same Box of most of the great people in the Country . . . In the middle of the square which is very spacious is a circuleer inclosure in which clumps of trees are planted which look like shrubbery as the trees are small and close together. Round them is the hedge which when cut has a very rural appearance. In the middle is the King on horse back. The whole is laid out into walks and those who live in the square have a key to one of the gates which you may make use of for to walk.[86]

Her second letter, written roughly a month later, was less impressionistic and more descriptive:

we are agreeably situated here in a fine open square, in the middle of which is a circle inclosed by a neat [iron] grated fence; around which are lighted every night about sixty Lamps. The border next the fence is in grass, the circle is divided into five grass plots. One in the mid[d]le is a square upon which is a statue of G[e]orge 2d. on horse back. Between each of the plots are gravel walks and the plots are fill[e]d with clumps of low trees thick together which is call[e]d Shrubbery, and these are surrounded with a low Hedge, all together a pretty effect.[87]

The erection of the railings at Grosvenor Square shortly after 1774 may have been in part encouraged by the prevalence of crimes of violence which were often reported as taking place in 'Hanover, Cavendish, Bloomsbury and other Squares'.[88] In 1767 a notice in the *Gazette and New Daily Advertiser* advised that 'as robberies often happen in the Squares of this metropolis, and the inhabitants of Squares are generally persons of distinction and property, they should concur to appoint and pay four extraordinary watchmen, that one may be placed at each corner of a square with handsome watch-houses, and every watchman well cloathed and armed, as in Germany'.[89] The residents of Grosvenor Square did not, however, appoint a special watch, but relied upon the officers employed by the Vestry to invigilate the square from their watchhouse in Mount Street.

At neighbouring Berkeley Square, on the other hand, the inhabitants found it necessary to enforce stricter measures. In 1756 the Vestry of St George Parish arranged that watchmen of the square and streets entering into it should call the half-hours for two months; and in the following year six night-watchmen were placed about the square calling at regular intervals. By 1766 the residents despaired of their precautions of increased surveillance, and intermittent repairs to the fence-wall around the central area and petitioned for, and were granted, a private Act to enclose and 'adorn' the square.[90]

The refurbishment of the square began in May 1766:

By order of the nobility and gentry in Berkeley-square, the workmen are to begin on Monday next, according to a plan ap[p]roved at Gwynn's tavern in Berkeley-square. There is to be a grass-plat in the middle, a gravel walk round, and iron palisadoes; but there is no statue or bason in the middle. The undertaker of the work has engaged to finish it completely for £7000.[91]

It was subsequently reported in July of the same year that:

The workmen have begun to inclose the interior part of Berkeley-square with a brick wall; a great part of the foot paving is already finished; it is eight foot in breadth; and from the curb of the foot-paving to the wall now building is forty feet for the coaches and carriages, which is paving with the Aberdeen Granite. The walls of the north and south ends of the square, are formed in the manner of a crescent or semi-circle; and the inclosed part will be laid out and planted after the manner of Grosvenor-square.[92]

The square was still incomplete the following June, when the 'grand plan' for improving the central area was 'entirely laid aside as they could have no bason of water, the square being ten feet lower at the South end than the north'. The new scheme proposed 'finishing [it] with a handsome green walk next the railing, then a terras walk, and the rest laid out in a grass plat'.[93] At the request of the inhabitants three watch-houses were erected around the periphery of the square in 1767, and an equestrian statue of King George III was placed at the centre of the garden in 1772.[94]

Secure enclosure was certainly utmost in the minds of the 'Gentlemen Residents of Fitzroy Square' when on 24 April 1815 they met

to take into consideration the present state of the Square; and particularly of the vacant ground situate on the North and West sides of the Square; part of which is now occupied as a cow yard; another is about to be used as a yard for dust; and the larger space Westward is the play-ground of children of the lowest classes, and is otherwise generally covered with stagnate pools of water, serving to make the air unhealthy.[95]

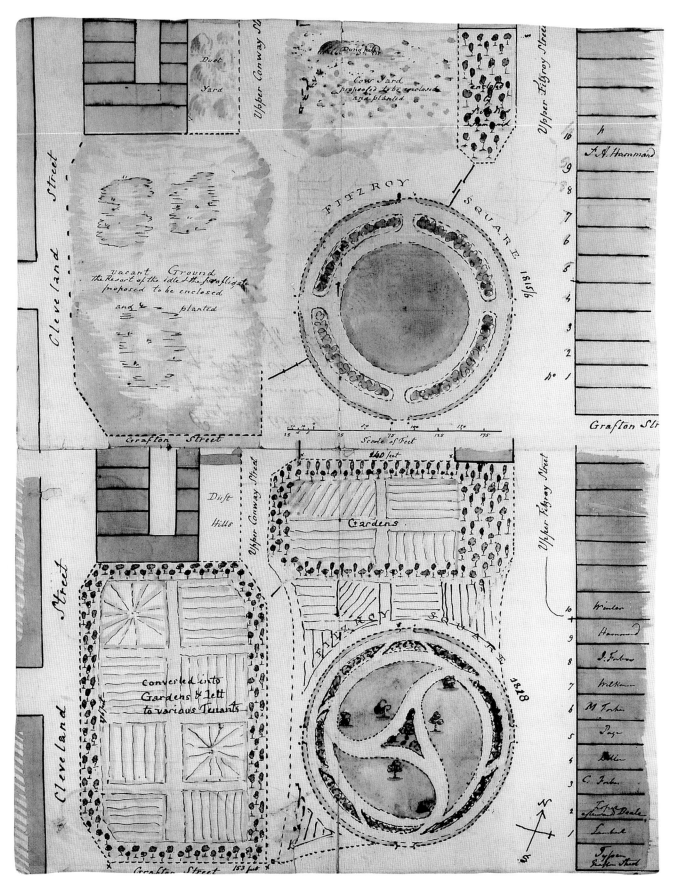

212 Unidentified draughtsman, plans of Fitzroy Square gardens and environs before (1815/16) and after (1818) improvements, pencil, pen and watercolour wash, *c*.1818. Fitzroy Square Frontages.

213 Jean-Claude Nattes, view of the south-east corner of Fitzroy Square gardens, pencil, pen and watercolour wash, c.1808. Guildhall Library, Corporation of London.

Although the square had been formed, and the central garden planted by 1798, two sides of the development remained incomplete. Initially the residents attempted to shut out the nuisances that took place on this vacant ground by erecting fencing and gates, as well as by forming a small plantation northwest of the central garden. When by 1815 these unruly wastes were still undeveloped, they were resolved to lease this 'Resort of the Idle & the Profligate' and to convert it into gardens.[96] That spring Colonel James Drinkwater was commissioned to prepare a plan for the 'alteration' of the central garden, as well as a proposal for the improvement of the vacant ground (figs 212 and 213). The scheme was hastily adopted by the residents, and building work began immediately: in the course of one year the railings and palings were repainted, the paths were recast and resurfaced, and new trees and shrubs were planted.[97] The wastes were let to Thomas Webb, a 'scavenger' of Pancras Street, Bedford Square, who at his own expense drained the ground, enriched the soil and 'formed it into a Garden ornamented with Trees'.[98]

Having improved considerably the physical surroundings, the residents invoked a range of measures that were intended to maintain and enhance the propriety of the square: in 1816 admittance into the square garden was restricted to 'Residents of the Square and their Inmates', and 'all dogs' were excluded; in 1839 smoking was banned in the gardens; and in 1843 the residents voted to 'secure the constant daily attendance of a Steady Man, who, beside working as a Gardener, should be distinguished by a laced Hat, or other distinctive Dress; & being appointed a Constable should have authority to exclude improper Persons & preserve order in and around the Square'.[99]

The design and policing of squares was not only intended to obviate infrequent and unorganised acts of antisocial behaviour, but also attempted to ensure that mass intrusion or disturbance would not take place. Squares, like large open public spaces, were seen as potential sites for large gatherings of 'massive, disruptive, fiercely acute or wickedly capricious, crowds'.[100]

In the turbulent environment of the late eighteenth

214   R. Banks, *The Manner in which the Queen proceeded daily from Lady Francis's House, St James's Square, to the House of Lords*, etching, 1810. Private collection.

century and the early nineteenth century there was among city dwellers a particular fear of riots. While the relatively orderly crowds which assembled at elections, civic events, royal and military celebrations, political meetings and demonstrations were considered destructive and antisocial, they were less threatening than spontaneous inchoate protests which took place in hitherto unpursued processional routes or meeting places. This form of behaviour induced panic because of the implications of a break of routine.

The inhabitants of London's squares had witnessed a range of sporadic disorders. For instance, in 1792 the 'decorative windows' of John Wilkes's house at 35 Grosvenor Square received the attention of the 'Mount Street rioters', and in 1815 an angry crowd opposed to the Corn Law 'proceeded to break the windows and tear up some of the area railings' of Lord Eldon's house in Bedford Square. The ground-floor apartments of the Lord Chancellor's house were destroyed while he and his family fled into the adjoining gardens of the British Museum, where they sought shelter with the soldiers who then guarded the museum. By contrast, however, the huge concourse of people which assembled in St James's Square in the summer of 1820 to observe the daily progress of Queen Caroline to her trial at the House of Lords was orderly (fig. 214).

Perhaps the most memorable public disturbance took place in June 1780, when London was gripped by a calamitous mob, which in the course of a few days burnt down several prisons and damaged over a hundred houses. The riots began as demonstrations in support of the anti-Catholic bigot Lord George Gordon, after whom they are now named, but degenerated into an unwieldy revolt. Over 11,000 militia and 1,000 officers were drafted in to quell the disturbances – most of whom were stationed in the City, St James's and Hyde Parks, and the gardens of the British Museum.[101] The West End, however – with a few notable exceptions – appears to have emerged relatively unscarred. A map drawn up after the riots were over marks in coloured ink the disposition of troops and strategic points within the capital, and goes some way to explaining this anomaly. Foot patrols were stationed in Red Lion, Bloomsbury and Queen's Squares, as well as in Lincoln's Inn Fields; horse patrols encircled the immediate precincts of Cavendish, Portman, Hanover, Leicester,

Soho and Manchester Squares; and the neighbourhoods of St James's, Grosvenor, Berkeley and Golden Squares were surrounded by lines of troops (fig. 215).

It was, of course, difficult to defend squares and their inhabitants from such large-scale and exceptional depredations without invoking emergency measures. It is, however, interesting to observe that, on a day-to-day basis, secure enclosure and costly garden improvements did not ensure the orderliness and respectability of gardens. In some instances the measures which were taken to protect and embellish the gardens were remarked to detract from their beauty. In 1725 Red Lion Square was portrayed by Sutton Nicholls as a hospitable and tidy enclosed garden, cast into four plots edged with

dwarf trees. This view is confirmed by an account of 1740 – four years after the square had received its Act – which described the square as 'one of the smallest in Town, but agreeably planted with Trees'.[102] By 1768 there had been further changes: it was now 'a handsome Area enclosed, which in its Centre is adorned with a lofty Obelisk placed upon a Pedestal'.[103] However, by 1771, Stewart, with characteristic disdain remarked:

Red Lion Square, elegantly so called . . . does not make us laugh; but it makes us cry. I am sure, I never go into it without thinking of my latter end. The rough sod that 'heaves in many a mouldering heap', the dreary length of the sides, with the four watch-

215 Unknown draughtsman, *Disposition of the Troops and Patrols in and adjoining London during the Gordon Riots the beginning of June 1780*, engraving with annotations. Guildhall Library, Corporation of London.

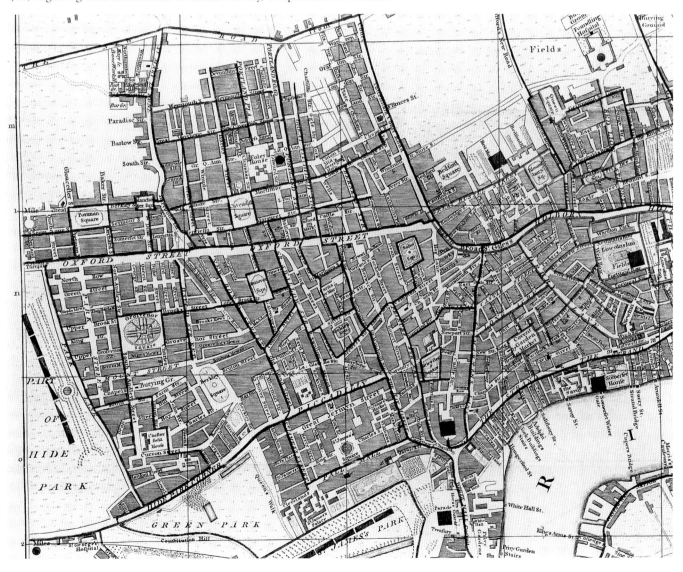

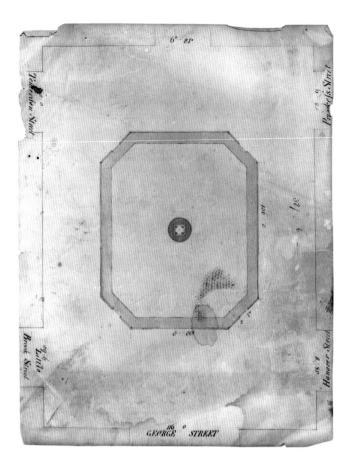

keep" must have first conceived the design'.[120] He asserted, moreover, that this metaphor 'might yet have been improved, by a thought taken from one of the most flagrant perversions of that taste that was ever exhibited to publick view'. He referred to the gardens of the deposed King Stanislaus of Poland, at Luneville ('one of the richest and most delightful countries in Europe, full of real pastoral objects and rustick images'), where the the true qualities of the place were 'degraded' by 'sticking up clock-work mills, wooden cows, and canvas milk-maids, all over his grounds'. This, he pro-

217 Plan of Hanover Square, pen, pencil and watercolour wash, *c*.1751. Dashwood Archives, West Wycombe Park. This plan outlines a proposal for the refurbishment of the square which focussed on the erection of a three-tier monument in the central garden. The fifty-foot structure would have formed a conspicuous eye-catcher in one of London's most celebrated vistas.

218 John Boydell, *A View of St Georges Church, Hanover Square, from Conduit Street, London,* engraving, 1751. British Museum, London. This view shows why in the eighteenth century the 'vis[t]a' down George Street was considered to be 'one of the most interesting in the whole city'. At this time there was a clear view looking north through Cavendish Square garden to the hills of Highgate and Hampstead. The gap on the north side of Cavendish Square was filled in 1771.

A View of S.t Georges Church Hanover Square, from Conduit Street London. Vue de l'Eglise de Saint George dans le Carré de Hanover, près du Coté Rüe Conduit à Londres.

London Printed for In.o Boydell Engraver Cheapside.

219 Edward Dayes, *Queen Square*, pen and pencil with watercolour wash, 1786. Paul Mellon Collection, Yale Center for British Art, New Haven. It was noted in 1802 that, however pleasant the garden of Queen Square might be, it was 'but small compensation for the loss of the beautiful view of Hampstead and Highgate'.

posed, was a 'precious thought' for Cavendish Square: 'imitation here would appear with greater propriety that nature itself. I would therefore recommend it to the next designer of country-in-town to let all his sheep be painted. And I think if a paste-board mill, and a tin cascade, were to be added it would compleat the rural scene'.[121]

The spectacle at Hanover Square (figs 217 and 218) was, to him, no less preposterous. It was:

neither open nor inclosed. Every convenience is railed out, and every nuisance railed in. Carriages have a narrow, ill-paved street to pass round in, and the middle has the air of a cow-yard, where blackguards assemble in the winter, to play at hussle-cap, up to the ancles in dirt. This is the more to be regretted, as the square in question is susceptible of improvement at a small expence. The buildings are neat and

uniform. The street from Oxford road falls with a gentle descent into the middle of the upper side, while, right opposite, George street retires, converging to a point, which has a very picturesque effect; and the portico of St. George's church seen in profile, enriches and beautifies the whole.[122]

Despite his abhorrence for the concept of *rus in urbe*, and gardens in general, Stewart acknowledged the status of the open ground at the centre of the square as an intermediate category; this intermediate status rendered the garden a discomfiting category for the critic, who insisted on the need to establish a sharp distinction between the urban and the rural.

His attack on *rus in urbe* illustrated how the context of many squares had changed since the early eighteenth century, and the extent to which by the early 1770s some squares, conceived upon the grandest lines, were struggling to reconcile the layout and function of their central areas with their new surroundings.

Stewart draws our attention, in particular, to the failure of some early eighteenth-century initiatives which had been trumpeted at the time as the 'amazing scene of new foundations, not of houses only, but as I might say of new cities, new towns, new squares, and fine buildings, the like of which no city, no town, nay, no place in the world, can show'.[123] This report referred to what might be called the 'second wave' of square building in London, and probably included Hanover, Cavendish, Queen (built 1708–20; fig. 219), and Grosvenor Squares. Each of these squares had been contrived to benefit from the obvious affiliation with both town and country, having at least one side which opened into neighbouring fields. This illusion – whether deliberate (Queen Square) or unintentional (Grosvenor Square) – funnelled *rus* into the city.

By the 1770s Hanover and Cavendish Squares were, however, absorbed into the dense urban fabric and their strong visual links with the countryside were substantially diminished.[124] This retreat of the countryside appears to have galvanised what Stewart condemned as 'preposterous' country-in-town scenes, such as the introduction of meadow grass and sheep into the 'butcher's pen' of Cavendish Square.[125] His satirical descriptions of the intrusion of animals into urban settings voiced the assumption that the function of the squares was ill-resolved, and that this form of urban garden was now, in fact, to be seen as quite distinct from the countryside.[126]

This 'fine Enfilade thro' the two squares' was, nevertheless, in other respects a triumph.[127] The ensemble contributed considerably to making the square an element of improved street design from the mid-eighteenth century onwards, and helped usher in the full potential of the application of the square to English urbanism – where the square and its derivative forms – crescents, circuses and polygons – were used to form sequences of planned open spaces.[128] As fine, open, geometrical figures which served as versatile links and pivots in the town plan, squares were no longer solely perceived in isolation, but as elements which, when employed in combination, formed and forged a framework which informally integrated new and existing street patterns and estate developments to create order and spaciousness in the ever-expanding and unstructured mosaic of the city.

In 1766 John Gwynn proposed that new quarters of town should be planned with regular buildings intermingled with open squares, octagons and circuses, which in his own words promoted 'novelty of design, elegance and spaciousness'. He expressed regret that a 'range of squares' had not been built many years earlier to link the West End with neighbouring quarters of town (fig. 220). Had these squares 'been formed, each of the same size with Grosvenor-Square, with streets corresponding from the new road to Piccadilly one way, and other at right angles with them, instead of that heap of absurdity and confusion . . . it would certainly have been more profitable, as well as more elegant and convenient'.[129]

His advice was, however, heeded by the next generation of town planners, such as George Dance Junior. Dance introduced the circus into a plan he proposed for roads in Southwark and Lambeth linking the Thames bridges (1768); and at St George's Circus he created a monumental circus in the form of a crossing, foreshadowing the building of Piccadilly and Oxford Circuses. In the same year he laid out the ensemble of America Square, the Crescent and the Circus, just off the Minories in the City. This was followed in 1769 by the planning of Finsbury Square, and subsequently Alfred Place (off Tottenham Court Road).

Most of these spaces were not in themselves conceived as garden squares, but 'places', or open figures, which recollected – however modestly – the great squares of Rome, Vienna and Paris.[130] Their practical function was to provide open space and air. Nevertheless, to create a figure with an open central area was to establish the infrastructure required for square; and as we have seen, gardens were often developed as elaborations of these spaces which were constantly in a state of flux, responding to changes of use and, more importantly, to changes in context.

LATE GEORGIAN SQUARES

These squares, or quadrangular places, contain the best and most beautiful buildings of London: a spacious street, next to the house, goes all round them, and within that there is generally a grass-plot, fenced in with iron-rails, in the center of which, in many of them, there is a statue, sometimes equestrian and gilt.[131]

What we have now come to know as the garden square – 'an open space, of a square figure (or a figure approximating to the square), houses on each of the four sides, and an enclosed centre, with turf, a few trees, and it may be flowers or a statue' – was, as we have seen, a

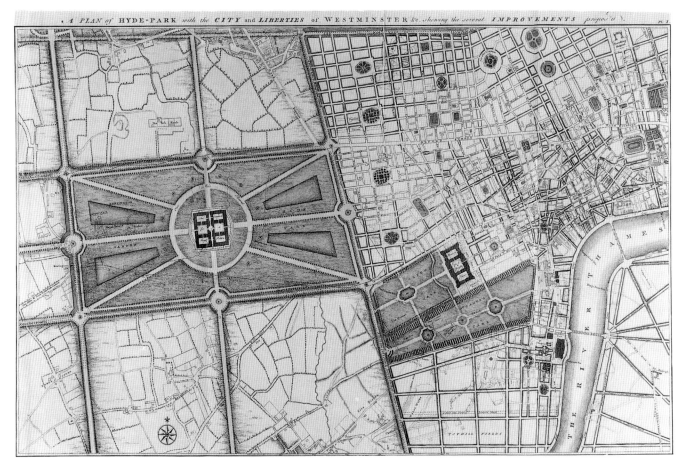

220   Unknown artist, 'A Plan of Hyde-Park with the City and Liberties of Westminster &c showing the several Improvements pro-pos'd', etching from John Gwynn, *London and Westminster Improved, Illustrated by Plans* (1766), plate 1, opp. p. 132. Paul Mellon Collection, Yale Center for British Art, New Haven.

relatively new concept in the eighteenth century.[132] Only towards the end of the eighteenth century do we begin to find their central areas of many of the city's squares described in such terms, and the gardens promoted as desirable elements to residential development for 'inhabitants of the first respectability'. By this time some of extensive planted gardens had begun to thrive in the few squares into which they had been introduced, and were credited as bestowing a degree of picturesqueness upon their settings.

Gardens were generally perceived to be neater, more convenient, more orderly and beautiful as the surroundings beyond the circumference of the garden rails were improved through the introduction of regulated improvements of artificial lighting, paving and watch-patrols, which were enforced both by the trustees of the squares and the parochial authorities. To these criteria of respectability should be added the character of the buildings which surrounded the central area: squares which received the highest commendations were often those which, like Grosvenor Square, were 'surrounded with elegant houses'.[133] Indeed, the character of a square was seldom described without reference to its context.

From the early eighteenth century onwards many critics advocated strict uniformity of building on all sides of a square. Although this objective was seldom achieved, it did not cease to be an important criterion for evaluating the success or failure of a square. For instance, it was remarked in 1783 that although Portman Square was a 'magnificent area' it was 'a pity . . . that the ground landlord did not confine his tenants to build according to a uniform plan! Or if symmetry, magnificence and public order, be objects of no value, why does he not let out the area in the center to every one who has money to build a house, or a dog-kennel?'[134] The impulse to create the impression of four palace fronts, arranged symmetrically upon a large open figure, had a profound effect on the layout of the central garden: the

221   Thomas Malton, 'Grosvenor Square', aquatint and engraving with hand colouring from *Picturesque Tour Through the Cities of West-minster and London* (1800), pl. 91. Paul Mellon Collection, Yale Center for British Art, New Haven. In 1807 the garden of Grosvenor Square was described as having a pleasant distribution of shrubs and trees, which 'have a very picturesque effect in every point of view' to the extent that the 'gilt equestrian effigies of George i. is nearly obumbrated [overshadowed] by the neighbouring foliage, as seen from the sides of the square'.

residents perceived their gardens as large axial flower gardens. In fact, many West End garden layouts from the mid-1770s to the late eighteenth century resembled pleasure grounds of rural landscape gardens – gardens found beneath the windows of country houses: Grosvenor Square, Berkeley Square and Lincoln's Inn Fields had extensive shrubberies, and the gardens of Portman and Leicester Squares were laid out as spacious parterres. These garden layouts served to reinforce the primacy of their surrounding architecture.

Gardens in these squares were kept strictly exclusive to preserve their respectability, grandeur and magnificence. As we have seen, from the early eighteenth century a square's secure and conspicuous enclosure was regarded as essential, as 'it preserves it from the rudeness of the populace'.[135] This exclusivity did not, however,

in the eyes of Gwynn, Stewart or other subsequent improvers, render the gardens less significant in the context of the metropolis. On the contrary, they were considered to be 'public places' in so far as they lay in the public realm, and they contributed to the convenience and propriety of the whole city and its residents.[136] This sentiment became particularly true as the gardens in the centres of squares were able to compete with their immediate and neighbouring built surroundings in terms of the bulk and stature of their planting.

In so far as squares were seen as capable of improving the 'dignity of character' of their surroundings, we should not be surprised to find that towards the end of the eighteenth century the promise of central gardens – and views, or direct access to them – often succeeded in bolstering the image of the newly formed square.

More and more it was acknowledged that 'the verdant foliage and evergreen turf on earth, and the ever-varying features of our rarely cloudless sky, freely revealed by the opening amid a forest of houses, lend a charm to every square; and simple as these elements be, they are susceptible to an infinite multiplicity of *nuances* of character'.[137]

The desirability of most respectable squares encouraged a proliferation of others throughout town. Few, however, as Sir John Soane remarked in 1813, achieved the dignity of the grand essays, such as Grosvenor Square (fig. 221): the majority were debased by insubstantial architecture which resulted in 'monotonous houses forming many of the streets and squares'.[138] It was, nevertheless, a measure of their ubiquity and their success that by the late eighteenth century squares were often discussed in terms of their relationship to one another, and compared in terms of their relative success or failure, and the degree of dignity or disgrace they conferred on their inhabitants and their environs.

William Henry Portman's ensemble of Portman Square and its surrounding streets was among the earliest speculations to have applied the principled town planning so esteemed by Gwynn – where a square with a garden at its centre had a direct link with Grosvenor Square to the south (fig. 222).[139] The square, which had 'some houses which would have done honour to Grosvenor Square', was laid out from 1761 and formed the nucleus of the Portman estate.[140] From 1774 the square was linked to the newly built Manchester Square, which was built upon the same estate some hundred yards to the north-east. Both squares were dignified with a garden soon after they were formed.[141]

Mecklenburgh and Brunswick Squares, as they are now known, were a more coherent, and less episodic, speculative undertaking (fig. 223). The squares originated as the 'principal features of attraction' of a strategic development plan prepared by the architect Samuel Pepys Cockerell for the Foundling Estate in 1790.[142] This initiative, however, failed to eclipse the development

222 Thomas Malton, *View of Portman Square's North Side*, aquatint and engraving with hand colouring, 1813. Guildhall Library, Corporation of London. The gardens of Portman Square were described in 1822 as 'a mere wilderness of foliage, and has a very pleasing effect, not a little improved by the Turkish ambassador, who often enjoyed the air within, surrounded by part of his train'. The ambassador, in fact, kept a moveable kiosk, which was regularly transported around the gardens so as to catch a glimpse of the sun.

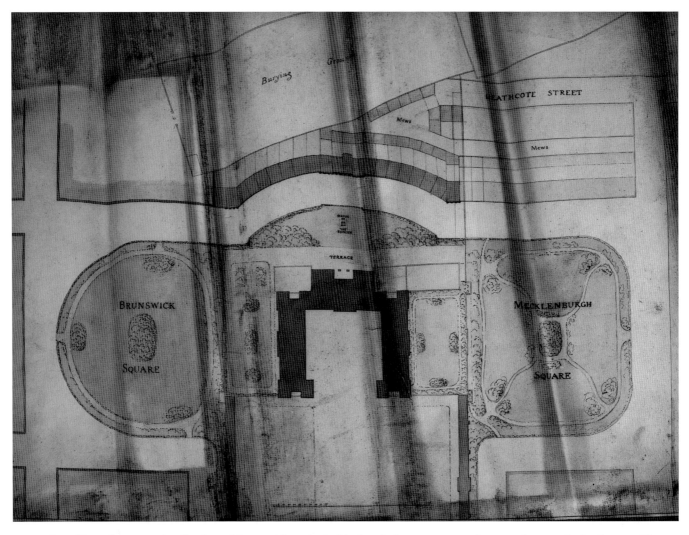

223 The office of S. P. Cockerell, plan of Brunswick and Mecklenburgh Squares, pen and watercolour wash, April 1811. Thomas Coram Foundation for Children, London.

of the neighbouring Bedford Estate. Bedford Square (begun 1776) launched the new building offensive of the Duke of Bedford's estate in Bloomsbury, and precipitated the transformation of the area into what has been called a *quartier des carrés* – or 'the Bedford Square group': 'a whole nucleus of squares, all comely, and some elegant, but all modern and middle-class' (fig. 224).[143] This paroxysm of building caused Francis Douce to remark in about 1796 from his house in Upper Gower Street that 'we have too many squares. At this time 4 new squares had started up in the course of a year in my neighbourhood'.[144]

Between 1800 and 1817 James Burton built Russell Square and Burton Crescent (now known as Cartwright Gardens; fig. 225), and from 1820 to roughly 1835

Thomas Cubitt built the fabric, and undertook the design and planting of the gardens of Gordon, Torrington, Woburn, Tavistock and Euston Squares. The squares – which were described in 1844 as 'all new, spruce and uninteresting' – were supplied with plants from Cubitt's own nursery ground – a commercial concern formed specifically for planting gardens in squares, and those of individual houses.[145]

By 1800 both the Bedford and the Grosvenor Estates had generally adopted a policy which required that speculative lessees of building land in squares should be responsible for the enclosure and planting of the gardens in the midst. The cost of the new gardens was underwritten by the estate, which was in turn reimbursed by the street commissioners. There were, however, numer-

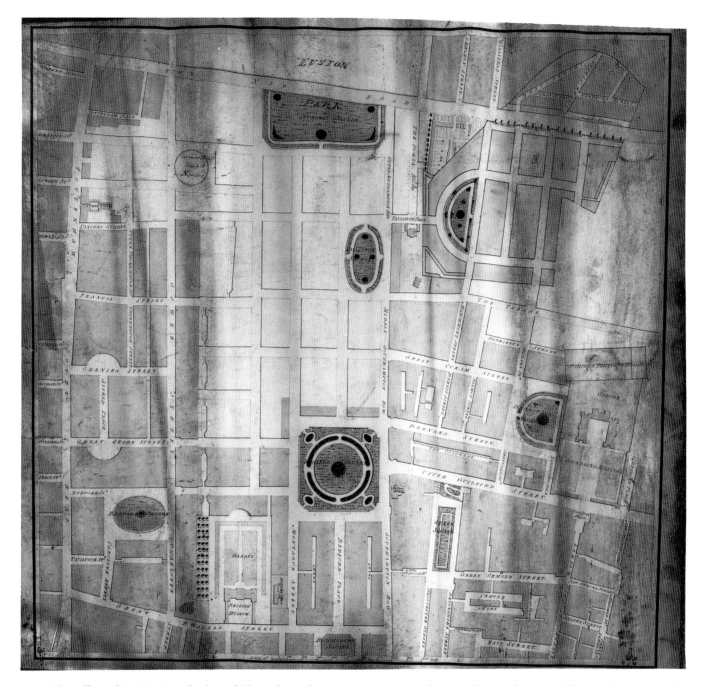

224   The office of S. P. Cockerell, plan of Bloomsbury showing squares, pen and watercolour wash, *c*.1815. Thomas Coram Founda-tion for Children, London.

ous exceptions. At Russell Square, for instance, the area was laid out under the provision of an Act of Parliament of 1801, whereby:

> the owner of the fee-simple of the Square, together with certain other specified persons, was appointed for five years to carry out the Act; and afterwards the

owner of the land and the occupiers of the houses in the Square were appointed Commissioners for regu-lating the central gardens, &c., the exclusive use of which is vested in the owner and aforesaid occupiers. Towards the formation of the garden the Commis-sioners were empowered to levy a rate upon the houses not exceeding 1s in the £ per annum on the

225 Robert Chantrell, *Perspective view of Burton Crescent*, pen and watercolour wash, *c*.1817. Sir John Soane's Museum, London. Now known as Cartwright Gardens, near King's Cross Station.

yearly rentals or values of the houses, and for maintenance a further rate not exceeding 6d. in the £ per annum.[146]

In many cases the estates allowed their surveyors to recommend garden lay-outs which could be accepted at face value, or modified at the discretion of the speculator. So long as the garden was enclosed and planted, and the scheme was completed within its budget, it met with the estate's approval. Nevertheless, some landowners who were more attuned to the advantages of imaginative and modern garden design, were quick to recognise the inadequacies of the speculators' garden schemes. Although invariably cheaper than those proposed by their respective surveyors, the layouts were often uninspired, and unresponsive to the new demands placed on the squares to provide for both private and public enjoyment.[147]

From the late eighteenth century onwards, the planting in the centres of squares became increasingly naturalistic, and there was a new emphasis placed on landscaping. Many of London's immured and orderly gardens were dramatically metamorphosed into informal, naturalistic scenes: straight paths were serpentinised, and walls and palisades were replaced by open iron railings through which passers-by could glimpse velvet lawns, luxuriant shrubberies and clumps of foliage and

flowers. 'Open iron railings' – a relatively new form of fencing for squares – did much to open the scenery of 'shrubbery-walks and grass-plats', which 'afforded very seasonable relief, the eye being wearied of the sameness of colossal piles of bricks and mortar'.[148] François Philippar, a French visitor to London in the late 1820s, reported that *places publiques* or 'Squarres' were 'all ornamented in the centre with gardens encircled by railings; a method which presents the advantage of attenuating the severity which is inherent in the regular layout of the enclosure' (figs 226–8).[149] James Peller Malcolm noted the change in character of many of the city's squares attributed to new railings and more luxuriant planting when he remarked in his *Anecdotes* (1808) that 'pure air so essential to the preservation of life, now circulates through the *new* streets; squares calculated for ornament, health and the higher ranks of the community are judiciously dispersed, and their centres converted into beautiful gardens'.[150]

Designers of the new gardens drew on theories of the picturesque and used them as a means of confronting, in aesthetic terms, the problem of creating gardens in town. They supported their arguments by proposing theories which reconciled aesthetic categories which had previously been opposed to one another – the sublime *versus* the beautiful; the wild versus the cultivated and the ordered; and the general *versus* the par-

226 François Philippar, 'Habitations anglaises devant lesquelles se trouve un petit jardin', etching from *Voyage Agronomique en Angleterre, fait en 1829* (1830), pl. I. Royal Botanic Gardens, Kew.

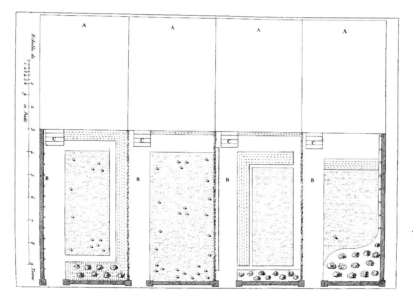

227 François Philippar, 'Plan de quatre jardins qui se trouvent devant les habitations anglaises; nous les avon nommés jardins de ville', etching from *Voyage Agronomique en Angleterre, fait en 1829* (1830), pl. II. Royal Botanic Gardens, Kew.

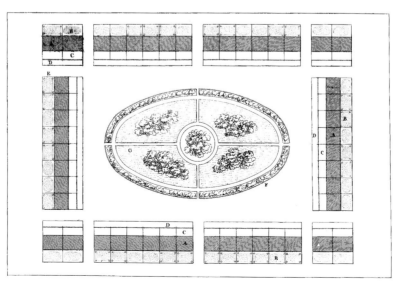

228 François Philippar, 'Plan d'une place de la ville de Londres (Squarre)', etching from *Voyage Agronomique en Angleterre, fait en 1829* (1830), pl. III. Royal Botanic Gardens, Kew. The French traveller's reconstruction of a typical London square is somewhat idealised.

ticular. As such, the unchecked growth of garden plants and trees was no longer perceived as a potential threat to the harmony, grandeur and uniformity of the surrounding buildings, but vaunted as a necessary complement to architectural urbanity and sophistication.

Hermann von Pückler-Muskau remarked in 1814 that the city's 'beautiful squares' were a 'great ornament to London'.

County and town in the same spot is a charming idea. Fancy yourself in an extensive quadrangular area surrounded by the finest houses, and in the midst of its delightful plantations, with walks, shrubberies, and parterres of fragrant flowers, inclosed with an elegant iron railing, where ladies arranged in all the splendour of fashion are taking the air; where children sweet as Loves chase one another; and growing beauties, with chequered silk cords in their showy hands, skip like Zephyrs among the roses, by plying the string over head and under foot, straight and cross-wise, with a grace and pliancy you have no conception of; then you will have a faint representation of those private promenades. Private they are, because they are constantly locked up for exclusive use of a number of families who have keys to their entrances.

Thus the inhabitant of the square has a rural prospect before his eye, without having to leave his house.[151]

The imitation of a 'rural prospect' was, as we have seen, a longstanding objective of the designers of gardens squares. It was, however, only in the last decade of the eighteenth century that it was no longer always considered important to have clear vistas across the gardens to the opposite side of the square – the view could be embowered by foliage. Inhabitants and observers alike desired the gardens to express 'a degree of maturity'.[152]

A genuine concern for the development of handsome central gardens prompted both the Duke of Bedford and Earl Cadogan to engage the professional services of Humphry Repton. The latter planned the gardens of Russell Square (before 1806; fig. 229) and Bloomsbury Square (c.1807) for the 5th and 6th Dukes of Bedford respectively, and Sloane Square for the 1st Earl Cadogan (c.1806).[153] At Bloomsbury Square, however, Repton's proposals were rejected by the trustees. The commission was instead given to Thomas Barr, who was asked by the inhabitants to adopt part of Repton's plan.[154]

The 6th Duke of Bedford took a great interest in the planting of the gardens of his estate's squares, and was

'in this, as every other matter concerning the Estate . . . the final arbiter of taste'.[155] An account of 1829 records that the duke 'went through Gordon Square the other day, and thinks the outside shrubbery quite consistent with his plan of decorating the interior. He thinks it wants thinning. When the time comes – have the trees planted according to the Duke's plan'. On the duke's insistence a double row of limes was planted at the same square; and at Torrington Square the garden was planted with a variety of 'Forest Trees and shrubs of large growth', including sycamore, birch, ash, Spanish chestnut, 'Scarlet Flowering' horse chestnut, lime, Eastern and Spanish planes, lilacs, thorns and flowering cherries.[156]

In 1790 the residents' committee at Soho Square embarked upon an 'improvement' of the central garden, which entailed 'trenching the Borders, the clumps, altering the Walks, [planting] two Rows of Quick Setts within the Iron railing, [and planting] Trees and Shrubs'. William Malcolm & Son, nurserymen from Stockwell, supplied and planted the garden in early 1791. Among the trees and shrubs planted in the garden were laurel, *Viburnum tinus*, phillyrea, honeysuckle, box, euonymus, peaches, cherries, laburnums, yew, almonds, azaleas, sweet briars and roses. The choice of plants was doubtless influenced by Sir Joseph Banks, who was a member of the Garden Committee.[157] Views of the square by Buonarotti Papworth and Jacques-Laurent Agasse (1816 and 1822) show that the garden in Soho Square had been transformed to picturesqueness by the replanting of the 1790s (figs 230 and 231). The new, naturalistic planting pleased Sir Charles Bell at number 34, who reported in 1811 that he was very pleased with his house, and especially 'the walk in the drawing-room looking down on the green and trees of the square'.[158]

Such picturesque planting was not unique to Bloomsbury's squares. In 1790 the basin in Lincoln's Inn Fields was filled in 'after much debate and opposition among the inhabitants', and the gardens were restructured into a naturalistic scene. The gardens of Berkeley Square were also remodelled: whereas 'the area of this quadrangle was till very lately an uninteresting slope of grass', in about 1800 'the inhabitants, sated with the sameness of the scene, entered into a resolution of planting shrubs and trees around the enormous pedestal which supports the equally enormous equestrian statue of his present Majesty . . .' (fig. 232).[159]

At another 'pleasing inclosed grass plat on the side on an hill', not half a mile away, a similar remodelling took place. In 1790 the gravel walks and the grass plots of Leicester Square were banished; the much derided

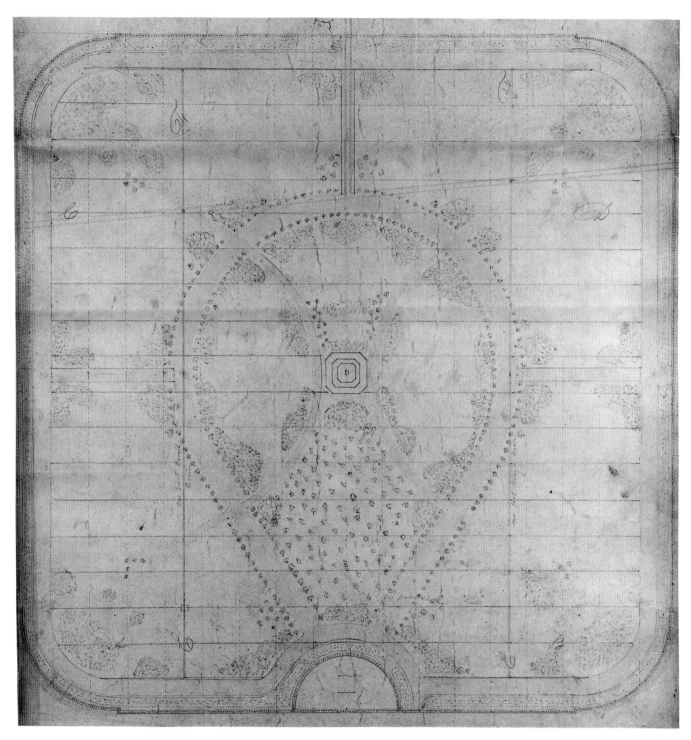

229   Humphry Repton, sketch design for the garden of Russell Square, pencil, 1804. Woburn Abbey, Bedfordshire. James Britton described the central garden in 1806 as 'one of the largest and most handsome in London . . . Broad streets intersect it at the centre and angles, which not only adds to its beauty, but removes an objection made by some to squares in general, by securing a thorough ventilation . . . The extensive enclosure in the centre is a miniature landscape-garden, combining beauty and variety'.

satisfy the mind'; in other words, they should provide a structured natural setting for passive public recreation and public instruction – particularly the pursuit of botany.

Putting forward his own model for a 'public square', Loudon recommended that such a feature of the urban topography should be fluidly integrated into the community in a way that surpassed the earlier models' fusion of art and nature (fig. 237). The formula of 'nature in the midst of art' was transmuted into 'art in the midst of nature' – the emphasis on garden boundaries should be diminished, and un-gated sunny and umbrageous garden paths should traverse spacious lawns and large plant beds and dissolve into the mosaic of the surrounding streets. Loudon's engraving of his model square had a powerful centrifugal thrust; the result of which was that the garden setting – formed with common sorts of plants, singular for beauty, fragrance and luxuriant growth, planted following the principles of natural scenery – suffused its built environment. Moreover, the fashion for public statues was proposed to be supplanted by a convention of installing a 'centrical covered seat and retreat', as the point of convergence for the community, and the hub of the picturesque whole.[171]

Loudon's achievement was to have galvanised ordinary citizens to think about garden squares in terms of their role in the metropolitan plan – as one of dozens of interactive parts of a whole coherent system. The square – which at the level of planning was simply an unelaborated open green space – was assigned a complex function and purpose in the structure of the city. It was not, however, assigned a fixed visual image. Although Loudon proposed ways in which to reform

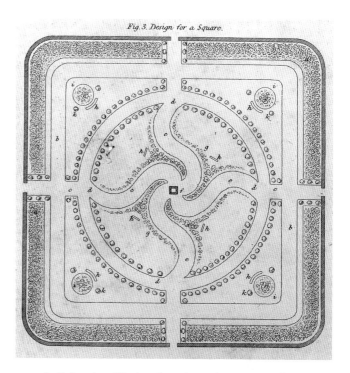

237   J. C. Loudon, 'Design for a Square', engraving from *Hints on the Formation of Gardens and Pleasure Grounds* (1812). The Lindley Library, Royal Horticultural Society, London. Loudon's general earliest published model for the design of a garden square.

the layout and treatment of squares, his foremost objective was to cultivate in his readers a desire to question, improve and adapt his ideas to their personal requirements. There was no propriety of design for a garden. He commented in the *Encyclopaedia of Gardening* (1822) that 'a small city square might be laid out in terraces, like the Isola Bella, or the gardens of Babylon . . .' Indeed, the tide of picturesqueness had changed the face of many squares across town; Sloane Square (from 1771) had been formed to approximate a hummocky woodland, and Edwardes Square, Kensington (1811–19), had been laid out in 1820 with winding vales by A. Aglio, 'an eminent landscape painter'.[172]

Humphry Repton also approached the subject of garden square design as a 'Public concern', and took 'a sort of Pride in contributing to the Embellishment of the Capital'. His views on London squares were based upon 'plain common sense improved by observation & experience'. He remarked that the 'Artist' of a garden 'area' had to treat the square both as a '*public* object' and a private garden. Repton presumably developed his concept of the propriety of garden squares from about 1805, after he was entrusted with the layout of Russell Square by James Burton.[173]

235 (*facing page top*)   'Cavendish Square', aquatint and engraving with hand colouring from Thomas Malton, *Picturesque Tour Through the Cities of Westminster and London* (1800), pl. 89. Paul Mellon Collection, Yale Center for British Art, New Haven. Wilhelm von Archenholz remarked in 1789 that 'the squares in London offer such objects to the eye as announce the opulence and good taste of the inhabitants: those who reside there, besides this, have the advantage of breathing a pure air, and are never disturbed by any noise'.

236 (*facing page bottom*)   *Lincoln's Inn Fields coming in from Great Queen Street*, lithograph, 1810. British Museum, London. In 1790 the basin in Lincoln's Inn Fields was filled in, and the gardens were restructured into a naturalistic scene. James Britton remarked in 1806 that 'the extent of the gardens is about eleven acres, equal to the space covered by the base of the largest Egyptian Pyramid'.

238 George Scharf, *View taken from N°.19 Bloomsbury Sqr*, pencil, *c.*1826. British Museum, London. Hermann von Pückler-Muskau remarked in 1814 that London's 'streets are large and lightsome, generally intersected at right angles, and disclosing to the views either of its stupendous bridges over the Thames, or the culminating top of a tower, or the smiling verdure of a square'.

In a letter of March 1807 in which Repton defended his rejected proposal for Bloomsbury Square he elaborated upon the 'Reasons upon which the Plan was founded' (fig. 238). He first explained the public objectives of his scheme, proposing to create a 'Walk around the Area for convenience & in compliance with the general custom of all other Squares', which was 'defended from without & ornamented on the inside by the margin of Shrubs by which it is accompanied'. His 'one great object' of the plan was to 'keep open the View from Holborn thro' Bedford Place to the statue forming a fine Enfilade thro' the two squares – such as prevailed from Cavendish Square thro' Hanover Square to the Portico of St George's'. He considered that the 'two great *private* uses of all Squares are space for the children & a Pleasure Ground for the inhabitants of the Square'. In so far as 'evergreen and winter plants will not bear the air of a City', he recommended planting a shaded walk of lime trees 'like that in Russell Square'. His final recommendation was to introduce some 'tall trees' to increase the 'apparent dimensions' of the ground by partial concealment. He remarked, 'that as a small lake appears large, by the Intervention of Islands, so a small area is increased by the interruptions thrown in the way of viewing the whole at once'.[174] Repton concluded:

A few years hence, when the present patches of shrubs shall have become thickets, – when the present meagre rows of trees shall have become an umbra-geous avenue, – and the children now in their nurses' arms shall have become the parents or grandsires of future generations, – this square may serve to record, that the Art of Landscape Gardening in the beginning of the 19th century was not directed by whim or caprice, but founded on a due consideration of utility as well as beauty, without a bigotted [*sic*] adherence to forms and lines, whether straight, croocked, or serpentine.[175]

Repton's contemporary John Nash promoted an aesthetic of domesticity with aspirations to grandeur. In October 1817 he prepared a plan for the redesign of the central area of St James's Square. Although the square had undergone a series of minor changes over the years – grass had replaced the gravel witin the railings (1759), the octangular railing was replaced by one of circular form (1799), and gas lamps replaced the oil lamps 'round the ring' (1817) – it was the first general rearrangement of the central area since 1727.[176] Nash's involvement at the square was significant: he was the private architect to the Prince Regent (and from 1820 to King George IV), adviser to the Surveyor-General of the Works, and had since 1811 been instrumental in the planning of the new residential area in Regent's Park. Nash, above all, was a master of scenographic art, and an outspoken critic on the subject of landscape propriety.[177]

Under Nash's supervision the central area of the square was enlarged, and a 'screen of plantations' was laid

239   Decimus Burton, *Design for Planting the Area of the two Crescents at the End of Portland Place*, pen with watercolour washes, *c.*1819. Westminster City Archives, London.

out, 'extending round the interior of the railing of about ten feet in width'.[178] After further discussions with the architect in 1818, a fence was thrown up around the large circular sheet of water in the centre of the enclosure and new planting was laid out. Nash, who appears to have engaged in regular consultations with the trustees of the square (without payment), was in 1822 supervising the erection of a covered garden seat to his design in the garden.[179]

The remodelled garden was an advertisement of the architect's preferred treatment for 'planted squares', which he described in 1822 as 'ornamental enclosures . . . like subscription tea gardens for *genteel* subscribers', surrounded by 'ornamental plantations on the outer boundary . . . [for] . . . breaking the uniformity and monotony of the straight lines of rows of houses'.[180] The planning of the gardens entailed the arrangement of 'ornamental plantations and walks & seats' within an iron-railed enclosure, and was based upon his particularised notion of the picturesque.

It was not, as Elmes noted in 1827, the picturesque according to the 'Gilpin School', although Nash's gardens inside Park Crescent (fig. 239) and Park Square (both laid out and planted by 1824) were crammed with picturesque devices: 'meadering walks', 'ambrosial shrubs', 'velvet turf', 'gay flowers', and 'serpentine walks'.[181] The aesthetic owed more to the principles of Uvedale Price, and, in particular, that which distinguished 'architecture in towns' as 'principal and independent'. Nash attempted to distinguish the buildings by setting them amidst 'considerable bodies of plantation', without subordinating them to the landscape.[182] This was not easily accomplished as the perception of the central space, and the effect of the garden setting were often constrained by the nature of its enclosure and overwhelmed by the architectural surroundings. As Price remarked on the subject in 1796: 'in a street, or square, hardly anything but the front is considered, for little else is seen . . . the spectator, also being confined to a few stations, and those not distant, has his attention entirely fixed on the architecture, and the architect.'[183] Nash subsequently applied the same principles to the gardens.

Nash neither suggested that buildings in squares should be obscured by trees, nor that the views across the central area should be totally obstructed. He had, for instance, only recommended the planting of shrubs at St James's Square; trees were introduced only in 1825, after he had ceased to advise the trustees, and it was decided to introduce 'a few Forest Trees' – limes and laburnums were ordered to be planted.[184]

'GENUINE SQUARES', 'NEW SQUARES' AND 'PLACES'

There was, by the 1830s, as little consensus on the 'correct' landscape treatment for the central gardens in squares as there had been in the early eighteenth century. For instance, Jonas Denis asserted in the *The Landscape Gardener* (1835) that there prevailed an 'egregiously tasteless disposition of the areas in public squares':

> Of all subjects for arrangement of plantations [in both town and country], areas of squares are most perplexing, from the difficulty of commanding an ornamental view from each of the four lines of surrounding houses. The inhabitants should be presented with the refreshing verdure of an open lawn in each direction, terminated by foliage not in one unbroken mass, but admitting through two or three apertures perspective display of the ulterior verdure. Trees should be evergreen and sparingly admitted, the foliage being principally composed of evergreen shrubs, supplying shade and shelter to an included curved walk, furnished with appropriate seats. Against the rail should be planted a hedge of wild holly uninviting to cattle, and including a walk of four feet width surrounded by privet backed by laurel. Viewed from the opposite side of the square, these graduated tints will be displayed, while the walks will be concealed.[185]

This aesthetic debate about gardens had, however, little influence on the popularity of squares as a constituent to urban residential development. By the early nineteenth century the success of the garden square was guaranteed, and undeniable. Until 1750 there had been only twenty-three London squares, thirteen of which had been developed before 1700 – and these were primarily distributed in the West End.[186] By 1800 another fourteen had appeared which were sprinkled around Westminster on the Cadogan, Church Commissioners, Portman, Conduit-Mead, and Bedford estates. However, between 1800 and 1850 the number of squares swelled to one hundred and fourteen, with the addition of seventy-six new garden enclosures occurring throughout the metropolis – from the De Beauvoir Estate (Hackney) in the east, to the Ladbroke Estate (Kensington) in the west, and from the Southampton Estate (Camden) in the north, to the Duchy of Cornwall Estate in the Oval, Kennington.

Charles Knight, who in 1844 remarked that 'in all the suburbs squares are now springing up like mushrooms', devised a typology in an attempt to distinguish the 'great diversity in the character of squares, simple though the elements be that comprise them'. The typology was published in his essay entitled 'The Squares of London', and the basis of his nomenclature was broadly social and geographical; it did, however, take account of a square's extent, its natural topography, historical associations, function, airiness and its position relative to neighbouring streets and buildings. The author classified squares into four 'grand divisions'. The first embraced all the squares west of Regent's Street, which he called 'fashionable squares'; the second and third divisions included squares situated between Regent Street on the west, and Gray's Inn Lane and Chancery Lane on the east – Holborn and Oxford Street forming a line of demarcation between them; and the fourth division encompassed squares south of Oxford Street, which 'having once been the seats of fashion, and still bearing upon their exterior the traces of faded greatness, have descended to become haunts of busy trading life'. To these 'grand divisions' he appended two 'sub-divisions': squares north of Holborn inhabited by the 'aristocracy of the law, among whom mingle wealthy citizens and the more solid class of *literati*'; and the 'obsolete, or purely City squares'.[187]

Knight's spirited narrative compares dozens of London squares, ranging from the city's oldest and witheringly ostentatious to the melancholy products of failed speculations. Praise and delight constantly alternate with criticism and condemnation as he jumps about the metropolis in pursuit of squares and their derivatives. However, unlike the authors of earlier commentaries on the subject, Knight places the square in the context of the whole range of metropolitan improvements: they are discussed in terms of their relationship to parks, sewers, building densities, streets and circulation. For instance, Belgrave Square is 'situated between town and country. The houses are already becoming sensibly less dense, like a London fog, as one approaches the outskirts. Hyde Park behind it: St James's Park intervenes between it and town; the great thoroughfares in the vicinity have more of the road in them than the street. In such a neighbourhood a square confined enough to allow the height of the house being felt in proportion to the extent of the ground-plan would convey a sense of confinement – of oppression to the lungs, though in the heart of town it would feel a relief' (fig. 240).[188]

facing page Detail from fig. 219.

The Garden, the Picturesque and the Disruption of Urban Decorum

THE METROPOLITAN PICTURESQUE

PREVIOUS CHAPTERS have discussed the town garden largely in terms of its harmonious integration into the urban fabric – or how the apportionment of building land for the creation of openings before or behind a house contributed to its protection and 'convenience'. I have, however, touched only briefly upon how the town garden was perceived in the wider arena of metropolitan improvements, and upon its relationship to what we now know as the suburban garden.

The role of landscape in the creation of a new civic aesthetic has been widely acknowledged.[1] Stephen Daniels has put it succinctly when he remarked that from the early nineteenth century onwards, 'along main roads into provincial cities, smart metropolitan styles of architecture and landscaping displaced the more vernacular looking work of builders and gardeners'. The pattern, he argues, was derived from the 'highly cultivated, prosperous looking scenery of manicured fields, ornamented farms, new or refashioned parks and grounds' of the English countryside.[2] Nowhere was this more evident than in London, and nowhere in the metropolis was this style more playful and innovative than in Regent's Park: here the architect, 'master pragmatist' and 'virtuoso of scenographic art', John Nash, addressed the town garden directly – both in aesthetic terms and as an important element in daily life.[3]

The story of London's metropolitan improvements during the period 1786–1830 has recently been rewritten. J. Mordaunt Crook has argued that Nash was engaged not in a smooth exercise of master-planning – as assumed by earlier historians – but in a process of 'muddling through' by 'instinct and luck'. Nash's

approach, in other words, is presented by Crook as 'episodic, protracted, fragmented, inconclusive'.[4]

Crook's view is supported by the many letters that Nash wrote, engaging in debate with developers and the Office of Woods and Forests over numerous aspects of the Regent's Park scheme. The pragmatic approach adopted in these letters was, of course, consistent with most of the assumptions about town gardening charted in my previous chapters: throughout the eighteenth century the town garden was seen as a space defined and managed with reference to a range of disparate arguments and principles. These arguments and principles, however, were never, in earlier writings, marshalled with the same sense of purposefulness: while Nash did not attempt to formulate any coherent body of theory himself, he did assume that the practice of town gardening ineluctably propels the gardener into an explicit and active engagement with theoretical debate. In discussing specific practical questions raised as the scheme for Regent's Park progressed, Nash took for granted that it was necessary to formulate and endorse his arguments through reference to the discourse of aesthetic theory – in particular the theory of the picturesque, as expounded, for example, by William Gilpin and Uvedale Price.

Where principles of design are invoked in earlier discussions of the town garden, they are normally seen not as an active element in the planning process, but, as has been shown in chapter 2, as a minor ingredient in the rhetoric of marketing employed by landlords and speculative builders. Such principles, moreover, are seldom elaborated in a manner that acknowledges the existence of a body of aesthetic theory that might prove directly relevant to specific planning decisions.

Nash, on the other hand, formulated a range of explicit arguments about the development of the gardens of Regent's Park. His involvement in the scheme began in 1806 when he was appointed to the post of Architect at the Office of Woods and Forests.[5] He arrived on the scene sixteen years after the government had realised the potential of the redevelopment of the London Crown Estate to raise much needed revenue, and after William Pitt had set in motion no less than twenty statutory reports that were intended to galvanise a concerted programme of urban reform.[6] The architect's picturesque sensibilities were not, however, applied until the autumn of 1810, when he submitted, in collaboration with his colleague James Morgan, a plan for the redevelopment of the 543-acre Marylebone Park (later Regent's Park) Estate in North London.

Nash's views on this aesthetic theory were formed during the early 1790s, at which time he engaged in dialogue and debate with Thomas Johnes, Uvedale Price and Humphry Repton.[7] These views were refined over the succeeding decades, most notably under the influence of his friend Sir John Soane, who invoked the picturesque to exploit the potential of 'the Principles of modern Decorative Landscape Gardening' to improve civic architecture and planning.[8] Like his contemporaries, Nash appropriated and applied the principles of the picturesque as they offered a means of incorporating within the same landscape contrasting categories – such as the sublime and the beautiful, the wild and the cultivated, and the general and the particular.

The practical usefulness of the theory of the picturesque, for Nash, lay partly in its concern with a particular problem raised by the planning of the park: the problem of how to assimilate domesticity and individual idiosyncracy within a framework of public magnificence. The role of palatial buildings as private dwellings, Nash assumed, would necessarily determine, to some extent, the aesthetic options and strategies of design available to the planner. In emphasising and exploring the relation between public and private, Nash developed a series of principles which can be seen as establishing a specific concept of the 'metropolitan picturesque'.[9]

In earlier decades, in contrast, the town garden was seen as disrupting theoretical speculation on aesthetic questions, rather than extending the range of such speculation. During most of the eighteenth century the garden was seen as threatening the much vaunted ideal of urban propriety: as a space in which individual whim could be freely indulged, the garden – and particularly the front garden – had the power to compromise the orderliness and regularity essential to public decorum. This suspicion was increasingly registered from the 1760s onwards, when small gardens became popular constituents in the town plan: their ubiquity was perceived by some architectural theorists as destabilising.

The initial response of architectural theorists was not to develop some more complex approach to the aesthetic problem posed by the small garden, but simply to dismiss the town garden as an irritating anomaly, and define it as too small and too marginal to provoke extensive theoretical speculation and debate. As has been shown in earlier chapters, John Gwynn, James Stewart and Thomas Malton's reproachful criticisms suggest that the town garden, when it subverted the pursuit of 'publick magnificence', was capable of arousing strong emotions. Gwynn remarked in 1766 that the provision of an 'intermediate space' between the house and the road was likely to be 'encumbered' by a garden and its wall, which, he exclaimed, defeated the 'original intention', creating 'confusion and deformity, extremely unbecoming the character of a great and opulent city'.[10] While gardens were very often attached to urban dwellings from the 1760s onwards, and were seen as desirable for ventilation and other practical purposes, they were not seen as spaces that could be readily managed by reference to the prevailing principles of architectural taste. It was only at the end of the century that the judicious use of vegetation was defined as a positive element within urban planning. Such a change of assumptions about the town garden can be charted in a range of contexts, such as the Grosvenor Estate in Pimlico or the Archbishop of Canterbury's estate in Lambeth, as discussed in chapter 2. It is in Nash's correspondence, however, that this change of outlook becomes most dramatically apparent.

What is striking about Nash's exposition of the metropolitan picturesque, then, is that he saw it as a body of theory of direct practical relevance to the town garden. His theoretical concept of the small garden contrasted sharply with those of earlier writers, who generally regarded such a small urban space as incapable, or even unworthy of rigorous aesthetic consideration. As has been argued in previous chapters, the eighteenth-century town garden was usually considered as a mere 'opening', the layout of which was guided by a range of fragmented and often contradictory principles. Nash elevated the garden to a place within debates about town planning.

Nash, in fact, was neither a great proponent of town

gardening, nor a champion of the small town garden; he did, none the less, develop a rigorous landscape aesthetic, which, of necessity, addressed the town garden. Foremost in his civic vision was the exclusion of social and aesthetic vulgarity through the manipulation of buildings and landscape: trees and shrubs, paths, roads, fencing and lighting were boldy deployed in order to 'shut out the irregular and ugly parts of town'.[11] Unlike many of his contemporaries, and the developer James Burton in particular, Nash was content neither to perpetuate landscape solutions which had been borrowed unashamedly from the rural pleasure ground, nor to plagiarise the conventional 'ornamental plantations' of town gardens or garden squares. He formulated instead a new civic aesthetic of 'Park scenery' which rose to the challenge presented by the urban context.

The parameters of the scheme had, in fact, been set by John Fordyce, Surveyor-General of Land Revenues, who conceived of the competition as an opportunity to implement a grand plan which would endow the park with a unified and comprehensive metropolitan consistency. His vision of the aesthetic, social and spatial organisation and structure of the park was detailed in a memorandum of 1809, which conveyed both general and particular recommendations – many of which later formed the basis for Nash's revised plans of autumn 1811. The new urban precinct was to comprise housing, churches, markets, monuments, roads, canals, lighting and sewerage, and was to be linked to Mayfair, Charing Cross, Marylebone, Whitehall and Westminster 'by a bold network of new thoroughfares'.[12]

Nash and Morgan's first submission borrowed extensively from an aborted proposal of 1809 prepared by John White. Although the scheme was largely geometrical in plan, it made minor concessions to the picturesque and evidently expressed sufficient civic dignity and public amenity to please the Treasury (fig. 241). The architects were, none the less, requested to revise their plans to show a reduction in the housing density and a greater area of land given over for public use.

Fordyce declared that it was essential that the park should be readily absorbed, and ultimately integrated, into the metropolis as a whole. The largest of the dwellings that he proposed to deploy within the pale were to be what he called 'country houses' – although they were, in fact, capacious suburban villas. These were to be skilfully assimilated into the landscape, in the sense that their picturesque qualities should survive any future diminution of the insulating parkland: the dwellings should adapt to what Fordyce considered to be the

inevitable encroachment of the metropolis. As the tide of building closed in on the park, the leases would be surrendered, the open parkland built over at an increased density, and the one-time 'country houses' would become 'mere well-planted town houses'.[13]

Nash's revised scheme proposed a pronounced integration of urban architecture with natural scenery, and displayed what he called 'variety': 'the successive combination of Building and rural scenery' (fig. 242).

It is humbly submitted that the double Circus on the Apex of the ground in the middle of the Park, the river-like lake of water in the Valley which will surround it, the stateliness of the ornamental Canal [the formal reservoir, or 'bason'], with its slopes, terraces, balustrades and fountain, now proposed on the summit of the eastern side of the Park, the range of handsome houses that will overlook it, the two ample Crescents open to the Park on its Northern boundary, the extensive line of houses on the Southern boundary, will all be objects of grandeur, suited to the great extent of the Park which they will surround; and when combined with the rural and picturesque scenery of the Park itself, formed by the intermixture of Trees, Lawn and Water (provided that in the grouping of them a general unity of Park-like character is preserved), as great a variety of beautiful forms, comprehended in one magnificent whole, will be produced, as the mind can conceive.[14]

The architect declared that his scheme embraced three practical 'leading principles'. The first was 'to create inducements for the Public, and particularly the higher classes of the Public, to establish themselves in Mary-le-bone Park, and to found these inducements on causes likely to be permanent; and this it is proposed to effect by creating Scenery that will attract the Public, and secure to the houses the enjoyment of that Scenery; at the same time making it select, by shutting out all connexion with the inferior streets, approaching it only through the wide and handsome Communications of Baker-street at the West, and Portland Place at the East'. The second principle was to make the elevated ground of the park 'contribute to the beauty and salubrity of the Metropolis'; and the third principle was to raise revenue for the Crown.[15]

Nash's belief that the production of a picturesque effect required a carefully adjusted combination of domestic buildings and natural scenery is evident in his clashes with his friend the builder James Burton. Their first confrontation took place over the design and layout

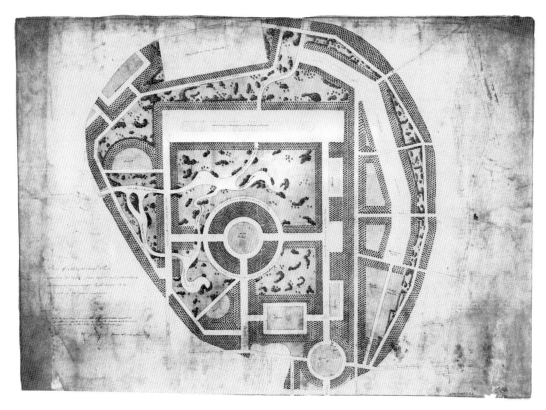

241 John Nash, *Plan of Marylebone Park*, pen and watercolour wash, signed and dated 'John Nash, Dover Street, March 1811'. Public Record Office, Kew.

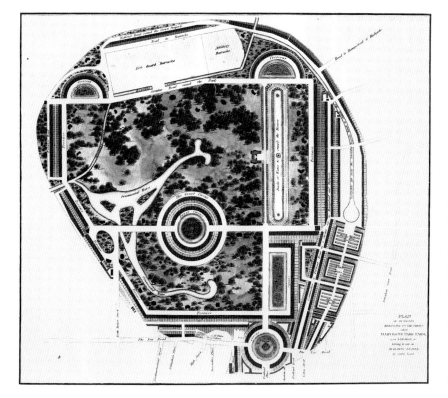

242 John Nash, 'Plan of an Estate belonging to the Crown called Marylebone Park Farm . . .', lithograph published in the First Report of the Commissioners of Woods, Forests and Lands Revenues, 1812. Public Record Office, Kew. Nash's reworking of his earlier plan of 1811.

243　W. Deeble after Thomas Hosmer Shepherd, 'Cornwall Terrace, Regent's Park', etching from *Metropolitan Improvements* (1827). Yale Center for British Art, New Haven.

of Cornwall Terrace, between 1820 and 1821. The latter was the first terrace to be raised on the edge of Regent's Park, and was the most urban of the palatial ranges that were to be built there. It was to be the only terrace on the park built without a slip of 'intermediate' garden space to separate it from the Outer Circle road (fig. 243).

The ease with which Nash moved between the practical and the theoretical is demonstrated by the wording of his objections to Burton's plan to build two houses at the eastern end of Cornwall Terrace, instead of planting the grounds there:

> It is to be regretted that Mr Burton has attached two Houses at the Eastend of the handsome line of houses which he has built, if he had planted the ground at the *Eastend* as he has at the westend, the grandeur arising from the unity of the Elevation would have been preserved . . . Magnificent as these ranges of buildings are in themselves that impression would be greatly diminished if the individuality of the design is not preserved by intermediate plantations – if they join they become a street surrounding a large plot of

ground instead of spacious Palace like buildings embellishing a park.[16]

The vegetation, Nash suggested here, was to increase the effect of architectural sublimity by supplying the qualities that Price termed the 'grandeur of intricacy'.[17] The same principle is affirmed in another letter, concerned with the York Terraces (1822–3) – the next to be built on the edge of the park: 'I think the magnificence of the effect of that range will depend on its being separate and distinct from any other – but on account of the forward state of the buildings and not disapproving of the Elevations & on assurance from Mr Burton that the small space he has left at the eastend of that range shall be planted as thick as possible with high poplars clustered together & brought forward to the road – I did not make any Complaints.'[18]

In a letter to the Commissioners of Woods and Forests in 1823 Nash criticised Burton's siting of Cornwall Terrace, suggesting that 'fewer houses should have been built in order that a considerable body of plantation might have distinguished and insulated the general range of buildings'.[19] The architect did not propose that the individual houses should possess small gardens; he argued instead that the range should have been embowered in a carefully planned garden.[20]

Nash was resolute that the York Terraces, which formed the 'great central Entrance to the Park', should be imposing and spacious, and that there should be 'no divisions in the gardens of the houses to denote individuality but the whole should appear as one entire building . . .' (fig. 244).[21] Once more, however, Burton proposed that Nash's guidelines should be rejected, and he put forward a plan to implement the conventional estate planning strategy which he had applied with great success to his developments in Bloomsbury. Nash reported that the builder proposed

> to take the Land within the rails of the Park enclosure northward to the ornamental water and from the Bridge road to the road leading northward from Baker Street – & separate the same from the other part of the Park by a sunk fence & to lay out the ground in *ornamental Plantations and walks . . . for the use of the inhabitants of the several houses opposite* – with permission to erect one or two low *ornamental Pavilions* thereon at once serving the purpose of *seats &* gardeners tool houses.[22]

The scheme displeased the architect, who railed that 'such a disposition of the Park ought not to be entertained even for a moment'.

> The objections are numerous – the first and the leading objection is the departure from the original purpose of forming a Park for which reason the few Villas to be allowed within its area are to have their small shrubberies surrounded by thick plantations of forest trees to *conceal* them as being *out of harmony with the Park Scenery* – and that the passenger in riding round the Park might recognise nothing but a Park – the next is – if such *ornamental plantations, walks & seats* should be allowed in the instance proposed it is impossible even to hope that it could be extended to the whole of the Park and its incongruity in that case must be felt and would be censured by every person who should possess common sense.[23]

'The gardens', he said, would resemble 'subscription Tea gardens for *genteel* subscribers', and the 'plantations will be likened to the Circus in Portland Place, to Russell Square and other ornamentally planted enclosures' (fig. 239). While this type of 'public garden' was appropriate 'for breaking the uniformity and monotony of straight rows of houses' on the 'outer boundary' of the park, it was inappropriate for the area 'within the Park enclosure'. Nash, furthermore, denounced Burton's scheme as impractical: no sooner would he complete the undertaking than he would care 'as little for the plantations in question as he does for the planted squares he has made in Bloomsbury'.[24] The architect, then, objected to the idea that the magnificence of the park should be compromised by the creation of private pleasure grounds within it. He objected, too, to a scheme in which decisions about the design were to be made by builders, who, as mere artisans, were both disinclined and ill-qualified to reflect upon questions of aesthetic theory.[25] In particular, he deplored the proposal to relinquish the responsibility of garden design and garden maintenance to 'the uncertain and capricious covenants of precarious and speculating individuals who might hire or buy them of Mr Burton'.[26]

The danger that Nash identified in his remark upon Burton's scheme was that the magnificence of the park as a whole might be destroyed by a distressing eruption of vulgarity: a lapse of taste occasioned by a conspicuous display of expenditure. In his remarks Nash invoked a vision of pretentious disregard of the simple and sublime that was implicit in many late eighteenth-century writings and was explicitly elaborated by Richard Payne Knight in his poem *The Landscape* (1794):

> Curse on the shrubbery's insipid scenes!
> Of tawdry fringe encircling vapid greens;
> Where incongruities so well unite,
> That nothing can by accident be right;
> Thickets that neither shade nor shelter yield;
> Yet from the cooling breeze the senses shield:
>
> Prim gravel walks, through which we winding go,
> In endless serpentines that nothing show;
> Till tir'd, I ask, *Why this eternal round?*
> And the gard'ner says, *'Tis pleasure ground,*
> *This pleasure ground!* astonished I exclaim,
> *To me Moorfields as well deserve the name:*
> Nay, better; for in busy scenes at least
> Some odd varieties the eye may feast,
> Something more entertaining still be seen,
> Than red-hot gravel, fringed with tawdry green.[27]

Nash, in the end, got his way. In 1823 Burton was commissioned to build the western range of York Terrace on the condition that he obeyed his critic: he was instructed to 'set his houses back [from the road] and form such quadrangular [garden] areas in front'; and that the proposed 'plantations and walks and rails cannot

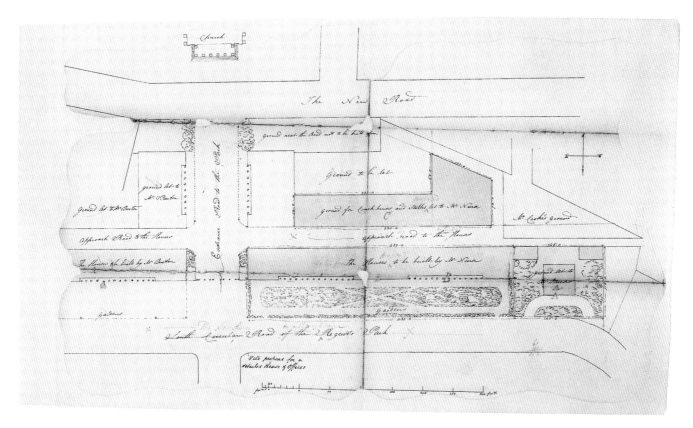

244   John Nash, sketch plan of the York Terraces, Regent's Park, pen and pencil with watercolour wash, 1822. Public Record Office, Kew.

245   T. Barber after Thomas Hosmer Shepherd, 'York Terrace, Regent's Park', etching from *Metropolitan Improvements* (1827). Yale Center for British Art, New Haven.

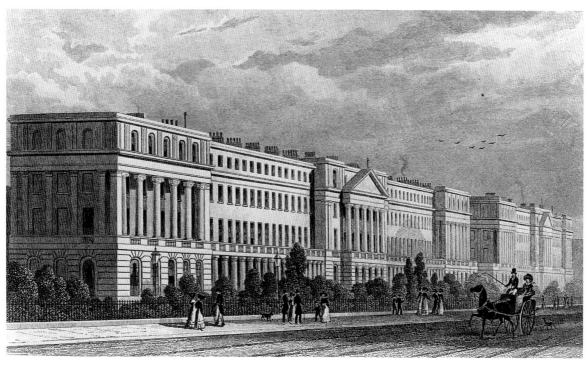

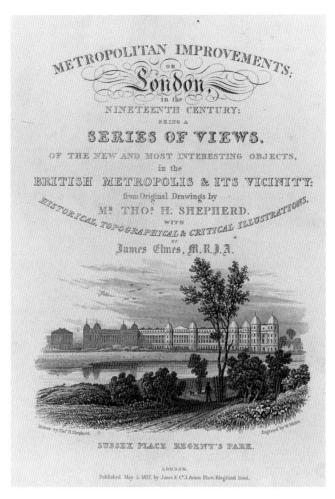

246 William Wallis after Thomas Hosmer Shepherd, 'Sussex Place, Regent's Park', frontispiece etching from *Metropolitan Improvements* (1827). Yale Center for British Art, New Haven. Elmes remarked that 'in elevation it presents a singular contrast to the chaster beauties of the other terraces and palaces, by which it is surrounded'.

be compared with the planted squares in the different parts of the town which are surrounded on all sides by housing, the proprietors of which are bound to keep them up'.[28] Burton proposed a seventy-five-foot set-back of 'Pleasure Grounds attached to the Houses' – in other words, a 'general garden' that was to remain the property of the inhabitants, as opposed to the earlier plan for a garden sold off to speculators (fig. 245). This was the format subsequently adopted by William Nurse for the eastern range of the terraces. The final design of the plantation plans and the enclosing iron palisading were doubtless the handiwork of Nash. The latter proclaimed that the plan, on one hand, would gratify the desire of each tenant to have use of a small piece of ground, and on the other would not diminish the

dignity of the park entrance. The provision of the garden ground was, of course, contingent on the enforcement of restrictive covenants which often prohibited 'the making of any alterations *whatsoever* in the laying out of the Garden'.[29]

As already noted, Nash saw the park as a scheme from which undesirable social elements were rigorously excluded. Those who were to enjoy its amenities – the polite – were offered the pleasure of participating in a fantasy of aristocratic, mildly exoticised grandeur (fig. 246). James Elmes remarked in *Metropolitan Improvements* (1827):

What a prospect lies before us? splendour, health, dressed rurality and comforts such as nothing but a metropolis can afford are spread before us. 'Trim gardens,' lawns and shrubs; towering spires, ample domes, banks clothed with flowers, all the elegancies of the town, and all the beauties of the country are co-mingled with happy art and blissful union. They surely must all be the abodes of nobles and princes! No, the majority are the retreats of the happy free-born sons of commerce, of the wealthy commonalty of Britain, who thus enrich and bedeck the heart of the empire.[30]

While it is generally acknowledged that the architecture of the park was devoted to the evocation of unbridled fantasy, it was the gardens and the landscape – and the setting of the buildings in these elements – that provided the focus for the theoretical programme that endorsed this fantasy.[31] The park required a landscaped infrastructure that was, as Fordyce had earlier remarked, at once capable of sustaining its 'unity of Park-like character' in the face of incursions of building and a steadily increasing building density.[32]

The remaining ground [not occupied by terraces and villas] in front of the [outer] road to be laid out and planted as Lawns or Parks; the road to be separated from the scenery by a sunk fence . . . affording the houses that may be built on the ground between the Road and the boundary line Views over those Lawns and Parks: and it is presumed, that those who are tempted to build or purchase houses by the sides of the dusty roads at the outlets of the Town, for the sake of looking over fields or gardens, often naked and without trees, with the continual apprehension of those fields and and gardens being also covered with buildings, and their prospects destroyed, will prefer to establish themselves by the side of a Road faced with such dressed Scenery as it is proposed to make round Mary-le-bone Park, and which will be continually improving as the Plantations flourish, and the view of which their houses cannot be deprived.[33]

Nash sought to guarantee the enduring integration of landscape scenery in the urban setting. Like Price, he devoted considerable attention to arboriculture, and was sympathetic to the latter's assessment that 'it is in the arrangement and management of trees that the great art of improvement consists':

> trees have a bold, lively and immediate effect on the eye [and] they alone form a canopy over us, and a varied frame to all other objects, which they admit, exclude, and group with, almost at the will of the improver . . . their beauty is compleat and perfect in itself, while that of almost every other object requires their assistance . . . it is perhaps from their possessing . . . variety and intricacy . . . in so eminent a degree, that trees are almost indispensably necessary to picturesque scenery.[34]

Nash had initiated the planting programme for the park as early as 1811 – at which time it lay mostly in pasture – to give 'the advantage of so many years growth while the buildings are in progress'.[35] By 1816 over 14,500 trees had been planted by three competing firms of nurserymen – an undertaking which gave the park an air of cultivated amenity before ever a single house or terrace was built.[36] Elmes suggested that Nash and the commissioners had invoked the wisdom of Cato the Elder who declared, in his book on rural life *On Agriculture*, that 'when we intend to *build*, we ought to deliberate; but when our intentions are to *plant*, we should not deliberate, but *act*'.[37]

The trees were planted in two distinctive patterns: the first was in regular plantations of alternating pairs of forest trees on sites designated for future building (tree species included plane and birch, larch and Spanish chestnut); these trees could be cut as timber and sold when the plots were selectively cleared for building. The second involved planting a series of random naturalistic thickets of more ornamental trees and shrubs, most of which were to remain undisturbed. It was, of course, implicit in Nash's reasoning that many aspects of the landscape would be felicitously improved by accidents of nature. This complemented the improver's prerogative of clearing and pruning trees which either impeded development, or needed to be carefully managed 'because they flourished too much, and have grown so

as to mar the planter's intention'. Here again Nash concurred with Price, who remarked that upon such occasions 'we must be cruel to be kind, or the trees will spoil one another; there will be no variety, no play of form or outline, but a mere crowd of plants, a uniform mass of foliage'.[38]

Despite his concern with overall effect, Nash wished to preserve garden boundaries; although he proposed to obscure them by means of erecting 'invisible fences', ha-has and hedges, he considered them essential for the protection of a premises.[39] Boundaries – the most conspicuous and maligned attribute of the town garden – were also, in fact, essential constituents in the picturesque strategy of creating and manipulating prospect. The picturesque eschewed the aesthetic of unmixed sublimity produced by limitless vistas – vistas had to be controlled and framed; or, as Price argued, 'it is on the shape and disposition of its boundaries that the picturesque in great measure must depend'.[40] As seen in chapter 2, a prospect was previously defined as a scene which offered the promise of control, rather than its actuality. The prospect of a garden from a balcony or a portico was therefore desirable: in Payne Knight's opinion it offered 'domestic convenience'.[41] When the spectator assumed the same vantage point to take in a sweeping extent of the landscape, however, the prospect was declared to dull the gratification of experiencing the intricacy of the scenery at first hand by introducing the 'very possibility of comprehending it all at once'.[42]

No less important to Nash's picturesque vision was the act of moving through the landscape – picturesque travellers were intended to conduct themselves over a network of smoothly surfaced 'McAdam patent' roads and paths through highly cultivated and prosperous looking scenery: to travel through the new park was to experience a moving panorama.[43] To this end Nash endorsed the principle that the 'Picturesque Point [of view] is always . . . low in all prospects';[44] the spectator was intended to feel a sense of being enveloped, or absorbed by the landscape, and the gardens were perceived as extensions of the park scenery into which the palace façades were also submerged and absorbed. This landscape treatment indulged the contemporary fashion for the prominence of a 'natural' foreground in preference to distant scenery: the foreground being, as Gilpin put it, the 'basis and foundation of the whole picture'.[45]

The pre-eminence of the foreground was not only a pictorial strategy; for inhabitants to feel safe and secure in the terrain that supplied them with their vantage point and foreground, they had to be given the exclusive rights to its enjoyment. Nash, for instance, supposed that 'many persons would consider the circumstance of Boats and Barges passing the [Regent's] canal as enlivening the Scenery'. This, however, was only true 'provided the Bargemen or People from the Boats were prevented from landing in the Park'.[46] Nash implied in his letter to the Commissioners in 1822 that the inhabitants, like picturesque tourists, were expected to engage in ceremonious vigilance by conducting promenades around and through the park, as if to mark out the extent of their defensible territory.

THE 'NEATNESS AND FRESHNESS' OF THE PARK VILLAGES

In a letter dated 18 June 1823 Nash put forward his first proposal for the development of picturesque settlement of houses in the last marginal acres of the Crown Estate in Marylebone. The plan for the Park Villages East and West was the final stage of Nash's speculative enterprises in and around the Park. Nash remarked:

these two plots being without the pale of the park and in the vicinity of the Barracks are only calculated for houses of the smallest class (4th rate houses) and it has occurred to me that if they were considered together as one plot of ground and the Houses though small scattered about in an irregular manner as Cottages with plantations between – a very delightful Village might be formed through which the canal would pass and if arranged with Taste and the Buildings truly to partake of the Cottage Character, the whole would become an ornamental feature and command, though humble, yet the better sort of class of people who require such small dwellings.[47]

Nash assessed the scheme retrospectively as 'a source of occupation and amusement' in his old age.[48] This casual remark helps to explain an apparent inconsistency in the planning of the Park Villages which was not evident in that of the park. The villages were treated very much as an exercise of caprice: there were, for instance, no explicit objectives to formulate a clear social programme, nor did Nash ever firmly commit himself to a well-resolved building plan.[49]

From its inception, the scheme was contrived as an assemblage of loosely arranged cottages sprinkled alongside two meandering village streets flanking the sides of the Regent's Canal (fig. 247). In the East Village many of the houses were paired or set in pairs at variable set-backs from the road, while in the West Village there was a higher proportion of larger, detached houses set in a similar natural landscape. Nash, however, equivocated over the proposed building density of the composition:

the principal of which is that the number of Houses be not limited but as such a restriction is meant to prevent the Village being crowded with houses I propose plots on which buildings may be erected be defined and set forth on the plan and a covenant entered into that no other part of the ground shall be built upon – such an arrangement (at the same time that it answers the purpose intended) will allow larger or smaller or grouped houses to be erected as individuals may require.[50]

He was, moreover, ambivalent about the scale and character of the dwellings: 'Specimens of the kind of Buildings [in the vignettes] intended to be erected may be varied or enlarged or lessened or otherwise grouped as shall be required by the Proprietors of them'.[51]

His prescriptions for the services and planting were, by contrast, precise; they were similar to those at Regent's Park. The whole building site was to be planted with a cover of trees and shrubs before the onset of any building, and the character and disposition of the new plantations were to be based on his conventional two-tiered planting system. The first planting zone embraced the roads and the fronts and sides of most of the dwellings (light green on the plan), and denoted 'open lawn to be kept in grass & planted with single [standard] trees which are scheduled in the leases & reinstated from time to time as they die or are destroyed – their use being to form & preserve the Village character'. The second zone (darker green) swathed the slopes of the canal and adjoined each house on at least one side. The purpose of these plantations was to 'screen the more offensive parts of the Cottages, separate them from each other & give intricacy to the scenery – the divisions between the Ground of the several Cottages are to be live hedges or Iron wire Fences but no close wood fences to be allowed'.[52]

The first dwellings were thrown up between May and September 1826 in Park Village East – but not to the plan of 1823.[53] Nash by this time had lost interest in the project, and the work was executed either by his office or a builder.[54] The houses which were erected – although a 'quaint set of variations on the styles' including castellated Tudor, broad-eaved Italian, Swiss, numer-

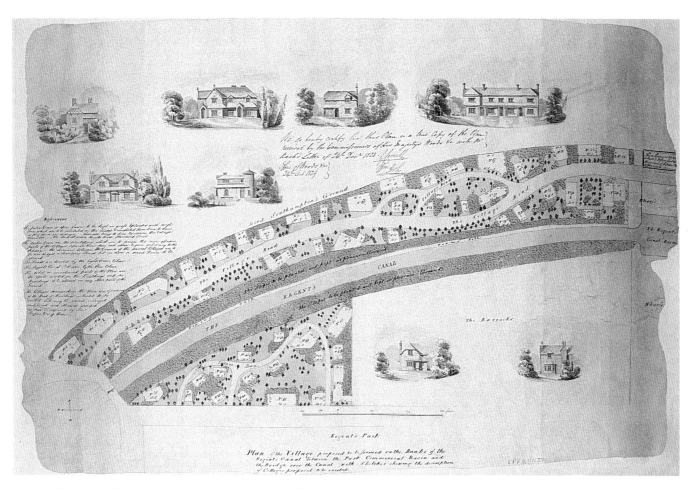

247 *Plan of the Villages proposed to be formed on the banks of the Regent's Canal*, pen and pencil with watercolour wash, 1823. Public Record Office, Kew.

ous variations of the classical vernacular 'and so rapidly descending to the nondescript', as John Summerson has put it, were not 'cottages', but substantial dwellings which came to be occupied by a cross-section of the middle classes (fig. 248).[55] They had lost the self-effacing character of houses in a rural village, and were not unlike what Nicol described in 1809 as the villas in the 'vicinage of the city . . . which may rather be termed *town houses*, and are often necessarily garrisoned in'.[56]

Through his process of aggrandisement the little cottages were transformed into miniature suburban villas: the streets were lined with double detached houses which were regularly spaced, closely set and the proposed 'invisible' enclosures of 'live hedges or Iron wire Fences' were rejected in favour of conspicuous and secure boundaries.[57] While the obtrusive barriers might have satisfied the inhabitants' need for privacy and protection, their presence banished the rural village character of the development, and reinforced its townishness.

The gardens were, moreover, not the 'cottage gardens', which Loudon declared would induce 'sober industrious and domestic habits . . . by creating that independence which is the best security against pauperism'. Nor was the average cottage inhabitant the rustic 'labourer', who typically occupied 'his own leisure hours in the operations of digging and planting, and those of his wife and children in hoeing, weeding and watering'.[58] The villages were inhabited by members of the professional and commercial classes. Park Village was none the less aesthetically in accordance with Loudon's vision of the appropriate expression for 'artificial villages': he regretted that on both sides of a public road a slip of ground should be apportioned to each 'villager' to allow him to build his own house and garden. The result would be a series of irregular buildings and individually laid out gardens.[59]

If the landscape framework of trees and closely set shrubs established and maintained the unity of the

248 W. Radcliff after Thomas Hosmer Shepherd, 'Park Village East, Regent's Park', etching from *Metropolitan Improvements* (1827). Yale Center for British Art, New Haven.

village setting, the private gardens diversified the scene through the introduction of spontaneity, idiosyncrasy, intricacy and variety. Likewise, upon the principle of association, the scene promoted what Price identified as 'the comforts and enjoyments of social life, pleasing the eye of civilized man'.[60]

The picturesque was concerned with composing pictorial views which combined the opposing categories of the sublime and the beautiful: on the one hand, an overwhelming grandeur, arousing awe and astonishment, and, on the other, a quality seen as pleasing and unthreatening, and often located in the social and the domestic.[61] In his terraces Nash was primarily concerned with maintaining grandeur, magnificence and sublimity; the Park Villages, on the other hand, through their evocation of unpretentious domesticity and through the small size of their individual gardens, emphasise elements in the picturesque more closely allied to the beautiful. Price recommended that a garden should be 'blended' and 'melted' together 'with a playful and airy kind of lightness, and a sort of loose and

sketchy indistinctness'.[62] He declared, too, that the association of 'neatness and freshness' was required 'immediately adjoining the dwellings of opulence and luxury, that everything should assure its character, and not only be, but appear to be dressed and cultivated. In such situations, neat gravel walks, mown turf, and flowering plants and shrubs, trained and distributed by art, are perfectly in character.'[63] The Park Villages closely follow these recommendations. Such qualities have provided the basis for a historical narrative in which the Park Villages supply a model for the subsequent development of the suburban garden.

'SMALL PLOTS' AND THE SUBURBAN GARDEN

Although the Park Villages have been placed by architectural historians at the beginning of the tradition of modern suburban development, few such scholars have discussed the relative importance of their small gardens.[64] Social historians and geographers, on the other hand, have for some years explored the role and meaning of 'smaller, non-utilitarian gardens' in the development of the suburban aesthetic and the demand for suburban living.[65] F. M. L. Thompson proposed in his essay 'The Rise of Suburbia' (1982) that the 'suburban life style of individual domesticity and group monitored respectability' could take hold only where the setting of the house was such that 'the family could distance itself from the outside world in its own private fortress behind its own garden fence and privet hedge and yet could make a show of outward appearances that was sure to be noticed by neighbours'. The individual garden was, he argued, among the greatest material aspirations of townsmen because it was an 'essential attribute of the single family house' – 'preferably one in front to impress the outside world with the display of a neatly-tended possession of some land, and one in the back for the family to enjoy'. 'It would' therefore, he suggested, 'be sensible to look at the suburban garden for the roots of the demand for suburban living, something which

brought the possibility of privacy and seclusion with it but which was desired in a straightforward way for its own sake because it was a piece of tangible evidence, however minute, that the dream of being a townsman living in the country was something more than just an illusion.'[66]

That the individual garden has been so closely associated with suburban living is to a large measure due to John Loudon, who from 1812 began to publish on the subject of 'laying out of small Plots of Ground' in the context of the metropolis. Such diminutive 'fourth-rate gardens' (fig. 249), as he later referred to them, became the central theme of his magisterial work *The Suburban Gardener* (1838), in which he declared that:

The enjoyments to be derived from a suburban residence depend principally on a knowledge of the resources which a garden, however small, is capable of affording. The benefits experienced by breathing air unconfined by close streets of houses, and contami-

249   Michael Serles, *Plan and Elevation of 3 Terraces of 58 Houses, Greenwich*, pen with watercolour wash, 1784. Royal Institute of British Architects, London. This design is an early example of the use of semi-detached houses in suburban estate development.

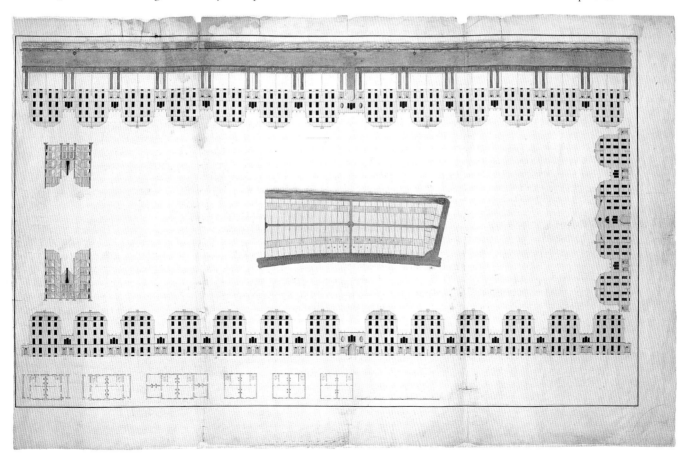

nated by the smoke of chimneys; the cheerful aspect of vegetation; the singing of birds in their seasons; and the enlivening effect of finding ourselves unpent-up by buildings, and in comparatively unlimited space.[67]

To appreciate the novelty of Loudon's model of the suburban ideal one must first be acquainted with the predecessors to the suburban garden. The town garden was initially the basis of his comparative analysis. This comparison was not lost on his contemporary readers, who were acquainted with such 'gardens in town' at first hand. But those who have subsequently used Loudon to frame the historical narrative of the suburban garden will not have been aware of the lively urban garden tradition which preceded it. The suburban garden has been presented as owing little to earlier urban gardening traditions – its appearance in the early nineteenth century transforming, as though by some extraordinary power to harness the aspirations of the age, the physical and social fabric of the common London house.

Loudon, himself, has contributed to this confusion: only once in his extensive outpourings did he compare the town garden to the suburban garden, or suggest that there might have been a notable distinction between the two traditions. In *The Suburban Gardener* (1838) he declared 'in a few words' that 'gardens in town' were 'calculated essentially for business and facility of enjoyment', whilst those in the 'suburbs of town are alone calculated to afford a maximum of comfort and enjoyment at a minimum of expense'.[68] In order to grasp the full force of this comparison we must refer back to his writings of 1812, when he confronted the town garden directly for the first time.

To recapitulate what has been said in an earlier chapter, Loudon published his thoughts on the layout of 'small Plots of Ground' in *Hints on the laying out of Gardens and Pleasure Grounds* (1812). His aim was to supply 'observations on the Mode of laying out small Plots of Ground' in the 'modern style'. This, he remarked, was a subject which had been 'almost wholly overlooked by modern writers on laying out grounds'. His view of 'Gardens for the Town' was not greatly different from Meager, Switzer, Langley, Dalrymple or Spence: small gardens were 'artificial situations' suited to the display of 'artificial forms'. 'It was', he said, 'natural for a mind acquainted with the powers of art, to suppose that professional assistance can effect little in laying out small gardens or places of a few acres; but this is to infer, that nothing can be beautiful that is not also extensive. Beauty or expression depend no more on dimension

than on expence, but are the result of a combination of parts forming a whole, calculated by fitness and utility to gratify the mind, and by its effect to charm the eye.' In laying out a 'small place', 'the artist will often meet with difficulties unknown in places of greater extent; since these, by their magnitude, naturally possess a certain greatness of character; while a small spot is a blank, depending for its effect wholly on the skill and ingenuity of him who undertakes to fill it up'.

Having established that small gardens could pose practical and aesthetic problems, he, perhaps rather surprisingly, proposed that the 'common mode of laying out spaces of this description in figures and compartments, after the manner of parterres' was 'well adapted' to such small plots. As works of 'undisguised art', town gardens were, in Loudon's mind, incapable of producing 'grandeur' and 'the simplicity of rural nature'; he advised his readers who wished to create gardens of a 'striking' character, to 'introduce either some grotesque or uncommon work of art, or a portion of the picturesque, or even rude scenery'.[69]

When Loudon was compiling *Hints*, he had not yet developed his concept of the suburban garden: extent of ground and expense of garden building and garden maintenance were the sole criteria for his analysis of the options open to metropolitan gardeners. In *The Suburban Gardener* he elaborated his vision of the suburban garden. Here the garden is presented in an entirely new light. Loudon put forward a view of the garden as a universal aspiration of domestic fulfilment, suggesting that the full development of suburban gardening was contingent on the equal participation of men, women and children in the manual labour of gardening (figs 250 and 251). The harmony of their combined labours, he implied, produced an idealised domesticity.

The suburban gardener, Loudon remarked, was 'generally his own gardener', and was by definition informed in the art of gardening and capable of carrying out the duties of a gardener, with or without the assistance of one. Gardening in the suburbs was, moreover, an inexpensive and enjoyable 'amateur' pursuit. There was, he remarked, 'a great deal of enjoyment to be derived from performing the different operations of gardening, independently altogether of the health resulting from this kind of exercise'.[70] Suburban gardening can easily be assigned a place within the pursuit of leisure that historians have seen as characteristic of British society from the late eighteenth century onwards.[71] At the same time, it was an activity that galvanised the impulse towards self-improvement; conscientious suburban gardeners,

Loudon assumed, would consult his own writings on the aesthetics and practice of gardening, and would be encouraged by these works to see gardening as more than a mere mechanical pursuit.

Loudon's remarks in *The Suburban Gardener* might suggest that there was a clear distinction between the town garden and the suburban garden: town gardens were old-fashioned, expensive and fussy conceits of 'avowed art' which 'harmonize[d] with their artificial surroundings'; suburban gardens, on the other hand, were places in which the family could escape from urban squalor to cultivate social harmony and sentimental domesticity in 'comparatively unlimited space'.[72]

250 Thomas Stothard, *Watering the Flowers*, pencil and watercolour, *c.*1810. Manchester City Art Galleries.

251 'Antony and Augustus; or, a rational education preferable to riches', engraving from Arnaud Berquin, *The Looking-Glass of the Mind* (1792 ed.), p. 158. British Museum, London. From the late eighteenth century children were encouraged to take an active interest in gardening. In Berquin's moral story children were taught that welfare and happiness were the product of a 'well-grounded education' – regardless of one's financial circumstances. This form of enlightened education included the healthy and robust activity of gardening.

The main problem for the reader who attempts to clarify the distinction between the two, however, is that Loudon defines the suburban garden primarily in social terms, but hesitates to pursue the social determinants of town gardening beyond the employment of jobbing gar-

249

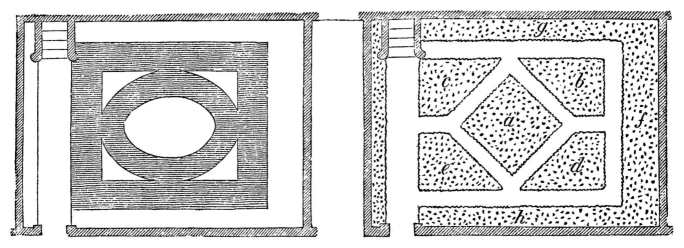

252　Plan of two 'fourth-rate gardens', engraving from J. C. Loudon, *The Suburban Gardener* (1838), p. 211. Loudon advocated low, formal layouts for front gardens as they did not compromise the ventilation of the house.

deners. Instead, he defines the town garden with reference to its aesthetic pitfalls. It is therefore difficult to determine whether Loudon perceives the two categories as entirely distinct, or whether he sees some overlap between the two.

When Loudon defines gardens with reference to their physical form, he compounds the confusion. In *The Suburban Gardener* he lumped all 'small Plots of Ground' under the category of the 'fourth-rate garden', and when discussing them he described, on one hand, new features of gardening on the peripheries of town, and on the other, features of an enduring tradition of town gardening (fig. 252). He perpetuated and revived a range of eighteenth-century conventions – the most notable of which was the layout of 'gardens, and parterres' in the 'ancient geometrical style of rural improvement'.[73] (The stylistic category invoked here is, in fact, explicitly named in *Hints*, and then silently dropped in *The Suburban Gardener*, in accordance with Loudon's more general revision of the history of gardening to exclude any sense of a continuing practice of town garden design.) He continued, moreover, to place considerable emphasis on the provision and treatment of garden boundaries.

Suburban gardens became, of course, a great deal more visually conspicuous than their urban predecessors – partly because they were usually larger in area, and also because they were often enclosed by lower and less solid structures, such as hedges and fences, as opposed to brick walls and palings. More ground was also generally given over to 'insulating' the better classes of houses by the provision of a more spacious gardens in

front than had generally been allotted to dwellings in the eighteenth century. Larger front gardens were intended to increase the airiness of a premises, and Loudon's endorsement of the low and flat style of parterres doubtless reflected his desire to ensure that the house remained well ventilated.

Like his predecessors, however, Loudon continued to assess gardens with reference to the urban ideal of public magnificence. When discussing the disposition of front gardens in town, he suggested that while 'there is little danger of the gardens of the wealthy being neglected . . . it is of great importance to the advancement of gardening, that the art should be displayed to as great a perfection as possible in those gardens which are most universal; which are continually under the eye of a large city population; seen by the whole country-inhabitants when they visit the towns; and which chiefly come under the eye of foreigners'.[74]

This injunction serves to remind us that the town garden was an awkward concept which was not readily assimilated into the urban aesthetic. Its anomalous character has determined its curious double mode of existence since the early nineteenth century: as, on one hand, a lively, continuing practice within the vernacular tradition and, on the other, a concept consigned to the very periphery of all writing about gardens. Town gardens continued to be formed in the metropolis throughout the century – indeed, in 1875 the tradition was reinvigorated with the passing of the Public Health Act, which gave local authorities the right to specify house layouts, the width of streets and the spaces around domestic buildings. The provision of small paved courts,

THE MOMENTOUS QUESTION.

Paterfamilias (who is just beginning to feel himself at home in his delightfully new suburban residence) interrupts the Wife of his Bosom.
"'SEASIDE!' 'CHANGE OF AIR!!' 'OUT OF TOWN!!!' WHAT NONSENSE, ANNA MARIA! WHY, GOOD GRACIOUS ME! WHAT ON EARTH CAN YOU WANT TO BE GOING 'OUT OF TOWN' FOR, WHEN YOU'VE GOT SUCH A GARDEN AS *THIS!*"

253   George Du Maurier, 'The Momentous Question', engraving from *Punch, or the London Charivari*, 2 September 1871.

yards or gardens then became for the first time a statutory requirement.

These little spaces were no longer, however, called town gardens, but suburban gardens, gardens of 'houses in streets', or 'small gardens', and were invariably referred to in association with attributes of the eighteenth-century city, such as geometrical planning, or squares and crescents. The town garden, then, as an explicitly formulated concept, was almost entirely excluded from all works addressing the theory and practice of gardening. This exclusion, none the less, is never quite complete. Many nineteenth-century writings acknowledged urban gardens, fleetingly and half-dismissively, as spaces for the eruption of endearing caprice and engaging archaism.

A comic illustration of 1871 from *Punch* (fig. 253), portrays the determined pursuit of leisure within the gardens of a 'delightfully new suburban residence'. Much of the irony and poignancy of this representation, however, is derived from the contrast between the desires and aspirations of the residents – a family in which the wife dreams of 'change of air', and the husband eagerly brandishes a watering-can – and the extreme spatial constraint of the setting in which these desires are expressed: the garden walls scarcely separate the little plot from the presence of the neighbours.[75]

Throughout the nineteenth century the town garden was, in fact, viewed as a lively but archaic and anomalous element, which belonged to another era. Loudon implied in 1812 that to modernise the layout of 'Gardens for the Town' was to breathe life into a system of gardening so remote as to bring to mind the 'ancient plans and treatises' of Leonard Meager (1670) and Batty Langley (1727).[76] Dickens, as has been shown, was no less critical, portraying town gardens in *Dombey and Son* (1848) as unfashionable and unlovable relics from the 'powdered head and pig-tail period'; and in 1872 a contributor to *The Garden* remarked that when 'modern citizens of Cockaigne' formed their small gardens, they imitated the 'meagre formal prettiness of the old Keepsake, or Souvenir fashion – a prim, pruned, and, as it were, starched and whaleboned beauty'.[77]

11 Switzer, in fact, made no distinction between urban and sub-urban gardens. He remarked that 'when Town-Gardens are mention'd, 'tis not thereby meant Gardens in or very near *London*, but those that are four, five, six, or seven Miles out of Town, wither the Fatigues of the Court and Senate often force the illustrious Patriots of *Great-Britain* to retreat, and breathe the sweet and fragrant Air of Gardens; and these are generally too much penn'd up'. *Nobleman, Gentleman, and Gardener's Recreation*, vol. 1, pp. xxx, xxix.

12 For a description of the growth of the London nursery trade see Harvey, 'Mid-Georgian Nurseries'.

13 Ware, *Complete Body of Architecture*, p. 649.

14 Kames, *Elements of Criticism*, vol. 3, pp. 305–6.

15 Ware, *Complete Body of Architecture*, p. 649.

16 Walpole, 'Essay on Modern Gardening', p. 535.

17 'London Gardens'.

18 Switzer, *Nobleman, Gentleman, and Gardener's Recreation*, p. xxvi.

19 *Common Sense*, no. 150 (1739).

20 In Dickens's *Dombey and Son* (London, 1848), Mr Dombey is described as living in a house of 'dismal state' on the 'shady side of a tall, dark, dreadfully genteel street in the region between Portland Place and Bryanstone Square'. His 'little garden' – probably planted some time in the late eighteenth century – was but 'a gravelled yard, where two gaunt trees, with blackened trunks and branches, rattled rather than rustled, their leaves were so smoke-dried'. *Dombey and Son* (1900), p. 14. Originally published in monthly numbers from October 1846 to April 1848.

21 Dickens, *Nicholas Nickleby* (1986 ed.), p. 66.

22 Dickens, *Nicholas Nickleby* (1986 ed.), p. 66. 'Blacks' were particles of soot.

23 'London Gardens'.

24 'London Gardens'.

25 'London Gardens'.

CHAPTER 1

1 This chapter attempts an iconology as Erwin Panofsky defined it, an 'iconography turned interpretive'. While iconography 'in the narrower' sense was the identification of conventional, consciously ascribed symbols, iconology probes a deeper stratum of meaning. It excavates the 'intrinsic meaning' of a work of art 'by ascertaining those underlying principles which reveal the basic attitude of a nation, a period, a class, a religious or philosophical persuasion – unconsciously qualified by one personality and condensed into one work of art'. Panofsky, *Studies in Iconology*, p. 14; and 'Iconography and Iconology', pp. 57–8, 55, 64, 65. For a discussion of an iconological approach to map reading see Harley, 'Meaning and Ambiguity'.

2 John Strype, *Survey the Cities*, bk 2, chap. 1, vol, 1, p. 1.

3 Ibid., pp. 1, 2.

4 Ibid., p. 2.

5 Daniel Defoe, *A Tour*, vol. 1, pp. 327, 328–9.

6 Fairchild, *City Gardener*, p. 6.

7 Fairchild, *City Gardener* pp. 67, title-page, 7, 69, 8.

8 Fairchild *City Gardener*, p. 58.

9 Sir Hans Sloane's *Horti sicci* (The Herbarium, Natural History Museum, London) comprises 337 numbered volumes, and includes the herbarium collections of Plukenet, Petiver, Buddle, Uvedale and many others. Two such collections are: 'Plants gathered in the Fields and Gardens about London about the year 1682 for my own [Sir Hans Sloane] and Mr Courtenir's collections' (H.S.9), and 'Botanicum hortense arborum *Jac. Petiver* in which are Specimens of trees in Gardens

about London with Petiver's Synonima in his *Botanicaum* mostly referred to Mr Ray', *c.*1716? (H.S.180). There are upwards of thirty specimens in the *Horti sicci* which were gathered in Fairchild's garden at Hoxton between 1700–1720; there are, likewise, dozens of annotations which describe how particular plants flourished at the nurseryman's garden.

10 Fairchild, *City Gardener*, p. 44.

11 Ibid., pp. 44, 45.

12 Ibid., pp. 50–51.

13 Ibid., pp. 51, 51–2.

14 Ibid., pp. 52, 16, 17, 19. Careful pruning is claimed to have given a 'good Prospect of Figgs this Year, at the Reverend Dr *Bennett's* Garden at *Cripplegate*; and near the same Place there are now large Figg-Trees growing well, tho' they have very little Air'. Ibid., pp. 52–3.

15 Ibid., pp. 17, 57, 53–4.

16 Ibid., pp. 17–18, 54–5, 56–7.

17 Ibid., pp. 18, 19–20, 19.

18 Ibid., p. 54.

19 Ibid., pp. 59–70.

20 For a discussion on 'Abundance' see Bryson, *Looking at the Overlooked*, pp. 96–135.

21 Fairchild, *City Gardener* pp. 62–3.

22 Ibid., p. 7.

23 Summerson, *Georgian London*, pp. 111–12.

24 Harley, 'Maps, Knowledge and Power', p. 292.

25 Ibid., p. 291.

26 [Bramston], *Art of Politicks*, pp. i, 261.

27 *Kalm's Account*, p. 85.

28 See *The A to Z of Regency London*, introduction by Paul Laxton, and Laxton, 'Horwood's Plan'.

29 A tenter ground is a ground occupied by tenters for stretching cloth, etc.

30 Laxton, 'Horwood's Plan', pp. 236–7.

31 In its numbering of premises it was unmatched until the 1930s.

32 See Harley, 'Meaning and ambiguity', pp. 28–9.

CHAPTER 2

1 John Claudius Loudon, *The Suburban Gardener* (1838), pp. 6, 1. Much of the material presented in *The Suburban Gardener* appeared in the *Gardener's Magazine* from 1835 onwards: for instance in vol. 10, pp. 489–95; vol. 11, pp. 509–613; and vol. 12, pp. 66–9.

2 Loudon established these parameters in *Hints*, p. 1; they were subsequently included among the criteria that determined the character of what he referred to as the 'fourth-rate garden'.

3 Loudon, *Suburban Gardener*, pp. 170–71.

4 Loudon, *Suburban Gardener*, p. 284.

5 Loudon, *Suburban Gardener*, p. 180.

6 Summerson, *Georgian London*, pp. 38–83. Olsen, *Town Planning*.

7 Muthesius, *English Terraced House*, p. 18.

8 Oglander, *Admiral's Wife*, p. 80; Oglander, *Admiral's Widow*, p. 37.

9 Robertson was arrested for non-payment of outstanding invoices to her carpenter Mr Martyr, who pressed charges for arrears totalling £1,200 for the manufacture of an aviary, garden seats, a swing. *Life and Memoirs of Miss Robertson*, pp. 24–5, 35.

10 The term 'estate', meaning either a rural or urban land-holding, is uniquely English, and reflects the distinction between *rus* and *urbs* that was for a long period ambiguous. The distinction first became blurred with the disappearance of city walls at the beginning of the sixteenth century. It was further dissolved by similar patterns of property ownership in both the country and the city; the leading rural estates were

very often the principal developers of the urban estates. An urban estate was often a large freehold owned by a single landlord and managed by the freeholder himself or by a trusteeship. Covent Garden (1630) was the first of a succession of speculative estate developments planned and managed by hereditary landlords.

The basis for leaseholding was that plots were disposed of at low ground rents to building speculators on long leases with the understanding that the lessee would build, at his own expense, a house or houses of substantial character. Once what was agreed upon was built, the lessee would keep the buildings and in many cases the garden walls in good repair according to the terms of his agreement with the freeholder. At the expiry of the lease all buildings and property reverted to the ground landlord, who could then choose to re-let on repairing leases (to cover dilapidations) or have the building or buildings demolished and lease the property for new construction. The interest of the freeholder was simply to preserve the reversionary value of the estate to sustain subsequent generations through greatly increased hereditary landed wealth.

11 Olsen, *Town Planning*, pp. 19–20.

12 Summerson, *Georgian London*, p. 98.

13 Daniel Defoe, *A Tour*, vol. 1, p. 316.

14 *SOL*, vol. 40, p. 99.

15 Seymour, *Survey*, vol. 2, p. 667.

16 Sale particulars for a house in Grosvenor Square in 1798 state that the plot was 36 by 200 feet and contained a 'large garden'. (BOD, G.A. fol.A.260 (144)).

17 *SOL*, vol. 40, pp. 222, 256.

18 Estate Plans Books, and Block Plans (nineteenth century), Archives of the Howard de Walden Estate, London. Mr Christie's, auction notice, 3 June 1795 (BOD, G.A. fol.A259 (148)); Skinner, Dyke & Co., 24 January 1805 (BOD, G.A. fol.A.260 (166); other plots appear, from auction notices, to average about 36 by 100ft.

19 *Grub Street Journal* (28 March 1734), no. 222.

20 Summerson, *Georgian London*, p. 111. It also marked the decline of the early Georgian building boom which began in the late 1730s and reached its ebb in the war period 1743–5. [Stewart] *Critical Observations*, p. 28.

21 James, *Theory and Practice*, p. 17.

22 Gwynn, *London and Westminster Improved*, p. 79.

23 Dorey, 'Sir John Soane's Courtyard Gardens'; Glenorchy Account Books, ref. no. GD 112/21/77 & 78, National Archive of Scotland; Harris, *William Chambers*, p. 222; Stroud, *Capability Brown*, pp. 179, 159; Longstaffe-Gowan, 'History of Spencer House Garden', p. 46.

24 Ware, *Complete Body*, pp. 345–6.

25 Thomas Rawlins referred to gardens in his *Familiar Architecture* (1768), p. xv, when laying out the townhouse. He called the back of the town house, like the back of a country house, the 'garden front'.

26 Ware, *Complete Body*, p. 345.

27 Ware remarked that 'ground-rent is so dear in *London* that every method is to be used to make the most of the ground-plan'. Ware, *Complete Body*, p. 346.

28 See Cruickshank and Burton, *Life*, pp. 74–96.

29 Two kinds of lavatory were employed in the eighteenth century, the privy and the water-closet; the former consisted simply of a primitive latrine, whereas the latter included a lavatory-pan that could be flushed with water, usually from a tank but sometimes directly from a water pipe. See Cruickshank and Burton, *Life*, p. 87.

30 Ware, *Complete Body*, pp. 346, 322.

31 Ibid., pp. 323, 322.

32 Richard Boyle, 2nd (and last) Viscount Shannon, youngest son of the Earl of Cork.

33 Hewlings, 'Leoni's Drawings'.

34 An auction particular of 1726 records that two houses in St James's Street, Westminster, possessed gardens behind the houses, 'with vaults under the garden'. BOD, John Johnson Collection, F.1.Med. (94).

35 Ware, *Complete Body*, p. 347.

36 These privies and their plumbing still survive.

37 Ware, *Complete Body*, p. 636.

38 Purchas, 'Maurice-Louis Jolivet's Drawings'.

39 West inhabited the house from 1774 until his death in 1820. Leigh Hunt referred to artist's garden as 'West's Italian garden'. Hunt, *Autobiography*, vol. 1, p. 158.

40 Ibid., vol. 1, pp. 147–8.

41 Ibid., p. 151.

42 Only part of Adam's scheme was executed as Grant suffered considerable financial embarrassment in 1774.

43 Light-wells and vents were common to most gardens built upon leads.

44 See Knox and Longstaffe-Gowan, 'Town Garden Design', and *SOL, St James's Westminster*, vol. 32, pt 2 (1963), pp. 500–5.

45 Letter to George Montague, 18 May 1748, *Private Correspondence of Horace Walpole*, 1820, vol. 1, p. 172.

46 The 'large family house' is described in 1802 as 'displaying TWO superb ELEVATIONS or FRONTS, the one in Old Burlington Street [to the east], the other in Cork Street [to the west]'. Mr Christie, auction prospectus for the premises of Sir John Call, Bart. deceased, February 4, 1802. BOD, G.A. fol.A261 (91).

47 The house stood near the present location of Marble Arch, and was later known as 23 Hyde Park Place. It was demolished in 1901.

48 Ware, *Complete Body*, p. 323.

49 Fairchild refers to small gardens as occurring in 'very close places', *City Gardener*, pp. 18, 54–5, 57, 45.

50 Contemporary sale notices published in the local press corroborate the ubiquity of forecourts.

51 *Kalm's Account*, p. 85.

52 Fairchild, *City Gardener*, pp. 52, 50, 52.

53 The 'airy', as its name suggests, was a light-well which gave light and ventilation to the basement.

54 It was reported in *The Grub Street Journal* (1734; no. 252, 1) that forecourts had been 'lately built in *Arlington Street*'.

55 Ware, *Complete Body*, p. 323.

56 Mr Christie, Edgware Road, 1791; Edmund Drayton, Raven Row, Mile End, 1805 (BOD, G.A. fol.A262 (4)); Mr Christie, no. 4 Fitzroy Square, 31 October 1799 (BOD, G.A. fol.A260 (38)).

57 Gwynn, *London and Westminster*, p. x.

58 Typical auction details for suburban dwellings. Mr Christie, Tyndall Place, Islington, 20 July 1798 (BOD, G.A. fol.A264 (182)).

59 Gwynn, quoting from a passage in *The Rambler*, on his title-page to *London and Westminster Improved* (1766).

60 Summerson, *Georgian London*, p. 121.

61 Gwynn, *London and Westminster*, p. 78.

62 Ibid., pp. x–xi.

63 Ibid., pp. 81, 78.

64 Ibid., p. xi.

65 A 'messuage' is a term used to describe a dwelling-house with its outbuildings and curtilage and the adjacent land assigned to its use.

66 Mr Robins, Judd Place, Somers Town, 1803 (BOD, G.A. fol.A260 (127)); Mr Smith, Judd Place East, June 1804 (BOD, G.A. fol.A260 (226)); Skinner, Dyke & Co., York Buildings,

New Road, 1805 (BOD, G.A. fol. 262 (290)); Mr Greenwood, East Side of City Road, 1802 (BOD, G.A. fol. A259 (186)); Mr Willock, Cumberland Place, New Road, 1805 (BOD, G.A. fol.A262 (290)).

67   [Pückler-Muskau], *Letters from Albion*, vol. 1, pp. 157–9.

68   Philippar, *Voyage*, pp. 30–31; translation from the French by the author.

69   Loudon, *Encyclopaedia* (1828), 5th edition, item no. 7292.

70   Ibid., item no. 7292.

71   Ibid., item no. 7426.

72   See Barrell, *Birth of Pandora*, chap. 3: 'The Public Prospect and the Private View: The Politics of Taste in Eighteenth-Century Britain', pp. 41–61.

73   Spence, *Observations*, anecdote 606, vol. 1, p. 252.

74   Switzer, *Ichnographia*, vol. 3, p. 14.

75   Mr Christie, advertising premises on south side of Pall Mall, 22 May 1799 (BOD, G.A. fol.A261 (116)); Mr Christie, advertising a house at 24 Nottingham Place, St Marylebone (west side), 31 May 1797) (BOD, G.A. fol.A261 (84)); Mr Christie, advertising Tyndall Place, Islington, 20 July 1798 (BOD, G.A. fol.A264 (182)).

76   Mr Winstanley, advertising 6 Devonshire Place, east of Portland Place, 11 May 1802 (BOD, G.A. fol.A259 (245)). Skinner & Dyke, advertising 5 Colebrook Row, Islington, 10 July 1799 (BOD, G.A. fol.A264 (186)).

77   Switzer, *Ichnographia*, vol. 3, p. 14.

78   There are many accounts in the local press of 'Good Houses' with gardens 'looking into' parks or neighbouring gardens. See the *Daily Courant*, Thursday 29 March 1716 for descriptions of houses in Pall Mall and Bond Street. Mr Christie, advertising house in Pall Mall, 22 May 1799 (BOD, G.A. fol.A261 (116)); Mr Christie, advertising house in Lower Grosvenor Place, 25 November 1802 (BOD, G.A. fol.A260 (328)); Skinner & Dyke, advertising 6 Lower Grosvenor Place, Pimlico, 8 March 1802 (BOD, G.A. fol.A260 (327)).

79   *Spectator*, no. 411 (21 June 1712); Barrell, *Birth of Pandora*, Bermingham and Brewer, *Consumption of Culture*.

80   Repton, *Fragments*, pp. 323, 334–5.

81   'Happiness drawn rather from Prospect than Possession – exemplified in the history of Euphanor', in *The Mirror*, no. 37 (Edinburgh, 1 June 1779), p. 1.

82   Christie's, advertising a house in Park Lane, near Hertford Street, 1800 (BOD, G.A. fol.A261 (131)); Mr Christie, advertising Holderness House, Park Lane, 28 January 1802 (BOD, G.A. fol.A261 (132)); Mr Farebrother, advertising 9 Montague Place, 24 March 1806 (BOD, G.A. fol.A261 (24)).

83   BOD, G.A. fol.A261 (131).

84   *Constat Books*, CRES, 6.79/H4, pp. 32–6.

85   Lord William Gordon (1744–1823) was Deputy Ranger of St James's and Green Parks from 1778 until his death.

86   In 1790 there were five dukes, four earls, two baronets and one count resident in Piccadilly – many of whom were very influential courtiers. CRES. 6.79/H4, 34.

87   CRES. 6.79/H4, p. 36.

88   Restrictive building covenants were not always enforced by urban landlords. They did, for instance, maintain the original character of the Bedford Estate (Olsen, *Town Planning*, p. 108.) This practice may have begun as early as the seventeenth century, although most documented cases tend to occur from the late eighteenth century.

89   29 August 1806, p. 148 (GEP 1409/5/4); GEP (1818), Mr Auriol lived at 131 Park Street (1409/5/7, p. 105) (MS).

90   Mr Willock, 15 May 1805 (BOD, G.A. fol.A260 (131)).

91   GEP (1766) (1409/5/2, numbers 306, 307, 310).

92   Mr Christie, Corner of Duke Street, Grosvenor Square, 23

May 1804 (BOD, G.A. fol.A259 (164)); Peter Coxe, Burrell & Foster, advertising Egremont House, Piccadilly, 13 February 1806 (BOD, G.A. fol.A261 (151)); Christie's, 5 November 1801, St James's Street, Park Place (BOD, G.A. fol.A262 (47)).

93   Repton, *Sketches*, p. 58.

94   Mangles, *Floral Calendar*, p. 27.

95   See Loudon's *Suburban Gardener*, pp. 177–80, for a thorough disquisition on the subject of aspect.

96   Repton, *Fragments*, p. 55.

97   Loudon, *Encyclopaedia*, article no. 1177.

98   Robert Noyes, 'Advice on the Management of a Fine House', *The Gentleman's Magazine* (1753), pp. 529–30.

99   Projecting balconies, awnings and verandahs were also at times described as obstacles to views. For instance see GEP (1814) 1049/5/5, pp. 36, 303; *SOL*, vol. 39, pt 2, 42.

100   Christie's, 28 January 1802, Holderness House, Park Lane (BOD, G.A. fol.A261 (132)).

101   Mangles, *Calendar*, p. v.

102   [Southey], *Letters*, vol. 1, p. 124.

103   GEP, 1409/5/4, 7 March 1806.

104   Ware, *Complete Body*, 323.

105   Ibid., p. 328.

106   Repton, *Fragments*, p. 53.

107   Evelyn, *Diary*, vol. 3, p. 375.

108   Evans, 'Jacques Rousseau'; Jackson-Stops, *English Arcadia*, pp. 7–8.

109   Now the Royal Foundation of St Katherine.

110   Schwab and Nurse, 'Butcher Row'. I am grateful to Roger Bowdler for this reference.

111   Ware, *Complete Body*, p. 346.

112   Peter Coxe, Burrell & Foster Auctioneers (BOD, G.A. fol.A260 (149)).

113   Oglander, *Admiral's Widow*, p. 164.

114   GEP, 1 October 1819, 1409/5/7, 462.

115   Gwynn, *London and Westminster*, p. 17.

116   Improvements to lighting and paving in London during the eighteenth century are charted in Cruickshank and Burton, *Life in the Georgian City*, pp. 3–22.

117   Previous acts had merely been feeble attempts to enforce long-standing personal obligations of individual householders to pave and maintain in good repair the pavement and street in front of their own door.

118   So immense was the success of the paving enterprise and its various related improvements that in 1787 the scheme was described as 'an undertaking which has introduced a degree of elegance and symmetry into the streets of the metropolis, that is the admiration of all Europe and far exceeds anything of the kind in the modern world'. George, *London Life*, p. 108.

119   The rear garden at no. 3 was described in 1777 as possessing a 'serpentised path well pav'd betwixt two ovalls embellished with a profusion of flowers'; and the neighbouring garden at no. 2 was three years later was described as 'a spacious garden neatly laid out on a most approved and convenient plan, planted with fine fruit trees and shrubs'. Uncatalogued papers of the Worshipful Company of Drapers, London.

120   The Act covered the parishes of St John Wapping and St George in the county of Middlesex.

121   Drapers' Company, ref. Y.180–242.

122   Drapers' Company, ref. 23212–15.

123   *Temporalities*, 1805, Archbishop of Canterbury's Estate in Lambeth, Lambeth Palace Library, TC.73, items 26, 39.

124   GEP, 1409/10/Box 6/2, 27 December 1793 (no. 201).

125   Nor was the practice limited to creation of small private gardens: in 1826 the Commissioners of Woods, Forests and Land Revenues enclosed 'a space of Ground behind the

Houses in Piccadilly Terrace and Hamilton-Place, and in front of Park-Lane, which was the resort of idle and disorderly persons, and, in its former state, a great and general nuisance'. It was 'formed into an Ornamental Garden' and it was proposed that 'those, whose Houses are in its immediate neighbourhood, shall have access to this Garden, on payment of a stipulated Annual Sum towards the Expense of keeping it up'. *5th Report, Commissioners of His Majesty's Woods, Forests, and Land Revenues*, 1826.

126 Agreements stress that these enclosures were not to be considered as 'occupations'.

127 GEP, 1409/5/2, 8 January 1796, 8.

128 GEP, 29 April 1808 (no.864), vol. 3, 219 (1409/5/3).

129 Longstaffe-Gowan, 'History of Spencer House Garden'; and CRES 6/88. Freeboard was the nine-foot wide margin of land which lay outside a park wall which remained in possession of the Crown. The land could not be built upon without special dispensation.

130 GEP, 1409/5/1, 13 March 1789.

131 GEP, 1409/5/1, 21 February 1794 (no. 209), 22.

132 GEP, 1409/5/4, 7 March 1806 (no. 772), 118–19.

133 Lambeth Palace Library, ED.1919, 182–88.

134 Principal sources of property sale particulars include the Gough Additional Manuscripts and the John Johnson Collection at the Bodleian Library; the Heal Collection at Camden Local History Library, Swiss Cottage; the Guildhall Library Manuscripts Department, and Westminster City Archives. Newspapers which have been examined include the *London Gazette*, *Daily Advertiser*, *Postman*, *Daily Courant*, *General Advertiser*, *London Evening Post*, *Morning Chronicle* and *London Advertiser*, *The Times*, *London Record* and *Sunday Gazette*.

135 *Daily Advertiser* (7 January 1745; 6 January 1752).

136 Mr Christie, 5 May 1801 (BOD, G.A. fol.A262 (112)); Messrs Greenwood & Co., 22 May 1806 (BOD, G.A. fol.A262 (43)).

137 No. 24 Basinghall Street was possibly among the larger gardens in the City, being '48 ft square'.

138 *Daily Advertiser* (18 January 1745).

139 BOD, G.A. fol.A259 (186).

140 Mr Graham, 13 July 1797 (BOD, G.A. fol.A262 (99)).

141 Skinner & Dyke, 2 June 1801 (BOD, G.A. fol.A260 (121)).

142 Mr Crosby, auctioneer, 5 October 1802 (BOD, G.A. fol.A259 (149)).

143 Winstanley Auctioneers, 20 May 1795 (BOD, G.A. fol.A260 (134)).

144 *Daily Advertiser* (21 January 1752).

145 Christie, 18 June 1801 (BOD, G.A. fol.A260 (184)); Messrs Greenwood & Co., 22 May 1806 (BOD, G.A. fol.A262 (43)); Skinner, Dyke, Skinner, 11 April 1799 (BOD, G.A. fol.A260 (243)); Mr Christie, 16 May 1805 (BOD, G.A. fol.A262 (42)).

146 Mr Herring, 18 July 1796 (BOD, G.A. fol.A265 (226)); Mr Thorn, 11 Mach 1806 (BOD, G.A. fol.A261 (104)); Skinner & Dyke, 1 August 1794 (BOD, G.A. fol.A263 (36)); Skinner & Dyke, 8 July 1794 (BOD, G.A. fol.A260 (322)).

147 Loudon, *Suburban Gardener*, p. 313.

148 GEP (1409/5/8) (1819), p. 345. Robertson did not, however, comply with Porden's demands. By refusing to observe the estate's policy of enclosing the ground in front of the new buildings before construction, Porden refused to grant Robertson further leases for development in neighbouring Wilton Street.

149 GEP, 1409/5/8, p. 371.

150 Hobhouse, *Thomas Cubitt*, p. 502.

151 Loudon, *Suburban Gardener*, p. 172.

152 Ibid., p. 182.

153 Ibid., pp. 183, 182–3.

154 Ibid., pp. 170–489.

155 Ibid., 11, 181.

156 Ibid., 131, 132.

157 Ibid., 173, 172.

158 Ibid., 173–4.

159 A 'dust hole' was a 'pit, lined with brick or stone, for such rubbish as will rot into manure'. Loudon, *Suburban Gardener*, p. 174; Phillips, *Sylva Florifera*, vol. 1, p. 21.

160 Loudon, *Suburban Gardener*, p. 174.

161 *Hints* was innovative in both format and content. The large quarto publication and the range of gardens it presented were aimed at a wide audience of self-educated, self-improving gardeners, craftsmen and middle-class householders. By diffusing such knowledge, Loudon spared his readers the expense of consulting nurserymen, or hiring builders to lay out and build their gardens. The book is neither a pattern book, nor a gardening manual: its dozens of plates illustrate a range of modern garden designs succinctly described in terms of design without the traditional complement of the sciences of horticulture, surveying and mathematics.

162 Loudon, *Hints*, p. 2.

163 Loudon, *Suburban Gardener*, pp. 184–5, 284.

164 *Gardeners Magazine* (1834), p. 493; Loudon, *Suburban Gardener*, p. 288; *Gardeners Magazine* (1834), pp. 489–95.

165 In gardens 'common to several houses connected together in a row' Loudon felt that the 'character of the whole should determine the character of the parts'. *Suburban Gardener*, p. 294.

166 Loudon appends the following condition to his remark: 'there is scarcely any limit to the kind of objects that may be introduced into a front garden': 'provided these conditions are kept in view in introducing them: first, that they never interfere with the unity and propriety of the expansion, or effect of the scene to which they belong; secondly, that they be not such as will be much injured by the action of the weather; and, thirdly, that due preparation be made for them by some description of architectural or gardenesque basement, plinth, or pedestal'. *Suburban Gardener*, p. 289.

167 Fairchild, *City Gardener*, p. 62.

168 If this figure was not agreeable, Fairchild suggested (p. 62), then a 'model might be made from some of the Waterworks in *Versailles* Gardens, to be fixed at Pleasure to the Water-Pipe, and changed for others if we saw convenient'.

169 Mr M. Palmer, 13 June 1805 (BOD, G.A. fol.A262 (103)).

170 Knight, *London*, vol. 6 (1844), p. 205. In 1823 Henry Phillips had compared town gardens grown on leads to the hanging gardens of Babylon. *Sylva Florifera*, vol. 1, pp. 14–15.

171 Loudon, *Suburban Gardener*, pp. 283–4.; Loudon, *Encyclopaedia*, item no. 7428.

172 'Description of a Rustic Fountain and Rockwork lately erected in the Garden of Mr. Thomas Andrews, at Peckham, by Mr. Benjamin Andrews', *Gardener's Magazine* (1838), pp. 463–4.

173 Knox, 'Joshua Brookes's Vivarium'.

174 Phillips, *Sylva Florifera*, vol. 2, pp. 253–4.

CHAPTER 3

1 See Hutcheson, *An inquiry*; Burke, *Philosophical Enquiry*; Kames, *Elements of Criticism*; Whatley, *Observations*; Alison, *Essays*.

2 Garton, *Practical Gardener*, introduction.

3 Switzer, *Nobleman, Gentleman*, pp. xxix, xiii–xiv.

4 Switzer, *Nobleman, Gentleman*, pp. xxix–xxx.

5 Ibid., pp. xiii.

6 Although written in the 1750s the work was not published until 1774.

7 [Dalrymple], *Essay*, pp. 5, 24–5.

8 *Hints*, p. vi. Loudon refers to Alexandre-Jean-Baptisite Le Blond, who adapted and republished Dézallier d'Argenville's *Theory and Practice of Gardening* in 1728.

9 Loudon, *Hints*, p. vi.

10 Ibid., p. vii.

11 Ibid., p. 2.

12 [Dalrymple], *Essay*, p. 24.

13 Ibid., p. viii.

14 This opinion is shared by John Dixon Hunt in 'Reckoning with Dutch Gardens', p. 55, who quotes Turner, *English Garden Design*, p. 57.

15 See Hunt and de Jong, *Anglo-Dutch Garden*; Jacques and van der Horst, *Gardens of William and Mary*; and de Jong and Dominicus-van Soest, *Aardse Paradijzen*.

16 Hunt, 'Reckoning with Dutch Gardens'.

17 Switzer, *Ichnographia Rustica*, vol. 1, p. 8.

18 Miller, *Gardeners Dictionary*, 7th ed., see 'Gardens'.

19 *Kalm's Account*, p. 85; Fairchild, *City Gardener*, pp. 50, 52.

20 Meager's 'easie and plain directions, very useful for a Learner, how to level and bring a Garden into some Order and Form' were first published in *The English Gardener*.

21 See Woodbridge, *Princely Gardens*, chaps 3 and 4.

22 Worlidge, *Systema-Horticulturae*, p. 18.

23 See 'Konstige Modellen van France Parterris', in van der Groen, *Nederlandtsen Hovenier*. This book commended French-inspired flower gardens. It is, however, worth noting that Dutch town gardeners generally adhered to the simplicity of the traditional, functional rectilinear plan for their modest premises in spite of the availability of sophisticated designs.

24 Switzer, *Ichnographia*, vol. 2, pp. 150–51.

25 Schama, *Embarrassment of Riches*, p. 62.

26 Hunt and de Jong, *Anglo-Dutch Garden*, p. 248.

27 Delany, *Autobiography*, vol. 1, first series, p. 476; and vol. 2, second series, p. 422.

28 Hunt, 'Reckoning with Dutch Gardens', pp. 42–4.

29 The gardens of the Officers' Terrace at Chatham Dockyards were the subject of a paper presented by the author at a Dumbarton Oaks Colloquium on the History of Landscape Architecture (1990) which was published as 'Private Urban Gardening in England, 1700–1830: On the Art of Sinking', pp. 47–75.

30 A. J. Dézallier d'Argenville was a Parisian naturalist, collector and exponent of the French formal style of gardening. D'Argenville's *La Théorie et la Pratique du Jardinarge* first appeared anonymously in Paris in 1709, where in several years it went through five further editions. Three editions were issued at The Hague, and the English translation by John James (Clerk of the Works at Greenwich) also reached a third edition as late as 1743.

31 Kames, *Elements*, vol. 1, pp. 376, 214; Kames also remarked 'The space marked out for a small garden, is surveyed almost at one view; and requires a motion of the eye so slight, as to pass for an object that can be comprehended under the largest angle of distinct vision. If not divided into too many parts, we are apt to form the same judgement of each part; and consequently to magnify the garden in proportion to the number of its parts'. Ibid., p. 215.

32 Switzer, *Nobleman, Gentleman*, p. xx.

33 Switzer, *Ichnographia*, vol. 1, p. 12.

34 The Spence Papers are held in the Osborn Collection at the Beinecke Rare Book and Manuscript Library, Yale University. For a reasonably comprehensive survey of his work see King, 'Joseph Spence of Byfleet', pts 1–4.

35 Philip Southcote (1699?–1758) – Spence's neighbour at Byfleet – had a considerable influence of the development of the late work of Spence. Southcote, credited as the 'founder' (Walpole's word) of the *ferme ornée*, was celebrated for his discriminating, innovative and informed amateur horticultural expertise. His emphasis on flowers and colour in natural gardening (attributed to his knowledge of English landscape painting) played a significant role in Spence's theoretical and practical work.

36 Johnson, *History*, p. 213.

37 Wright, *Joseph Spence*, p. 117.

38 Letter to the Revd Mr Wheeler (1751). Spence remarked to Wheeler 'you ask me too what I have done to my own ground in particular [Byfleet]. This might be answered in four words: I found it all confined, gloomy, regular and flat, I have made it appear less flat, quite irregular, light and open'; Spence, *Observations*, vol. 2, p. 650.

39 Published in French in 1749. The letter convinced Spence that 'they [the Chinese] seem to exceed our late best designers in the natural taste almost as far as those do the Dutch taste, brought over in to England in King William's time'. Spence, *Observations*, vol. 2, p. 647.

40 In his letter to Wheeler he warned him that although he had set down what rules he thought might be most helpful, nine parts in ten of their success would depend upon their application. Spence, *Observations*, vol. 2, p. 646.

41 Spence, *Observations*, vol. 1, anecdote 1110, p. 419.

42 *Gentleman's Magazine*, vol. 39 (1769), p. 577.

43 These are the only ones known to the author. See Joseph Spence papers, Osborn Collection, Beinecke Rare Book and Manuscript Library, Yale University.

44 There are many encomiums on the amiability and liberality of Spence. The cleric himself was aware of his own propensity to help others. He was compelled to caution himself with the following reflection, which although apparently smug, is probably sincere: 'Benevolence is more a Passion, than a Virtue in me; & ought to be watcht, almost as much as a Vice; (to keep it, either from Impertinence, or Impropriety)'. Wright, *Joseph Spence*, p. 149.

45 Although this plan has not been drawn by Spence, it is presumably based on his recollections of Le Sage's garden in Paris.

46 The inscription on the top right of the plan suggests that the layout was also considered appropriate for Baron Atkyns's substantial suburban garden at Fulham (50 by 180 feet).

47 Wright, *Joseph Spence*, p. 66.

48 Spence, *Observations*, vol. 2, anecdote 1354, pp. 497–8. The first part of *Gil Blas* appeared in 1715.

49 Ibid., p. 498.

50 See Leatherbarrow, 'Character, Geometry and Perspective'.

51 Williams, 'Sir John Dalrymple'.

CHAPTER 4

1 This subtitle is derived from the third chapter of James, *Theory and Practice*.

2 Midway through his career Spence developed and refined his series of garden precepts, or 'materials' for the process of garden composition. This exercise was carried out in 1751 at the behest of his friend the Reverend Mr Wheeler, who wished to know the procedure to laying out a garden. It is possible that Spence intended his articles to comprise a section of his book to be entitled 'Tempe: or Letters Relating to Gardens in All Ages: and More Particularly to the Method of Making the Grounds and Country Pleasing All Round One, so Happily Introduc'd of Late Among Us'. Spence, *Observations*, vol. 1 anecdote 1113, p. 1113. The articles were published posthumously. For a transcription

of Spence's 'Materials for Designing a Garden' see Spence, *Observations*, vol. 2, pp. 645–52.

3 James, *Theory and Pracice*, p. 15 – quoting Dézallier d'Argenville.

4 Ibid.

5 Spence, 'Materials for Designing a Garden', Joseph Spence Papers, Osborn Collection (OSB MSS 4, Box 9) Beinecke Rare Book and Manuscript Library, Yale University.

6 Spence's first precept, Letter to the Reverend Wheeler (on gardening), 1751. See Spence, *Observations*, vol. 2, pp. 646–7.

7 Meager, *Compleat English Gardner* (1704), p. 92. Meager's *English Gardener*, first published in 1670, was in eleventh edition by 1710. Charles Marshall, like many, was using virtually the same formula for small garden design in the late eighteenth century.

8 See Meager, *Compleat English Gardner* (1704), pp. 92–5. Worlidge applied a similar technique to laying out gardens. See *Systema-Horti-Culturae*, p. 17.

9 James, *Theory*, p. 15.

10 Switzer, *Ichnographia Rustica*, vol. 1, p. xxvii.

11 Meager, *The English Gardener*; Langley, *Practical Geometry* and *Builder's Compleat Assistant*; Rutter and Carter, *Modern Eden*; Ware, *Complete Body of Architecture*.

12 James, *Theory*, p. 16.

13 Breaks, *Complete System* p. 385. Worlidge had said more or less the same thing in *Systema Horti-Culturae*, p. 17.

14 Rutter and Carter, *Modern Eden*, p. 215.

15 Switzer *Ichnographia*, vol. 2, p. 144.

16 Kames, *Elements*, vol. 3, pp. 305–6.

17 This was a principle taken for granted by eighteenth-century garden designers, including Switzer, Langley and Bradley. Whatley's book was written in 1765 and published in 1770.

18 Whatley, *Observations*, p. 137.

19 Joseph Addison, *The Spectator*, no. 414 (25 June 1712).

20 Hutcheson, *An inquiry*, pp. 37–8.

21 Precept no. 3 made allowances for 'regularity' near the house.

22 James, *Theory*, p. 17.

23 Rutter and Carter, *Modern Eden*, p. 212.

24 Kames, *Elements*, vol. 3, p. 313.

25 Addison, *The Spectator*, no. 412 (23 June 1712). Variety had been a cornerstone to Pope's theory of landscape gardening.

26 Kames, *Elements*, vol. 1, p. 401.

27 Addison, *The Spectator*, no. 412.

28 Whatley, *Observations*, p. 16.

29 'Curiosity is derived from the pleasure of experiencing novelty – but it is a superficial affection, and cannot be sustained – soon exhausts the variety which is commonly to be met with in nature; the same things make frequent returns, and they return with less and less of any agreeable effect'; Burke, *Philosophical Enquiry*, p. 42.

30 [Dalrymple], *Essay*, p. 25. This book, written in the 1760s, has been attributed to Sir John Dalrymple by Robert Williams, see 'Sir John Dalrymple'. It has also been attributed, less reliably, to Isham Parkyn. Spence owned a copy of Dalrymple's *Essay*. Williams, 'Sir John Dalrymple', p. 144.

31 Hill, *Works*, letter to Lady Walpole of 30 May 1734, vol. 1, p. 251.

32 Hill, *Works*, vol. 1, p. 253–4.

33 Hill, *Works*, vol. 1, p. 256, letter to Lady Walpole of 8 June 1734.

34 See further Longstaffe-Gowan, 'William Stukeley's Travelling Gardens'.

35 Precepts 2, 5, 6, 8, 10 and 13 deal directly or indirectly with views.

36 John Tracy Atkins (d. 1773), barrister-at-law, was the third son of John Tracy of Stanway, Gloucestershire. In 1755 he was appointed cursitor baron of the Exchequer. He adopted the name Atkyns, probably on account of the legal eminence of his grandfather Sir Robert Atkyns (1621–1709), one-time lord chief baron of the Exchequer.

37 I am grateful to Lord Neidpath for determining the location of this garden.

38 Quotations from Spence's plans of the Exchequer Garden.

39 Mark Laird claims that it is conceivable that the ideas of studs is derived from Francis Bacon, or Timothy Nourse who wrote of 'little Heaps, in the Nature of Mole hils . . . with Some Red Roses . . .'. He refers to John Harris's article 'Some Imperfect Ideas'.

40 Notes on reverse of third plan for Exchequer House.

41 James, *Theory and Practice*, pp. 17–18. A 'Quincunce', or quincunx, was a group of five trees–four of which occupy the corners, and the fifth the centre of a square or rectangle.

42 Rutter and Carter, *Modern Eden*, p. 212.

43 James, *Theory and Practice*, p. 18.

44 Rutter and Carter, *Modern Eden*, p. 212.

45 Switzer recommends doing this in *Ichnographia*, vol. 2, p. 144.

46 Spence Papers (OSB MSS4, Box 9), 'Miscellaneous Items of interest to one whose hobby is gardening'.

47 Other types of parterres which could be found in town gardens until the end of the eighteenth century were 'mixed', cutwork and embroidery (most of the designs of which were the legacy of Mollet).

48 [Pluche], *Spectacle*, vol. 2, p. 27.

49 [Pluche], vol. 2, p. 27.

50 James, *Theory and Practice*, p. 20.

51 Spence, *Observations*, anecdote 1072.

52 Marshall, *On the Profession*, p. 33. The notion of the *enfilade*, which circumscribes the perimeter of the garden, is explained in Switzer; See *Ichnographia*, vol. 1, pp. 6–8.

53 James, *Theory and Practice*, p. 18.

54 Rutter and Carter, *Modern Eden*, p. 214.

55 James, *Theory and Practice*, p. 18.

56 Ibid.

57 Other things to be shut out included bad air and disagreeable objects. Spence, 'Materials'; Langley, *New Principles*, pp. iv–v.

58 Langley, *New Principles*, pp. iv–v.

59 Langley, *New Principles*, pp. iv–v; Switzer, *Ichnographia*, vol. 2, pp. 154–5.

60 James, *Theory and Practice*, p. 108; Switzer, *Ichnographia*, vol. 2, pp. 150–51.

61 Spence, 'Materials'; From Precept no. 4.

62 Kames, *Elements*, vol. 1, p. 377. Pope himself favoured a mixture of contrasting scenes, where symmetry could be found along with the irregular and unexpected feature; moreover it mattered little whether such devices were artificial or natural. James reinforced this remark when he claimed that in organising the ground you should 'observe, in placing and distributing the several Parts of a Garden, always to oppose one to the other: For Example; a Wood to a Parterre, or a Bowlinggreen'; James, *Theory and Practice*, p. 20.

63 [Dalrymple], *Essay*, p. 24.

64 Spence, *Observations*, p. 411; Kames, *Elements*, vol. 3, p. 300.

65 John Johnson Collection, BOD, b.59(28).

66 Hunt and de Jong, *Anglo-Dutch Garden*, p. 49.

67 Miller, *Dictionary* (1731), see 'Fountains'.

68 Hatton reported in 1708 that 'there are several [fountains] in the Gardens of the Nobility, Gentry and Merchants', but he did not describe their whereabouts. [Hatton], *New View*, vol. 2, p. 786.

69 Fairchild, *City Gardener*, p. 62.

70 James, *Theory and Practice* (1728 ed.), p. 292.

71 For an illustration of Rysbrack's oil on canvas *A View of Richmond Ferry from the Town Wharf*, see *Prospects of Town and Park*, pp. 38–9. The picture is in possession of the Museum of London.

72 Spence, *Observations*, pp. 415–6. See Spence's *Polymetis*.

73 [James Ralph], *A Critical Review* (1734), p. 36.

74 *Man at Hyde Park Corner*, introduction.

75 [Ralph], *Critical Review*, p. 34.

76 For attacks on the excessive use of garden sculpture, see, for example, Switzer, *Ichnographia*, vol. 1, pp. 310–18; Garrick and Colman, *Clandestine Marriage*, Act II, scene in Sterling's garden; Robert Lloyd, 'The Cit's Country Box' (1756), *Connoisseur*, no. 135.

77 Switzer, *Ichnographia*, vol. 1, pp. 311, 316.

78 Earl of Cork, *Connoisseur*, no. 113 (Thursday, 25 March 1756).

79 See further Pincot, *Essay*; Kelly, *Mrs Coade's Stone*.

80 For an analysis of symbolism in Stukeley's town gardens see Longstaffe-Gowan, 'William Stukeley's Travelling Gardens'.

81 See Precepts 12, 13, 15, 16, and addendum C.

82 King, 'Joseph Spence of Byfleet', pt iii, p. 41. From Precepts 15 and 16; see Spence, *Observations*, p. 426.

83 Langley, *New Principles*, p. 183.

84 Laird, 'Approach to Conservation', p. 46; and Laird, *Flowering of the Landscape Garden*, pp. 45–53, 102–9, 124, 191–2.

85 Worlidge, *Dictionarium rusticum*, see 'Garden'.

86 Laird, 'An Approach', p. 46.

87 Ibid., 45–6.

88 Spence produced his first plan for the flower-garden in August 1751. There are two other plans, one dated 30 March 1762, the other undated.

89 This plan has traditionally been represented as being for Lady Falmouth's house in Stratton Street. A contemporary Rate Book records, however, that she lived in Albemarle Street.

90 The table is possibly like those illustrated in Langley, *City and Country Builder*, pl. cxlix: 'Marble tables for Arbours and Gardens'.

91 Annotations on Falmouth garden plan.

92 See Langley, *New Principles*, p. xv. Switzer remarked that Sir William Temple had early on stressed the combined knowledge of the science and surveying and mensuration with the rules of painting guaranteed that the designer was able to anticipate, profit from and play with the effects created by illusion and perspective. Switzer (1741/2), vol. 2, p. 185.

93 In Spence's notes for the 'Materials for Designing Gardens', Spence Papers (MSS 4 Box 9), Beinecke Rare Book and Manuscript Library, Yale University.

94 *City Gardener* (1722), *Catalogus Plantarum* (1730); *Curtis's Botanical Magazine* (from 1787), supplied Londoners with 'A Catalogue of Trees and Shrubs, both *Exotick* and *Domestick*, that are Hardy enough to bear the Cold of our Climate in the open Air, and are propagated for Sale in the Gardens near London'; Loudon, *Suburban Gardener*, pp. 177–489.

95 Curtis, *Flora Londinensis*, p. 11, fn.

96 For detailed accounts of Southcote's planting style see Laird, *Flowering of the Landscape Garden*, pp. 191–2, 194, 196.

97 The term 'garden' had specifically referred to an enclosed piece of ground devoted to the cultivation of flowers, fruit or vegetables.

98 Spence, 'Materials', elaboration of Precepts 5 and 8. Spence remarks that 'Boundaries . . . seem to imprison you'.

99 Ware, *Complete Body*, p. 320.

100 Switzer, *Ichnographia*, vol. 3, p. vii. Although Switzer here referred to country houses, the same practice was common in the city.

101 Rutter and Carter, *Modern Eden*, p. 213.

102 Gwynn, *London and Westminster*, pp. 12–13.

103 'Cit' is short for citizen, a townsman or 'cockney', as distinguished from a countryman, or to a tradesman or shopkeeper as distinguished from a gentleman.

104 'The Cit's Country Box', *Connoisseur*, no. 135 (26 August 1756).

105 Horace Walpole, letter to the Countess of Ossory, 26 December 1763, *Letters*, vol. 9, pp. 429–30.

106 *Connoisseur*, no. 135 and 33 (1754).

107 Spence, *Observations*, pp. 648–9.

108 Curtis, *Flora Londinesis*, vol. 1, Ligustrum vulgare, note. The contributors to the Catalogus Plantarum (1730) suggest that privet was not as commonly grown as a hedge plant in London as it used to be. Miller reported in his *Dictionary* (1768) that privet was 'frequently cultivated in the nurseries near London, to furnish the small gardens and balconies in the city, it being one of the few plants which will thrive in the smoke of London'.

109 Notes accompanying Boleby garden plan (1766).

110 James, *Theory and Practice*, p. 72. A cabinet was an outdoor/garden room; or the most retired place in the finest apartment of a building, 'set apart for writing, studying, preserving things very precious'. Chambers, *Cyclopædia*.

111 Spence suggests that lattices and arbours are still desirable when he drew up his plan for the Ablemarle Street garden in 1753. His arbours are 'natural' – meaning that they are formed with branches of trees (usually Dutch lime with hornbeam), hoops and lattice work to construct covered galleries, porticos, halls, and green 'vistoes'. See Chambers, *Cyclopædia*.

112 Miller, *Dictionary* (1737), see 'Arbours'.

113 Chambers, *Cyclopaedia*.

114 *Gentleman's Magazine*, vol. 39 (1769), p. 576.

115 It is unknown when this practice became popular, but it may have been derived from the earlier Dutch convention (in Amsterdam and Rotterdam only) of painting the walls of small domestic 'canal gardens'.

116 *SOL, Mayfair*, vol. 39, p. 27.

117 See Dorey, 'Sir John Soane's Courtyard Gardens'.

CHAPTER 5

1 This chapter is based on my article, 'Proposal for a Georgian Town Garden' (1987). I have, since this time, had time to reconsider the garden, and have made numerous amendments to the text. I am particularly grateful to Mark Laird and John Harvey for making available their typescript for an article entitled 'The Garden Plan for 13 Upper Gower Street, London: a conjectural review of the planting, upkeep and long-term maintenance of a late eighteenth-century town garden.' The latter appeared in German translation in *Garten Kunst Geschichte* in 1994.

2 *Gentleman's Magazine*, 104, pt 2 (1834), p. 213.

3 In 1823 Douce inherited a considerable legacy upon the death of the sculptor Joseph Nollekens.

4 Douce lived at various addresses after he left Upper Gower Street in 1806; he returned to Upper Gower Street to live between 1827 and 1832. *Gentleman's Magazine*, 104, pt 2 (1834), and *SOL*, vol. 21, p. 83.

5 Gardening and botanical books which are mentioned in their correspondence include: Pliny the Elder, *Natural History*; Curtis, *Botanical Magazine* (from 1787); John Parkinson, *Paradisi in sole paradisus terrestris* (1656 ed.); William Turner, *Herbal* (1568), and James Abercrombie, *Every Man his Own Gardener*. Douce possessed a number of gardening books, all of which were collected for their antiquarian value. The 'Catalogue of the Printed Books and Manuscripts bequeathed by Francis

Douce Esq. to the Bodleian' (1840) lists his collection of anti-quarian gardening books. Among them, he owned Pliny's *Natural History* (1476 and 1539 editions), Davy Brossard, *The Country-mans Recreation* (1654); *The Expert Gardener* (1654); Geofroy Linocier, *L'histoire des plantes* (1584); John Evelyn, *Sylva* (1664, 1670, 1776 eds.); Nicolas de Bonnefons, *The French gardiner* (1675); John Evelyn, *Kalendarium Hortense* (1699); and Jean de la Quintinie, *L'Art ou la manière particulière et seure de tailler les arbres fruitiers* (1699).

6   Douce wrote: 'Pour le marriage je voudrais bien prendre votre conseil. Je me flatte que j'aurais bien de quoi cultiver la femme, mais pour le jardin, le dequoi n'est pas si facile à trouver.' Richard Twiss to Francis Douce, 7 December 1790, BOD, Douce, d. 39, fol. 25; and Douce to Twiss, BOD, Douce d. 39, fol. 27. *Candide* is a story of a rational protection against the basic evils of the world.

7   Twiss, *Life of Lord Chancellor Eldon*, vol. 1, p. 355.

8   The house was built on the 'six-acre field' of the Southampton Estate in 1790/91. It was renumbered sometime in the nineteenth century to 112 Gower Street. The house was demolished after 1949 to make way for the Darwin Building, University of London.

9   Twiss to Douce, 28 November 1791 (BOD, Douce c.11, fol. 18–21). Twiss annotated his letter to Douce with an inventory and sketches of the tools necessary for gardening.

10 Twiss presumed that the property of 13 Upper Gower Street was 25 feet wide and 100 feet long, inclusive of the house and the mews buildings. The real dimensions of the ground were roughly 25 by 165 feet, of which the back garden would have measured 25 by 110 feet. Twiss remarked in his letter of the 28 November 1791 that he was unfamiliar with Douce's property. The plan was drawn at a scale of four foot to an inch.

11 Twiss to Douce, 28 November 1791 (BOD, Douce c.11).

12 Note on garden plan, BOD, Douce c.11.fol 18–21. The tools included 'a hoe, another sort of do., a hand hoe, a light rake set with eight teeth in wood, a large and small watering pot, a small stone roller, a hammer, and a pruning knife'. Notes on garden plan, BOD, Douce c.11.fol 18–21.

13 Twiss to Douce, 28 November 1791 (BOD, Douce c.11).

14 Notes on Douce's garden plan, BOD, Douce c.11, fol. 18–21. Douce's garden faced east.

15 Both Lee and Loddiges were famous nurserymen: Lee was the author of *Introduction to the Science of Botany* (London, 1760) and had a nursery in Hammersmith; Loddiges was the proprietor of a nursery in Hackney. Miller was the greatest British gardener of the period, author of *The gardeners dictionary* (1731), and Gardener to the Apothecaries Garden at Chelsea between 1722 and 1770. Douce was acquainted with Loddiges and Lee. Twiss to Douce, 13 June 1791 (BOD, Douce d.39).

16 Twiss to Douce, 13 June 1791 (BOD, Douce d. 39, fol. 32.)

17 The author referred specifically to the eighth edition of Miller's *Dictionary* of 1768.

18 *Gentleman's Magazine*, vol. 61, pt 1 (1791), pp. 414–15.

19 Fairchild, *City Gardener*, p. 6.

20 *Gentleman's Magazine*, vol. 61, pt 2 (1791), p. 619. The Wood Street Florist wrote again in September to advise his readers how to prepare their gardens for the winter, recommending that 'in the course of the next month take into the house, or put into a frame covered with glass, all his geraniums, myrtles, &c. which require housing . . .' Advice was also given on sowing seeds for the following spring (vol. 61, p. 800).

21 *Gentleman's Magazine*, vol. 61, pt 2 (1791), p. 800.

22 Smith, *Nollekens*, vol. 1, pp. 30–31.

23 Laird and Harvey, 'The Garden Plan for 13 Upper Gower Street', p. 202. If the garden layout was impracticable, and

hypothetical, it was doubtless calculated, as Voltaire remarked of his own purpose in Candide, 'to bring amusement to a small number of men of wit'.

24 Alexander Pope, recorded in Spence's *Observations* (vol. 1, pp. 619, 256–7, dated '1728?'): 'I have sometimes had an idea of planting an old Gothic cathedral, or rather some old Roman temple, in trees. Good large poplars, with their white stems, cleared of boughs to a proper height, would serve very well for the columns, and might form the different aisles, or peristylums, by their different distances and heights.'

25 Town dwellers did not generally dry their washing on hedges or bushes as was the habit in the country, but hung it on lines. In town gardens the standard arrangement was a set of fixed posts with connecting lines which were assembled only on wash days. Loudon recommends the practice of employing the socket and post clothes-line as the most fashionable solution to drying clothes in the town. When the posts were not in use he suggests that they were stored in a garden shed, after being aired in the sun; Loudon, *Suburban Gardener*, p. 176.

26 Laird and Harvey, 'Garden Plan', p. 18.

27 Walpole, 'Essay', p. 524. This shortcoming may be due to the fact that Twiss did not know that it was possible to exploit the view eastwards. It is, however, possible that Douce advised Twiss to ignore the view, anticipating that it might soon be lost through the encroachment of new streets. The prospect was obscured by buildings by the late 1830s. Walpole, 'Essay', p. 522. Douce visited Strawberry Hill and Horace Walpole on 3 September 1789. See further Lewis, *Correspondence of Horace Walpole*, vol. 12, p. 234.

28 In September 1794 Twiss wrote to Douce to request information on 'Treillages' (BOD, Douce d. 39, fol. 72). Douce was well informed on the subject of Antique sculpture. His library contained sixteen important treatises (the earliest dating from 1575), as well as numerous contemporary works including Spence's *Polymetis*. Douce kept a commonplace book to record his observations on statuary ('Notes on statues'). He made memoranda and plans during his visits to Thomas Hope's Duchess Street collection (n.d.), and Charles Townley's collection in Queen Anne's Gate (1786 and 1794).

29 Twiss to Douce, 28 November 1791 (BOD, Douce c.11, fol. 18).

30 Twiss to Douce, 4 August 1790 (BOD, Douce d. 39, fol. 32), and Twiss to Douce 7 December 1790 (BOD, Douce d. 39, fol. 25) quoting from Parkinson's *Herball*.

31 The Cloaca Maxima was the famous drain formed by Tarquinius Priscus, fifth king of Rome, to drain the marshy land of the Valbrum. Twiss 'laid' unwanted books and musical scores in his own 'temple' (in other words, he threw them down it).

32 His opinions are recorded in various memoranda, commonplace books and notebooks including 'Maxims and opinions', 'Miscellanies I' and II, 'Bigarrures modernes', or 'Modern blunders, defects, absurdities and inconveniences' (1793–1833), BOD, 'Cogit. Extemp.' and 'Cogit. miscell.' (begun 1795).

33 Rogers, *Douce Legacy*, p. 10.

34 'Miscellanies II', BOD, Douce e. 35, fols 14–16, n.d.

35 The inconveniences included the inefficacy of the police in maintaining the peace; the inadequacies of the system of leasehold tenure; and the distraction of bell ringing - the 'curse of civilized men', and the 'silly useless nuisance, [and] the amusement of fools.'

36 'Maxims', BOD, Douce e. 33, fol. 19, n.d.; 'Miscellanies II', BOD, Douce e. 35, fol. 7, n.d.; 'Maxims', BOD, Douce e. 33, fol. 12, n.d.

37 'Miscellanies II', BOD, Douce e. 37, fol. 3, n.d.

38 The house is described as a 'very Substantial and Commodious

Leasehold Dwelling House, with Coach House, Stabling for four horses, and Suitable Offices, Desirably Situated, No. 13 on the East Side of Upper Gower Street, Bedford Square.' Mr Christie Auctioneers, 1806 (BOD, GA.fol.A.262(196)).

39 The WC was probably installed c.1805 – some years earlier than his neighbour Mrs Peters at no. 34.

40 *Dictionary of National Biography* (1973), p. 1161.

41 BOD, Douce d. 39, fols 46, 48 and 70.

42 This is not surprising, for although Douce had an interest in botany, he did not, in fact, share Twiss's infatuation with the art of gardening; furthermore, Twiss indicates in his correspondence that he feared that as early as March 1791 he was in danger of surfeiting his correspondent 'as much ab[ou]t Botany now, as I used to do about chess' (BOD, Douce d. 39, fol. 36). Unfortunately most of Douce's private correspondence was destroyed after his death at his own behest. There are, therefore, no replies to Twiss's many letters.

43 Voltaire to Mme Du Deffand, April 1760 see A. Owen Aldridge, *Voltaire and the Century of Light* (Princeton, 1975), p. 259. There are several references to *Candide* in Twiss's letters.

CHAPTER 6

1 Garton, *Practical Gardener*, introduction; and Longstaffe-Gowan, 'Private Urban Gardening', pp. 48–50.

2 'On the Life of a Jobbing Gardener – By Mr Archibald M'Naughton, of Hackney', *Gardener's Magazine*, pt 1 (September 1826), article v, p. 26.

3 Ernest Arthur Ebblewhite, 'The Worshipful Company of Gardeners', typescript (n.d., c.1930?), London Guildhall Library, MS 3396A.

4 Bradley, *General Treatise of Husbandry*, vol. 1, p. 347. The Company, or 'Mystery' as it was known, had flourished from the fifteenth century.

5 Webber, *Early Horticulturists*, and Welch, *History of the Company of Gardeners*.

6 The Company described these categories in 1701, when it petitioned Parliament to enforce its Charter and bye-laws. Ebblewhite, 'Company of Gardeners', p. 7.

7 Bradley, *Treatise*, vol. 1, p. 348.

8 Switzer remarked in *Nobleman, Gentleman* (pp. xviii–xix), that 'Northern Lads, which whether they have serv'd any Time in this Art or not, very few of us know anything of, yet by the Help of a little Learning, and a great deal of Impudence, they invade these *Southern* Provinces'. He had much to say about 'the Poison of these audacious Empiricks in Gardning'.

9 The Company of Gardeners does not possess an extensive archive; what papers they have are on deposit at the Guildhall Library.

10 Switzer, *Nobleman, Gentleman*, p. xvii.

11 Switzer, *Ichnographia*, vol. 1, pp. xxii–xxvi; Bradley, *Treatise*, vol. 1, p. 347.

12 Ebblewhite, 'Company of Gardeners', p. 7.

13 London and Wise remarked in 1699 that: 'Men who call themselves Gard'ners, and of them not a few, who having wrought at labouring work at the new making of some Ground, or in a Garden, where a great many Hands are employed; and after the youth beginner hath exercised the Spade and the Barrow for twelve Months or thereabouts, then puts on an Apron, sets up for a professed Gard'ner, and a place he muct have; he hears some honest Country Gentleman is in London, and wants a Gard'ner, he goes to him and tells him his story of what great matters he is capable of, and that he hath been new making of such a ground, may be he gets a favourable Letter, or at least some recommendation from some of those sellers of Trees

before mention'd; for then he is hired'. 'An Advertisment to the Nobility and Gentry', in De la Quintinie, *Compleat Gard'ner*.

14 Switzer, *Nobleman, Gentleman*, p. xviii.

15 Ibid., p. xvii.

16 Fairchild, *City Gardener*, p. 66.

17 Ibid., p. 69.

18 Ibid., pp. 66–7.

19 Ibid., p. 67. George London and Henry Wise, for instance, had given the same advice in 'An Advertisement to the Nobility and Gentry' published in their edition of de la Quintinie's *Compleat Gard'ner*.

20 Switzer, *Nobleman, Gentleman*, p. xvii.

21 In particular the *London Gazette, Daily Courant, Daily Advertiser, General Advertiser, London Evening Post, Morning Chronicle,* and *London Advertiser, The Times* and the *London Record or Sunday Gazette*.

22 *Daily Advertiser* (19 April 1745).

23 *Morning Chronicle, and London Advertiser* (4 February 1789).

24 *Daily Advertiser* (5 May 1760).

25 *London Evening Post* (10 October 1747).

26 Private accounts of Sir Thomas Hanmer from 1713 to 1730, MSS Bunbury (E18/660.2), Suffolk Record Office, Bury St Edmunds. Symonds was employed by Hammer from c.1723 to 1730. Hanmer was Speaker of the House of Commons.

27 Glenorchy Account Books, ref. no. GD 112/21/77 and 78 (National Archive of Scotland). Glenorchy, later 3rd Earl of Breadalbane, was an MP. He lived at 46 Grosvenor Square until 1738.

28 Bedford Office Papers, memoranda of 1806–7, 1813; BOD, GA.fol.A259(56).

29 Loudon, *Encyclopaedia*, section 2, articles 2070, 2071 and 2081. There are numerous earlier attempts to classify the various categories of gardeners – for instance, that employed by the Company of Gardeners from the early seventeenth century. These, however, distinguish gardeners by the produce they deal with, rather than the nature of their specific professional skills and duties.

30 Thomas Fairchild dedicated *The City Gardener* to the Governors of Bridewell and Bethlem. Besant, *London in the Eighteenth Century*, pp. 374, 544; *Reports from the Select Committees*, pp. 2–7.

31 For instance, between 1761 and 1768 eighteen boys from the Hospital were apprenticed in gardening and household business. All the applicants 'for a Boy out of the Hospital' were male and 'of the Protestant Religion', and most were 'Housekeepers'. None of the applicants was a serving gardener. London Library, Foundling Hospital Archives, applications for apprenticeships: ref. A/FH/A12/1/2/1-1/6/1. I am grateful to Julia Muir and Ruth McClure for their assistance with this material.

32 Various accounts including Switzer, *Ichnographia*, vol. 1, pp. xxx–xxxiii; Burnard, 'On the Remuneration of Gardeners'.

33 See Bradley, *General Treatise*, vol. 1, pp. 345–8; Marshall, *On the Profession*.

34 Campbell, *London Tradesman*, pp. 334–5.

35 Burnard, 'On Remuneration', p. 141.

36 *Sensitivus*, 'On the Treatment'.

37 Jobbers' private account books must have read like contemporary parochial rate books, or nurserymens' ledgers, in the margins of which were frequently scribbled the reasons for clients' defalcation: 'insolvent', 'presumed dead', and 'moved, left no forwarding address'. For examples see Colvill MSS (Minet Library, Brixton).

38 The 'Black Act', 9 George I, c.22 (June 1722), George III, c.36 (1765), etc.

39 Switzer, *Ichnographia*, vol. 1, p. xxiv.
40 M'Naughton, 'On the Life of a Jobbing Gardener'.
41 A number of articles were published in the *Gardener's Magazine* from 1826 to 1840 on the management of town gardens: Sylvaticus, 'Management of a Town Garden'; 'A would-be Suburban Gardener', 'Culture and a List'; Rutger, 'Some Remarks'.
42 John Loudon called these 'London contracts for plants'. [Loudon] *Greenhouse Companion*, p. vii.
43 The earliest reference I have thus far found on the business of plant contracting in London dates from 1747; *London Evening Post* (10 October 1747).
44 Cochran's shop was located at the corner of Duke and Chandler Streets, adjacent to Grosvenor Square.
45 In 1800 James Cochran entered a partnership with Thomas Jenkins, and the two men advertised as 'nurserymen, seedsmen and land surveyors in the New Road, Marylebone'. The neighbouring village of Paddington was renowned, like the East End, and the King's Road, for its many nursery gardens.
46 See Longstaffe-Gowan, 'James Cochran', pp. 58–9, for tables showing accounts of Cochran's business.
47 In hiring 'plants for the night', Cochran served 122 male customers, and 64 females (many were regular customers); and in outdoor garden work he served 48 male and 37 female customers. See Longstaffe-Gowan, 'James Cochran', p. 59, table 2.
48 In 1839 Mangles listed six 'reasonable' London nurseries who furnished balconies, glasshouses and interiors by contract: 'Mr Harrison of East Acton, Mr Dease of Westbourn[e]-road, Paddington, Mr Calder of Harrow-road, Mr White of Paddington Green, Mr Drake of Paddington Market, and Mr McArthur of Edgware-road; *Floral Calendar*, p. 71.
49 Thomas Fairchild, Stephen Switzer, Batty Langley and Philip Miller had been saying very similar things from the beginning of the eighteenth century.
50 William Aiton (1731–93), one of the most celebrated gardeners of his day, was in 1759 appointed superintendent of Kew. His book *Hortus Kewensis* (1789) described 5500 species, not only of plants grown at Kew, but almost all the species cultivated in England.
51 [Loudon], *Greenhouse Companion*, pp. 243–4.
52 Ibid., p. 243–4.
53 PRO, James Cochran MSS, C.111/132/1.
54 It had long been remarked that 'the turf of a London Garden requires to be renewed every year'. *Gardener's Magazine*, article v (April 1828), and Loudon, *Encyclopaedia* (1822).
55 PRO, Cochran MSS, C.111/133/1.
56 PRO, Cochran MSS, C.111/132/1.
57 [Loudon], *Greenhouse Companion*, p. 3.
58 PRO, Cochran MSS, C.111/B2/1; C.111/132/1.
59 PRO, Cochran MSS, C.111/B2/1.

CHAPTER 7

1 [Loudon], *Greenhouse Companion*, pp. 1–2. The anonymously published book was composed 'in conformity with the best written authorities, and according to what we have seen in our extensive observation and communications with botanical cultivators and nursery-men, in the neighbourhood of London and elsewhere. The work has also had the advantage of revisal by a nurseryman who is engaged in the culture of green-house and hot-house plants at his commercial establishment in the King's Road', pp. vi-vii.
2 Ibid., p. iii.
3 Meager, *Compleat English Gardner*, 10th ed., p. 137. Loudon coined the term 'town green-house' in *The Greenhouse Companion*.

4 *Gentleman's Magazine*, vol. 34 (1764), p. 207. It should be noted that many persons also considered that living flowering plants were also capable of impairing or destroying human health: not until the late eighteenth century did science dispel the notion that the 'effluvia' or 'vegetable steams' produced by plants were harmless. For a discussion on 'vegetable steams' see Longstaffe-Gowan 'Plant Effluvia'.
5 Meager, *Compleat English Gardner*, 10th ed., pp. 136–50; Worlidge, *Dictionarium Rusticum*, 'Green-House'; Evelyn, 'The Green-House and other Conservatories', in *Lady's Recreation*, pp. 103–8; Miller, *Gardeners Dictionary* (1731), and later editions.
6 Fairchild suggested that 'while the Fires are not in use' the chambers of a house could be 'adorned at once with living Plants', or that exotic plants such as 'Orange-Trees may be set Chimneys, or in the Windows'; *City Gardener*, p. 64.
7 Tod, *Plans*, description of pl. 4, p. 11.
8 Tod, *Plans*, p. 10.
9 Loudon, in fact, recommended 'Messrs. Bailey of London' in the *Greenhouse Companion* (p. 23); the ironmongers were 'patentees of sash for curvilinear hot houses' (*Pigot & Co., London and Provincial New Commercial Directory, for 1826–7*). He made reference to other persons experienced in the management of 'hot-houses' such as Mr Cushing at Hammersmith Nursery, and Messrs Loddiges at Sion House.
10 The wrought-iron glazing bar was patented by J. C. Loudon in 1816.
11 Repton, *Fragments on the Theory*, pp. 52–4.
12 [Loudon], *Greenhouse Companion*, p. 3.
13 Ibid., p. 241.
14 Ibid., pp. 24–5.
15 Ibid., p. 241. A case was often a small, portable, closely glazed container for growing plants. A plant cabinet was a projecting bay of a window designed to receive living plants. Chamber-stages were moveable tiered stands for the display of flowering plants; they were often set in or near windows, or in greenhouses.
16 Ward pioneered the Wardian Case, which was a closely glazed case devised for growing plants indoors, and as a means of transporting plants.
17 Loudon, *Suburban Gardener*, pp. 283–4.
18 [Loudon], *Greenhouse Companion*, pp. 22–3.
19 Ibid., p. 24.
20 Mangles, *Floral Calendar*, p. 37.
21 [Loudon], *Greenhouse Companion*, p. 36.
22 Ibid., p. iii.
23 Ibid., pp. 241–2.
24 Mangles, *Floral Calendar*, p. 70.
25 [Loudon], *Greenhouse Companion*, pp. 4–5, iii–iv.
26 Loudon, *Gardening for Ladies*, p. 244.
27 [Loudon], *Greenhouse Companion*, p. 2.
28 Davidoff and Hall, *Family Fortunes*, p. 451. Loudon designated the green-house as a work of art: 'the plants inclosed are in the most artificial situation in which they can be placed, and require constant and unremitting attention to counteract the tendency of that artificial state to destroy them'. *Greenhouse Companion*, p. 3.
29 [Loudon], *Greenhouse Companion*, pp. iii, 246–7.
30 Humphry Repton was commissioned by Richard Walker to fit up his house and garden at 17 St James Street, Piccadilly, for a masquerade in c.1803/4 – he did so by strengthening the floor and 'festooning the scaffolding with flowering garlands and coloured lamps'. Repton, 'Memoir,' Part Two, autographed draft, British Library, Add. MS 62112, 2, pp. 177–92.
31 Ribeiro, 'Mrs Cornelys', p. 49.
32 The Season was prescribed by the nobles and the sessions of

Parliament. In the early nineteenth century it was governed by the reigning monarch's official birthday. By court regulation, in 1818, it was decreed that the celebration of the Prince Regent's birthday was to be established arbitrarily as the 23 April – St George's Day (the Regent's birthday was 12 August).

33 See Orgel and Strong, *Inigo Jones*, vol. 1, pp. 6–11.

34 To complement a host's efforts the guests often dressed in rustic, foreign and antique raiment. Newspaper columns were glutted with descriptions of costumes which were worn on all occasions, especially at balls. At Sir Jacob and Lady Astley's ball of mid-June 1820 there were 'motley groupes of Spanish Grandees and their Donnas; Turks, Persians and Chinese Mandarins; Highland Chieftans and Captains of Banditti; Swiss peasants and flowergirls'. Others were wrapped in Roman robes, Persian sashes and obsolete court dress from the time of Henry VII. The nature of players' conversation, like their disguises, had barely changed since the Renaissance: there were lively exchanges of rehearsed enigmas, logogriphs, charades, rebusses, queries and transpositions. *Morning Post* (24 June 1820).

35 Nicol, *Villa Garden Directory*, p. 363 fn.

36 In grander households this responsibility was sometimes shared with the steward.

37 *Morning Post* (24 June 1818).

38 Several patrician customers switched their allegiance from Messrs Colvill and Harrisons's nurseries to Cochran, including the Duke of Grafton, the Earl Grosvenor, the Marquess of Cholmondeley, the Marchioness of Cornwallis, the Earl of Stair and the Duke of Leeds. Colvill MSS, Minet Library, Brixton; and Hewitt, Smith, Harrison and Cook MSS, LMA.

39 *Morning Post* (30 July 1821).

40 *Morning Post* (27 July 1820, and 24 June 1818).

41 *Morning Post* (15 June 1818).

42 *Morning Post* (5 June 1818).

43 *Morning Post* (6 June 1818).

44 *Morning Post* (5 June 1818).

45 Trollope, *Days of the Regency*, vol. 2, p. 85. I am grateful to the late Sir John Summerson for this reference. For an earlier account of the floral decoration of a 'grand mask gala', see Surr, *Winter in London*, vol. 2, pp. 215–23.

46 Loudon hoped that the greenhouse 'would be an appendage to every villa, and to many town residents a mark of elegance and refined enjoyment'; *Greenhouse Companion*, vol. 1, p. 250.

47 [Loudon], *Greenhouse Companion*, p. 248.

48 Ibid., pp. 248–9.

49 Ibid., p. 249.

50 Ibid., pp 249–50.

51 Wills, 'Plants for House Decoration', pp. 84–5.

52 The flow of luxury goods has only recently begun to generate historical analyses focused on patterns of distribution and private consumption, and on individual manufacturers' techniques for cultivating their clientele. See Bermingham and Brewer, *Consumption of Culture*; Brewer and Porter, *Consumption and the World of Goods*; Schama, *Embarrassment of Riches*; Weatherill, *Consumer Behaviour*; McKendrick, Brewer and Plumb, *Birth of the Consumer Society*.

53 *Gardener's Magazine* (1833), p. 63; (1828), p. 60.

CHAPTER 8

1 Strype's description of Bridgewater Square in 1720. He found the place 'very delightful'; *Survey*, vol. 2, p. 93.

2 Summerson, *Architecture in Britain*, p. 134. Summerson quotes an extract from a document which was issued by the 4th earl's son during the Commonwealth.

3 The layout also owed much to Jones's familiarity with formally designed Italian *piazze* with churches, such as those in Venice, Florence and Leghorn. The last example influenced Claude de Chastillon's layout of the Place Royale for Henry IV and Marie de' Medici.

4 The unbuilt south side of the piazza was credited from *c.*1664 as contributing to the airiness of the square; the earl's 'small Grotto of trees' was also praised. [Sorbière], *Relation d'un Voyage*, p. 34; Strype, *Survey*, vol. 2, p. 89.

5 The statue of Louis XIII by Daniele da Volterra and Pierre Biard the Younger was erected in the middle of the square in 1639. It was melted down at the time of the Revolution. Blunt, *Art and Architecture in France*, p. 256.

6 According to a petition of 1638 the Earl of Bedford had promised to pave the piazza and erect a statue of Charles I. This plan was not carried out, and a tree was planted in its stead; *SOL*, vol. 36, p. 79; and Churchwardens' Accounts of St Paul's Covent Garden (1657), WCA.

7 *SOL*, vol. 3, p. 7.

8 *Black Books* of Lincoln's Inn, vol. 2, pp. 439–40; *Register of Privy Council*, vol. 3, f. 45; *SOL*, vol. 3, p. 7.

9 *SOL*, vol. 3, p. 8.

10 *SOL*, vol. 3, p. 8, fn.

11 Jacques, 'Chief Ornament'.

12 *SOL*, vol. 3, p. 18. See pl. 6. for a view of the fields *c.*1683.

13 *SOL*, vol. 34, p. 432.

14 *SOL*, vol. 34, p. 433.

15 Harden deeds, LMA, X142, X145; Greater London Record Office (M) Acc.401/182–3.

16 *SOL*, vol. 34, pp. 79, 129–31, and Churchwardens' Accounts of St Paul's Covent Garden, WCA.

17 The square is recorded in leases of 1683 as 'King Square'. By this time the statue of Charles II had been erected in the centre of the square, which was presumably named in honour of the reigning monarch; *SOL*, vol. 33, p. 42.

18 *SOL*, vol. 33, pp. 42, 33.

19 PRO, C6/291/12.

20 Fairchild, *City Gardener*, pp. 17–18.

21 Strype, *Survey*, vol. 2, p. 87.

22 Westminster Cathedral, deed of 21 April 1684.

23 Royal National Ear, Nose and Throat Hospital deeds, 28 October 1685; see also *SOL*, vol. 31, p. 145.

24 PRO, c8/350/89.

25 Fairchild, *City Gardener*, p. 12.

26 Ibid., pp. 11–12. Bloomsbury Square was laid out in *c.*1661 by the 4th Earl of Southampton. The centre of the square was initially a market. It was laid to turf and enclosed in *c.*1700, and subsequently planted with trees and shrubs in *c.*1807.

27 Fairchild, *City Gardener*, pp. 13–14.

28 Ibid., p. 14. The author remarked that he was 'sensible that it may be very much improved'.

29 Fairchild's recommendations were not new. In 1712 John James had 'earnestly' recommended the planting of 'small Groves of Evergreens' in 'some Squares' as they would 'look very well when seen from the Building' and they would 'make a diversity from other Wood; which having lost its Leaves, appears quite naked all the Winter'; *Theory and Practice*, p. 18.

30 Fairchild, *City Gardener*, pp. 16–21.

31 Ibid., pp. 21–6.

32 Ibid., p. 27.

33 Ibid., pp. 27–34.

34 Fairchild does not prescribe a height for his hedges. They were presumably approximately eight feet, as were Alston's at Grosvenor Square Wilderness planted by *c.*1729/30; Fairchild, *City Gardener*, pp. 40–42.

35 For a similar wilderness plan see Strachey, 'Helmingham Plan', pp. 36–41.
36 Fairchild, *City Gardener*, title page.
37 *SOL*, vol. 36, p. 131.
38 Fairchild, *City Gardener*, pp. 42–3.
39 Ibid., pp. 41, 14, 42, 43.
40 *Foreigner's Guide*, p. 124. The first new squares to be built along the lines of Grosvenor Square did not appear in London, but in Bath. John Wood had spent two formative years in London (1725–7), and was well acquainted with the still incomplete development of Grosvenor Square, and the building activities on the neighbouring Cavendish-Harley Estate, when he began to formulate his design for Queen Square, Bath, in 1728. The enclosed garden, or as Wood called it the 'open area', proposed for the centre was an expansive and geometrical wilderness derived from Fairchild's *City Gardener*. For a thorough description of the garden at Queen Square see Wood, *Essay*, vol. 2, p. 345.
41 The layout of the square was prepared, or possibly modified by Charles Bridgeman by 1729. Willis, *Charles Bridgeman*, p. 30.
42 The remainder of the sum was allocated to drainage and legal fees.
43 GEP, Draft agreement of 1729, John Alston and Sir Richard Grosvenor, 1409/10/4, miscellaneous 6.
44 Articles of Agreement for the building of the garden of Grosvenor Square, 1729. GEP, 11409/10/4, miscellaneous 6.
45 Specifications included in 'Articles of Agreement for the building of the garden of Grosvenor Square'.
46 *Foreigner's Guide*, pp. 124–6.
47 James Ralph, *Critical Review*, pp. 108–9. For an interesting insight into Ralph, see Harris, *British Architectural Books*, pp. 381–4.
48 Published comments on the square from 1734 onwards treated the irregularity of the buildings as an excusable defect of the grand plan.
49 At the Restoration the land had formed part of the queen dowager's jointure, of which Lord St Albans was a trustee. The Bailiwick was the name given to the extensive tract of meadowland originally assembled by Henry VIII from the holdings of Westminster Abbey, the Convent of Abingdon and the Hospital of St James.
50 *Notes and Queries*, ser. 11, vol. 9, 14 February 1914, p. 126; and Chamberlayne, *Angliae Notitia*, p. 493.
51 *The Postman* (28–31 August 1703).
52 12 Geo. i, c.25, extract. So considerable was the accumulation of debris that 3,792 cubic yards of soil from the surface of the square were removed when it was replanned in 1727. SJST, 15 March 1726/7. For a detailed description of activities which have taken place in the square from the late seventeenth century onwards see Forrest, *St James's Square*, pp. 18–53, 80–88.
53 12 Geo. i, c.25, extract. The precedent had been established in 1707 when a bill had been brought in 'for beautifying and preserving the Square called Lincoln's Inn Great Fields'. Nothing, however, came of it; *House of Commons Journals*, xv, 272.
54 Correspondence of James Brydges, 1st Duke of Chandos, 12 March 1726 (Huntingdon Library) quoted in Forrest, *St James's Square*, pp. 29–30; SJST, 23 June 1726. The Trustees of St James's Square assembled for the first time in June 1726.
55 SJST, 7 February 1727, London Library. The basin was lined with clay and finished with a bed of flints.
56 The water was initially supplied by the New Company of York Buildings.
57 SJST, 6 February, 15 March 1726/7.

58 *London in Miniature*, p. 203.
59 SJST, 6 February, 15 March 1726/7.
60 *SOL*, vol. 29, p. 79, fn.
61 SJST, 9 May, 2 October 1728, May 1733. The Act authorised the Trustees to bring male-factors before the justices, whereby upon conviction the offenders were obliged to forfeit twenty shillings for dumping rubbish in the square, and £50 for encroachment. Although there were no restrictions imposed on the flow of pedestrian and other traffic through the square, there was a penalty of ten shillings for hackney coachmen caught standing or plying for hire in the square. While the constables could keep vagrants at bay, they were generally unsuccessful in dealing with the perpetrators of 'improper behaviour' (unelaborated). It was, understandably, beyond the capability of most beadles to contend with civil disorder – such as marches, riots or other gatherings of large crowds, which occurred sporadically from the late seventeenth century to the early nineteenth century. Disturbances include the Papist Riots (1688), 'Wilkes and Liberty' Riots (1768), Gordon Riots (1780), Corn Law Riots (1816) and the great nuisances caused by the crowds which assembled for the regular processions made by Queen Caroline to Westminster when she was undergoing her trial for adultery.
62 Among them [Ralph], *Critical Review*, p. 32.
63 The garden in the square was initiated and managed by the landowner until 1770 when the Square received its own Act.
64 *Foreigner's Guide* (1740); and [Stewart], *Critical Observations*, pp. 14–15.
65 *London in 1710* (1934), p. 132, and [Ralph], *Critical Review*, p. 28.
66 8 Geo. ii, c.26, extract.
67 *London and Westminster Guide* (1768). There had been several plans to redesign the central area of the square. At the end of the seventeenth century Mr Cavendish Weedon of Lincoln's Inn proposed 'two noble design[s] for beautifying [of] Lincoln's Inn Fields'; *SOL*, vol. 3, p. 20.
68 *Country Journal* (16 April 1737), and [Ralph] *Critical Review*, p. 30.
69 MS plan of Leicester Fields, 1737. Kings Topographical Collection, British Library, Maps, KT xxii.
70 The statue had been modelled by C. Buchard in about 1716 for the 1st Duke of Chandos and erected in the garden of his house at Cannons. *SOL*, vol. 34, p. 433.
71 *The London and Westminster Guide*. The stone statue attributed to John van Nost was erected in 1753, and was of the then reigning monarch, George II.
72 [Ralph], *Critical Review*, pp. 101–2.
73 MSS Portland, Soho Square Bundle. Nottingham University.
74 *SOL*, vol. 33, p. 51.
75 Ralph, *New Critical Review*, p. 169.
76 Gwynn used the term 'coop'd up brick walls' when he referred to gardens being concealed from the street by high opaque barriers. Gwynn, *London and Westminster Improved*, p. 81.
77 Richardson, *Charles Grandison*, 125.
78 [Ralph], *Critical Review*, pp. 108–9.
79 [Stewart], *Critical Observations*, pp. 9–10 (For a discussion on the attribution of this book please refer to Harris *British Architectural Books*, pp. 168–9). The rhetoric employed by the various commentators was very similar; John Gwynn referred the 'clumsy brick piers in Grosvenor-Square, which are incumbrances' [which] should be removed'. *London and Westminster Improved*, p. 80 n.
80 In the second revised edition of Ralph's book it is observed that 'all the squares in London, at present, have their areas inclosed by neat iron railing'; *New Critical Review*, p. 173.

81 Feldborg, *Dane's Excursions*, p. 11.

82 14 Geo. iii, *c*.52, extract.

83 This plan, in the Kedleston (Derbyshire) Archives, was brought to my attention by Tim Knox; its attribution to Richardson has been made by Geoffrey Fisher at the Courtauld Institute. The plan is doubtless the scheme for the garden refurbishment proposed by the trustees of the square in 1774. It would appear to have been commissioned by Assheton Curzon, later 1st Baron and 1st Viscount Curzon. Curzon lived at 66 Brook Street – just off Grosvenor Square – between 1759 and 1820, and was presumably a trustee of the square. Richardson was working for Curzon at Kedleston in the early 1770s.

84 Horwood's representation of the garden on his *Plan* (1792) corroborates the layout of the garden to the Kedleston plan.

85 Moritz, *Travels*, letter of 17 June 1782.

86 Ryerson, *Adams Family Correspondence*, vol. 6, December 1784 – December 1785, p. 242: Abigail Adams to [her sister] Mary Smith Cranch, *circa* July–August 1785. The Adamses took up residence in Grosvenor Square in June 1785.

87 Ryerson, *Correspondence*, vol. 6, p. 277; Abigail Adams to Mary Smith Cranch, 15 August 1785.

88 *Public Advertiser* (14 July 1755).

89 *Gazette and New Daily Advertiser* (14 March 1767).

90 6 Geo. iii, *c*.56 (Private Act).

91 *Gazette and New Daily Advertiser* (10 May 1766).

92 Ibid. (17 July 1766).

93 Ibid. (11 June 1767).

94 Vestry minutes, 2 and 11 June 1767; *Annual Register*, 1772, p. 132. The statue was executed by the French sculptor Beaupré, under the direction of Joseph Wilton, RA, sculptor to the King. Johnson, *Berkeley Square*, p. 191.

95 Drapers' Company, Fitzroy Square Frontages, Minutes of the Inhabitants, 24 April 1815.

96 The land was let from William and James Adam, who held the head-lease from Lord Southampton.

97 The gardener, Mr Maxfield, superintended the garden work, which cost £200.

98 Although Webb was encouraged to grow vegetables he was not permitted to plant 'Cabbages, Turnips, Onions, or Leeks, or any other vegetable that might be considered offensive by the Residents of the Square'. Drapers' Company, Minutes, Memorandum of Agreement, 18 September, 1815.

99 Drapers' Company, Minutes, 11 May 1816; 19 July 1839; 5 May 1843.

100 For an analysis of the behaviour and spatial distribution of crowds in England's four largest provincial towns for the period 1790–1835 – an analysis of direct relevance to the eighteenth-century understanding of the topography of the metropolis – see Harrison, 'Symbolism'.

101 *Notes and Queries*, vol. 9, 2nd ser., p. 292 (14 April 1860).

102 *Foreigner's Guide*, p. 118.

103 *London and Westminster Guide*, p. 29.

104 [Stewart], *Critical Observations*, pp. 13–14.

105 Ibid., p. 15.

106 Ibid., pp. 1–2.

107 *London and Westminster Improved* was the climax of a vigorous campaign to raise the reputation of English artists by establishing a national academy to nurture national talent and by 'promoting the advancement of grandeur and elegance' in public building. Gwynn began publishing the aims of his campaign in 1749. Behind a great many of the suggestions in *Critical Observations* is Gwynn's *London and Westminster Improved*, which is duly commended as 'the most judicious and well-digested plan that has been yet proposed'. [Stewart], *Critical Observations*, p. 40.

108 See also [Stewart], *Critical Observations*, p. 2. The important difference between the two treatises was that Stewart was an ardent advocate of urban expansion, whose ultimate purpose in writing his book was to counter the objections made by Gwynn and others against further aggrandisement of the metropolis. Harris, *British Architectural Books*, p. 170.

109 [Stewart], *Critical Observations*, p. 7.

110 Ibid., pp. 8–9. Gwynn remarked 'not one is to be found that is regularly built, on the contrary it is hardly possible to conceive anything more confused and irregular than the generality of them are'; *London and Westminster Improved*, p. 80.

111 [Stewart], *Critical Observations*, p. 14.

112 Jenner, *Town Eclogues*, eclogue 4, p. 26.

113 [Stewart], *Critical Observations*, p. iv.

114 Rarely, until the late eighteenth century, was it felt that these four elements were balanced, and that there prevailed a 'regularity' throughout in the structures, and 'neatness' of the gardens. St James's Square was among the first garden squares to be praised for its handsome regularity.

115 [Stewart], *Critical Observations*, pp. 7–8. Gwynn had made similar recommendations for the treatment of areas 'in the midst' of squares. Gwynn, *London and Westminster Improved*, p. 80.

116 [Stewart], *Critical Observations*, p. 8.

117 Ibid., p. 21.

118 *London and Westminster Guide*. Lord Chandos's house, begun in 1724 to a design by Edward Shepherd, was never completed; Lord Foley's house was demolished in 1814 to make way for the New Street (Regent Street); and Harcourt House (Lord Bingley's) built in 1722 to designs by Thomas Archer, was demolished in 1906.

119 [Stewart], *Critical Observations*, pp. 10–11.

120 Ibid., pp. 10–11.

121 Ibid., pp. 11–12.

122 Ibid., pp. 12–13.

123 *Applebee's Original Weekly Journal*, 14 September 1725. Derived from Defoe's description of 1720.

124 The gap on the north side of Cavendish Square was filled in 1771, thereby terminating the open 'vis[t]a' from Hanover Square; the last building carcases were erected in Grosvenor Square by 1731; and the open views to the north gained from Queen Square were obstructed by the erection of houses in Upper Guilford Street by *c*.1795.

125 The sheep in Cavendish Square were evicted in 1771, soon after the erection of the statue and the completion of Mr Tuffnell's houses on the north side of the Square. Archer, '*Rus in Urbe*', p. 162.

126 This was not, of course, unique to squares; other urban garden and landscape settings produced a similar sense of anomaly, and a distressing confusion of symbolic categories. For instance, one foreign observer was in 1710 surprised to find that St James's Park contained neither woodland nor birds, but 'merely avenues' of trees, and a considerable number of grazing cattle and deer. *London in 1710*, p. 12.

127 'Mr Repton/Letter to the Trustees of Bloomsbury Square/ March 3rd 1807', in Private Correspondence xiii.G.10 [in Hardwicke file], Sir John Soane's Museum.

128 John Wood's extemporised projections in Bath were also influential, and entailed linking Queen Square with the Circus (from 1754) by Gay Street (begun 1750) to form a sequence of planned open space.

129 Gwynn, 'with a view therefore to this great defect', proposed a design for a great new square with a 'circular area . . . of seven hundred feet in diameter' – which he compared to the Circus at Bath – near Whitfield's Tabernacle in Tottenham

130 Dance had over six years' architectural training in Italy between 1758 and 1764. For nearly fifty years he 'exercised an enlightened supervision over the growth and redevelopment of the City'. Colvin, *Biographical Dictionary*, p. 249.

131 Moritz, *Travels* (1798 ed.), p. 36.

132 Knight, *London*, vol. 6, p. 193.

133 Lambert, *History and Survey of London*, vol. 3, p. 532.

134 Ralph, *A New Critical Review* (1783), p. 175.

135 [Ralph], *Critical Review*, p. 30.

136 [Stewart], *Critical Observations*, p. 2.

137 Knight, *London*, vol. 6, p. 193.

138 Watkin, *Soane Lectures*, p. 649.

139 Gwynn was doubtless referring to Portman Square when he recommended that new squares should be formed along the lines of Grosvenor Square. He projected such a new square, adjacent to Portman Square, as a pendant to Grosvenor Square north of Oxford Street. Refer to Gwynn's plan of Westminster 'shewing several improvements propos'd' (Portman Square was still being formed at the time).

140 Soane's Royal Academy Lecture XI, first presented March 1815. See Watkin, *Sir John Soane*, p. 649.

141 A church was originally planned for the centre of Manchester Square. It was never built, and a garden was laid out in its place.

142 The squares were originally proposed to have 'basons of water in each'.

143 Knight, *London*, vol. 6, p. 199.

144 BOD, Douce e.35/fol.29.

145 Knight, *London*, vol. 6, p. 199; Hobhouse, *Thomas Cubitt*, pp. 58–82. Hobhouse coined the term *Master Builder* to describe Thomas Cubitt (1788–1855), whose building enterprise was pioneering, and whose success gained him the reputation of having established the first modern building firm. Cubitt was engaged in many great schemes of urban development, including the Duke of Bedford's Bloomsbury estate, and the 'Five Fields' district (later known as Belgravia) for Lord Grosvenor.

146 Chancellor, *History of the Squares of London*, p. 212.

147 For Russell Square, Burton's plan was estimated to cost £2,570 and Gubbin's (Lord Bedford's surveyor), £3,000; the alternative prices for Tavistock Square were £1,650 and £1,850. Olsen, *Town Planning*, p. 52, fn.

148 Feldborg, *Dane's Excursions in Britain*, p. 11. 'Sundry portions' of brick walls were substituted by 'open Iron Railings' around the edges of Hyde Park and Green Park in 1826. *Fifth Report of the Commissioners* (1826), p. 14.

149 Philippar remarked: 'En Angleterre toutes les places publiques sont ornées, au centre, d'un jardin entouré de grilles'. He described the placing of gardens in squares as 'Cette méthode, qui offre l'advantage d'atténuer la sévérité qu'offre cette régularité de construction . . .' *Voyage Agronomique*, pl. iii.

150 Malcolm, *Anecdotes* (1808), p. 472.

151 [Pückler-Muskau], *Letters*, pp. 132–3.

152 Hughson, *London*, vol. 4, p. 372.

153 Carter, Goode and Laurie, *Humphry Repton*, p. 156.

154 The 'walk & belt of shrubs' of Repton's plan were recommended by the trustees as features to be adopted. Woburn Abbey, Bedford Estate Papers, letter dated 8 August 1807. For a detailed description of the development of Russell and Bloomsbury Squares see Daniels, *Humphry Repton*, pp. 181–2.

155 Hobhouse, *Thomas Cubitt*, p. 71.

156 Ibid. In 1850 George Scharf, who lived at 1 Torrington Square, recorded on a sketch that the square was planted with 'Plain Liburnum Lillac and Elm Plane Lilac [and] Sycamore'.

157 British Museum, Add. MSS 39167 g(2) ff. 143–6. Regular garden maintenance was in 1796 known to have been carried out by 'James Alexander, of No. 35 Wardour Street, Gardener'.

158 *The Letters of Sir Charles Bell* (1870), p. 101; see also pp. 187–8 n., 227, 232, 327.

159 Malcolm, *London Redivivum*, vol. 4, p. 331.

160 The central garden of Leicester Square as it is portrayed in Hodges's painting of *c*.1790 suggests that the new planting scheme approximated that of the Elysian Garden (begun in the early 1780s) at Audley End. William Tompkins depicted the latter in a minutely detailed painting of 1788. See Laird *Flowering of the English Landscape Garden*, pp. 341–50.

161 S. Rawles's engraved view was published in 1801.

162 Hughson, *London*, pp. 400–1. Euston Square was the 'Bedford Nursery'. For a detailed history of Russell Square see 'The Historical Development of Russell Square', report prepared by Land Use Consultants, May 1997.

163 *Lady Morgan's Memoirs*, vol. 2, p. 432.

164 Papworth, *Select Views*, p. 36. The servants, of course, had access to keys to the gardens.

165 Their behaviour caused 'considerable annoyance' to inhabitants of the square, whose garden 'was intended to be used for the preservation of quiet & respectability', and was 'maintained for the comfort & recreation of the Families of Residents contributing to its support & chiefly frequented by the Ladies and Children'. Drapers' Company, Minutes of the Inhabitants of Fitzroy Square, 1 April 1837.

166 Drapers' Company, Minutes, 1 April 1837, 19 July 1839. The appearance and general demeanour of the Belgian Minister Monsieur van de Weyer's maidservant had begun to affront residents as early as spring 1836.

167 London, *Encyclopaedia* (1822), p. 1030.

168 Hobhouse, *Thomas Cubitt*, p. 71.

169 The Society was unable to make the garden entirely public because of the restrictions of the Act of 1735. The Act was repealed in 1894. *SOL*, vol. 3, p. 21.

170 Loudon, letter to the editor, dated 22 December 1803, in *Literary Journal* 2, 12 (31 December 1803), cols. 739–42. The private residential squares of London – despite their apparent failings – had been promoted by Gwynn and Stewart in the eighteenth century as conspicuous and outstanding displays of grandeur in the metropolis, which demonstrated the superior advantages in England (over France) of private enterprise – of public improvements that spring initially from the spirit of the people.

171 Loudon, *Encyclopaedia*, item 2041, 'Public Squares'. For a discussion on the fashion for the erection of statues in squares see [Stewart], *Critical Observations*, p. 19 fn.

172 Loudon, *Encyclopaedia*, item 2041.

173 'Mr Repton/Letter to the Trustees of Bloomsbury Square/March 3rd 1807', in Private Correspondence XIII.G.10 [in Hardwicke file], Sir John Soane's Museum.

174 'Mr Repton/Letter to the Trustees of Bloomsbury Square'.

175 Repton, *Inquiry*, p. 64.

176 SJST, 4 May 1759, 14 May 1799; 28 June 1816; 7 June 1817.

177 For a recent interpretation of Nash's urban picturesque aesthetic, see Crook, 'Metropolitan Improvements', p. 96.

178 SJST, 2, 4 September 1817.

179 SJST, 4 July 1822.

180 Letter from John Nash to Alexander Milne (Secretary of the Commissioners of Woods, Forests and Land Revenues), dated 24 January 1822. CRES, uncatalogued correspondence with

181 Elmes, *Metropolitan Improvements*, p. 88.

182 MS letter from John Nash to Alexander Milne dated 2 January 1823 (CRES uncatalogued).

183 Price, *Essay*, vol. 2, p. 207.

184 SJST, 28 June, 4 July 1825.

185 Denis, *Landscape Gardener*, pp. 74, 40.

186 Hatton calculated in 1708 that London had 'twenty Squares, mostly very large and pleasant'; there were, therefore, more squares than there were 'Markets for flesh; fowls, &c.' (15), markets for cattle (2), and for corn (3); colleges (4); chapels (20); bridges (5); and 'Gates in the [City] Walls' (15). [Hatton], *New View*, vol. 1, p. iii.

187 Knight, *London*, vol. 6, pp. 194–5, 195.

188 Ibid., p. 205.

189 Ibid., p. 196.

190 Wryrardisbury, 'Squares and Villas', p. 606.

CHAPTER 9

1 Daniels, *Repton*, pp. 28, 207–9; Andrews, 'Metropolitan Picturesque'; Fredericksen, 'Metropolitan Picturesque'; Arnold, 'Decimus Burton'.

2 Daniels, *Repton*, p. 28.

3 Crook, 'Metropolitan Improvements', p. 96.

4 For an account of the planning and building of Regent's Park see Summerson, *John Nash*, pp. 55–74, 114–29; or Crook, 'Metropolitan Improvements', pp. 78–87.

5 No less important a circumstance took place in 1806 in the same government department in rural Herefordshire: Nash's friend Uvedale Price was made the first and last Deputy Surveyor of the Forest of Dean. Nash and Price were friends and ardent exponents of the picturesque. See Crook, 'Metropolitan Improvements', p. 78.

6 There was a great need to maximise revenue during this period of 'royal extravagance and unprecedented wartime expenditure'. See ibid., p. 77.

7 The extent of Nash's contribution to the development of picturesque houses and gardens during this period has been explored by David Whitehead, who initially presented his findings in 'Repton and Nash: A Picturesque Partnership, made in Hertfordshire 1790–95', at the colloquium 'Romanticism and the Picturesque' (Gregynog Hall, 1 July 1991). The concept of the picturesque was first formulated by William Gilpin in the 1770s as a means of extracting aesthetic pleasure from the natural, or 'wild' landscape. It was subsequently transferred to landscape gardening through the writings of Uvedale Price and Richard Payne Knight, where it came to be applied as a means of viewing and interpreting contrived landscape scenery – or, as Price remarked in 1794, of appraising 'every object, and every kind of scenery, which has been, or might be represented with good effect in painting'; Price *An Essay*, p. 34; see also Knight, *The Landscape*.

8 'Lecture x: Gardens and City Plans', in *Lectures on Architecture*, ed. Arthur Bolton (1929), p. 152. Soane argued in this Royal Academy lecture of 1815 that the new generation of planners and architects had much to learn from ornamental gardening. What was needed to inject life into London's streets were such garden attributes as irregularity, contrast and surprise.

9 The term 'Metropolitan Picturesque' is attributed to Malcolm Andrews, who employed the term in his essay 'The Metropolitan Picturesque', pp. 282–98. See also Fredericksen, 'The Metropolitan Picturesque', who argues that the 'Picturesque City' was a 'distinct urban model that, while not traditionally avant-garde, represents an important configuration of landscape theory and city construction which profoundly shaped modern architecture and planning'.

10 Gwynn, *London and Westminster Improved*, pp. x–xi. See 'A Discourse on Publick Magnificence', ibid., pp. 1–22.

11 John Nash to Alexander Milne, 18 January 1822. CRES 2/771.

12 Crook, 'Metropolitan Improvements', p. 79.

13 Uncatalogued correspondence, CRES, Carlton House Terrace.

14 Surveyor-General Land Revenues, Report of 1812, p. 113. Extract from Nash's letter of 1811 addressed to the Commissioners, regarding the 'permanent inducements' essential to successful planning of Marylebone Park; *First Report of the Commissioners of Wood, Forest and Land Revenue* (1812), App. 12G, 113.

15 John Nash, addressed to the Commissioners, 30 August 1811, reproduced in the *First Report of the Commissioners* (1812), p. 113.

16 John Nash to Alexander Milne, 17 April 1822 (CRES 2/771).

17 Price, *An Essay* vol. 2, pp. 238–9. The intricacy was intrinsic in the succession of contradictory attributes of uniformity, greatness of dimension and grandeur, juxtaposed with the irregularity of nature, and the particularity of the smallest elements of the composition – namely the domestic premises.

18 Nash to Milne, 14 January 1823 (CRES 2/771).

19 Nash to Milne, 4 Jan 1823 (CRES 2/771). It should be noted that in many instances Nash's correspondence survives in different versions in the CRES files.

20 John Nash to the Commissioners, 17 April 1822 (CRES 2/771). Nash obliquely invokes Price's remark that 'magnificent buildings', such as 'palaces, adorned with porticos and balustrades' are picturesque; 'though in a less degree: for new buildings have a unity of tint, and sharpness of angle, which render them unfit for painting, unless when mixed with trees or some other objects, which may break and diversify their colour, and graduate and harmonize their abruptness of their lights and shadows'. *An Essay*, p. 153.

21 Nash to Milne, 17 April 1822 (CRES 2/771).

22 Nash to Milne, 18 January 1822 (CRES 2/771).

23 Nash to Milne, 18 January 1822 (CRES 2/771).

24 Nash to Milne, 24 January 1822 (CRES 2/771).

25 For an account of the distinction that Nash is drawing here – a distinction between the judgement of the man of taste and that of the artisan – see Barrell, *Political Theory of Painting*, pp. 13–18.

26 Nash to Milne, 18 January 1822 (CRES 2/771).

27 Knight, *The Landscape*, bk 3, lines 219–234. The term 'pleasure ground' in the eighteenth century usually referred to the 'most extensive area of ornamental planting within the wider landscape garden. It was essentially distinct from the park and, being a *locus amoenus*, was separated from utilitarian enclosures . . . [and] very often it contained one spot primarily devoted to shrubs, the shrubbery, as well as one spot principally dedicated to flowers . . . the flower garden.' See Laird, *Flowering of the Landscape Garden*, pp. 12–13.

28 Nash to Milne, 24 January 1822 (CRES 2/771).

29 Dead files (uncatalogued), Notes on the proposed layout and planting of York Terrace, April 1822, Crown Estate Commissioners, Carlton House Terrace. Nash proposed stringent covenants to protect the landscape settings of the Park terraces.

30 Elmes, *Metropolitan Improvements*, p. 21.

31 Nash declared that in order to stage his fantasy he required the landscape contrived on the principles of the picturesque. He reflected, for instance, that as the park increased in beauty through a maturing landscape, so too did the odds increase of attracting occupants of good character and quality. *Second*

respect to the building of York Terrace presently in possession of the Crown Estate Commissioners.

Report of the Commissioners of Woods, Forests and Land Revenue (1816), app. 20, p. 113.

32 *First Report of the Commissioners of Woods, Forests and Land Revenues* (1812), App. 12.G, p. 113.

33 Detailed explanation of John Nash's first scheme, addressed to the Commissioners, dated 30 August 1811, reproduced in the *First Report of the Commissioners* (1812), p. 86.

34 Price, *An Essay*, p. 209.

35 Elmes, *Metropolitan Improvements*, p. 20.

36 William Malcolm and Jenkins and Gwyther completed most of the forest tree plantations, and Lee and Kennedy supplied most of the ornamental stock (CRES 2/745).

37 Elmes, *Metropolitan Improvements*, p. 20.

38 Letter of Uvedale Price to Lady Beaumont, dated 10 January 1820. Coleorton Papers, Pierpont Morgan Library, New York.

39 Humphry Repton and Walter Nicol, for instance, believed that well-placed boundaries were essential for the definition of a garden, and for the protection of a premises.

40 Price, *Essay*, p. 81.

41 Knight, *Landscape*, p. 82.

42 Malkin, *Scenery, Antiquities, and Biography*, p. 344.

43 For records of the road surfaces used at Regent's Park see *Minute Books* (1824–9), Archives of the Crown Estate Paving Commissioners, Regent's Park.

44 Mason, *Poems of Mr Gray*, p. 360n.

45 Gilpin, *Three Essays*, p. 127.

46 App. 12B, p. 87.

47 CRES 2/778. Nash included a map of the property and not a site plan (MP 1905 (1)), PRO.

48 Nash, *A Statement* (1829); copy in the possession of Sir John Summerson. In 1823 Nash was seventy-one years old.

49 Nash's scheme for Blaise Hamlet was the precedent for the Park Villages. Completed in 1811, the Hamlet was an assemblage of 'picturesque' cottages for the poor and aged, designed by Nash for John Scandrett Harford, a Quaker banker of Bristol. The rustic cottages were grouped around a small green – each semi-secluded, and irregularly placed, so as not to advertise the philanthropy of the proprietor. See Temple, *John Nash*.

50 CRES 2/778. The plan referred to is shelved at MPE 911 (PRO).

51 MPE 911 (PRO). The Commissioners objected to this proposal fearing that it might threaten the villages' low building density. Van Sickle, 'Review', p. 6.

52 From legend of Plan of December 1823, MPE 911 (PRO).

53 Van Sickle. 'Review', p. 6. Villa numbers 1, 6/8, 10/12, 14 and 16 were those erected in this period. By 1837 all building sites but five (in Park Village East) had been taken and built upon.

54 Nash's successor, and the heir to his practice, was James Pennethorne.

55 Summerson, *John Nash*, p. 129.

56 Nicol, *The Villa Garden Directory*, p. 4.

57 Nicol remarked: 'The whole should appear light and airy; nor should the place be *boxed in* by high walls or hedges'. Ibid., p. 3.

58 Loudon, *Encyclopaedia* (1822), p. 1203.

59 Loudon, *Treatise*, pp. 145–6.

60 Price, *An Essay*, vol. 2, p. 153.

61 The category of the beautiful, defined by opposition to the sublime, was introduced by Edmund Burke, in his *Philosophical Enquiry into the Origins of the Sublime and the Beautiful* (1757); most late eighteenth-century and early nineteenth-century writings on aesthetic matters take for granted the two opposing categories, and treat them as obvious points of reference.

62 Price, *An Essay*, vol. 2, p. 147.

63 Price, *An Essay*, vol. 2, p. 153.

64 Saint, 'Quality of the London Suburb', pp. 15–16; Saunders, *Regent's Park*, pp. 86–7, 133; Summerson, *John Nash*, pp. 128–9.

65 Davidoff and Hall, *Family Fortunes*, pp. 370–75; Davidoff, L'Esperance and Newby, 'Landscape with figures'.

66 Thompson, 'Introduction', pp. 8, 15. Thompson speculated that the 'desire for individual gardens' was surfacing among 'suburbanites' in the 1790s, at 'just about the time when building suppliers chose to put the article on the market'. The countryside was 'ceasing to be feared or despised as boorish, backward, or hostile, and was coming to be admired by cultivated opinion as the home of all that was natural and virtuous'.

67 Loudon, *Suburban Gardener*, p. 1.

68 Ibid., p. 10.

69 Loudon, *Hints*, pp. vii, 37.

70 Loudon, *Suburban Gardener*, pp. 4, 2.

71 See further McKendrick, Brewer and Plumb, *Birth of the Consumer Society*, pp. 265–86.

72 Loudon, *Hints*, p. viii; *Suburban Gardener*, p. 1.

73 Loudon, *Hints*, p. vii. A number of plans for small gardens published in *Hints* were republished in *Suburban Gardener*.

74 Loudon, *Encyclopaedia*, item no. 2034: 'The Common Front Garden'.

75 Donald Olsen remarked that the most satisfactory suburb gave the householder 'the maximum of privacy and the minimum of outside distraction'. *Growth of Victorian London*, pp. 210–16.

76 Loudon, *Hints*, p. vi.

77 Dickens, *Dombey and Son*, London, 1900, p. 14; 'London Gardens', p. 95.

78 Butts reports that this spectacle was 'a little to the scandal of wondering neighbours, on more than one occasion'. *Blake Records*, G. E. Bentley, Jr, ed. (Oxford, 1969), pp. 53–4; see also Peter Ackroyd, *Blake* (London, 1999), pp. 157–8.

Select Bibliography

UNPUBLISHED SOURCES

Unpublished Reports

Ebblewhite, Ernest Arthur, 'The Worshipful Company of Gardeners', typescript, [*c*.1930?], Guildhall Library, MS 3396A

Fredericksen, Andrea, 'The Metropolitan Picturesque: Associating Ideas in Modern London'. Ph.D. dissertation, University of California, Los Angeles, 1997

Laird, Mark, 'An Approach to the Conservation of Ornamental Planting in English Gardens, 1730–1830', MA thesis (Institute of Advanced Architectural Studies), York, 1984

Land Use Consultants, 'The Historical Development of Russell Square', May 1997

Van Sickle, W. H. H., 'Review of the Building History of the Park Villages', September 1985, Crown Estate Commissioners

Welch, Charles, 'A History of the Company of Gardeners' (1890), Guildhall Library, Corporation of London

Whitehead, David, 'Repton & Nash: A Picturesque Partnership, made in Hertfordshire 1790–95'. Paper presented at *Romanticism and the Picturesque*, Gregynog Hall, Newtown, Wales, 1 July 1991

Manuscripts

London

BRITISH LIBRARY: DEPARTMENT OF MANUSCRIPTS
George Scharf Drawings (1820–50) (Add. 36489A)
Repton, *Memoir*, Part Two, autographed draft (Add. 62112)

BRITISH MUSEUM: DEPARTMENT OF PRINTS AND DRAWINGS
Dorothy George Collection
George Scharf Drawings (Books 1–6; Solander Boxes 17A–17E; Sketchbooks 198 A24–25)

THOMAS CORAM FOUNDATION (FOUNDLING ESTATE)
Building Committee Minutes (1790–1801)
Records of the Meetings of the General Committee (1788–1791)
Minutes of the General Court (1767–1802)
Uncatalogued plans

CROWN ESTATE OFFICE, CARLTON HOUSE TERRACE
Uncatalogued correspondence (*c*.1800–1830)
Dead files (uncatalogued): notes on the proposed layout and planting of York Terrace, Regent's Park, April 1822

CROWN ESTATE PAVING COMMISSIONERS, REGENT'S PARK
Minute Books (1824–29)

DRAPERS' COMPANY
Francis Bancroft's Charity MSS: Mile End Road (*c*.1738–1819)
John Edmanson's Charity MSS: Mile End Road (*c*.1707/8–1819)
Greenwich and Charlton Estate MSS: Queen Elizabeth's Row (*c*.1773–1819)
John Jolles's Estate MSS: Betts Street (*c*.1785–1819)
Pemel's Charity MSS: Whitechapel Road (*c*.1698–1819)
Walter's Charity MSS: Newington Butts (*c*.1783–1819)

FITZROY SQUARE FRONTAGES (manuscripts currently in the care of the Georgian Group, London)
Accounts of Receipt and Expenditure, Fitzroy Square (1806–43)
Minutes of the Meetings of the Inhabitants, Fitzroy Square (1815–43)

GUILDHALL LIBRARY
Papers regarding the Bishop of London's Estates (1770–1819)
Auction notices, MSS 18,795

THE HONOURABLE SOCIETY OF LINCOLN'S INN
Black Books of Lincoln's Inn

HOWARD DE WALDEN ESTATE
Block Plans of the Duke of Portland's Estate in St Marylebone (*c*.1805–1865)
Series of Ground Plans for Individual Houses on the Duke of Portland's Estate in St Marylebone (*c*.1812–1960)
Series of Terms of Contract for Individual Houses on the Duke of Portland's Estate in St Marylebone (*c*.1812–1960)

LAMBETH PALACE LIBRARY
Temporalities (1805) (TC 73)

'Survey of an Estate called the 21 Acres situate in Lambeth' (TC 76)

'Plan of the Archbishop of Canterbury's Estate [in London]' (1812) (TD 210)

LONDON LIBRARY
Minutes of the Trustees of St James's Square (1726–1825)

LONDON METROPOLITAN ARCHIVES
Hewitt, Smith, Harrison & Cook MSS, nurserymen: Kensington, Middlesex (1775–1827) (B/HRS)
Harden deeds X142, X145; (M) Acc.401/182-3.
Foundling Hospital Archives: applications for apprenticeships (A/FH/A12/1/2/1-1/6/1)

MERCERS' COMPANY
Lady Mico's Almshouse Charity MSS: St Dunstan's, Stepney (c.1680–1700)

MINET LIBRARY, BRIXTON
James Colvill MSS, nurseryman: Chelsea (1797–1907) (IV/39)

NATURAL HISTORY MUSEUM
Petiver, James, 'Botanicum hortense arborum in which are Specimens of trees in Gardens about London with Petiver's Synonima in his Botanicum mostly referred to Mr Ray', c.1716? (H.S.180)
'Plants gathered in the Fields and Gardens about London about the year 1682 for my own [Sir Hans Sloane] and Mr Courtenir's collections' (H.S.9)
Sloane, Sir Hans, *Horti sicci*

PUBLIC RECORD OFFICE, KEW
Records of the Crown Estate Commissioners and their predecessors
James Cochran MSS, nurseryman: London (1812–20) (C111/132-3)

ST PANCRAS LIBRARY, SWISS COTTAGE
Heal Collection
J. F. King 'Panorama of the Kentish Town and Highgate Roads' (1848–55)

SIR JOHN SOANE'S MUSEUM
Drawings of Plans for Townhouses (John Soane Case, shelf C, Folio VIII): Plan of the Ground and one pair floor of a house in Gower Street belonging to Mrs Peters (f.54); The Earl Fortesque, 43 Hill St., Berkeley Square: Plan of Basement floor with proposed alterations (f.68); Sir John Seabright, Bart., 19 Curzon Street, 21 October 1807 (f.65)
Mr Repton/Letter to the Trustees of Bloomsbury Square/ March 3rd 1807', in Private Correspondence XIII.G.10 (Hardwicke file)

VICTORIA AND ALBERT MUSEUM
Gillow and Co. Papers (E.12-105/1952; E.351-43/1955)

WESTMINSTER CITY ARCHIVES
Accounts of the Church of St Paul's Covent Garden

Grosvenor Estate Papers: Mayfair, Belgravia and Pimlico (accession 1049)
Articles of Agreement for the building of the garden of Grosvenor Square, 1729 (1049/10/4, misc. 6)

WORSHIPFUL COMPANY OF GOLDSMITHS
Morrell's Charity MSS: Hackney (1703–1808)
Bowes' Charity MSS: Woolwich (c.1771)
Goldsmiths' Company Almshouses MSS, East Acton (c.1808–1855)

Outside London

BEDFORD ESTATE, WOBURN ABBEY
Estate papers of the Duke of Bedford's estate in Bloomsbury (c.1770–1840)
Memoranda (c.1790–1810)

BEINECKE RARE BOOK AND MANUSCRIPT LIBRARY, YALE UNIVERSITY, NEW HAVEN
Joseph Spence Papers (OSB MSS 4)
'Plan: for a Parsonage Flower Garden: August 31, 1751' (Box 6, Folder 167)
'Stratton Street' (1744) (Box 6, Folder 203)
'Plan of a Garden for a house in Buckingham Gate, London' (1747) (Box 5, Folder 164)
Two plans of Robert Dodsley's Garden in Richmond (1753) (Box 6, Folder 198)
'John's Plan: for Baron Atkyns's at Fulham' 10 April 1753 (Box 6, Folder 177)
Plan of a Garden for Exchequer House, 10 April 1753 (Box 6, Folder 175)
Plan of a Garden for Exchequer House, 10 April 1753 (second of five draft plans) (Box 6, Folder 175)
Plan of a Garden for Exchequer House, 10 April 1753 (third of five draft plans) (Box 6, Folder 175)
Plan of a Garden for Exchequer House, 11 April 1753 (fourth of five draft plans) (Box 6, Folder 175)
Plan of a Garden for Exchequer House, 16 April 1753 (fifth of five draft plans) (Box 6, Folder 175)
Plan for Lady Falmouth's Garden in Stratton Street [Albemarle Street], Piccadilly (1744) (Box 6, Folder 188)
Stephen Duck, Detail of treillage for Spence's Garden at Byfleet, Surrey (c.1750–52) (Box 5, Folder 166)
Plan of Dr Noel Broxholme's garden, Bond Street, London (1743) (Box 5, Folder 163)

BODLEIAN LIBRARY, OXFORD UNIVERSITY
Francis Douce MSS (Special Collections and Western Manuscripts) (1790–1833)
John Johnson Collection of ephemera: auction prospectuses, c.1700–c.1900
Gough Additional Manuscripts: auction prospectuses, c.1700–c.1900 (G.A. fol. A259–A265)
Gough Maps: drawings and engravings collected by William Stukeley

Grohmann, J. G., *Ideenmagazin für Liebhaber von Gärten (Recueil d'Idées nouvelles pour la décoration des jardins, etc.)* (Leipzig, 1796–1811)

Grosley, P. Jean, *Londres*, 4 vols (Lausanne, 1774)

Gunnis, Rupert, *Dictionary of British Sculptors, 1660–1851* (London, 1954)

Gwynn, John, *London and Westminster Improved* (London, 1766)

Halfpenny, William, and John, Robert Morris and T. Lightoler, *The Modern Builder's Assistant* (London, 1757)

Hall, Elisabeth, and Jean Lear, eds, 'Chatham Dockyard Gardens', *Garden History*, vol. 20, no. 2 (Autumn 1992), pp. 132–52

Hall, Ivan, 'Box, Privet and Point Plants: The Urban Gardens of Georgian Westminster', *Westminster History Review*, vol. 1 (London, 1997), pp. 22–7

'Happiness drawn rather from Prospect than Possession – exemplified in the history of Euphanor', in *The Mirror: reflecting Men and Manners*, no. 37 (Edinburgh, 1 June 1779; London, 1786), pp. 1–6

Harding, Jane, and Anthea Taigel, 'An Air of Detachment: Town Gardens in the Eighteenth and Nineteenth Centuries', *Garden History*, vol. 24, no. 2 (1996), pp. 237–54

Harley, J. B., 'Meaning and Ambiguity in Tudor Cartography', in Sarah Tyacke, ed., *English Map-Making, 1500–1650: Historical Essays* (London, 1983), pp. 22–45

Harley, J. B., 'Maps, Knowledge, and Power', *The Iconography of Landscape*, ed. Dennis Cosgrove and Stephen Daniels (Cambridge, 1988), pp. 277–312

Harris, Eileen, *British Architectural Books and Writers, 1556–1785* (Cambridge, 1990)

Harris, John, *Sir William Chambers* (London, 1970)

Harris, John, 'Some Imperfect Ideas on the Genesis of the Loudonesque Flower Bed', in *John Claudius Loudon and the Early Nineteenth Century in Great Britain* (Washington, DC, 1980)

Harrison, Mark, 'Symbolism, "Ritualism" and the Location of Crowds in Early Nineteenth-Century English Towns', in Denis Cosgrove and Stephen Daniels, eds, *The Iconography of Landscape* (Cambridge, 1988), pp. 194–213

Harvey, John, *Early Nurserymen* (London, 1974); first published as 'Mid-Georgian Nurseries of the London Region', *Transactions of the London and Middlesex Archaeological Society*, vol. 26 (Penzance, 1975), pp. 293–308

Harvey, John, 'The Georgian Garden: Nurseries and Plants', *The Georgian Group: Report and Journal, 1986* (1987), pp. 55–66

Harvey, John, *The Nursery Garden* (London, 1990)

[Hatton, Edward], *A New View of London; or an Ample Account of that City, in Two Volumes, or Eight Sections*, 2 vols (London, 1708)

Henrey, Blanche, *British Botanical and Horticultural Literature before 1800*, 3 vols (London and Toronto, 1975)

Hewlings, Richard, 'Leoni's Drawings for 21 Arlington Street', *The Georgian Group Journal 1992* (1992), pp. 19–31

Hill, Aaron, *The Works of the Late Aaron Hill Esq., in four volumes* (London, 1753–4)

Hobhouse, Hermione, *Thomas Cubitt: Master Builder* (London, 1971)

Hughson, David [Edward Pugh], *London*, 6 vols (London, [1804–15])

Hunt, John Dixon, and Erik de Jong, eds, *The Anglo-Dutch Garden in the Age of William and Mary, Journal of Garden History*, vol. 8, nos 2 and 3 (1988) [special double edition]

Hunt, John Dixon, 'Reckoning with Dutch Gardens', *Journal of Garden History*, vol. 8, nos. 2 and 3 (1998), pp. 41–60

Hunt, Leigh, *The Autobiography of Leigh Hunt*, 3 vols (London, 1850)

Hutcheson, Francis (the Elder), *An inquiry into the original of our ideas of beauty and virtue* (Dublin, 1725)

Jackson-Stops, Gervase, *An English Arcadia, 1600–1990* (London, 1992)

Jacques, David, '"The Chief Ornament" of Gray's Inn: The Walks from Bacon to Brown', *Garden History*, vol. 17, no. 1 (Spring 1989), pp. 41–67

Jacques, David, and Arend Jan van der Horst, eds, *The Gardens of William and Mary* (London, 1988)

James, John, *The Theory and Practice of Gardening* (London, 1712)

Jenner, Charles, the Younger, *Town Eclogues* (London, 1772)

Johnson, Basil Henry, *Berkeley Square to Bond Street* (London, 1957)

Johnson, George W., *A History of English Gardening* (London, 1829)

Jong, Erik de, and Marleen Dominicus-van Soest, *Aardse Paradijzen: De tuin in de Nederlandse kunst 15de tot 18de eeuw* (Ghent, 1996)

Kalm's Account of his Visit to England on his way to America in 1748, Joseph Lucas, trans. (London, 1892)

Kames, Lord [Henry Home], *Elements of Criticism*, 3 vols (1762)

Kelly, Alison, *Mrs Coade's Stone* (Upton-upon-Severn, 1990)

King, R. W., 'Joseph Spence of Byfleet', part 1, *Garden History*, vol. 6, no. 3 (Winter 1978), pp. 38–64

King, R. W., 'Joseph Spence of Byfleet', part 2, *Garden History*, vol. 7, no. 3 (Winter 1979), pp. 29–48

King, R. W., 'Joseph Spence of Byfleet', part 3, *Garden History*, vol. 8, no. 2 (Summer 1980), pp. 44–65

King, R. W., 'Joseph Spence of Byfleet', part 4, *Garden History*, vol. 8, no. 3 (Winter 1980), pp. 77–114

Knight, Charles, ed., *London*, 6 vols (1841–4)

Knight, Richard Payne, *The Landscape: A Didactic Poem in three books* (London, 1794; second edition, 1795)

Knox, Tim, 'Joshua Brookes's Vivarium: An Anatomist's Garden in Blenheim Street, W1', *The London Gardener*, vol. 3 (1997–8), pp. 30–34

Knox, Tim, and Todd Longstaffe-Gowan, 'A Town Garden Design for 29 Old Burlington Street, Westminster', *Georgian Group Journal 1991* (1991), pp. 36–40

Lady Morgan's Memoirs: Autobiography, Diaries and Correspondence, 2 vols (London, 1842)

Laird, M., 'Ein Gartenplan für Upper Gower St. 13. London: Mutmassungen über Anlage, Pflege und Entwicklung eines Burgergartens im ausgehenden 18. Jahrhundert', in Erika Schmidt, Wilfried Hansmann and Jörg Gamer, eds., *Garten Kunst Geschichte: Festschrift für Dieter Hennebo zum 70, Geburtstag* (Worms am Rhein, 1994), pp. 82–94

Laird, Mark, *The Flowering of the Landscape Garden: English Pleasure Grounds, 1720–1800* (Pittsburgh, 1999)

Laird, Mark, and Harvey, John, 'The Garden Plan for 13 Upper Gower Street, London: A Conjectural Review of the Planting, Upkeep and Long-term Maintenance of a Late Eighteenth-century Town Garden', *Garden History*, vol. 25, no. 2 (Winter 1997), pp. 189–211

Lambert, B., *The History and Survey of London and its Environs*, 4 vols (London, 1806)

Langley, Batty, *Practical Geometry applied to the Useful Arts of Building, Surveying, Gardening, and Mensuration* (London, 1726)

Langley, Batty, *New Principles of Gardening* (London, 1728)

Langley, Batty, *The Builder's Compleat Assistant*, 2 vols (London, [1738])

Langley, Batty, *The City and Country Builder's and Workman's Treasury of Designs* (London, 1745)

Laxton, Paul, 'Richard Horwood's Plan of London: A Guide To Editions and Variants, 1792–1819', *London Topographical Record*, vol. 26 (1990), pp. 214–63

Leapman, Michael, *The Ingenious Mr Fairchild: The Forgotten Father of the Flower Garden* (London, 2000)

Leatherbarrow, David, 'Character, Geometry and Perspective: the Third Earl of Shaftesbury's Principles of Garden Design', *Journal of Garden History*, vol. 4, no. 4 (1984), pp. 332–58

Leigh, Samuel, *Leigh's New Picture of London* (London, 1824–5)

Le Livre, Audrey, 'Hoxton's Horticulturist', *Country Life* (3 November 1988), pp. 196–8

Life and Memoirs of Miss Robertson of Blackheath (London, 1802)

London, George, and Henry Wise, *The Retir'd Gard'ner, in Two Volumes. Vol. I. being a translation of Le jardinier solitaire* [by François Gentil], *Vol. II. containing the manner of planting and cultivating all sorts of flowers, plants, shrubs . . . being a translation from the Sieur Louis Liger* ['Le jardinier fleuriste et historiographe'] (London, 1706)

The London and Westminster Guide (London, 1768)

'London Gardens', *The Garden*, vol. 2 (1872), p. 95

London in Miniature (London, 1755)

London in 1710. From the Travels of Zacharias Conrad von Uffenbach, ed. and trans. W. H. Quarrell and Margaret Mare (London, 1934)

London Suburbs (London, 1999)

London's Pride, Mireille Galinou, ed. (London, 1990)

Longstaffe-Gowan, Todd, 'James Cochran: Florist and Plant Contractor to Regency London', *Garden History*, vol. 15, no. 1 (1987), pp. 58–9

Longstaffe-Gowan, T., 'Proposal for a Georgian Town Garden in Gower Street, London: The Francis Douce Garden', *Garden History*, vol. 15, no. 2 (1987), pp. 136–44

Longstaffe-Gowan, T., 'Plant Effluvia. Changing notions of human health in the eighteenth and nineteenth centuries', *Journal of Garden History*, vol. 7, no. 2 (1987), pp. 176–85

Longstaffe-Gowan, T., 'Private Urban Gardening in England 1700–1830: On the Art of Sinking', in *The Vernacular Garden* (Dumbarton Oaks, 1990), pp. 47–75

Longstaffe-Gowan, T., 'William Stukeley's Travelling Gardens: Itinerarium Curiosum: iter domesticum. An account of the gardens of William Stukeley', *Architectural Review*, vol. 190, no. 1130 (April 1991), pp. 78–83

Longstaffe-Gowan, T., 'Institutional Elysiums: London Almshouse Gardens, 1690–1810', *Georgian Group Journal* (1992), pp. 82–6

Longstaffe-Gowan, T., 'History of Spencer House Garden, 27 St James's Place', *The London Gardener*, vol. 1 (1995), pp. 40–48

Longstaffe-Gowan, T., 'Melancholy Little Gardens', *The London Gardener: or The Gardener's Intelligencer*, vol. 4 (1999), pp. 45–8

Longstaffe-Gowan, T., 'Melankolske små haver', *Guide London* (Copenhagen, 1999), pp. 69–75

Loudon, Jane, *Gardening for Ladies* (London, 1840)

Loudon, J. C., 'Hints Respecting the Manner of Laying out the Grounds of the Public Squares in London, to the Utmost Picturesque Advantage', *Literary Journal*, vol. 2 ([31 December] 1803), cols 739–42

Loudon, John Claudius, *A Treatise on Forming, Improving and Managing Country Residences*, 2 vols (London, 1806)

Loudon, J. C., *Hints on the Formation of Gardens and Pleasure Grounds* (London, 1812)

Loudon, J. C., *An Encyclopaedia of Gardening* (London, 1822; revised 1824; 1828, fifth edition)

Loudon, J. C., *The Suburban Gardener and Villa Companion* (London, 1838)

[Loudon, J. C.], *The Greenhouse Companion* (London, 1824)

Lyson, Daniel, *The Environs of London*, 4 vols and supplement (London, 1792–6)

McClure, Ruth K., *Coram's Children: The London Foundling Hospital in the Eighteenth Century* (London, 1981)

McKellar, Elizabeth, *The Birth of Modern London: The Development and Design of the City, 1660–1720* (Manchester and New York, 1999)

McKendrick, Neil, John Brewer and J. H. Plumb, *The Birth of the Consumer Society* (London, 1982)

Malcolm, J. P., *London Redivivum*, 4 vols (London, 1802–7)

Malcolm, James Peller, *Anecdotes of the Manners and Customs of London during the eighteenth century* (London, 1808)

Malkin, B. *The Scenery, Antiquities, and Biography of South Wales* (1804)

Malton, Thomas, *A Picturesque Tour Through the Cities of London and Westminster* (London, 1792)

The Man at Hyde Park Corner, Sculpture by John Cheere 1709–1787, exh. cat., Temple Newsam, Leeds, and Marble Hill House, Twickenham (London, 1974)

Mangles, James, *The Floral Calendar, Monthly and Daily, with miscellaneous details relative to plants and flowers, gardens and greenhouses, horticulture and botany, Aviaries, &c., &c.* (London, 1839)

Marshall, Charles, *An Introduction to the Knowledge and Practice of Gardening* (London, 1796)

Marshall, Charles, 'On the Profession of a Gardener . . . etc; Self Education of Gardeners – The Spirit of Education', *The Gardener's Magazine* (April, 1826), pp. 225–6

Marshall, John, and Ian Wilcox, *The Victorian House* (London, 1986)

Mason, William, ed., *The Poems of Mr Gray. To which are pre-fixed Memoirs of his Life and Writings* (London, 1775)

Mawe, Thomas, and John Abercrombie, *Every Man His Own Gardener*, tenth edition (London, 1784)

Mayhew, [Henry], and [A.] Mayhew, *The Greatest Plague in Life: or the adventures of a lady in search of a good servant, by one who has been 'almost worried to death'* (London, [1847])

Meager, Leonard, *The English Gardener* (London, 1670)

Meager, Leonard, *The Compleat English Gardner*, 10th edition (London, 1704)

The Microcosm of London, or London in Miniature, 3 vols (London, 1904)

Miller, Philip, *The Gardeners Dictionary*, first edition, 2 vols (London, 1731–9)

Miller, Philip, *The Gardeners Dictionary*, third edition (London, 1737)

Miller, P., *Gardeners Dictionary*, sixth edition (London, 1752)

Miller, P., *Gardeners Dictionary*, seventh edition (London, 1759)

Miller, P., *Gardeners Dictionary*, eighth edition (London, 1768)

Morgan, Lady, *Italy*, 3 vols (London, 1821)

Moritz, Carl Philip, *Travels, Chiefly on Foot, through Several Parts of England in 1782, translated into the English by a Lady* (London, 1795); another edition, William Mavor, *The British Tourists*, vol. 4 (London, 1798), pp. 1–138

Muthesius, Stefan, *The English Terraced House* (London, 1982)

Nash, John, *A Statement* ([London], 1829)

Neve, Richard, *The City and Country Purchaser and the Builder's Dictionary* (London, 1726)

Nicol, Walter *The Villa Garden Directory; or Monthly Index of Work to be done in Town and Villa Gardens* (Edinburgh, 1809)

Noyes, Robert, 'Advice on the Management of a Fine House', *The Gentleman's Magazine* (1753), pp. 529–30

Oglander, Cecil F., Aspinall, *Admiral's Wife – Being the life and letters of the Hon. Mrs. Edward Boscawen from 1719–1761* (London, 1940)

Oglander, Aspinall, *Admiral's Widow- Being the life and letters of the Hon. Mrs. Edward Boscawen from 1761–1805* (London, 1942)

Olsen, D. J., *The Growth of Victorian London*, second edition (London, 1979)

Olsen Donald J., *Town Planning in London: The Eighteenth and Nineteenth Centuries*, second edition (New Haven and London, 1982)

'On the Life of a Jobbing Gardener', *The Gardener's Magazine* (September, 1826), article v, p. 26

'On the ridiculous Consequence assumed from Superiority of Places of Residence', *The Monthly Mirror* (April 1803), pp. 238–40

The Original Picture of London, Enlarged and Improved: Being a Correct Guide to the Stranger, as well as for the inhabitant, to the metropolis of the British Empire together with a Description of the Environs, J. Britton, ed. (London, [1826])

Orgel, Stephen, and Roy Strong, *Inigo Jones: The Theatre of the Stuart Court*, 2 vols (London and Los Angeles, 1973)

Panofsky, Erwin, *Studies in Iconology: Humanistic Themes in the Art of the Renaissance* (Oxford, 1939)

Panofsky, E., 'Iconography and Iconology: An Introduction to the Study of Renaissance Art', in *Meaning in the Visual Arts* (Harmondsworth, 1970)

Papworth, John Buonarotti, *Select Views of London* (London, 1816)

Pepys, Samuel, *The Diary of Samuel Pepys*, Robert Latham and William Matthews, eds, 10 vols (London, 1970–93)

Philippar, François, *Voyage agronomique en Angleterre fait en 1829; ou Essai sur les cultures de ce pays comparées a celles de la France* (Paris, 1830)

Phillips, Henry, *Sylva Florifera: the shrubbery historically and botanically treated; with observations on the formation of orna-mental plantations, and picturesque scenery*, 2 vols (London, 1823)

Pincot, Daniel, *An Essay on the Origin, Nature and Uses and Properties of Artifical Stone* (London, 1770)

[Pluche, Noel,] *Spectacle de la Nature; or, Nature display'd . . . translated from the original French . . . by Mr Humphreys*, sixth edition, 4 vols (London, 1743–4)

Porter, Roy, *English Society in the Eighteenth Century* (London, 1982)

Price, Uvedale, *An Essay on the Picturesque as compared with the Sublime and the Beautiful* (London?, 1794–8)

Prospects of Town and Park, Colnaghi exh. cat. (London, 1988)

[Pückler-Muskau, Prince Hermann von], *Letters from Albion to a Friend on the Continent written in the years 1810, 1811, 1812 and 1813*, 2 vols (London, 1814)

Purchas, Anne, 'Maurice-Louis Jolivet's Drawings at West Wycombe Park', *Architectural History: Journal of the Society of Architectural Historians of Great Britain*, vol. 37 (1994), pp. 68–79

Quintinie, Jean de la, *The Compleat Gard'ner* (London, 1699)

[Ralph, James], *A Critical Review of the Publick Buildings . . . in and about London* (London, 1734)

Ralph, James, *A New Critical Review of the Publick Buildings . . . in and about London* (London, 1783)

Rasmussen, Steen Eiler, *London: The Unique City* (London, 1937)

Rawlins, Thomas, *Familiar Architecture* (London, 1768)

Reports from the Select Committees, respecting the Arts-Masters and Apprentices of Bridewell Hospital (London, 1799)

Repton, Humphry, *An Enquiry into Changes of Taste in Landscape Gardening. To which are added Some Observations on its Theory and Practice, including A Defence of the Art* (London, 1800)

Repton, Humphry, *Fragments on the Theory and Practice of Landscape Gardening* (London, 1816)

Ribeiro, Aileen, 'Mrs Cornelys and Carlisle House', *History Today*, vol. 28, no. 1 (January 1978), pp. 47–52

Richardson, Samuel, *Sir Charles Grandison*, Jocelyn Harris, ed. (London, 1972)

Robison, Sir John, 'Description of a Glass Case for growing Plants in Rooms', *The Gardener's Magazine* (1840), pp. 117–20

Rogers, David, *The Douce Legacy: An Exhibition to Commemorate the 150th Anniversary of the Bequest of Francis Douce, 1757–1834* (Oxford, 1984)

Rutger, Thomas, 'Some Remarks on the Suburban Gardens of the Metropolis, and the Mode of laying out and planting the Public Squares', *The Gardener's Magazine* (1835), pp. 513–17

Rutter, John, and Daniel Carter, *Modern Eden or the Gardener's Universal Guide* (London, 1767)

Ryerson, Richard Alan, ed. *Adams Family Correspondence*, 6 vols (Cambridge, Mass., 1993)

Saint, Andrew, 'The Quality of the London Suburb', in *London Suburbs* (London, 1999), pp. 9–29

Saunders, Ann, *Regent's Park* (Newton Abbot, 1969)

Schama, Simon, *The Embarrassment of Riches* (London, 1987)

Schwab, Irene and Bernard Nurse, 'Butcher Row, Ratcliffe, E.14', *Transactions of the London and Middlesex Archaeological Society*, vol. 28 (1977), pp. 231–51

Sensitivus, 'On the Treatment which Gardeners out of Place generally receive from Nurserymen, and the Consequences resulting therefrom', *The Gardener's Magazine*, part 3 (January, 1827), pp. 36–7

Seymour, Robert *A Survey of the Cities of London and Westminster* 2 vols, (London, 1734–5)

Shepherd, Thomas Hosmer, *London and its Environs in the Nineteenth Century, Illustrated by a series of Views from Original Drawings* (London, 1829)

Simo, Melanie Louise, *Loudon and the Landscape: From Country Seat to Metropolis, 1783–1843* (New Haven and London, 1988)

Smith, John Thomas, *Nollekens and his Times*, 2 vols (London, 1829)

Soane John, *Lectures on Architecture . . . 1809 to 1836*, Arthur Bolton, ed. (London, 1929)

Society of Gardeners, *Catalogus Plantarum* (London, 1730)

[Sorbière, Samuel de] *Relation d'un Voyage en Angleterre* (Paris, 1664)

[Southey, Robert], *Letters from England by Don Manuel Alvarez Espriella, Translated from the Spanish*, 3 vols (London, 1807)

Spence, Joseph, *Polymetis* (London, 1747)

Spence, Joseph, *Observations, Anecdotes, and Character of Books and Men collected from Conversation*, James M. Osborn, ed., 2 vols (Oxford, 1966)

[Stewart, John], *Critical Observations on the buildings and improvements of London* (London, 1771)

Strachey, Nino, 'The Helmingham Plan: An Eighteenth-century Survey of the Gardens at Ham House', *The London Gardener*, vol. 2 (1997–98), pp. 36–41

Stroud, Dorothy, *Capability Brown*, fourth edition (Over Wallop, Hampshire, 1984)

Strype, John, *Survey of the Cities of London and Westminster*, 2 vols (London, 1720)

Summerson, John, *Architecture in Britain, 1530–1830* (Harmondsworth, 1970)

Summerson, John, *Georgian London*, fifth edition (Harmondsworth, 1978)

Summerson, John, *The Life and Work of John Nash, Architect* (London, 1980)

Surr, Thomas Skinner, *A Winter in London; or, Sketches of fashion: A novel*, 3 vols (London, 1806)

The Survey of London (London, 1900–)

Switzer, Stephen, *The Nobleman, Gentleman, and Gardener's Recreation* (London, 1715)

Switzer, Stephen, *Ichnographia Rustica: or, The Nobleman, Gentleman, and Gardener's Recreation*, 3 vols (London, 1718)

Switzer, Stephen, *Ichnographia Rustica . . . The second edition with . . . Additions*, 3 vols (London, 1741/2)

Sylvaticus, Matthaeus, 'The Management of a Town Garden throughout the Year, in a Series of Monthly Directions', *Gardener's Magazine* (1828), pp. 59–60

Temple, Nigel, *John Nash and the Village Picturesque* (Gloucester, 1979)

Thomas, Keith, *Man and the Natural World* (London, 1983)

Thompson, F. M. L., 'Introduction: The Rise of Suburbia', in *The Rise of Suburbia*, F. M. L. Thompson, ed. (Leicester, 1982), pp. 2–25

Tod, George, *Plans, Elevations and Sections of Hot-Houses, Green-Houses, an Aquarium, Conservatories, &c.* (London, 1807)

Trollope, Frances, *The Days of the Regency* (London, 1848)

[Trusler, John], *Elements of Modern Gardening* (London, [1784])

Turner, Tom, *English Garden Design. History and Styles Since 1650* (Woodbridge, 1986)

Twiss, Horace, *The Public and Private Life of Lord Chancellor Eldon*, 3 vols (London, 1844)

Voltaire, F. M. A. de, *Candide* (London, 1759)

Walpole, Horace, 'Essay on Modern Gardening', in *The Works of Horatio Walpole*, vol. 2 (London, 1798); first published 1785

Walpole, Horace, *The Letters of Horace Walpole*, P. Cunningham, ed., 9 vols (London, 1890–91)

Walpole, Horace, *Horace Walpole's Correspondence*, Wilmarth S. Lewis, ed. (New Haven and London, 1933–83)

Ware, Isaac, *A Complete Body of Architecture* (London, 1756)

Watkin, David, *Sir John Soane: Enlightenment Thought and the Royal Academy Lectures* (Cambridge, 1996)

Weatherill, Lorna, *Consumer Behaviour and Material Culture in Britain, 1600–1760* (London, 1988)

Webber, Roland, *The Early Horticulturists* (Newton Abbot, 1968)

Welch, Charles, *The History of the Worshipful Company of Gardeners*, second edition (London, 1900)

Wells, H. G., 'The Door in the Wall', in *The Short Stories of H. G. Wells* (London, 1927)

Whatley, Thomas, *Observations on Modern Gardening* (London, 1770)

Williams, Robert, 'Sir John Dalrymple's "An Essay on Landscape Gardening"', *Journal of Garden History*, vol. 3, no. 2 (April–June 1983), pp. 144–56

Willis, Peter, *Charles Bridgeman and the English Landscape Garden* (London, 1977)

Wills, John, 'Plants for House Decoration', *Journal of the Royal Horticultural Society*, 15 (1893), pp. 84–5

Wood, John, the Elder, *An Essay towards the Description of Bath* (London, 1749)

Woodbridge, Kenneth, *Princely Gardens* (London, 1986)

Worlidge, John, *Systema-Horti-Culturae: or The Art of Gardening* (London, 1683)

Worlidge, John, *Dictionarium rusticum & urbanicum* (London, 1704); another edition 1717

Wright, Austin, *Joseph Spence: A Critical Biography* (Chicago, 1950)

W. S., 'Suggestions for a Society for promoting the Improvement of the Public Taste in Architectural and Rural Scenery', *The Gardener's Magazine* (1835), pp. 280–84

Photograph Credits